HEALTH CARE POLITICS, POLICY, AND SERVICES

A SOCIAL JUSTICE ANALYSIS

SECOND EDITION

Gunnar Almgren, PhD

SPRINGER PUBLISHING COMPANY
NEW YORK

Springer Publishing Company, LLC
11 West 42nd Street
New York, NY 10036
www.springerpub.com

Acquisitions Editor: Sheri W. Sussman
Senior Production Editor: Joe Stubenrauch
Composition: Techset

ISBN: 978-0-8261-0887-6
E-book ISBN: 978-0-8261-0888-3

Qualified instructors may request supplements by emailing textbook@springerpub.com
Instructor's Manual: 978-0-8261-9929-4

12 13 14 15/5 4 3 2 1

The author and the publisher of this Work have made every effort to use sources believed to be reliable to provide information that is accurate and compatible with the standards generally accepted at the time of publication. The author and publisher shall not be liable for any special, consequential, or exemplary damages resulting, in whole or in part, from the readers' use of, or reliance on, the information contained in this book. The publisher has no responsibility for the persistence or accuracy of URLs for external or third-party Internet websites referred to in this publication and does not guarantee that any content on such websites is, or will remain, accurate or appropriate.

Library of Congress Cataloging-in-Publication Data

Almgren, Gunnar Robert, 1951–
  Health care politics, policy, and services : a social justice analysis / Gunnar Almgren. — 2nd ed.
    p. ; cm.
Includes bibliographical references and index.
  ISBN 978-0-8261-0887-6 — ISBN 978-0-8261-0888-3 (e-book) — ISBN 978-0-8261-9929-4 (instructor's manual)
I. Title.
  [DNLM: 1. Delivery of Health Care—United States. 2. Health Services—economics—United States. 3. Health Services—history—United States. 4. Healthcare Disparities—United States. 5. Social Justice—United States. 6. Socioeconomic Factors—United States. W 84 AA1]
  362.10973–dc23

                                                                            2012023132

Special discounts on bulk quantities of our books are available to corporations, professional associations, pharmaceutical companies, health care organizations, and other qualifying groups.

If you are interested in a custom book, including chapters from more than one of our titles, we can provide that service as well.

For details, please contact:
Special Sales Department, Springer Publishing Company, LLC
11 West 42nd Street, 15th Floor, New York, NY 10036-8002s
Phone: 877-687-7476 or 212-431-4370; Fax: 212-941-7842
Email: sales@springerpub.com

Printed in the United States of America by Bang Printing.

To my wife Linda, in loving gratitude for the nearly four decades of life we have shared together. The best is yet ahead of us my love.

CONTENTS

FOREWORD

Three developments frame the contemporary importance of *Health Care Politics, Policy, and Services*, as well as explain the changes in content that have occurred since the first edition.

The salience and importance of a social justice framework have only grown, as ideological, political, and partisan differences have grown and crowded out a reasoned policy discourse. Having a justice framework, however derived, provides a moral and policy compass for the design of health care policy and services. Having a justice framework forces a reconsideration of the question of basic intent and rationale for health care coverage and services in our country.

In this book, the alternative frameworks are compared and contrasted, even down to the practical and critical analysis of the Patient Protection and Affordable Care Act (PPACA). Rawls, Sen, Nussbaum, Nozick, Marx, Daniels, and all the leading intellectual sources for understanding the public responsibility and appropriate design of health policy are critically interpreted in this work. These perspectives help us rethink our commitment to access, equity, particular mixes of health services, prevention and health promotion, and support for vulnerable groups such as the aged.

Second, the social science context has changed dramatically in the last five years, and the breadth of content in this book reflects this transformation. The contemporary analysis of health policy embodies the breadth of social sciences and public health, from history, to demography, to social epidemiology, to political economy, and ultimately back to the structure of health care organization and services. The modern practice of policy analysis is increasingly "transdisciplinary," and Gunnar Almgren's approach embodies this paradigm.

Finally, this book is published in the midst of all the turmoil, contention, and uncertainty of the PPACA. What is most compelling about the approach of this book is that it provides not just an understanding of what *is* in our complex health system, but how to think about the dynamics of the next period of debate and change. The PPACA is and will continue to be a work in progress, and what we need more than anything are tools for understanding its implementation and restructuring (legal, political, administrative). So much in this book, including the reanalysis of the justice implications of Medicaid coverage, helps us understand these dynamics. This process has just begun.

Gunnar Almgren speaks with a voice, and has produced an analysis of our health system that harkens back to the British tradition of social administration, social policy analysis, and population health, albeit brought to bear on the U.S. health system. Richard Titmuss, Martin Bulmer, Michael Marmot, and others in the British tradition brought a facile combination of moral insight, critical analysis, and social epidemiology to the understanding of health policy and health services. They combined methodological savvy, a belief in the importance of the empirical, and a grounding in what is ethical to the analysis of social and health systems. Professor Almgren is unapologetic in his moral voice, something our national discussion of health policy gravely needs.

So in many ways this book, like its first edition, is a "back to the future" analysis of the justice, organizational, and policy context of our current health services environment. Professor Almgren is bringing us back to first principles, by asking the relevant justice and ultimately moral questions about the purposes and design of health services.

His timely new edition occurs during the most consequential period of health reform and implementation of our lifetimes. Even though this book has "health care politics" in its title, it is a refreshing and thoughtful antidote to the clamor and rancor of our current "small p" political discussion of health policy and reform.

Edward F. Lawlor, PhD
Dean and William E. Gordon Distinguished Professor
Brown School
Director, Institute for Public Health
Washington University in St. Louis

PREFACE

The first edition of this book was written with the conviction that the health care policy courses, which serve as the policy foundation for students of the health professions, must go well beyond the traditional descriptive analysis of the health care system, or even other analyses of health care policy that are based upon particular disciplinary frameworks. Both the author and editors of the first edition shared the belief that there was a need for a book that would critically examine health care policy and the structure of the American health care system, in light of the prevalence of disparities in health and health care, and how different perspectives on social justice might lead to very different conclusions about the central purposes and boundaries of health care policy. Core to the purpose of the book's original edition, and this second revised edition, as well, is an ethos that the health care practitioners who have committed their careers and much of their lives to the health of others are those that must be at the forefront of the national dialogue on just health care policy. The practitioners are the experts in the professions that care for health, and therefore must be the strongest voice in health care policy. This book is intended to provide health care professionals with essential preparation toward that end.

This second edition of the book, published 6 years after the first, retains the basic structure of the original, and has been substantially revised as well. Consistent with the first edition, the book begins with a primer on alternative theories of social justice and their implications for the principles of just health care policy. The next four chapters provide a descriptive and critical analysis of the history of the U.S. health care system, health care financing, and the contemporary organization of health care. With these foundations in place, the next two chapters of the book, also as in the original edition, provide an analysis of health care disparities and the theoretical frameworks that inform our understanding of the determinants of disparities in health and health care. The final chapter provides both a political and principled analysis of health care reform.

The revisions in this second edition begin with the first chapter, which is expanded to include a synopsis of the Capabilities Approach to social justice developed by Sen and Nussbaum, and the rights to health care that are implied from this emerging theoretical framework. While the Capabilities Approach awaits development as a fully comprehensive theory of justice, it is widely regarded as the most innovative and influential paradigm of social justice of the current day. In particular, the Capabilities Approach challenges us to rethink the murky distinctions between rights to health and health care and other forms of fundamental human rights.

Thus, this new edition of the book now considers the moral foundations of rights to health care in accordance with five alternative social justice frameworks: Libertarianism, Utilitarianism, Marxism, Liberalism, and (new with this edition) the Capabilities Approach. Chapters 3 through 6, which cover the descriptive aspects of the health care system, contain extensive revisions that incorporate the most recently available data and developments in both health care financing and the organization of health care delivery. Chapter 7, which is devoted to the understanding of the theoretical determinants of health and health care disparities, has also been updated to take into account the emerging developments in social epidemiology theory and related empirical support.

The final chapter of this second edition is the most extensively revised, because at the point that the first edition was published in 2007 the national discourse on comprehensive health care reform was largely devoted to debates over *hypothetical* policy alternatives to the possibility of fundamental reform. As this second edition is published, the nation is grappling with the implementation of the most comprehensive health care reform undertaken in nearly 50 years—and the fundamental political and constitutional debates that have ensued in response. The final chapter of the book thus has four parts: (1) a summary of the political context of health care reform—both in historical and contemporary terms, (2) a descriptive synopsis of the Patient Protection and Affordable Care Act (PPACA) that considers its central aims and major provisions, (3) a political and principled analysis of the PPACA—the latter addressing how PPACA does or does not reflect a just approach to health care policy in accordance with the alternative theories of justice introduced in the first chapter, and (4) an approach to health care reform that would be most consistent with the framework of social justice that speaks most closely with the author's perspective—the theory of justice advanced by the late John Rawls.

Although this book is written with careful attention to the facts pertaining to the demography of health care and disparities in health care, it is neither neutral nor dispassionate with respect to the central purposes of health care policy. That is, this book is written with the conviction that health care policy is first and foremost a complex and multilayered problem of social justice. Whether or not the particular theory of justice that is favored by the author also resonates with most or even a small minority of readers, it is hoped that this one central idea engages us all.

ACKNOWLEDGMENTS

As with the first edition of this book, I wish to acknowledge the principled influence of my parents, Gayle and Peter. They each instilled in their children a strong sense of justice as basic fairness in all societal arrangements—decades before John Rawls formulated his theory around this moral idea. For the writing of this second edition, again as with the first edition, I am deeply indebted to my wife Linda for her enduring love and support. The task of writing this extensively revised book proved to be no less demanding than the writing of the first edition, and the big and little sacrifices required of her over the past several months were given freely, lovingly, and with a wonderful quality of partnership. Finally, I am very grateful for the generous support I have received from my editors at Springer Publishing Company: former Senior Editor Jennifer Perillo, Executive Editor Sheri W. Sussman, and Associate Editor Kathryn Corasaniti.

CHAPTER ONE

A Primer on Theories of Social Justice and Defining the Problem of Health Care

*T*he premise of this chapter is that relatively few students in public health, medicine, nursing, and social work have more than a superficial acquaintance with specific theories of social justice. Although this text employs a very specific (Rawlsian) social justice framework in its analysis of health care policy, the text's chosen perspective will be contextualized and highlighted by contrasting it with other dominant theories of social justice. In later chapters, the health care policy implications of the differing perspectives on social justice will be considered.

DEFINING THE PROBLEM OF SOCIAL JUSTICE

The term *social justice* has many uses and interpretations, but in its most basic and universal sense, social justice is a philosophical construct—in essence, a political theory or system of thought used to determine what mutual obligations flow between the individual and society. As such, social justice is distinct from the concept of individual justice, the latter pertaining only to obligations that exist between individuals (Rhodes, Battin, & Silvers, 2002). Also inherent in the concept of social justice, as it is generally construed within democratic societies, is the idea that civil society is predicated on the basis of a social contract that spells out the benefits, rights, and obligations of societal membership.[1] For example, at a very basic level, collective security as a benefit of membership in civil society is reciprocated through individual obligations pertaining to taxation and availability for military service.

Beyond these points pertaining to general definition, there is no absolute, generally agreed-upon notion of what defines or constitutes "social justice," either as process or as an outcome. Were that the case, the problem of social justice would be limited to one of social engineering—ways of organizing social institutions to assure that the individuals, groups, and organizations composing society act in "just" ways in accordance with the rules of "absolute, true, and universal" social justice. However, unlike a theocracy comprised of culturally homogenous and like-minded individuals ascribing to a shared moral and political philosophy, a pluralist democracy must accommodate diverse points of view on what mutual obligations exist, what rules for the governance of mutual obligations should be codified, and how limited resources should be distributed. Thus, in a pluralist democracy, the problem of social justice is twofold. First, there is the problem of achieving a conception of social justice that is mutually recognized and acknowledged by diverse individuals and groups as a legitimate basis for adjudicating claims on obligations and resources. Second, there is the problem of how to organize social institutions in accordance with the prevailing conception of social justice (Rawls, 2001).[2] This chapter is principally concerned with the first problem, namely, finding a perspective on social justice that accommodates fundamentally different world views, experiences, and interests.

ALTERNATIVE THEORIES OF SOCIAL JUSTICE

As implied by the general definition of social justice as a philosophical construct, there are very different theoretical perspectives pertaining to the principles used to determine what we as individuals are owed as members of society, and what we in turn owe society at large. A second point of theoretical diversity concerns the just distribution of limited resources, an aspect of social justice that is obviously central to health care policy. The social justice perspective that frames the analysis of health care policy in this chapter, that advanced by John Rawls, will be contrasted with four other different but highly influential theoretical approaches to social justice: Libertarianism, Utilitarianism, Marxism, and the Capabilities Approach.[3] In the review of alternative theories of social justice that follows, the primary bases of comparison will be each theory's fundamental claims pertaining to the nature and overall purpose of civil society, which obligations flow upward from individuals to society, which obligations flow downward from society to the individual, and the theory's essential basis for the just distribution of limited resources.[4]

It should be noted in the review that follows that the term "obligations" is used in a very broad sense to apply to all of those acts and actions that either individuals or social institutions have a responsibility to perform under the principles of a given theory of social justice. As we use the term obligations here, it is meant to apply to acts that might more narrowly be defined as "duties" rather than just obligations. A more detailed analysis of alternative theories would devote more attention to this distinction within each theory. However, for the limited purposes here, the more general application of the term "obligations" is acceptable.[5]

Broadly speaking, principles of social justice are of three general types: procedural, redistributive/compensatory, and distributive. Principles pertaining to *procedural justice* concern the fairness of the process for determining what is just, independent of the outcome. Principles pertaining to *redistributive/compensatory justice* are concerned with the determination and of punishment and compensation for wrongs, injuries, and losses. Principles that are concerned with the just allocation of limited benefits and resources pertain to distributive justice. This book is primarily concerned with this third type of social justice.

The Progression of Theories Considered: Emergent Theories of Justice as "Moral Improvements"

The order of theories reviewed is framed by philosopher William Talbott's thesis that the dominant theories pertaining to human rights and the political philosophy of just governance represent sequential stages in a progression of "moral improvements" (Talbott, 2010). Talbott, like Amartya Sen (2009), concedes that no human society is every likely to discover the perfect or optimal moral system. In absence of a perfect theory of social justice and scheme of human rights that is universally applicable across all cultural and historical contexts, we are therefore reliant upon approaches that compare the prevailing moral philosophies (and the societal arrangements that reflect them) against potential improvements (Talbott, 2010, pp. 17–18).[6]

In this vein, the human rights principles of Libertarianism thus emerged as a "moral improvement" over the principles of governance by monarchy, whereas the consequentialist justification of human rights embedded in Utilitarian principles emerged in the writings of J.S. Mill in the century following the American Revolution (J.S. Mills, *On Liberty*, 1859). The principles of a Marxist orientation to human rights and just governance, although they were established by Karl Marx and Friedrich Engels in their 1848 *Communist*

Manifesto, were not reflected in principles of governance until the Bolshevik Revolution in 1917.[7] The next theory of social justice and human rights to emerge was based upon the politics of Liberalism that were made manifest in the American Progressive movement and in the New Deal policies advanced by the Franklin Delano Roosevelt administration—and then later in the civil rights and social legislation of the Kennedy/Johnson administrations.[8] However, the Liberal theory of social justice and human rights was not formulated as a coherent moral system until John Rawls's (1971) *A Theory of Justice*.

The final dominate theory of social justice to be considered, the Capabilities Approach, emerged during the 1990s[9] in response to what economist and political philosopher Amartya Sen regarded as significant limitations of Rawls's Liberal theory of justice. Although Sen had a decades-long collegial relationship with Rawls and dedicated his most recent treatise on the Capabilities Approach (*The Idea of Justice*, 2009) to the memory of John Rawls, he questioned the moral priority that Liberalism places on the *means* of achieving human well-being (specifically a just scheme of resource allocation) as opposed to the *ends* to be achieved, which he defines as the human capabilities that will allow individuals the freedom to achieve well-being. In addition, Sen rejects Rawls's Liberal theory as being a "transcendental theory of justice," that is, a theory of justice that presumes justice can be achieved through the identification of the nature of "perfect justice" and the institutional arrangements that are presupposed to achieve what is either perfect or at least optimal (Sen, 2009, p. 6).[10] Instead, Sen advocates for an approach to the advancement of social justice that is *comparative* as opposed to abstract. That is, an approach to the conceptualization and advancement of social justice that is based upon "realization-based" comparisons between alternative real-world societal systems of governance, human rights, and social institutions—as opposed to the epistemological traditions in Western political philosophy that favor the use of thought experiments that presuppose the existence of a utopian ideal system of justice.[11]

The Libertarian Theoretical Perspective on Social Justice

The Nature and Overall Purpose of Civil Society

In the classical libertarian perspective, civil society is comprised of a network of natural and voluntary associations among autonomous and equal individuals that in various ways serve human needs (Boaz, 1997). In accordance with this perspective, societies must be governed, but only to the extent necessary to assure the protection of an explicit set of individual rights. As such, government's legitimate functions pertain only to basic protections against foreign or domestic threats to life, property, or the exercise of personal autonomy (Nozick, 1974). For example, governments can legitimately do such things as levy taxes to provide military and police protection, legislate and enforce laws against theft, fraud, and breach of contract, and restrain actions by individuals or groups that in other ways deprive or interfere with the essential civil and property rights of others.

In the dominant libertarian vision of civil society, collective wellbeing is best achieved through the exercise of individual free will and self-responsibility in the context of a laissez-faire market economy. A market economy, unrestrained by burdensome taxes and regulation, alleviates poverty and promotes commonwealth through technological innovation, job creation, and the efficient production and distribution of goods and services yielded by the free flow of labor and capital. To the extent there are individual misfortunes[12] that result in poverty (and family resources are absent), mutual aid societies and other charitable organizations exist as an outgrowth of voluntary cooperation and such factors as individual religious conviction. However, because illness, unemployment, and even old age are risks that are intrinsic to human social existence, it is the role and responsibility of individuals in a free and civil society to self-protect through (1) such market mechanisms as insurance and savings, (2) sharing of family resources, and (3) participation in voluntary networks of mutual aid and protection (e.g., churches, fraternal organizations).[13]

Which Obligations Flow Upward From Individuals to Society?

Core to libertarian philosophy is the premise that individuals have "full self-ownership," meaning that individuals have a *moral right* to grant or deny use of any aspect of their person on whatever basis they determine aligns with their preference, individual moral philosophy, or self-interest. It also means that *individuals have full immunity or protection against the "nonconsensual" loss of their rights to self-ownership*—except where the individual violates the rights of others (Vallentyne, 2004). A second core premise of libertarian social philosophy is that individuals also have the moral right to acquire *property rights* in external things (objects outside the person) that if acquired legitimately *are also immune from nonconsensual loss*.[14] A third and related core premise of libertarianism concerns the use of coercion by governments, institutions, or individuals. In accordance with this third core premise, it is not permissible to employ coercion or the use of force to either: (1) benefit the person, (2) benefit others, or (3) prevent third parties from violating the rights of others (Vallentyne, 2004, p. 1). A fourth core premise, mentioned previously, concerns the minimalist role of governments, in essence, the position that governmental functions should be limited to the protection of life, property, and the exercise of personal autonomy (Nozick, 1974). Collectively these premises imply that the obligations that flow from individuals to society are limited to those that involve overt or explicit consent, and in the case of individual obligations to the government, are limited to those essential for the preservation of collective security and individual liberty, such as taxation for national defense and law enforcement. Indeed, other than those obligations assumed under explicit and free consent, the only other obligations owed by individuals to society at large are those that involve a duty not to violate the essential rights of others (Vallentyne, 2004).[15]

Notably, libertarians do not dismiss the idea that individuals have moral responsibilities, or that various obligations do not arise from their status as moral actors. In the libertarian thought, it is entirely compatible for a libertarian to *voluntarily* hold herself to a stringent moral philosophy that requires that in every action she places the well-being of others before her own narrow self-interest. It is also the case that libertarians place great emphasis on the notion that the free agency carries with it the full burden of accountability for whatever good or evil might result from one's actions (Clarke, 2003).

The dignity that one has in virtue of being a free agent, then, consists in one's making a difference, by one's exercise of active control, in how things go in the world. It consists of one's actions (and some of their consequences) being attributable to the individual self as source and author, and, providing that one has an ordinary capacity to appreciate and act for moral reasons, in one's being responsible for one's actions (and some of their consequences).[16]

Although we can clearly read the foregoing account of libertarian free will as a heavy imperative that individuals should strive to do good in the world and should pursue existence as atomistic and egocentric beings, the distinct thread of libertarianism is retained through the exercise of free will in selecting one's individual moral philosophy. The central point of libertarianism concerning the obligations that flow from the individual to the society at large is that obligations toward others in society are a matter of free choice, other than the nonconsensual obligation or duty to not violate the libertarian rights of others (Vallentyne, 2004).

Which Obligations Flow Downward From Society to the Individual?

As implied by the preceding summary of the libertarian perspective on the flow of obligations from the individual to society as a whole, as well as the libertarian perspective on the nature of society, the obligations that flow downward from the society to the individuals would seem to be quite limited. If, as libertarians argue, civil societies are spontaneous entities comprised of a network of natural and voluntary associations (Boaz, 1997), then it is difficult to find any basis for assuming which (if any) obligations toward individuals actually encumber society at large. However, in the classic libertarian framework there are two kinds of obligations that flow from society to the individuals: those that pertain to the preservation of a limited set of natural rights and those that arise from voluntary social contracts between individuals and the organizations, institutions, and communities they choose to join.

In the utopian society described by classic libertarian theorist Robert Nozick (1974), individuals are free to form, enter, and exit any of a multitude of diverse communities, each expressing a different vision of what values should govern individual lives and what values should govern communal relationships. As stated by Nozick (p. 312), there is no utopian society writ large with a single encompassing vision of ideal social existence, but rather a utopian society that is a collection of many different kinds of utopias that serve different individual preferences. In this vision of society, individuals are at liberty to choose which community to join or leave; membership in any one community can entail a large set of restrictions on individual freedom and extensive mutual obligations between the individual and the community at large. Accordingly, an individual may choose to join a highly socialistic community, or at the other extreme, may choose to join a highly laissez-faire community having minimal constraints on individual behavior and very few mutual obligations.[17] Thus, libertarian theory really does not oppose the idea that an extensive set of entitlements and obligations can flow downward from society to the individual (or vice versa), per se, just as long as those more extensive entitlements and obligations are a function of a social contract enacted by voluntary membership in a community comprised of other like-minded individuals.[18]

In contrast to this benign view of the entitlements and obligations that might arise in voluntary communities, libertarians consider entitlements and obligations that flow through any kind of central government to be inherently suspect, if not pernicious. The philosophical basis for this libertarian aversion to central government is typically attributed to John Locke's *Second Treatise of Government* written in 1690, wherein Locke argues that (1) individuals possess an essential set of natural rights that precede the formation of governments, (2) governments are formed to protect natural rights, and (3) governments that exceed their protectionist role and impinge on individual rights lose their basis of legitimacy (Boaz, 1997; Nozick, 1974). Although there are strains of libertarianism that are willing to extend the protectionist role to equality of opportunity (Otsuka, 1998; Vallentyne, 2004), advocates of classic libertarianism emphasize the idea of the "minimal state" described previously—one that is limited to "the functions of protecting its citizens against violence, theft, and fraud, and to the enforcement of contracts" (Nozick, 1974, p. 26).

Libertarian theory is popular among individuals who, for various reasons (and often good ones), believe governments do things badly. However, in the classic libertarian framework, the reasons why governments are inefficient (and even pernicious) are tied to issues of human diversity and political pluralism. According to this line of reasoning, if it is presumed that individuals have a natural right to live life as they choose (as long as their actions are not harmful to the natural rights of others), and that society is comprised of individuals having diverse preferences and beliefs about what constitutes personal security and the requisites of happiness, then how is it possible to sustain a form of government that serves all individual ideologies and preferences? The answer is that central governments in fact cannot, and that by some method (be it democratic or authoritarian), central governments are bound to select and impose duties, mutual obligations, and limits to freedom that force some individuals to conform to the social ideologies of others. The objection to the central government being the purveyor of mutual social obligations, as opposed to communities and other voluntary forms of human association, is that individuals cannot "opt out" and seek other alternatives short of renouncing citizenship and fleeing—which itself defeats the very purpose of having a central government.

The Utilitarian Theoretical Perspective on Social Justice

The Nature and Overall Purpose of Civil Society

Classic utilitarians, like libertarians, assume that society is founded upon, and to a large extent justified by, voluntary relationships formed for purposes of mutual advantage (Barry, 1989; Roemer, 1996). It can be said that the origins of the utilitarian perspective on social justice begins with Aristotle's notion of distributive justice, which in essence views the just distribution of the goods and benefits of society as a legitimate function of the state (Miller, 2002). That being said, Aristotle himself was not in any sense a utilitarian, because his criteria for the just distribution of goods and benefits rest on the merits of the individual rather than upon the *principle of utility*—the latter being the hallmark of classic utilitarianism introduced in its full form by John Stewart Mill in his (1863) essay titled *Utilitarianism*.[19] In simple form, this principle states that utility (whatever is valued as a good thing) should be distributed in accordance with whichever scheme yields *the maximum good to the maximum number of people* (Rescher, 1966). The principle of utility, taken at face value, suggests that civil society should be organized in highly rationalistic terms (some would say even in calculated terms) to achieve the maximum social good for the most number of persons. Accordingly, the primary problem of distributive justice becomes one of economics, or in the words of eminent economist John Roemer, that system of resource allocation "which maximizes the sum total of utility over persons" (Roemer, 1996, p. 5).

Taken to this extreme, the doctrinaire utilitarian society would be relatively unconcerned with problems of either extremes of deprivation or extremes of abundance, as long as *the maximum good to the maximum number* outcome is served. While one might question the political viability or moral basis of such a system of social organization and governance, in effect this utilitarian doctrine has been underscored and emphasized as a rationale for a number of economic and social policies that clearly benefit some groups over others, such as tax policies that by many accounts contribute to rising concentrations of wealth via such arguments as "a rising tide lifts all boats" (Pizzigati, 2005). The remarkable level of acceptance among Americans for this line of argument suggests that utilitarianism in fact has broad intuitive appeal as a significant foundation for social policy on a variety of fronts, including health care.

Which Obligations Flow Upward From Individuals to Society?

To get to an idea of which obligations flow upward from individuals to society (and vice versa), three concepts are key. First is *consequentionalist theory*, in essence, theories that hold that individual obligations are a function of their outcomes. The second key concept is the ethical principle of *rule utilitarianism*, meaning in essence that the rightness or wrongness of acts are evaluated in accordance with a set of rules that themselves have (over time) managed to achieve the maximization of the common good. Third is the now familiar idea of the *social contract*, described earlier as the idea that civil society is predicated on the basis of a social contract that spells out the benefits, rights, and obligations of societal membership. Thus, in accordance with the utilitarian premise that the ultimate function of society is the promotion of the maximum level of common good, the primary basis for determining the social rules (e.g., laws, social policies, civic duties) is whether or not they are genuinely intended for the common good—even if one's own happiness and well-being (or utility) are compromised. Conversely, this also implies that utilitarian ethics do not obligate one to act in accordance with rules that do not serve the maximization of the common good.

As an example, consider a tax that is levied for road construction, under the premise that there is a consensus among voters that building a particular arterial is essential to commerce and public safety. Even though a utilitarian citizen may not drive or even personally agree that the proposed arterial is needed, she is obligated to pay her share of the taxes because the decision to build the road was determined (1) by the rules of democratic process (presumably adopted because they maximize the common good) and (2) the utilitarian justification that the proposed road itself serves to maximize the common good. However, suppose that it is shown that the proposed road is actually an overly priced boondoggle, put before the voters to benefit a select contractor with a lot of political influence. Would our citizen-utilitarian still have the ethical obligation to pay the taxes levied for the boondoggle arterial? If the voting process itself were not corrupt, the answer would seem to be yes—the premise being that accountability to the outcome of the democratic process remains justified under the ethical principle of *rule utilitarianism*. If, on the other hand, both the democratic process was not adhered to and the road project was not in service of the common good, then our utilitarian citizen will not in any sense violate her ethical principles by refusing to pay taxes for the road because there is no aspect of social contract that was not violated (however, she still might be thrown in jail).

The only other general obligations that flow upward from individuals to society are those that concern restraint from doing evil or harm, or *negative utilitarianism*. Simply stated, there is a utilitarian principle that also states that the rightness of actions should be also evaluated by producing the least harm to the least number of people, or performing actions that prevent the most harm to the most number of people. Accordingly, a social contract that is consistent with utilitarianism can also include obligations that are aimed at either constraining harmful behavior or even obligating the individual to perform duties that are aimed at preventing harm. As an example, it is legitimate from a utilitarian perspective that a village obligates every person who is physically capable to help pile sandbags along a river that is on the verge of flooding. From a health care policy perspective, negative utilitarianism underscores the justification of rules governing personal health behavior—including sexual conduct.

Which Obligations Flow Downward From Society to the Individual?

Utilitarianism does not prescribe a specific set of societal obligations toward individuals, but rather provides general ethical criteria for the evaluation of the laws and other social policies that distribute the benefits and resources of society. In this sense, though, Utilitarian theory is an extremely potent determinant of societal obligations. Consistent with the ethical obligations of individuals, Utilitarian principles hold that social arrangements and actions should (1) maximize the sum of happiness and well-being over the most number of persons, (2) do the least harm to the least number of persons, or (3) prevent the most harm to the most number of persons. By strict Utilitarian standards, this suggests that governments are not ethically obligated to respect any aspect of individual autonomy, happiness, or well-being that runs counter to the maximization of the general good of all—per the ruthless utopia depicted in Aldous Huxley's (originally published in 1932) *Brave New World* (Huxley, 1998).

However, most Utilitarian thinkers promote a strain of utilitarianism that recognizes that there are some limits to the utilitarian principle where the so-called natural rights of individuals are at stake, such as life and liberty. For example, few Utilitarian ethicists condone violent actions of governments or individuals that take the lives of innocents in order to prevent the deaths of many others, or suggest a rigid application of a strict cost–benefit analysis to the provision of all forms of health care. Rather, most Utilitarian thinkers temper their utilitarianism with other fundamental considerations of justice that are not themselves derived from Utilitarian theory, such as recognition of a minimum subsistence threshold for the distribution of essential goods. Along this line, distributive justice philosopher Nicolas Rescher (1966) proposed a "qualified utilitarianism" that adds *all other things being equal* to the basic "greatest good to the greatest number" principle of utility—these other things referring to other relevant principles of justice (Rescher, 1966, pp. 115–117).

A Marxist Theoretical Perspective on Social Justice

There is no single Marxist theory of social justice per se, but rather a variety of interpretations of how the extensive political and historical works of Karl Marx and Friedrich Engels (spanning the 19th century from 1841 to 1895) led to an implicit theory of social justice. The Marxist theory of social justice that is selected for this chapter is explicated in Rodney Peffer's (1990) *Marxism, Morality, and Social Justice*, which many would agree is a rigorous and exhaustive treatment of this subject.[20] However, it should be noted and emphasized that any scholarly interpretations of Marxist thought are generally (and often hotly) contested among Marxists and non-Marxists alike. As such, Peffer's Marxist theory of social justice stands as an exemplar of a Marxist social justice framework rather than the definitive Marxist theory of social justice.

The Nature and Overall Purpose of Civil Society

The central tenet of Marxist theory is *historical materialism,* which stated in the simplest terms claims that the particular social arrangements that comprise different forms of society (social systems) are determined by the modes of production that are dominant in any given historical epoch. Over time, less efficient social systems (those that fail to maximize the dominant mode of production) give way to social systems that are more efficient with respect to the maximization of production (Peffer, 1990). The image of society that became the basis for Marxist theory was 19th century England; a social system with a rigid class structure and ruthless class oppression that was greatly transformed by the Industrial Revolution that had taken place over the preceding 100 years. Thus, class exploitation and conflict lie at the heart of the Marxist perspective of the nature of society and constitute a central theme of contemporary Marxist writings pertaining to issues of social justice.

Although it can be said that the Marxist[21] perspective on the nature of society rests upon an explicit theory of economic determinism and class conflict, the classic Marxist perspective on the overall purpose of civil society can be gleaned only indirectly—since neither Marx or Engels can be said to have produced a unified moral theory.[22] However, one can gain a foothold on the Marxist conception of the purpose of society by examining (1) the central themes of Marx's critiques of 19th-century social systems, (2) the fundamental merits of the communist social system Marx viewed as morally superior to capitalism, and (3) the Marxist criteria for a morally justified revolution—as argued by Peffer (1990). Concerning the first point, insomuch as Marx viewed the capitalist social systems as pernicious and exploitive because a large segment of society suffers poverty and fails to find personal fulfillment or freedom and self-determination, it can be assumed that Marx regarded such things as legitimate claims or expectations of everyday citizens. Regarding the second point (the relative virtue of the communist social system over others), Marx's famous dictum that such a system would assure that "each contributes according to their ability and receives according to their need" strongly suggests themes of equity and commonwealth as core purposes of society (Wolff, 2003). Finally, as Peffer's interpretation of Marxist theory of social justice would have it, people have a legitimate basis for rebellion where governments: (1) fail to secure basic rights of well-being, (2) fail to secure "maximum equal liberty" among citizens, (3) fail to provide equality of opportunity, or (4) fail to eliminate unjust social and economic inequalities.[23]

Marxist thinkers differ greatly on the extent to which the social systems they endorse or believe will incorporate all aspects of doctrinaire Marxism. Peffer's approach to a Marxist theory of social justice rests upon the model of a "democratic, self-managing socialist" society, which he argues is the social system that is most able (in the current historical epoch) to fulfill the Marxist principles of social justice he puts forth. In such a society, the core tenets of socialism (that productive property is socially owned rather than privately owned and the formally working class is elevated to the ruling class), are joined with the political authority of the democratic state (Peffer, 1990, pp. 11–12). Notably, Peffer suggests that democratic, self-managing socialist society can either function as a socialist command economy or a socialist market economy as a matter of simple pragmatism rather than ideology—the choice should be whichever form is most efficient and compatible with the principles of social justice derived from Marxist theory. Briefly stated and somewhat paraphrased, Peffer's Marxist theory of social justice has four core principles:

1. Each person's rights to security and subsistence shall be respected
2. There is to be a maximum system of equal basic liberties, which at minimum must include:
   Freedom of speech and assembly.
   Freedom of conscience and thought.
   Freedom of the person.
   Personal (as opposed to productive) property rights.
   Freedom from arbitrary arrest and seizure.
3. Equal rights to opportunity of position attainment and participation in decision making within all social institutions of which one is a part.
4. Social and economic inequalities are justified if and only if they:
   Serve to benefit the least-advantaged member of society.
   Fall below a level that undermines equal worth of liberty or the good of self-respect (Peffer, 1990, p. 418).

Which Obligations Flow Upward From Individuals to Society?

In contrast to the libertarian and utilitarian frameworks reviewed previously, included and explicit in the Marxist social justice perspective, is the positive right of subsistence (see the first principle). Broadly defined, subsistence refers to being provided the material essentials necessary to sustain life (food, shelter, clothing). However, as explicated by Peffer, the positive right of subsistence is meant to *guarantee* each member of society "a minimum level of material well-being including basic needs, such as, those needs that must be met in order to remain a normal functioning human being" (Peffer, 1990, p. 14). Positive rights that involve material resources are inherently reciprocal—meaning that as individuals not only do we benefit from the guarantee of some minimum level of our own welfare, but we also assume specific obligations and duties toward the basic welfare of others.

The second of the Marxist principles is basically consistent with the obligations individuals assume toward the natural rights of others as advocated by libertarians, except for the limited definition of property rights that excludes ownership of property that has a productive function. The third and fourth principles imply that individuals are also obligated to surrender their individual interests where their personal interests significantly clash with collective equity in the material, social, and political spheres of opportunity, and where their individual interests conflict with social and economic equalities more generally.

In sum, these principles imply that individuals assume not only a moral burden for the basic well-being of others, but also the significant individual obligations that are necessary to promote the ethic of egalitarianism in all spheres of public and productive life.[24] As stated by Peffer, these principles convey a "natural duty" that extends to the support and promotion of just social institutions (p. 15).

Which Obligations Flow Downward From Society to the Individual?

Akin to Libertarian theory, under Peffer's interpretation of Marxist social justice principles, society is obligated to respect and protect the so-called natural rights of individuals, those that pertain to fundamental liberties such as freedom of speech, thought, association, and dominion of one's person and personal property (see the second principle). However, in contrast to the Libertarian perspective and as pointed out previously, the Marxist social justice principles do not suggest that society is obligated to respect or protect property rights that are in any way linked to the productive capacities of society—the latter being subject to collective ownership. Like other theories of social justice that assume an implicit social contract as the basis for legitimacy of political authority (the corollary of which provides the basis for legitimate revolution), the Marxist perspective obligates society to sustain and protect rights to personal security, that is, the provision of protections against coercive actions of others (individuals, institutions, or states) that would unjustly deprive the individual of life, liberty, or personal property. A distinctly Marxist societal obligation pertains to the provision of subsistence at a level necessary to sustain normal human functioning, which in the classic context of Marxist theory would suggest a subsistence level that is sufficient to preserve individual human dignity (e.g., no poor farms, no slums, or other accoutrements of abject poverty).

As specified in the third principle, the Marxist social justice framework places significant emphases on society's obligation to promote and protect equity of opportunity for both status attainment and participation in political decision making, consistent with the liberal social justice framework to be described shortly. However, the thread that is distinctly Marxist in Peffer's social justice framework is the emphasis (in the third principle) on equal rights of participation in all social decision-making processes within *all* social and economic institutions of which one is a part. As Peffer (1990, pp. 401 and 404) states it, the Marxist approach to social justice extends the principle of collective self-determination beyond the political realm to all other realms of social and economic structure—most particularly the workplace. In practical application, the third principle argues that society has the obligation to restrain such social organizations as schools, workplaces, and social service agencies from engaging in nondemocratic forms of governance, and conversely, to positively promote democratic governance in such organizations.

The final set of societal obligations (embedded in the fourth principle) pertains to the eradication of *unjust* social and economic inequalities. Since this principle holds that there are very restricted circumstances under which social and economic inequalities can be considered just, it would seem that society is obligated to eliminate as much as possible all the social and economic inequalities that fall outside of the narrow circumstances specified. The exceptional circumstances are specified in the Difference Principle, a cornerstone of Rawls's theory of social justice. In essence, the difference principle holds that *only those social and economic inequalities that provide the greatest benefit to the least-advantaged members of society are just* (Rawls, 2001, p. 2). The Marxist modification of the Difference Principle (as postulated by Peffer) narrows the criteria for "just" social and economic inequalities by limiting the application of the Difference Principle to *only* those social and economic inequalities that do not undermine the social bases of self-respect. To illustrate, the original Difference Principle would suggest it is "just" to reward a manager with a higher salary for the same number of hours of work if this arrangement provided the most material benefits to the least advantaged of workers. The Marxist modification of the Difference Principle would suggest that the higher salary must not only produce the most benefits to the least advantaged, but also must not be so much higher as to undermine the social bases of respect for the other workers.

The Rawlsian "Justice as Fairness" Liberal Theoretical Perspective on Social Justice

As acknowledged and explained earlier in the preface, Rawls's theory of social justice has been selected as the central social justice perspective of this text. The social justice theory of John Rawls, referred to by Rawls as a "justice as fairness" approach to a theory of social justice (1985), is also commonly regarded as the classic Liberal theory of social justice. As explained by Rawls (p. 224), his theory of social justice is intended to be a *political* theory of social justice; that is, a moral conception of justice that applies to the political, social, and economic institutions of society as distinct from a moral system that applies to the actions of individuals. Notably, Rawls considers his theory of social justice to be limited to and specifically for the special case of a modern constitutional democracy (Rawls, 2001, p. 14). According to Rawls (1985, pp. 226–227), the central challenge of a political theory of social justice in the context of constitutional democracy is to reconcile the inherent pluralism that a free and democratic society promotes with the imperative to create *a public conception of justice*—the latter described as a "mutually recognized point of view from which citizens can adjudicate their claims of political right on their political institutions or against one another" (Rawls, 2001, p. 9).[25]

The Nature and Overall Purpose of Civil Society

Consistent with the social contract doctrine of Locke and his predecessors, Rawlsian social justice theory views the purpose of society as a cooperative social and political arrangement conceived and enacted for mutual advantage. As described by Rawls, his essential concept of society is that of *a unified and fair system of cooperation for reciprocal advantage between free and equal individuals* (Rawls, 2001, p. 22). Notably, Rawls speaks of society only in political terms and as a political conception, which in essence is a closed system of coercive authority (and hopefully optimal mutual benefit) that one involuntary enters at birth and exits at the point of death (p. 40).[26] Because Rawls limits his theory to the case of modern constitutional democracies, his theoretical conception of society places a strong emphasis on society's inherently and irreversibly pluralistic nature (Rawls, 1996). As an extension of this idea, Rawls rejects the notion that "cooperation for mutual advantage" implies society can be or should be communal in nature—because pluralism, optimal individual liberty, and a genuine general communalism cannot all three jointly coexist.[27]

Although Rawls's ideal society is founded upon the moral principles of individual liberty and equality, his theory acknowledges that democratic societies do not (and in fact cannot) assure an equal distribution of advantage and resources across all members of society. That is to say, even among democratic societies conceived on principles of equality and fair reciprocity, there exists an inherent hierarchy of advantage and various forms of social and economic inequalities that arise from arbitrary forces of history and individual endowments. However, pluralism, hierarchies of advantage, and social and economic inequalities do not preclude the evolvement of a society that is both "well ordered" and fundamentally just, a point that brings us to central concepts and principles of Rawls's theory of social justice.

As described by Rawls's, a *well-ordered society* is one governed and regulated by *a public conception of justice*, described previously as a "mutually recognized point of view from which citizens can adjudicate their claims of political right on their political institutions or against one another" (Rawls, 2001, p. 9). The paradox involves the achievement of "a mutually recognized point of view," or set of universally sanctioned justice principles in a society that is (1) inherently pluralist in culture and ideology and (2) already weighted with differences in relative advantage and political interest. To do so, Rawls builds his theory of social justice on a framework of six core concepts (described by Rawls as his "fundamental ideas") and two principles. In keeping with Rawls's presentation of his ideas (Rawls, 2001), we begin with a review of his six fundamental ideas.[28]

The first fundamental idea, *society as a fair system of cooperation*, was described previously as Rawls's essential concept of society, that is, "a unified and fair system of cooperation for reciprocal advantage between free and equal individuals" (Rawls, 2001, p. 22).

The idea of *free and equal individuals* (identified by Rawls as the fifth of his six fundamental ideas) is more complex than it appears. As explained by Rawls, it actually incorporates core conceptions of citizenship that originate with the writings of Aristotle in ancient Greece (see Rawls, 2001, p. 24 and pp. 142–143). Central to the Aristotelian idea of citizenship in a democratic society is full access to social and political participation and engagement in all the rights and duties that accompany citizenship. In the just society of Rawls, being "free and equal" requires that one has the capacity to fulfill the role requirements of active social and political citizenship as conceptualized by Aristotelian philosophy. The radical element of the Rawlsian notion of "free and equal" is the idea that freedom and equality cannot exist independently of the right and capacity to engage in all aspects of citizenship. For example, under this more restricted notion of free and equal citizenship, persons who are unable to exercise the right to vote (whether through physiological incapacity or electoral process manipulation) cannot be called free and equal.

A third fundamental idea of Rawls theory of social justice is the concept of *a well-ordered society*, which in its essence is a society governed by a generally recognized and broadly accepted "public conception of justice"—an idea mentioned in the introductory paragraph on Rawls's theory of justice as "a mutually recognized point of view from which all citizens can adjudicate their claims of political right on their political institutions or against one another" (Rawls, 2001, p. 9). In essence, "a public conception of justice" requires that there is some core set of principles of justice that are known, recognized, and accepted by all members of society. It further means that all members of society have an individual sense of justice that enables them to understand and apply the broadly shared principles of justice as they function in the social and political roles of citizenship.

Also, as pointed out earlier, there is a central paradox in this conception having to do with pluralism—how can a society comprised of culturally and politically diverse individuals with distinct individual moral identities be expected to universally know, recognize, and accept *any* principle of social justice, let alone a fully explicated public conception of justice involving multiple principles? Rawls deals with this paradox by suggesting that citizens have two kinds of commitments and attachments that "specify their moral identity"—those that pertain to their conceptions of political and social justice and those that pertain to more personal aims (Rawls, 2001, p. 24). In contrast to moral attachments that are tied to more personal aims, the moral commitments and attachments that are tied to individual conceptions of political and social justice are more amendable to the achievement of some "overlapping consensus" among otherwise highly diverse individuals.

Although Rawls does not list his concept of an "overlapping consensus" as one of his six fundamental ideas, it is in fact core to his theory of social justice. In essence, an "overlapping consensus" refers to a political conception of justice that does not derive from any particular comprehensive religious or political doctrine—but derives sufficient support from diverse and often opposing religious, political, and moral doctrines to attract a critical mass of adherents and to endure over time (Rawls, 2001, p. 32). Simply stated, an overlapping consensus involves the rules of justice that diverse peoples can agree upon.[29]

A fourth fundamental idea of Rawls's theory of social justice refers to *the basic structure of a just society*. First and foremost, it should be emphasized that "the basic structure of society" is the end object and central subject of Rawls's theory of social justice. As described theoretically, the basic structure of society is the "background social framework" that provides the structural context for political and social cooperation between the various individual elements and associations that compose society. As such, the basic structure involves such institutions and processes as a political constitution, specification of property rights, the economic system, and the social and political constructions of the family system (Rawls, 2001, p. 10). Critical to Rawls's theory of social justice is the idea that the principles of social justice *do not necessarily* determine the actions of the particular associations and institutions that compose society. For example, families may choose to adopt a set of duties and obligations for children that, outside the family context, would be generally interpreted as unfair and pejorative elsewhere—just as churches, employers, and social clubs might. The principles of social justice can indeed determine or trump the policies and actions of families and social organizations, but only where the general principles of social justice are clearly at stake. For example, a parent may choose to ground a child as punishment for some minor transgression without violating political principles of social justice. However, denial of the child's needed medical care as punishment does—because the latter involves fundamental concerns pertaining to the particular social obligations assumed by parents under any reasonable scheme of social cooperation, as well as the basic rights the child holds as a prospective citizen.[30]

A fifth fundamental idea of Rawls's theory introduces *the idea of the original position*, which, like the other fundamental ideas thus far discussed, has layers of complexity that are left unaddressed in this limited rendition of Rawls's theory of justice. Briefly stated, however, the "original position" involves the necessary and sufficient conditions for arriving at a "just" agreement that determines the structure of "a fair system of cooperation between free and equal citizens." That is to say, the original position refers to the point of view from which the social contract is negotiated and agreed upon. An original position that promotes fairness has formidable requisites that go beyond ordinary considerations of coercion and overtly unfair bargaining advantage. In essence, the ideal original position for the creation of a just social contract must be completely objectified—uninfluenced by immediate social contingencies, historical advantages, or any social factor that contributes to the bargaining advantage of any particular individual or group. This condition of unfettered objectivity is referred to by Rawls as the "veil of ignorance," emphasizing the point that the truly objective pursuit of fairness can be achieved only with complete absence of information about the effect of the agreement on any particular individual or group.[31]

The sixth and final fundamental idea that rounds out the foundation of Rawls's theory is *the idea of public justification*. "Public justification" is described by Rawls as a central feature of a well-ordered society that "establishes a shared basis for citizens to justify to one another their political judgments: each cooperates, politically and socially, with the rest on terms that all can endorse as just" (Rawls, 2001, p. 27). Rawls very deliberately makes a distinction between public justification and either (1) assent to the merits of valid argument or (2) what he terms "mere agreement" to a political judgment. The latter two are outcomes, whereas public justification is more truly a process of political engagement between free and equal citizens that yields a consensus on more fundamental principles of justice and related crucial aspects of the basic structure of a just society (Rawls, 2001 pp. 29, 46). In Rawls's theory of justice, the process of public justification is central. By extension, basic structural arrangements may be considered adequate and just to the extent they optimize the capacity of all individuals to participate in this process. This particular point has significant implications for a number of social institutions—including basic education and health care.

The Rawlsian model of a just society is shaped by two essential principles of justice, which for convenient reference are referred to as (1) the Equal Basic Liberties Principle and (2) the Difference Principle. The Equal Basic Liberties Principle simply states that "Each person has the same indefeasible claim to a fully adequate scheme of equal basic liberties, which is compatible with the same scheme of liberties for all" (Rawls, 2001, p. 42). Although Rawls devotes significant attention to the delineation of which individual liberties are considered basic, on its face this first principle is consistent with a number of other theories as well as popular ideas of social justice. On the other hand, the Difference Principle (briefly described earlier in Peffer's Marxist theory of social justice) is far more unique and nuanced.[32] It reads as follows:

> Social and economic inequalities are to satisfy two conditions: first, they are to be attached to offices and positions that are open to all under fair conditions of equality of opportunity; and second, they are to be the greatest benefit to the least-advantaged members of society (Rawls, 2001, p. 42).

The Difference Principle, while it acknowledges that inequalities are unavoidable and in some instances even functional, sets a very high bar for justification. First, that privilege in status and power cannot be just if inherited or otherwise conferred in a process that does not provide equity of opportunity for all persons. In pragmatic terms, this principle implies that social class standing and the resources that accompany social class are under most circumstances inherently unjust—whether or not the privileged status in question ultimately serves a greater benefit to the least advantaged. In this regard, Rawls is careful to make the point that "fair equality of opportunity" in its moral weight precedes "the greatest benefit to the least advantaged," which is the other essential justification embedded in the Difference Principle (see Rawls, 2001, p. 43). Second, as previously stated, even where privileged status arises through a fair and equitable process of selection, it is deemed just only if it continues to benefit most those that are most marginalized in society. Although a more complete discussion of the health policy implications of Rawls's two principles of social justice will take place in the chapters that follow, it is easy to see how the Difference Principle might be applied to the analysis of status, power, and income inequalities that are embedded in the hierarchy of the health professions.

Although the preceding paragraphs have sketched the main framework of Rawls's theory of social justice and vision of a just society, it is also important to reference the four-part process through which principles of justice are formulated and adopted. In Rawls's model of an optimally just society, the essential principles of justice are identified and adopted during the first stage by the various parties to the agreement[33] behind the previously described veil of ignorance—in essence, to assure as much as possible that the principles adopted are unbiased with respect to the interests of particular persons or groups. In the second stage, described as the "constitutional convention" stage, the specific political arrangements that optimally serve the essential principles of justice are adopted—with some knowledge of and attendance to the nature and interests of various groups composing the body politic. In the third, "legislative" stage, specific laws are enacted that are either required or permitted by the principles of justice adopted in the first stage, and in the fourth stage the laws that are enacted at stage three are interpreted, applied, and followed in the respective roles of elected officials, administrators, the judiciary, and ordinary citizens (Rawls, 2001, p. 48). In essential respects, Rawls's ideal process serves as a justification of the historical process that yielded the American constitutional democracy—with the notable exception of a "veil of ignorance" during the first stage.

Which Obligations Flow Upward From Individuals to Society?

Under the Rawls's theory of justice, the obligations that flow from individuals to society either derive from obligations accounted for by the principle of fairness or derive from what he terms "natural duties" (Rawls, 1971). According to the general principle of fairness explicated in his original theory, individuals are accountable to the obligations imposed by social and political institutions when two conditions are met: the institution is "just" in that it satisfies the two fundamental principles of justice; and the individual in question has either voluntarily accepted the benefits of or taken advantage of the personal opportunities afforded by the arrangement (Rawls, 1971, pp. 111–112). As Rawls would have it, under such restricted criteria only a limited number of individuals have obligations that derive from such voluntary arrangements—public office holders and ordinary citizens that have clearly advanced their interests by accepting particular institutional arrangements. A classic case of the latter might be the extraordinary obligations physicians assume to provide emergency aid to victims of injury, irrespective of the opportunity for payment.

On the other hand, the obligations that fall under the rubric of "natural duties" apply to all persons under the general circumstances of a legitimate social contract. While Rawls suggests there are many "natural duties," those he highlights in his original theory and later writings include the duties of justice, fair play, mutual aide, and nonmaleficence (Rawls, 1971, 1999). Briefly stated, the principle of justice requires individuals to both support and comply with the just institutions of society that apply to each individual's circumstances. The principle of justice also "constrains [the individual] to further just arrangements not yet established, at least when this can be done without too much cost to ourselves" (Rawls, 1971, p. 115). The closely related duty of fair play holds that individual participants in the various social institutions that exist for purposes of mutual benefit, if they accept the rules of the institution as just or fair, are obligated to act in accordance with the rules of the institution.[34] The duty of mutual aid, as described by Rawls, involves helping another person when that person is in need or jeopardy, "provided one can do so without excessive risk or loss to oneself" (Rawls, 1971, p. 114). Finally, the duty of nonmaleficence (or do no harm) requires that individuals not engage in actions that either do harm to another person or are the cause of unnecessary suffering.

Of the aforementioned natural duties, the most radical departure from other theories of social justice is the clause of the duty of justice that obligates individuals to be advocates of social change. A principle of justice that "constrains [the individual] to further just arrangements not yet established" implies very directly that any individual's passive acceptance of unjust aspects of social structure or unjust institutions is in essence a violation of their duty of justice—even if the individual had nothing to do with the creation of the structural injustice in question. This aspect of Rawls's theory imposes a very different lens on the analysis of health and health care policy than is typically afforded, as will be evident in later chapters.

Which Obligations Flow Downward From Society to the Individual?

The obligations that flow downward from society to the individual are not systematically delineated by Rawls so much as they are discussed in reference to three general domains of social justice: *equal basic liberties, fair equality of opportunity,* and *equal distribution of primary goods.* Although equal basic liberties and fair equality of opportunity are subsumed under equal distribution of primary goods, a more complete sense of the societal obligations toward the individual is gained through some explication of all three general domains of social justice. Given its primacy, the first to be considered will be *equal distribution of primary goods.*

As the term "primary goods" implies, these are the political, social, and material benefits of society that are deemed to be the most core or essential.

The most specific definition of primary goods provided by Rawls identifies primary goods as those "things needed and required by persons seen in the light of the political conception of persons as citizens who are fully cooperating members of society, and not merely human beings" (Rawls, 2001, p. 58). As originally described (1971), primary goods were said by Rawls to encompass rights and liberties, opportunities and powers, and income and wealth. In later writings, primary goods were assigned to five more elaborately described categories that include basic rights and liberties that are the essential institutional conditions for the adequate development and the full and informed exercise of the two moral powers of free and equal persons:[35] the freedom to pursue opportunities that are consistent with individual ends; power and authority; income and wealth; and "the social bases of self-respect"—meaning those aspects of basic institutions that are essential to self-worth (Rawls, 2001, p. 58).

Rawls offers two approaches to the explication of "basic liberties." One approach delineates an explicit list of basic liberties that is either logically derived from Rawls's first principle of justice (Martin, 1985) or based upon a historical survey of common basic rights among the most successful democratic regimes (Rawls, 2001). As noted by Martin (1985), the "explicit list" approach yields what is commonly regarded in the United States as the basic civil rights: the right to vote, freedom of speech and assembly, liberty of conscience, the right of property, and the protections against arbitrary arrest, servitude, and seizure of property that are established by the rules of due process. The other approach is analytical rather than explicit. In essence, basic liberties are defined generally as those basic rights and liberties "that provide the political and social conditions that are essential for the adequate development and full exercise of the two moral powers of free and equal persons" (Rawls, 2001, p. 45). Although the latter approach may not yield a radically different set of basic rights and liberties from those delineated in the first, it does build in more possibility of contextual adaptation and dynamic evolvement.

The final domain of societal obligations toward the individual considered here, "fair equality of opportunity," is conceded by Rawls to be difficult and fraught with ambiguity. However, the explicit inclusion of this idea in Rawls's second principle of social justice clearly establishes its central place in Rawls's theory of social justice. As suggested by Rawls (2001, p. 43), the idea of "fair equality of opportunity" can best be understood if contrasted with the idea of "equality of opportunity" in the formal or legalistic sense. In the formal or legalistic sense, equality of opportunity involves institutionalized rules and practices that leave offices, occupations, and social positions open to all persons who have the requisite abilities and credentials. Although this might be de jure equality of opportunity, de facto equality of opportunity involves a far more complex appraisal of a given individual's genuine prospects; given such factors as the impediments (or privileges) of social class background, stigmatized social characteristics, and access to the other material and social benefits that are determinate of the opportunity in question. In stating that a just society owes each person "fair equality of opportunity" to offices and social positions that is commensurate with his or her natural endowments and motivations (Rawls, 2001, pp. 42–44), Rawls very directly lays not only the groundwork for an array of individual claims on society, but a radical social and political agenda as well.[36]

Taken to its logical end, the idea or principle of "fair equality of opportunity" produces an expansive set of societal obligations that flow to individuals (and particular groups) that in large part are determined by the sources and extent of their accumulated disadvantage. For example, interpreted in this light, "fair equality of opportunity of education" implies a special and particular set of obligations pertaining to the schools that serve the poor that is the complete opposite of the current patterns of social investment in education. Finally, the "fair equality of opportunity principle" also entails significant implications for health and health care-related entitlements, a crucial point that will be taken up in the concluding section of this chapter.

The Capabilities Approach to Social Justice

As discussed at an earlier point this chapter, the Capabilities Approach to social justice and human rights was formulated by Amartya Sen in a series of lectures, essays, and books during the final decades of the last century in large part as a critique of Rawlsian Liberalism's resource-based principles of justice. While Sen acknowledges the enormous influence of John Rawls on his development of the Capabilities Approach to social justice (Sen, 2009), he does not regard the Capabilities Approach as either a refinement or extension of Rawlsian Liberalism—nor should we. While there are many areas of convergence between Rawlsian Liberalism, and the Capabilities Approach, the points of departure are fundamental. To recapitulate points made in the beginning of the chapter, the Capabilities Approach argues: (1) that the conceptualization and realization of social justice is advanced through a comparative epistemology as opposed to reliance upon an abstract transcendental theory of justice, (2) that approaches to social justice that focus on *means* (resources, ideal institutional arrangements) as opposed to *ends* (the realization of human capabilities) are less effective in the advancement of human possibilities and freedoms, and (3) that theories of justice that are predicated on an idealized social contract overlook both problems of exclusion and impact of globalization on local social conditions and human rights. These three points of departure between Liberalism and the Capabilities Approach are not the only ones, but in many respects they are the most crucial.

While the basic tenets of Capabilities Approach were formulated by economist Amartya Sen, this theoretical framework for the consideration and advancement of social justice is often referred to as Sen and Nussbaum's Capabilities Approach in acknowledgement of philosopher Martha Nussbaum's crucial contributions to the substantive aspects of the human capabilities that are to be the moral object of a just society. The synopsis of the Capabilities Approach to social justice that follows will begin with an overview of Sen's fundamental ideas concerning the nature of justice and the means of advancing it, and then will summarize Martha Nussbaum's ideas concerning the "ten central human capabilities" that are essential to the achievement of social justice. Finally, the implications of Sen and Nussbaum's Capabilities Approach for the nature and purpose of a just society, the obligations that flow upward from individuals to society, and the obligations that flow downward from society to the individual will be considered.

In contrast to the theories of social justice thus far reviewed, the Capabilities Approach is regarded as a conceptual framework that can be applied to a range of normative concerns related to human rights and human well-being rather than a precise and comprehensive theory of social justice (Robeyns, 2011; Sen, 2009), including the particular concern that is the project of this book—just health and health care policy. As succinctly stated by Robeyn's (2011, p. 1) foundational to the Capabilities Approach "are two normative claims: first, that the freedom to achieve well-being is of primary moral importance, and second, that freedom to achieve well-being is to be understood in terms of peoples' capabilities, that is, their real opportunities to do and be what they have reason to value."[37] It should also be stated that although Sen is critical of the use of equity as a general criteria of justice, he also holds that considerations of equity must be central to any theory of justice (Sen, 2009, p. 296).

So, if the advancement of peoples' capabilities is the primary lens through which we consider and compare alternative social arrangements (government political structures and processes, social policies and social institutions), how is the advancement of human capabilities accomplished? The Capabilities Approach argues that human capability is developed through the interplay of four essential causal components: individual endowments, individual needs, external physical and social conditions, and individual agency (Venkatapuram, 2011). Thus, the evaluation of alternative social arrangements entail how they take into account and affect all four causal components of human capability, as opposed to one or two to the exclusion of others.[38]

Figure 1.1 provides a very basic sketch of the central idea and some essential concepts that are crucial to the understanding of the Capabilities Approach to the advancement of human rights and social justice. As the diagram shown in Figure 1.1 suggests, the Capabilities Approach to the advancement of social justice would consider the ways in which specific social policies and institutional arrangements, as they adapt to individual needs and endowments, might either advance or retard human capabilities, generally defined as the "real" opportunities or possibilities of persons to "be" or "do" that which is valued (Robeyns, 2011) or realize the achievement of functioning in accordance with how one wishes to pursue life (Venkata-puram, 2011). The Capabilities Approach also places significant emphasis on *conversion factors*, that is, those factors (personal, social, environmental) that help an individual convert or transform endowments and resources into capabilities and functionings (the beings and doings of living life).[39] For example, a paraplegic woman may have the intelligence and training to compete for employment as a computer programmer, but her realization of that opportunity (her capability) is contingent on various conversion factors; personal, social, and also environmental (Robeyns, 2011). The personal conversion factor might be her skills and confidence in encounters with disability prejudice and discrimination, the social conversion factor might be national employment discrimination policies that make it more difficult for prospective employers from rejecting her application on the basis of her paraplegic condition, and the environmental conversion factor might be the local "built environment" for disabled persons — the existence of sidewalks with wheel chair accessible ramps that would enable her to get from her house to the nearby public bus stop. The public bus fleet itself would then be required be wheelchair accessible, as a matter of social policy (a social conversion factor).

As also shown in Figure 1.1, capabilities (as real opportunities/possibilities to be able to "be" or to "do") do not in and of themselves determine specific functionings or achievements. In accordance with Sen's core idea of "capabilities as freedom," capabilities allow the individuals be, do, and achieve that which they have reason to value (Sen, 2009). "[I]t may be appropriate to think that the claims on individuals on the society may be best seen in terms of freedom to achieve (given by the set of real opportunities) rather than actual achievements" (Sen, 2009, p. 238). Thus Figure 1.1 shows, in accordance with the Capabilities Approach, specific functionings are heavily determined by value preferences that may be either primarily individual or cultural in origin. As Robeyns (2011) observes on this crucial point: ". . . the notion of

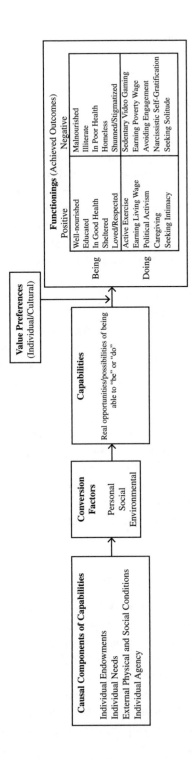

Source: Author's compilation.

Figure 1.1 *Heuristic diagram of "Capabilities Approach" theoretical framework for comparative social justice.*

functionings is a conceptual category that is in itself morally neutral" (p. 5). That is, the appraisal of whether a specific function is either "good" or "bad" is made in the context of the real possibilities/opportunities available to the person, an understanding of the individual and cultural value preferences that are reflected in the function, and the normative theory being applied.

For example, taken at face value assuming the functions of caregiver to an aging parent is generally regarded as positive functioning, in comparison with neglecting the needs of an aging parent in order to pursue various forms of narcissistic (self-centered) gratification (spending the weekend at a spa or meeting a lover in Las Vegas). However, what if we interjected cultural values and expectations that make it more incumbent on the individual in question (who happens to be the only daughter) to be primary caregiver of the parent, as opposed to another equally healthy and equally available sibling (who happens to be the only son)? Whether or not the choice of caregiving is regarded as a positive function might then be subject to several contextual considerations, including the normative lens being applied. Seen through the historical and normative lens of sociologist Evelyn Nakano Glenn (*Forced to Care: Coercion and Caregiving in America*, Nakano, 2010), we would first question the extent to which daughters of aging parents typically possess (as a capability) genuine autonomy or the freedom to choose between caregiving and self-gratification. Even should this capability be granted, we then might question whether there is equity of personal autonomy between the hypothetical daughter and son in this situation, given deeply entrenched cultural beliefs that daughters more than sons are "natural caregivers." The appraisal of the relative equity and fairness of the choices between the son and the daughter might then turn on the normative framework (religious teachings, communal expectations, or particular theory of justice) being applied. It is for this reason that the Capabilities Approach holds that questions of justice are best seen in light of human capabilities, as opposed to achieved outcomes (Sen, 2009).

The Nature and Overall Purpose of Civil Society

Since the Capabilities Approach functions as a comparative framework as opposed to a comprehensive theory of justice, it offers no explicit vision of the perfect civil society. Rather, it primarily concerns itself with the relative merits of specific societal arrangements (political, economic, and social structures) as they affect people's freedom to achieve well-being, understood in terms of peoples' capabilities—their real opportunities to do and be what they have reason to value (Robeyns, 2011; Sen, 2009). So it could be said as a general statement that while the Capabilities Approach sees human societies as inherently diverse in their structures, cultural foundations, priorities, and visions of purpose, the primary moral aim lens through which to view alternative societal forms is the extent to which they either advance or impede people's freedoms to achieve well-being; understood as their real opportunities (capabilities) to do and to be what they have reason to value.

Which Obligations Flow Upward From Individuals to Society?

In contrast to the other theories of justice considered, the Capabilities Approach as it is thus far developed has little to say about specific duties and obligations that flow from individuals to the society at large (Robeyns, 2011). However, Sen (2009, p. 19) places strong emphasis on the idea that with the realization of capabilities (the power to do things), comes accountability for our actions and also demands for duties. We should then wonder of course; to which specific duties are persons obligated and to whom are these duties owed? The only duty Sen speaks to specifically and consistently (and even then in very general terms) is the duty of reducing injustice in the world. As stated multiple times in his most recent explanation and defense of the Capabilities Approach (*The Idea of Justice*, 2009): "... [I]f someone has the power to make a change that he or she can see will reduce injustice in the world, then there is a strong social argument for doing just that ..." (p. 205). Sen also takes pains to point out that this general duty of justice arises from the power to effect change, as opposed rationales based on either mutual advantage or other forms of contractarian reasoning. As to the question, "To whom are duties owed?," Sen argues that to the extent that the power to effect change crosses various kinds of boundaries and borders (families, neighborhoods, communities, and nation states), so does the duty to reduce injustice (Sen, 2009, pp. 170–173).

Which Obligations Flow Downward From Society to the Individual?

While it should be apparent at this point that the Capabilities Approach holds that there is a manifest obligation of society to foster the real opportunities (capabilities) of individuals to do and be what they have reason to value, Sen has consistently resisted specifying which human capabilities matter most or would be a universal priority for all societies (Robeyns, 2011; Sen, 2009; Venkatapuram, 2011). These arguments he has left to others, most notably to feminist philosopher Martha Nussbaum (*Women and Human Development: The Capabilities Approach*, Cambridge University Press, 2000a). Nussbaum's version of the *Capabilities Approach* identifies 10 central human capabilities that together comprise the minimum and essential list of individual entitlements in a just society. Because Nussbaum's list of 10 central capabilities are the most exhaustive, definitive, and frequently referenced by the proponents and critics of the Capabilities Approach, they are cited in their entirety from Nussbaum's (2000a) *Woman and Human Development* (pp. 78–80):[40]

CENTRAL HUMAN FUNCTIONAL CAPABILITIES

1. **Life.** Being able to live to the end of a human life of normal length; not dying prematurely, or before one's life is so reduced as to be not worth living.
2. **Bodily Health.** Being able to have good health, including reproductive health; to be adequately nourished; to have adequate shelter.
3. **Bodily Integrity.** Being able to move freely from place to place; having one's bodily boundaries treated as sovereign, that is, being able to be secure against assault, including sexual assault, child sexual abuse, and domestic violence; having opportunities for sexual satisfaction and for choice in matters of reproduction.
4. **Senses, Imagination, and Thought.** Being able to use the senses, to imagine, think, and reason—and to do these things in a 'truly human' way, a way informed and cultivated by an adequate education, including, but by no means limited to, literacy and basic mathematical and scientific training. Being able to use imagination and thought in connection with experiencing and producing self-expressive works and events of one's own choice, including religious, literary, musical, and so forth. Being able to use one's mind in ways protected by guarantees of freedom of expression with respect to both political and artistic speech, and freedom of religious exercise. Being able to search for the ultimate meaning of life in one's own way. Being able to have pleasurable experiences, and to avoid nonnecessary pain.
5. **Emotions.** Being able to have attachments to things and people outside ourselves; to love those who love and care for us, to grieve at their absence; in general, to love, to grieve, to experience longing, gratitude, and justified anger. Not having one's emotional development blighted by overwhelming fear and anxiety, or by traumatic events of abuse or neglect. (Supporting this capability means supporting forms of human association that can be shown to be crucial in their development.)
6. **Practical Reason.** Being able to form a conception of the good and to engage in critical reflection about the planning of one's life. (This entails protection for the liberty of conscience.)

7. **Affiliation. A.** Being able to live with and toward others, to recognize and show concern for other human beings, to engage in various forms of social interaction; to be able to imagine the situation of another and to have compassion for that situation; to have the capacity for both justice and friendship. (Protecting this capability means protecting institutions that constitute and nourish such forms of affiliation, and also protecting the freedom of assembly and political speech.) **B.** Having the social bases of self-respect and nonhumiliation; being able to be treated as a dignified being whose worth is equal to that of others. This entails, at a minimum, protections against discrimination on the basis of race, sex, sexual orientation, religion, caste, ethnicity, or national origin. In work, being able to work as a human being, exercising practical reason and entering into meaningful relationships of mutual recognition with other workers.

8. **Other Species.** Being able to live with concern for and in relation to animals, plants, and the world of nature.

9. **Play.** Being able to laugh, to play, to enjoy recreational activities.

10. **Control Over One's Environment. A. Political.** Being able to participate effectively in political choices that govern one's life; having the right of political participation, protections of free speech and association. **B. Material.** Being able to hold property (both land and movable goods), not just formally but in terms of real opportunity; and having property rights on an equal basis with others; having the right to seek employment on an equal basis with others; having the freedom from unwarranted search and seizure.

Among the many caveats that Nussbaum applies to her list of 10 human capabilities, two are particularly crucial. First, that the structure of a society's political and social institutions should be chosen with the intention of creating a minimum "threshold level" of each of these capabilities (p. 75). Second, that there is no order of priority or preference that would advance one of these central human capabilities over the other (Nussbaum, 2000b).

CONCLUDING COMMENTS: ALTERNATIVE THEORETICAL PERSPECTIVES ON "THE RIGHT TO HEALTH CARE"

The Nature of Positive Rights

Political theorists and moral philosophers make a distinction between *negative rights* and *positive rights*. Negative rights involve constraints on others to not impede our actions and preferences, do something to us, or take something from us. Negative rights also mostly apply to the actions of the state or governments and thus are commonly known as "liberty rights." Positive rights pertain to what is owed to us or what we can legitimately claim we should be provided. The "right to health care" typically is construed as a positive right, something society owes the individual as either an implied or an overt provision of the social contract. As it is conventionally understood, the right to health care entails a societal obligation to furnish individuals and/or populations with some established array of health care services that may be preventative, curative, or even restorative (Hessler & Buchanan, 2002). Debates about the "right to health care" can be roughly divided between those that are focused on whether *any* right to health care exists, and those that concern the scheme of specific entitlements and limits that derive from the right to health care. While only the former are considered in this brief discussion, alternative social justice perspectives on specific entitlements will be considered later in the text in the context of health care reform.

As readers might have concluded by now, the five social justice perspectives considered in this chapter (Libertarian, Utilitarian, Marxist, Liberal, and Capabilities Approach) indeed differ on their appraisal of health care as a basic right. Some theoretical perspectives go even further, by extending their arguments to entitlements or positive rights to not just health care, but to health itself. In this final section of Chapter 1, these alternative theoretical perspectives on the right to health care will be briefly summarized, and then the chapter ends with a review of the reasons for choosing the "Justice as Fairness" Liberal theory of John Rawls as the optimal framework for the analysis of just health and health care policies.

Five Theoretical Perspectives on Positive Rights to Health and Health Care: Their Essential Distinctions

The Libertarian Perspective on Health and Health Care Rights

The libertarian perspective, primarily because it is concerned with constraining the authority of the state, conceptualizes a very minimal social contract that clearly excludes any semblance of a right to health care. Notably, it presumes that persons who prefer a more extensive array of reciprocal obligations than provided by the minimalist state will self-select into the kind of human communities and voluntary associations that best fit their preferences (Nozick, 1974). Core also to the classic libertarian perspective is the idea that as the risks to human existence are generally known and individuals exist as autonomous and self-responsible beings, it is incumbent on individuals and not governments to seek ways to self-protect and mitigate risk.

As applied to health care, this suggests that the prudent individual will assure the provision of adequate health care (in accordance with their personal tastes) through such voluntary mutual benefit associations as nonprofit health insurance funds or commercial health insurance. Although a variety of challenges to this perspective are put forth concerning the plight of the more vulnerable populations (children, elderly, and disabled), the classic libertarian perspective denies at every turn that there exists any general positive right to health care.

The Utilitarian Perspective on Health and Health Care Rights

The second social justice perspective considered, utilitarianism, also does not establish health care as a basic right—but utilitarian theory does leave open the possibility that health care might be defined as a universal entitlement that is established by social policy. It was stated earlier in this chapter that utilitarianism does not prescribe any specific set of societal obligations so much as it provides the general ethical criteria for the evaluation of social policies that distribute the benefits and resources of society. Under the utilitarian ideal, if some scheme of universal basic health care were indeed proposed as an obligatory function of government, its ethical justification would turn on two criteria: (1) whether or not the agreed upon processes of deliberation and public consent had been followed and (if so) (2) whether or not the principle of utility had been satisfied in the proposed scheme, meaning that the proposed universal health care scheme distributes health care in a manner that yields *the maximum good to the maximum number of people* (Rescher, 1966) Notably, utilitarianism is the ethical perspective that is most consistent with public health analysis of the more advanced and desirable health care systems—in essence, those systems of health care that yield the highest levels of average population health. If the health care systems that yield the highest levels of population health also happen to provide universal access to health care,[41] this provides a utilitarian argument in favor of a universal positive right to health care. However, if the evidence were to suggest that the utility principle is best served by a more selective entitlement to health care, then the utilitarian perspective would argue against a universal positive right to health care.

The Marxist Perspective on Health and Health Care Rights

Marxism is far less equivocal, although like most other political theorists and social philosophers of his day, Karl Marx did not speak directly of a right to health care. However, the ideal, if not a general positive right to health care, has been the centerpiece of every regime in history predicated on Marxism.

This is so for a variety of reasons, the most fundamental of which are that Marxist principles call for both the collective ownership of the system of health care and the elimination of any disparities in the rewards of labor. That is, the health care system exists as a "mode of production" that involves labor and ergo collective ownership, and health care (if not provided outright by the state) is generally construed as a reward of labor. Although Marx theorized different principles of distribution at different stages in the evolvement of the communist state (Peffer, 1990, p. 78), perhaps his most infamous quote, "From each according to his ability, to each according to his needs" (Marx, 1938, p. 10), refers to the state of affairs he envisions in the final evolution of the communist society. As a statement of the Marxist ideal, this if nothing else establishes a positive right to health care as a clear tenet of any reasonably Marxist theory of social justice. Thus, the Marxist theory of social justice explicated earlier in the chapter (Peffer, 1990) specifies (under its principle pertaining to universal security and subsistence rights) a universal positive right to basic medical care (see Peffer, 1990, pp. 418, 420).

As a final point on framing the Marxist perspective on health care, it must be said that Marxism was the first theory of social justice to establish theoretical linkages between economic injustices, class structure, and injustices in the distribution of health. In classic Marxist theory, poor health is seen as consequent to the capitalist social system, because the capitalistic system directly spawns detrimental and demoralizing living and working conditions, and further, undermines the physical and mental health of workers through processes of disempowerment and alienation (Peffer, 1990, p. 52). Moreover, Marxist critiques of the organization of health care in market economies generally see their health care systems as inherently exploitive and reinforcing of class structure. In general, Marxist theorists directly and often quite coherently link the basic social and economic structure of a given society, the distribution of health and disease, and the organization of the health care system.

The Rawlsian "Justice as Fairness" Liberal Perspective on Health and Health Care Rights

As acknowledged in the Preface of this book, the "Justice as Fairness" liberal perspective of John Rawls will frame the analysis of health and health care policy alternatives that will follow in later chapters.[42] For this reason, as well as the observation that this perspective's application to health and health care policy has been more developed in recent decades, more space is devoted to a review of this theoretical perspective's view of health and health care rights.

The General Argument. In his original *Theory of Justice* (published in 1971), John Rawls did not directly deal with the question of a positive right to health care, and did not include health care among either his list of basic rights or primary goods. However, in his final theoretical formulation (written just before his death), Rawls unequivocally conceded that medical care might be regarded as the equivalent of a primary good (i.e., among the political, social, and material benefits of society deemed most core or essential to a just society):

> "…. provision for medical care, as with primary goods generally, is to meet the needs and requirements of citizens as free and equal. *Such care falls under the general means necessary to underwrite fair equality of opportunity* [italics added in this text for emphasis] and our capacity to take advantage of our basic rights and liberties, and thus to be normal and fully cooperating members of society over a complete life. (Rawls, 2001, p. 174)

Beyond this one crucial statement though, Rawls left the task of extending his theory of justice the specifics of health and health care rights to others, most notably to philosopher Norman Daniels (1981, 1985, 2002, and 2008). While in his earlier extensions of Rawls's liberal theory of justice Daniels limited the "fair equality of opportunity" argument to the specific provisions of a positive right to health care, in his most recent extension of Rawls's theory Daniels connected the "fair equality of opportunity" principle to health itself. In making the argument that health itself (and not just health care) is an essential precondition to "fair equality of opportunity," Daniels opens the door to an array of positive rights (social entitlements) that clearly go well beyond the original version of Rawls's liberal theory of justice. In his more recent extension of Rawls's theory of justice, Daniels also bridges Rawlsian Liberalism to some key premises of Sen and Nussbaum's Capabilities Approach (Daniels, 2008; Venkatapuram, 2011).

As most recently argued by Daniels (2008), health (which necessarily includes health care) has special moral importance in a just society because health is crucial to the development and protection of "fair equality of opportunity"—a central tenet of Rawls's theory of justice. As a next step, Daniels (2008, p. 42) then defines health as "normal human functioning," and "health needs" as "those things we need to maintain, restore, or provide functional equivalents (where possible) to normal species functioning (for the appropriate reference class by age and gender)." Critical to Daniels' approach is the connection made between "normal human functioning" and what he terms "individual shares of the normal opportunity range," that is, an equitable share of "the array of life plans persons can reasonably choose in a given society" (p. 59). Thus, moral claims to social provisions for health (and ergo health care) are based on the following progression of ideas:

SIX HEALTH NEEDS→ NORMAL HUMAN FUNCTIONING→ NORMAL OPPORTUNITY RANGE→ EXERCISE OF CHOICE IN LIFE PLANS

The "six health needs" that Daniels argues are essential to normal human functioning (pp. 42−43) are as follows:

1. Adequate nutrition
2. Sanitary, safe, unpolluted living and working conditions
3. Exercise, rest, and such important lifestyle features as avoiding substance abuse and practicing safe sex
4. Preventative, curative, rehabilitative, and compensatory personal medical services (and devices)
5. Nonmedical personal and social support services
6. An appropriate distribution of other social determinants of health

Clearly, this very broad list of "health care needs" implies a formidable array of positive rights (or social entitlements) as preconditions to the normal human functioning that Daniels argues is essential to the realization of "fair equality of opportunity." Although it can be argued that the social entitlements suggested by the first, second, and fourth "health needs" are largely subsumed in Rawls's final formulation of his theory of justice (2001), the other health care needs and their related entitlement are a far more radical extension of Rawls's. In particular, by including "an appropriate distribution of the social determinants of health" as a de facto precondition to fair equality of opportunity, Daniels argues that the demands of social justice must include rights and entitlements that (1) reduce the disproportionate risk of disease and disability and (2) endeavor to promote normal functioning and "thus assure [individuals] the range of opportunities that they would have in absence of disease or disability" (Daniels, 2008, p. 58).

Special Considerations and Caveats

There are a few considerations and caveats of Daniels' (2008) extension of Rawls's Liberal theory of justice that are particularly worthy of mention, even within this very brief synopsis of his ideas and arguments. These include the rationale for and limits to entitlements for the frail aged and disabled, implications for the approach to the financing of health care, procedural considerations in defining and realizing a "right to health," and addressing the problem of individual responsibility for health (pp. 155–158).

Starting with the issue of entitlements to social and health care services for the frail aged and disabled, the basis of such entitlements is the preservation, so far as it is reasonably possible, the normality of function that is essential to fair equality of opportunity (p. 62). There are some forms of care that are simply obligatory to humane societies even where "normality of functioning" is not achievable; these would include care of the terminally ill, the mentally ill, and the severely disabled (p. 62). Where states of disease progression and/or disability are extreme, while the "worst off" have a high priority for social resources relative to others, the setting of limits is appropriate in accordance with a fair process of deliberation that establishes "accountability for reasonableness" (p. 148). This fair process of deliberation must also address what for any society constitutes the "normal range of functioning."[43]

With respect to health care entitlements generally, the guiding principle must be one that takes into account all other resource requirements of a just system, that is, other entitlements necessary to sustaining an active and productive workforce, the dependency and educational needs of children, and providing for the range of other social needs that occur over the lifecourse (p. 63). A distinction is also made between those health care entitlements that are disease based, linked to the alleviation of suffering, and directly linked to the preservation/restoration of "normal functioning"—as opposed to health care entitlements that might enhance functioning to a higher range of normal or enhance opportunities beyond an essential threshold (pp. 149–152).

The issue of health care finance, of course, is particularly crucial. The current system of health care finance in the United States, as examined in more detail in Chapter 3, is a mixed private and public approach that combines employment-based insurance with a publicly funded (and highly permeable) health care safety net. Even should all provisions and entitlements of the Patient Protection and Affordable Care Act be ultimately implemented, significant barriers to health care remain that are correlated with race, ethnicity, and social class. While Daniels leaves the question of a public vs. private approach to the financing of health care open to a range of solutions,[44] he is unequivocal on the central principle that "fair equality of opportunity" requires universal access to health care for all that is devoid of all obstacles—financial, geographic, racial, and so on (p. 143). The question as to whether unfettered universal access to an adequate array of essential health care services can be achieved by a mixed public and private system will be revisited in the final chapter of the book.

The final special consideration to be examined in light of Daniels' extension of Rawlsian Liberalism is the problem of personal responsibility for health. As Daniels rightly points out, as tempting and intuitively logical as it might seem to insist upon personal accountability for detrimental health behaviors (e.g., smoking, excessive consumption of high-fat foods), detrimental health behaviors correlate with (1) various forms of discrimination and disadvantage and (2) social policies foster that detrimental health behaviors. For example, the obesity epidemic among school children affects lower income children disproportionately, is fostered by the economic incentives of the fast-food industry, and reflects the impact of an electronic culture that emphasizes television and video games over active exercise. Because the problem of determining the precise share of individual agency across a wide range of detrimental health conditions is exceedingly difficult (if not altogether intractable), Daniels argues that accountability sanctions should be focused on behavioral choices that are detrimental to others (p. 157). This approach would justify higher taxes on tobacco products, high-fat foods, tanning salons, and a range of other products and services that represent or foster detrimental health behaviors—but is very different from reducing health care subsidies for conditions that are tied to detrimental health behaviors.

The Capabilities Approach Perspective on Health and Health Care Rights

The most recent and comprehensive account of how the Capabilities Approach applies to rights and entitlements to health and health care has been published by Sridhar Venkatapuram (*Health Justice*, Polity Press, 2011). Building on the definition of health developed by Lennart Nordenfelt (1987) that defines health as the ability to achieve vital goals and the 10 central human capabilities identified by Martha Nussbaum (2000a), Venkatapuram (2011) defines the "Capability to be Healthy" as a person's ability to achieve or exercise a cluster of basic capabilities and functioning—which in turn are understood as a "meta-capability" to achieve and exercise Nussbaum's 10 central human capabilities (p. 143).[45] In the language of the Capabilities Approach, a "meta capability" is defined as "an overarching capability to be and to do things that make up a minimally good human life in the contemporary world." (p. 20). By logical extension, the capability to be healthy (as a "meta-capability") would therefore necessitate conceptualization of a right to health as a "cluster-right," that is an entitlement that can only be realized through a combination of other rights, claims, privileges, protections, and powers (p. 163). So, rather than defining the right to health as a rigorously justified and finite set of specific health and health care rights, the Capabilities

Approach challenges us to discern in the context of any given society, the particular "rights, claims, privileges, protections and powers" that are essential and instrumental to Nussbaum's 10 central human capabilities.

This is a formidable undertaking that awaits to be pursued in a comprehensive and systematic way—though Venkatapuram promises to do so in future works (pp. 236–238). As a critical first step to this project, Venkatapuram provides a deeply insightful conceptualization of "health rights" that delineates "health rights" into four categories (pp. 182–183). The first category is health rights that are specific to particular diseases and disabilities (e.g., renal dialysis entitlements for end-stage kidney disease), and the second health right category is for "health-affecting" goods and services (e.g., as in the public health infrastructure, adequate nutrition, and basic health care). The third category of "health rights" are other kinds of human rights that are shown to affect the health of persons (Sen has shown that freedom of expression is instrumental in preventing famines). Finally, there is a fourth category of "health rights" that derive from theories of justice (such as Rawls's right to "fair equality of opportunity").

Despite the daunting developmental challenges that await the systematic application of the Capabilities Approach to all the various forms of "health rights," this framework can and does provide a powerful moral lens through which policy alternatives can be compared. In fact, as argued by Sen (2009), this empirical comparative process is the optimal means of advancing just social policies.

The Choice of the "Justice as Fairness" Liberal Theory of Rawls as a Framework for Analysis of Health and Health Care Policy Alternatives: Four Essential Reasons

At an earlier point in this chapter, it was stated that the order of theoretical frameworks considered would be consistent with William Talbott's (2010) "moral progress" thesis—in essence, the idea that emerging theories of justice and human rights represent moral and legal improvements over prior approaches to questions of justice and human rights that are informed by human experience. This would suggest that, as a more recent theory, the Capabilities Approach is likely a moral improvement over the "Justice as Fairness" Liberal theory of Justice, and should therefore be the optimal framework for the moral analysis of health and health care policies that will follow in later chapters of this book. So why should this book select an analysis of health and health care policy that favors the "Justice as Fairness" Liberal theoretical framework (aka Rawlsian Liberalism) over the more recently emergent

Capabilities Approach? Without rejecting the idea that the Sen and Nussbaum Capabilities Approach holds the promise of a moral and legal progression over Rawlsian Liberalism, there are four reasons for retaining Rawlsian Liberalism as the optimal normative framework for the health and health care policy alternatives considered in subsequent chapters.

First, unlike Rawlsian Liberalism, Sen and Nussbaum's Capabilities Approach has not as yet evolved to a comprehensive theory of justice (Robeyns, 2011), even by the judgement of its proponents (Sen, 2009; Venkatapuram, 2011). Second, also unlike Rawlsian Liberalism, the proponents of the Capabilities Approach have not as yet developed normative arguments that are specific to a number of knotty problems in health care policy (e.g., reconciling competing health care entitlement claims where resources are limited).[46] Third, although the proponents of the Capabilities Approach offer compelling arguments for rejecting an approach to the advancement of just social policies that is based upon the premise of a social contract, the national context of the analysis of health and health care policy undertaken in this book (the United States) is constitutional democracy with a market economy. That is, the de facto policy discourse on the justification and extent of health and health care entitlements in the United States is deeply embedded in the premise of a social contract and debates over the boundaries of inclusion. As a comprehensive theory of justice formulated specifically for the case of a constitutional democracy with a market economy, the Liberal perspective formulated by Rawls appears more readily applicable to some of the most crucial health and health care policy questions confronting the American body politic.[47]

The fourth and final reason for considering Rawlsian Liberalism as the preferable normative framework of this book brings us back to the idea of emergent theories of justice as moral progress. That is, Norman Daniels' most recent extension of Rawls's theory of justice to health and health care entitlements explicitly incorporates the central premise of the Capabilities Approach—human capabilities (as with opportunities) are essential to the exercise of freedom (Daniels, 2008, pp. 153–157). This further *development* of Rawls's theory of justice, informed by Sen's critique of Rawls's emphasis on the just distribution of resources to the neglect of actual capabilities, bridges a crucial difference between the Capabilities Approach and Rawlsian Liberalism. Although other critical differences remain, the perspective of this book is one that can be best described as a formulation of Rawlsian Liberalism that incorporates a particular concern with human capabilities. The most concise summary of this hybrid version of Rawlsian Liberalism is provided by its intellectual architect, political philosopher Norman Daniels: "In general, meeting health needs, however they arise, is important to protecting opportunity, and thus important to sustaining the capabilities of free and equal citizens" (2008, p. 157).

The ways in which we have either succeeded or failed to meet essential health needs, or even acknowledged them as a society, will comprise the next six chapters of this book. The final chapter will then consider the policy alternatives targeted at crucial health need deficits.

NOTES

1. The idea of the social contract, as it evolved through the essays of Hobbes, Locke, and ultimately Rousseau, holds that the only basis for the legitimate authority of governments and related social institutions is voluntary agreements between free and equal individuals.

2. The problem of social justice as it is defined here is based upon two critical concepts that John Rawls builds upon in his theory of social justice. The first is the idea of a *public conception of justice* and the second is the idea of a *well-ordered society*. According to Rawls, one requisite of a well-ordered society is that it is regulated by the prevailing public conception of social justice (see Rawls, 2001, p. 9).

3. Obviously, these do not comprise an exhaustive list of alternative social justice frameworks. Those chosen reflect the author's judgment of the most historically influential frameworks in terms of health care policy. Regrettably, this leaves out the analysis of some very compelling perspectives on social justice that are very relevant to health care.

4. The term "theories of social justice" is used broadly here, to apply to both well-developed theories of social justice (libertarianism, utilitarianism, and liberalism) and also theoretical frameworks that fall short of fully explicated theories of justice (Marxism and the Capabilities Approach).

5. In the literatures of political philosophy and moral philosophy, the definitional distinction between obligations and duties is contested ground. As Rawls would have it, obligations are incurred as the result of some voluntary action, whereas duties are acts that are "moral requirements" that apply to all persons irrespective of explicit consent or the moral status of the person (Steinberger, 2002).

6. William Talbott is Professor of Philosophy at the University of Washington. The ideas cited here are from Talbott's *Human Rights and Human Well-Being* (New York: Oxford University Press, 2010). Talbott's book argues for a universal set of human rights based on consequentialist moral reasoning. Regretfully, it is beyond the scope of this book to consider the theoretical arguments for rights to various forms of social insurance, including health insurance that Talbott brilliantly argues.

7. The point could be easily made that Marxism, both in theory and in practice, represented a retreat to tyrannical forms of governance rather than a moral improvement over Libertarian or Utilitarian principles of justice. However, elements of Marxist thought, especially egalitarianism and a particular attention to the moral preeminence of human dignity, represented advancements in moral reasoning that have been incorporated into later theories of justice.

8. The civil rights and social legislation that transformed Liberal ideology into national policies and institutions took place during the administration of Lyndon Johnson, and should be recognized as his presidential legacy. However, the administration of John F. Kennedy played a significant role in laying the social and political foundations of these triumphs of Liberalism.

9. Although the *Capabilities Approach* became well known through a series of publications by Amartya Sen and Martha Nussbaum in the 1990s (in particular Sen's [1992] *Inequality Re-examined*, Oxford: Clarendon Press, and Sen's [1999] *Development as Freedom*, New York: Knopf), the emergence of the *Capabilities Approach* are generally traced Sen's Tanner Lecture "Equality of What?", delivered at Stanford University in 1979.

10. Sen (2009) offers a number of other critiques of Rawls's Liberal theory of justice, in particular the limitations of a system of justice predicated on an abstract social contract that is presupposed to extend to all persons in a given society. In practice, as it has been formulated in all constitutional democracies, the social contract excludes groups and persons regarded as either inferior or as outsiders—both from the deliberations that establish specific provisions of the social contract and also from the rights and protections that are ultimately agreed upon. As a specific example, the authors of the U.S. Constitution and Bill of Rights were literate, White male property owners and slaveholders that excluded most of the nation's inhabitants from the rights and protections afforded by both documents. In addition, the social contract also presupposes that it applies to a nation state. However, in the context of global economic and political institutions, the rights and protections realized by the individual within any nation state are only partially determined within its borders. A perfect example of this is the 2012 mandates from the European Union and International Monetary Fund that dramatically forced the government of Greece to reduce the social welfare entitlements to its citizens.

11. The comparative "realization-based" epistemology advocated by Sen's *Capabilities Approach* focuses on the extent to which specific social institutions and political systems lead to either the advancement or retreat of "justice," which is defined in terms of the optimization of "human capabilities"—people's real opportunities to do and be what they have reason to value (Sen, 2009, pp. 6–10). These ideas will be discussed in more depth at a later point in the chapter.

12. Libertarians are loath to concede market failures, see Boaz (1997, pp. 256–260).

13. Libertarians decry the emergence of the welfare state and its displacement of social welfare functions that were formally assumed by other social institutions, most notably the family but also various types of mutual aid societies that have flourished throughout U.S. history. This point of view is hardly unique to libertarians, but this perspective is far more central to the libertarian views of the pernicious nature of government.

14. This generally means acquired in ways that do not violate the rights of others.

15. The strain of libertarianism presented here is the traditional form of libertarianism, sometimes called "right-wing libertarianism," which tends to be much more absolutist about unfettered individual appropriation of natural resources—and by extension, the negation of equality of opportunity. There are "left-wing" versions of libertarianism that recognize and accommodate issues of compensation and equality of opportunity, even to the extent of equality of access to personal welfare (see Otsuka, 1998).

16. See Clarke (2003, p. 7).
17. On this point see Nozick (1974, pp. 320–321).
18. "Like-minded individuals" is used here in a very limited sense, meaning persons with a similar social philosophy and set of preferences for human community. Nozick envisions his utopian communities as being comprised of highly diverse individuals in other dimensions, for example, in talents and occupational preferences.
19. It should be noted that John Stewart Mill did not himself introduce the basic utilitarian principle of "the greatest good to the greatest number of people." That is credited to the writings of English jurist and social philosopher Jeremy Bentham in 1776 (Fox, 1907). However, John Stewart Mill is credited with extending the utilitarian principle to a unified theory and popularizing utilitarian ideas among English intellectuals.
20. Published by Princeton University Press, Princeton, NJ in 1990.
21. For the limited purposes of this chapter, I will not discriminate between the particular contributions of either Marx or Engels to Marxist theory, but will refer to Marxism as incorporating the ideas of both.
22. In fact, Marx deliberately avoided moral arguments because he believed that moral systems of thought were themselves products of economically determined social systems rather than the foundations of social systems. Moreover, he regarded his work as empirical theory and not moral philosophy. However, it seems that he was unable to escape moral arguments altogether (on this observation, see Wolff's (2003) essay in chapter references).
23. See chapter reference on Peffer (1990, pp. 416–418 and 452). Peffer constructs his Marxist theory of social justice largely from Marx's idea of maximum equal freedom (explicated on p. 417 of Peffer, 1990) and the main tenets of John Rawls's theory of justice. As such, Peffer incorporates a modified version of Rawls's "difference principle," which in its original form holds that only those social and economic inequalities that provide the greatest benefit to the least-advantaged members of society are just (see reference for Rawls, 2001, *Justice as Fairness*, p. 42).
24. It should be noted that Peffer extends his Marxist principles of social justice to the international sphere, which he argues holds each individual to a "natural duty" to promote a "worldwide federation of democratic, self-managing socialist societies" (see Peffer, 1990, pp. 14, 15).
25. The version of Rawls's theory of social justice that is presented here is the most recent formulation, published in 2001 before his death the following year.
26. Obviously, individuals can generally choose to exit a given society through migration. However, even in democratic societies, exit through migration comes at a psychological and/or material cost that for many individuals is prohibitive. Thus, it is reasonable for theoretical purposes to treat even democratic societies as closed systems.
27. While society can be hospitable to an array of communal associations, society itself is too pluralistic to be communal absent the arbitrary imposition of a universal set of values and beliefs (see Rawls, 2001, pp. 198–199). On this point Rawls shares some common ground with classic libertarian theory.
28. For the sake of brevity, this chapter departs from Rawls's exact order of presentation.

29. For example, although Americans have diverse religious views on the personal circumstances that justify divorce, there is clearly "an overlapping consensus" that the state's interests in promoting and preserving marriage does not supersede the exercise of individual rights pertaining to the dissolution of marriage.

30. Rawls uses the denial of medical care of a child as an example of a situation where parental actions are constrained by political principles of social justice. See Rawls (2001, p. 10) on this point.

31. Had the ideal conditions prevailed in the framing of the U.S. Constitution, its authors would have known nothing of colonial history, the social characteristics of various groups of colonial Americans, or the history and characteristics of the continent's indigenous inhabitants. It is interesting to consider how some aspects of the document might have been different had this level of objectivity been achieved.

32. Although Peffer employed a modification of the Difference Principle in his version of a Marxist theory of social justice, the Difference Principle is original to Rawls. Peffer does not suggest Rawls derived his Difference Principle from Marx, but rather argues that there are aspects of the Difference Principle that are compatible with Marxist theory. On this point see Peffer (1990, pp. 368–369).

33. The term "parties to the agreement" refers to the representatives of free and equal citizens.

34. Rawls uses the example of the tax-dodger, who violates the duty of fair play when he accepts the benefits of government while not paying his share of the tax burden (see Rawls, 1999, footnote on p. 99). It seems that this example is not only apt, but, given Rawls's political philosophy, one very close to his heart.

35. The two moral powers Rawls refers to are in essence the moral exercise of political power, that is (1) the ability to understand, apply, and act from the principles of political justice and (2) the capacity for the conception of the good in accordance with individually selected belief systems or moral doctrines (see Rawls, 2001, pp. 18–19).

36. As Rawls notes (2001, p. 44), fair equality of opportunity means that the free market economic system, as one aspect of the basic structure of society, must be constrained to prevent excessive concentration of wealth and political power. In the contemporary context of the United States, this necessitates the redistribution of concentrated wealth—the equivalent of "class warfare" in the lexicon of conservative political discourse.

37. A normative claim is an "ought" statement or claim about what constitutes proper actions or states of being.

38. Some may object that some kinds of individual endowments (e.g., intelligence, developmental disabilities) are not a causal component of human capabilities that can be affected by social policies and social institutions. However, consider the well-documented impacts of sustained deprivation on the median physical stature of the North Korean population vs. the South Korean population.

39. In reading various accounts and interpretations of the role *conversion factors* in the causal model of capability (Pierik & Robeyns, 2001; Robeyns, 2011; Venkatapuram, 2011), I have found that conversion factors have been described as crucial to the transformation of resources into *both* capabilities and functionings. Since the idea that capabilities precede functionings is core to Sen's *Capabilities Approach* (Sen, 2009), consistent with logical inference I have placed the *conversion factors* shown in Figure 1.1 in advance of capabilities rather than functionings.

40. Nussbaum's 10 central human capabilities are also incorporated in Venkatapuram's (2011) application of the *Capabilities Approach* to health and health care entitlements, which is considered in the final section of this chapter.
41. In fact, according to World Health Organization data (in particular, see *The World Health Report 2000*), there is a strong correlation between universal access to health care and average population health outcomes. However, universal access to health care correlates with other aspects of social structure that appear to be determinants of more favorable population health. This point will be explored in great depth in later chapters.
42. The reasons for choosing this perspective over others, most particularly the Capabilities Approach, will be summarized at the conclusion of this chapter.
43. Daniels (2008, p. 146) points out that the criterion for "normal functioning" must take into account disease-specific impediments that deviate from the species' "normal functioning," and impediments that are most directly linked to a particular society's opportunity structure.
44. Daniels' specific statement on this central issue is as follows: "What forms of organization—public or private administration and financing—are implied is not a question to which just health provides a unique answer. There are probably an array of 'just enough' institutional structures that can provide the needed protection of opportunity" (2008, p. 144).
45. Nussbaum's 10 central human capabilities are listed on page 30.
46. As pointed out previously, Venkatapuram's *Health Justice* (Cambridge UK: Polity Press, 2011) is to date the most comprehensive development of the Capabilities Approach to moral claims to health and health care entitlements. However, even this groundbreaking book does not deal directly with some crucial specifics of health and health care rights and entitlements, in particular distributive concerns (e.g., the problem of competing claims to limited resources). To quote Venkatapuram on this point: "... this book is largely about the 'what' or metric of health justice and not about the 'how' or rules for distribution" (p. 237). Venkatapuram intends to deal with these issues in subsequent works, which might make the Capabilities Approach a more practicable framework for the analysis of health and health care policy than it currently is.
47. Despite this book's embracement of Rawlsian Liberalism as the optimal moral lens through which to examine our nation's health and health care policy alternatives, this is a choice made at a specific juncture in American social and political history, and also in the intellectual progression of theories of social justice. A later edition of this same book or one like it may well find that a more fully developed version of the Capabilities Approach will offer a superior accounting of the institutional arrangements and specific policies that are both realizable and consistent with the demands of justice.

REFERENCES

Barry, B. (1989). *Theories of justice*. Berkely, CA: University of California Press.

Boaz, D. (1997). *Libertarianism: A primer*. New York: The Free Press.

Clarke, R. (2003). *Libertarian accounts of free will*. New York: Oxford University Press.

Daniels, N. (1981). Health-care needs and distributive justice. *Philosophy and Public Affairs, 10,* 146–179.

Daniels, N. (1985). *Just health care.* New York: Cambridge University Press.

Daniels, N. (2002). Justice, health and health care. In R. Rhodes, M. Battin, & A. Silvers (Eds.), *Medicine and social justice.* New York: Oxford University Press.

Daniels, N. (2008). *Just health: Meeting health needs fairly.* New York: Cambridge University Press.

Fox, J. (1907). Benthanism. In J. C. Farley (Ed.), *Catholic encyclopedia on-line* (2003 ed., Vol. II). New York: K. Knight.

Hessler, K., & Buchanan, A. (2002). Specifying the content of the human right to health care. In R. Rhodes, M. Battin, & A. Silvers (Eds.), *Medicine and social justice.* New York: Oxford University Press.

Huxley, A. (1998). *Brave new world.* New York: Perennial Classics.

Marx, K. (1938). *Critique of the Gotha programme, by Karl Marx; with appendices by Marx, Engels and Lenin; a revised translation.* New York: International Publishers.

Martin, R. (1985). *Rawls and rights.* Lawrence, KA: University Press of Kansas.

Miller, F. (2002). Aristotle's political theory. In E. N. Zalta (Ed.), *The Stanford encyclopedia of philosophy.* Palo Alto, CA: University of Notre Dame Press.

Nakano, G. (2010). *Forced to care: Coercion and caregiving in America.* Cambridge, MA: Harvard University Press.

Nordenfelt, L. (1987). *On the nature of health: An action-theoretic approach.* Boston: Reidel Publishing Company; Norwell, MA, USA: Sold and distributed in the U.S.A. and Canada by Kluwer Academic.

Nozick, R. (1974). *Anarchy, state, and utopia.* New York: Basic Books.

Nussbaum, M. (2000a). *Women and human development: The capabilities approach.* New York: Cambridge University Press.

Nussbaum, M. (2000b). Aristotle, politics and human capabilities: A response to Arneson, Charlesworth, and Mulgan. *Ethics, 111,* 102–140.

Otsuka, M. (1998). Self-ownership and equality, a Lockean reconciliation. *Philosophy and Public Affairs, 27,* 65–92.

Peffer, R. G. (1990). *Marxism, morality, and social justice.* Princeton, NJ: Princeton University Press.

Pizzigati, S. (2005). The rich and the rest: The growing concentration of wealth: A labor economist sees peril as a tiny minority of the population accumulates more and more wealth. *The Futurist, 39*(4), 38–43.

Pierik, R., & Robeyns, I. (2001). *Dworkin on Sen: On the role of social mechanisms in egalitarian theory.* Retrieved March 6, 2012, from http://mora.rente.nhh.no/projects/EqualityExchange/Portals/0/articles/pierik1.pdf.

Rawls, J. (1971). *A theory of justice.* Cambridge, MA: Harvard University Press.

Rawls, J. (1985). Justice as fairness: Political not metaphysical. *Philosophy and Public Affairs, 14*(3), 223–251.

Rawls, J. (1996). *Political liberalism.* New York: Columbia University Press.

Rawls, J. (1999). *Collected papers.* Cambridge, MA: Harvard University Press.

Rawls, J. (2001). *Justice as fairness; a reformulation.* Cambridge, MA: Harvard University Press.

Rescher, N. (1966). *Distributive justice: A constructive critique of the utilitarian theory of distribution.* New York: Bobbs-Merrill.

Rhodes, R., Battin, M., & Silvers, A. (2002). Preface. In R. Rhodes, M. Battin, & A. Silvers (Eds.), *Medicine and social justice* (pp. vi). New York: Oxford University Press.

Robeyns, I. The capability approach. In E. N. Zalta (Ed.), *The Stanford encyclopedia of philosophy* (Summer 2011 Edition), URL = <http://plato.stanford.edu/archives/sum2011/entries/capability-approach/>.

Roemer, J. (1996). *Theories of distributive justice.* Cambridge, MA: Harvard University Press.

Sen, A. (1992). *Inequality re-examined.* Oxford: Clarendon Press.

Sen, A. (1999).*Development as freedom.* New York: Knopf.

Sen, A. (2009). *The idea of justice.* Cambridge, MA: Belknap Press of Harvard University Press.

Steinberger, P. (2002). Political obligations and derivitive duties. *Journal of Politics, 64*(2), 449–465.

Talbott, W. (2010). *Human rights and human well-being.* New York: Oxford University Press.

Vallentyne, P. (2004). Libertarianism. In E. N. Zalta (Ed.), *The Stanford encyclopedia of philosophy.* Palo Alto, CA: University of Notre Dame Press.

Venkatapuram, S. (2011). *Health justice.* Cambridge, UK: Polity Press.

Wolff, J. (2003). Karl Marx: Life and works. In E. N. Zalta (Ed.), *The Stanford encyclopedia of philosophy.* Palo Alto, CA: University of Notre Dame Press.

CHAPTER TWO

HISTORICAL EVOLVEMENT OF THE U.S. HEALTH CARE SYSTEM

A remarkable feature of the U.S. health care system is that, in many respects, it largely evolved in the absence of any strong role of government. Until the middle of the 20th century, American hospitals received very little investment or attention from either the state or the federal government, and the medical profession was, for all practical purposes, unregulated and unlicensed until the last decades of the 19th century. In fact, the government was not involved in the financing of health care for ordinary citizens (i.e., those not wards of the state, not covered by Indian treaties, nor veterans with war-related injuries) until private health care insurance plans had emerged as the dominant form of personal health care finance in the 1930s. Although federal financing and regulation of the U.S. health care system has now ascended to dominance, this is a relatively recent development spanning the past 60 years. Thus, this chapter is divided into two segments. The first is devoted to the emergence of the fundamental parts of the U.S. health care system: its hospitals, its professional labor force, and its system of employment-based health care insurance financing. The second segment of this chapter concerns itself with the historical evolvement of the federal government in health care, and ultimately the effects of federal legislation on the contemporary structure of the health care system.

HISTORICAL EVOLVEMENT OF THE BASIC COMPONENTS OF THE HEALTH CARE SYSTEM: HOSPITALS, DOCTORS, NURSES, AND HEALTH INSURANCE

A Brief History of the American Hospital System

The centerpiece of the American health care system is its roughly 5800 hospitals, of which just over three-quarters are either public or private not-for-profit (AHA, 2010). The majority of hospitals (almost 60%) exists as voluntary organizations and operate on a nonprofit basis, reflecting the philanthropic, ethnic, and religious origins of the American hospital.[1] Although there are many historical narratives of the evolvement of the American hospital system, the definitive history offered by Rosenberg's (1987) *The Care of Strangers*[2] suggests that the evolvement of the American hospital in its most essential features occurred over three distinct periods: the pre–Civil War period, from 1800 to 1850; the midcentury period, from roughly 1850 to 1870; and the critical 50-year-long era of hospital care expansion between 1870 and 1920 (Rosenberg, 1987). The history offered here will extend the American hospital's chronology to a fourth period, the second major expansion of the hospital care that occurred during the post–World War II era between 1946 and 1970.

The American Hospital in the Pre–Civil War Era

During the first century of the nation's existence, there was a very small number of hospitals, largely because hospitals existed to provide shelter and care for the destitute—those without the resources of either kin or community. In fact, the first census of hospitals in 1873 found only 178 hospitals with a collective capacity of less than 50,000 hospital beds, including those classified as mental hospitals (Rosenberg, 1987). The character of the early American hospital reflected the fact that medicine had very little to offer in the way of cure, and that most of what medicine did have to offer, either to heal an injury or help cure a disease, could more readily and more safely be provided in the home. The developmental progression of the American hospital, though more rapid in America than in Europe, essentially followed a similar path, from a specialized form of an almshouse to eventually a place of care and cure that served all segments of society (Starr, 1982, p. 151).

The immediate precursor of the early American hospital, the almshouse, existed as a shelter of last resort for the poor that (as the name implies) was created and supported as an extension of Christian charity. As such, almhouse residents were comprised of abandoned elderly, orphaned children, unwed mothers spurned by their families, the insane, and those too ill or disabled to work. Although some colonial almshouses developed what amounted to charity care wards for the sick and injured, the civic and religious leaders of colonial America's large cities did not consider the almshouse the appropriate place to care for those who, through no fault of character or moral defect, found themselves ill and unable to support themselves. Thus the earliest American hospitals had a common purpose: a place of refuge and care for the worthy poor. The early American hospitals that fit this description include Charity Hospital in New Orleans (1736), Pennsylvania Hospital in Philadelphia (1752), New York Hospital (1771), and Massachusetts Hospital in Boston (1821) (Rosenberg, 1987; Starr, 1982).

Religiously motivated charity was not the only stimulus for the founding of hospitals in early America; the need for public order was also a significant concern. The well-ordered city could not have sick and destitute immigrants collapsing in the doorways, the insane babbling in the market places, or the abandoned women delivering their newborns in the street. A third impetus to the founding of hospitals was tied to the various waves of new immigrants, who emigrated with both an ethos of "taking care of our own" and the reality of being in an alien city without the presence and care of kin in the event of illness or injury. Thus, the origins and affiliations of many 19th-century hospitals can be traced to the efforts of different ethnic societies and associations, such as Philadelphia's German Hospital, founded in 1860 (Rosenberg, 1987). A fourth source for the founding of hospitals was various faiths and religious orders, usually as an expression of religious mission but also in response to Protestant bigotry encountered in established hospitals. This was the story behind the founding of many of the early Catholic and Jewish hospitals. Finally, as the industrial revolution progressed, hospitals were organized by different industries, particularly among those industries like mining, textiles, and railroads that had high accident rates (Rosenberg, 1987).

The 1850–1870 Period: The Era of Hospital Reform

The main social purposes of the hospitals of the pre–Civil War period included the provision of shelter and care for the incapacitated poor, providing a social laboratory for the training of physicians, and as a means of discharging the obligations of religious piety. Medicine had very limited range of genuinely curative interventions, and death by contamination and infectious disease was common. Although Pennsylvania Hospital in Philadelphia was superior to most by the standards of the time, death rates from such routine surgeries as limb amputations exceeded 25% (Rosenberg, 1987). In 1869, the term "hospitalism" was coined by British physician James Simpson to refer to the septicemias, gangrenes, and other forms of infections that were endemic to hospitals of the pre-1870 era (Brieger, 1972). The sources of death from contamination and infectious diseases could be largely attributed to the absence of sterile surgical techniques, crowded ward conditions with an abundance of effluvia in open buckets, reuse of soiled linen, and poor ventilation.

Ironically enough, the transformation of the 19th-century hospital from an institution of last resort to an edifice of healing can largely be attributed to the lessons learned over two bloody wars, the Crimean War (1854–1856) and the American Civil War (1861–1865). Although the discoveries of pathogenic microbes and antiseptic techniques in the 1860s by Pasteur and Lister ultimately propelled the medical profession to the acceptance of germ theory, this acceptance was slow in coming and preceded by the pioneering hospital reforms advanced by Florence Nightingale. Nightingale, known more generally as the founder of the nursing profession, made at least equal contributions as a hospital reformer. Formally trained as a nurse, Nightingale volunteered her services to the British army as nursing supervisor during the Crimean War. Although Nightingale's reforms were not informed by germ theory, she believed disease and death were caused by overcrowding, poor food, the presence of filth, and poor ventilation. Under Nightingale's ruthless tutelage the British military hospitals became the models of hygiene and order and the death rates of British soldiers plummeted. Nightingale's *Notes on Hospitals*, published in 1859, contained the essential lessons on the organization of nursing and hospital reform that were adopted by the Union Army over the course of the Civil War (Brieger, 1972). As a result, during the final year of the Civil War over 1 million soldiers were treated in the military hospitals of the Union Army with a mortality rate of only 8% (Starr, 1982). The convincing successes of the Civil War military hospital, coupled with the tireless advocacy of Nightingale and her followers, by the early 1870s had fundamentally transformed the organization of the 19th-century American hospital and had also provided the basic foundations for the later professionalization of nursing.

The First Era of Hospital Expansion: 1870–1920

In the first survey of U.S. hospitals, conducted in 1873, there were 178 hospitals in existence. By 1920, the number of hospitals exceeded 4000 (Rosenberg, 1987). Although some of the growth in the number of hospitals can be attributed to population growth in the wake of massive immigration, the primary factors have to do with the ascendance of the medical profession, the effects of hospital reform on survival and recovery, and the marriage of the interests of the medical profession and private philanthropy.

By the 1870s, the gradual acceptance by the medical profession of germ theory and related developments in aseptic and antiseptic techniques were coupled with the development of surgical anesthesia—first used in 1846 to aid the surgical excision of a tumor (Brieger, 1972). The use of sterile techniques permitted patients to survive more complex and invasive surgeries, and anesthesia permitted both patients and surgeons to endure it. As a result, heretofore, fatal conditions such as appendicitis and abdominal tumors often became curable and successful surgery for a variety of conditions became more common (Cassedy, 1991). Parallel developments in clinical pathology and disease-specific diagnosis and treatment, coupled with innovations in surgery, gradually made the hospital the prime locus of curative medical practice for the most serious illnesses. With the invention of the x-ray machine in 1896, by the turn of the century hospitals had finally become embraced by the middle and upper classes rather than shunned by them. This, in turn, fueled a huge popular demand for hospital expansion and new hospital construction.

Despite the growth in demand for hospital care, neither states nor the federal governments had traditionally assumed more than a peripheral role in the construction of hospitals. Other than asylums for those deemed mentally ill and hospitals for the quarantining of those with diseases such as tuberculosis, states and the broad public saw hospitals as the business of municipal governments and private charities—largely because hospitals had functioned as a specialized form of the almshouse. Had the turn of the century medical profession no alternative for the funding of hospital expansion and construction but the government, it is likely that the hospital system in the United States would have evolved to a far more equal mix of voluntary and public hospitals—which, in turn, in later decades, could have tipped the balance in favor of a federalized system of health care insurance. History instead took another turn, one that involved the marriage of private philanthropy and medical free enterprise.

As noted by Starr (1982), philanthropy is the means by which personal wealth can be parlayed for social status and social influence. Throughout the nation's first century, hospitals had historically been a preferred destination for philanthropy, both because, more than other charities, they appeared to serve the "worthy poor" and because their boards of trustees brought together the elites of science and politics. Coincidentally, as the demands for hospital expansion escalated toward the close of the 19th century, the era of economic expansion known as the Gilded Age (1866–1901) had created a new class of wealthy elites (many of them immigrants) eager to transform their wealth to status and influence. Physicians, who by this same period became economically aligned with the growth of hospitals, were only too eager to turn to a source of hospital financing that would as much as possible keep government out of the business of health care. Where possible, physicians would often organize investor-owned hospitals that would rely on profits from private pay patients. However, the driving source of expansion was the voluntary hospitals that, while representing different kinds of ethnic and religious loyalties, nonetheless had the common thread of extensive reliance on private philanthropy.

The most significant exception to the general pattern of the nongovernmental funding of hospitals pertained to mental hospitals. Prior to the Civil War, the mentally ill that were not tolerated in almshouses were relegated to jails, and the almshouses that did tolerate the mentally ill were often themselves deplorable establishments. Through the revolutionary and tireless state-by-state campaign of social reformer Dorthea Dix (1802–1887), over the latter half of the 19th century the state mental hospital became the national pattern for the care of the mentally ill. Although state asylums are rightfully regarded as having a very dark history, during the latter half of the 19th century they were conceptualized as curative institutions that were a humanitarian alternative to the jails and poorhouses that heretofore had warehoused the mentally ill.

The Second Era of Hospital Expansion: 1946–1970

The economic consequences of the Great Depression and World War II had basically stagnated civilian hospital growth for nearly 2 decades, despite the continued increase of the national population. Despite the Truman administration's strong preference for amendments to the Social Security Act that would extend health insurance coverage to all Americans, there was a stronger political consensus in Congress to fund the expansion and modernization of the nation's hospitals. Moreover, federal investments in the expansion of hospitals in ways that would not invite federal control over the delivery of health care were more acceptable to the interests of the powerful American Medical Association (AMA) lobby. The result was the Hill–Burton Act of 1946 (formally titled the Hospital Survey and Construction Act of 1946), which involved a multibillion dollar infusion of federal dollars into the modernization and expansion of the nation's hospitals. Discussed in more detail later in this chapter, this legislation basically provided federal matching funds for the expansion of hospital capacity in accordance with plans administered by the individual states. Between 1947 and 1971, this legislation generated an estimated $9.1 billion in local and state matching funds in addition to the $3.7 billion federal investment, three quarters of these monies going for hospitals (Starr, 1982).

Other social forces that contributed to the expansion of hospital capacity during this era include suburbanization, the expansion of hospital insurance benefits, the post-WWII birthrate increase, innovations in hospital care technology that further fueled demands for hospital care, and parallel federal investments in the expansion of the health care labor force. As a result, by 1970, the number of acute care hospitals had peaked to more than 5800, of which just over 60% were not-for-profit (U.S. Census Bureau, 1972). Notably, by 1970, most hospitals had been upgraded to many of the basic architectural standards that are still in place today. That is, large wards had been replaced by semiprivate rooms, specialty care units (e.g., intensive care, telemetry, psychiatry) had become the industry standard, as had the physical structures to accommodate very sophisticated diagnostic and surgical technologies.

The Brief Overlapping Histories of Medicine, Nursing, and Health Insurance

The primary labor force components and the financing component of the health care system each have their own very complex histories, but in critical analysis their narratives must intersect and overlap. This is because the political economy of the American medical profession to a large extent fashioned the institutional characteristics of the nursing profession and the health insurance industry to serve the material interests of physicians. While recent decades have witnessed a sea of change in the level of professional autonomy and social status achieved by the nursing profession, and in many respects the practice of medicine is now subordinate to the bureaucracy of health insurance, the fundamental truth remains—both the nursing profession and the essential structure of health insurance exist (even in their current forms) in large part as derivatives of the political economy of the American medical profession.

The Medical Profession: The Colonial Period Through Abraham Flexner (1760–1910)

The 150-year period between roughly 1760 and 1910 spans the time from colonial medicine to the historical point at which it can be said that the American medical community had clearly emerged as a powerful profession with a coherent social and political agenda. The narrative that follows is very different from the countless other published histories of medical care that place emphasis on the ascendance of modern medical practice as a triumph of human achievement over ignorance and disease. Since this is about the policy-relevant aspects of medical history, the narrative offered here must tilt toward the role that the ascendance of the *medical profession* played in the unique structures of American health care policy—largely as portrayed in Paul Starr's eloquently documented 1982 classic, *The Social Transformation of American Medicine.*[3]

In the colonial America of the mid-18th century, there were at least a few thousand persons described as physicians, but only a small proportion them actually possessed medical degrees. In fact, the title of "doctor" was not generally used in the American colonies until a few years before the American Revolution (Twiss, 1960). By the year of the nation's founding in 1776, there were estimated to be 3500 physicians, of which 400 possessed medical degrees (Twiss, 1960). Persons who practiced colonial medicine typically learned their profession (such as it was) as an apprenticeship, a practice that continued well into the century that followed. The selection of persons for medical apprenticeships was at the individual discretion of practicing physicians, within broad normative criteria—that is, that the candidates be White, male, of good character, intelligent, industrious, and literate. It was also preferred that the prospective physician's family background be reputable and prosperous, though not necessarily wealthy. The following passage, quoted from a prominent early 19th-century physician's essays on medical education, is illustrative (Brieger, 1972, p. 10).[4]

> But it is not sufficient that boys selected for the study of medicine should have a good constitution, they ought, equally, to be endowed with vigorous and inquiring minds. Without these, whatever may be the appearance of success, they must at last make incompetent physicians ... A student of medicine should not only be of sound understanding but imbued with ambition. A mere love of knowledge is not to be relied upon, for the greatest lovers of knowledge are not infrequently deficient in executive talents and go on acquiring without learning how to appropriate.

Although race is not alluded to in this passage, that the candidate be White and generally Northern European was a given. In all other respects, this passage captures the essence of the ideal early American physician; a male of vigorous constitution, an inquiring mind, and a clear talent and disposition toward medical free enterprise.

The problem that plagued the early American medical profession, also alluded to in this passage, was that the ranks of those claiming to be physicians were polluted with incompetents and outright quacks. Broadly speaking, an incompetent physician is one who was practicing medicine in an honest state of perpetual ignorance, whereas quackery involves the willful pretense of knowledge and/or use of false credentials (Cassedy, 1991). Both involve issues of control over the professional credentialing process, and they undercut both the public confidence in professional medicine and the capacity of competent physicians (by the standards of the time) to earn a living. A related problem that retarded the legitimization of the early American medical profession was of course the limited state of medical knowledge and limited range of curative therapeutics. This, in turn, perpetuated the continued prevalence of folk medicine as the preferred alternative to the services of a physician, as well as reliance on other kinds of healers—ranging from mystics to women who, despite being spurned by the nascent medical profession, were gifted practitioners of the medical arts.

As the nation developed, the situation that characterized American medicine during the pre-1865 antebellum period can be described as a polyglot of competitive schools of therapeutic thought, some clearly outside the mainstream medicine of French and British origin and some embraced within. As noted by Cassedy (1991), these different "sects" of therapeutic belief tended to be aligned with social class. For example, homeopathic medicine (which emphasized personal attention and conservative use of pharmaceutical remedies) was preferred by the middle and upper classes. In contrast, rural and lower-class patients preferred therapies that were more aligned with their trust of folk remedies, eclectic medicine, and a botanically oriented system of medicine called Thomsonianism (Cassedy, 1991, pp. 36–39). Notably, neither the government nor university-sanctioned medical education in the form of medical schools played more than a peripheral role in the organization of the medical profession until after the Civil War.

With the ending of the Civil War, the medical profession entered what might be called its Enlightenment period, which like the Enlightenment era of 17th-century Europe was exemplified by the ascendance of intellectual and scientific achievement. As previously discussed in the section devoted to the development of hospitals, the significant advancements in surgery made possible by the application of antisepsis and anesthesia greatly contributed to the rising status of formally trained physicians—as well as contributed to a rising demand for their services. Although surgical anesthesia was an American innovation, most of the critical 19th-century advancements in medical science originated in Europe. Thus, the period immediately following the Civil War witnessed a vast increase in the numbers of Americans traveling to Europe to acquire education in the medical sciences, most of whom returned to ultimately populate the faculties of American universities and revolutionize the scientific foundations of American medicine (Cassedy, 1991).

The ground-breaking advancements in medical science of the post–Civil War period were complemented by demographic and economic developments that set the stage for the private practice of medicine to flourish. Rural or so-called horseback medicine had always existed as an economically marginal enterprise, both because of the range of travel involved in maintaining a medical practice and because barter rather than currency was often the medium of exchange. For medical practice to become lucrative, increased levels of population concentration, improvements in transportation, and the replacement of barter systems with currency all needed to evolve. These changes epitomized the 1865–1900 era of industrial expansion, Western migration, and immigration that transformed the nation to a modern industrial state. Thus, as the latter half of the 19th century commenced, the medical profession had science, demography, and industrial expansion on its side—what it lacked was organization and direct control of the credentialing process.

Although the market for the private practice of medicine was beginning to flourish, the period between 1865 and 1900 was rife with medical sectarianism. In the battles between different sects of medicine over claims to legitimacy and control over the credentialing process, the principal protagonists were homeopathic physicians, eclectics,[5] and the so-called allopathic physicians representing the orthodox medical traditions of Western Europe (Rothstein, 1972). Although numbers favored the adherents of allopathic medicine (they controlled 80% of the roughly 130 medical schools that existed in the late 19th century), no group was able to gain a particular advantage over the mechanisms of state licensure, which in any case were often devoid of adequate enforcement provisions (Rothstein, 1972; Starr, 1982). The AMA, which represented orthodox medicine, was itself too weak and divided during this period to enforce its sanctions against the local medical societies that failed to expel their eclectics and homeopaths. Clearly, unless medicine could ultimately speak with a unified voice, it could not gain firm control of its credentialing.

Ultimately, the AMA yielded to pragmatism, and in 1903 it adopted a revised version of its constitution that eliminated provisions that had heretofore excluded nonallopathic physicians. As a result, the AMA ranks swelled to the point where the organization could soon claim without serious challenge that it represented the national voice of the medical profession. This in turn gave the AMA the unity and political clout it needed to achieve uniform standards of medical licensure in each state, including dominion over what acts by the various groups of other healers constituted the illegal practice of medicine. Even more significantly, the AMA's new constitution (approved in 1901) created a structure whereby the membership and representation at the state and national levels required membership in the county medical society (Rothstein, 1972). In effect, this provision permitted the AMA to purge from its ranks any members who could not either gain or retain membership in its local medical society. Although this had the very desirable effect of ridding the profession of its quacks and incompetents, it also permitted the local medical societies to enforce nonscientific norms of membership having to do with gender, race, ethnicity, and political views that conflicted with the interests of unfettered medical free enterprise. Taken in tandem, these two developments assured that, for the critical decades to come, the medical profession remained largely the exclusive dominion of White male individuals— collectively committed to extending the profession's political influence and economic advantage.

As described by Paul Starr, the achievement of *professional sovereignty* refers to the capacity of a profession to extend and transform its authority into social privilege, economic power, and political influence (Starr, 1982, p. 5). In the case of the medical profession of the 20th century, it fully exploited its authority in the shaping of a health care system that yielded medicine its disproportionate share of economic rewards and social privileges. Although the achievement of the medical profession's unique level of authority is best left to the original teller of the tale, at minimum it required the acquisition of legitimate authority. In the case of medicine and many other professions, legitimate authority entails the possession of a universally recognized credential that represents mastery over a definitive body of knowledge. After it had achieved professional consolidation in the first years of the new century, the most significant problem confronting the AMA remained the weak claim to legitimate authority carried by the medical school diploma. Of the roughly 160 medical schools that were in existence at the turn of the century, at least half or more were either proprietary diploma mills devoid of anything akin to even a minimal medical education, or at the very least schools that were grossly deficient in faculty credentials, laboratories, and integration of clinical training.

The AMA dealt with the issue by turning to the Carnegie Foundation for the Advancement of Teaching, which in turn commissioned educational specialist Abraham Flexner to conduct an investigation of the nation's medical schools and make recommendations (Rothstein, 1972; Starr, 1982). Flexner visited 152 medical schools in the United States and 8 in Canada, the result of which was the infamous Flexner 1910 report on medical education (Cassedy, 1991). The report was a devastating critique of the state of American medical education and recommended that the training and credentialing of physicians be consolidated into a small number of top-quality schools. Although the AMA did not go as far as Flexner recommended, within a few short years the number of medical schools was cut in half, and those that remained were generally affiliated with universities, prestigious colleges, and teaching hospitals. Within 2 years of the publication of Flexner's report, about 80% of medical school graduates completed their training in hospital internships, thus cementing together the prestigious triad of universities, hospitals, and medical schools (Starr, 1982).

Gender, Medicine, and the Early Professionalization of Nursing

History abounds with ironies, among them the stark contrast between the historically subordinate status of the nursing profession and the invaluable contributions of nursing knowledge to the survival chances of hospitalized patients—all to the ultimate benefit of the medical profession's further achievements in occupational prestige and economic reward. As discussed previously in this chapter's section on the development of hospitals, Florence Nightingale was at once a pioneer of nursing and a pioneer of hospital reform. This makes sense, in that the boundaries between defining the body of knowledge and essential skills of nursing and the reform of hospital care were even more permeable in the 19th century than they are today. As Nightingale rationalized and organized the labor and training of nurses, she attacked with equal vigor and certainty the sources of disease and death endemic in the physical arrangements, food, supplies, and customary hygienic behaviors of the various ranks of hospital workers. Because the effects of Nightingale's efforts (in combination with later developments in anesthesia and antiseptic surgical practice), the mid-19th hospital was transformed from a death house to an institution of healing and hope.[6] In particular, surgery was transformed from a procedure of desperate resort to a curative miracle that only medical doctors trained in science and surgery could perform. Thus, the medical profession could at last differentiate itself from other kinds of healers in a way that was convincing to the general public.

These developments, which fostered both the ascendance of hospital care and the ascendance of the medical profession during the last quarter of the 19th century, also made hospitals the institutional locus of nursing training and credentialing. Paralleling the expansion of hospitals during the same era, between 1873 and 1900 the number of nurses' training schools had grown from 3 to 432 (Cassedy, 1991; Starr, 1982). Although many of Nightingale's principles of nursing education were largely incorporated into the structure and curriculum of hospital-based schools of nursing, Nightingale's philosophy of nursing education favored independent schools of nursing where only nurses trained nurses (Cope, 1958; Hobbs, 1997). Nightingale saw very clearly that in institutions dominated by male physicians, the knowledge and skills of women would be discounted and subordinated to the interests of both the medical profession and the extension of male privilege.[7] In fact, this became a dominant theme that burdened the evolvement of the nursing profession throughout most of the century that followed, and likely will continue to haunt the nursing profession until gender balance in all domains of medicine is realized.[8] The precepts of Nightingale's philosophy of nursing education were no match for the medical profession's financial interests in having a ready source of essentially free hospital labor, thus the hospital school model of nursing training prevailed for decades to come. Although the exploitation of cheap labor was in many respects the primary reward of the hospital training school model, the real damage to both the nursing profession and the evolvement of the health care system was in the long-term effect of this institutional arrangement—the subordination of autonomous nursing knowledge and practice to the interests of the medical profession.[9]

Medicine and the Early Evolvement of Health Insurance

Until nearly the end of the 19th century, the concept of health insurance was not generally known and certainly not an issue of any significant political concern. As late as the last quarter century of the 1800s, most hospitals that existed were already charitable institutions of last resort, and the primary locus of medical practice was the patient's home. Those unable to afford the services of a private physician either did without (which was often the safest road to recovery), bartered what they could for a physician's services, or they sought medical care at a "dispensary."[10] Medical dispensaries, such as almshouses, originated in England as a form of charitable provisions for the poor. Their primary function was to provide medical care for the poor as an alternative to hospital care, and to provide the medical profession with human grist for medical education.[11] In this way, the 19th-century medical dispensary was the forerunner of the emergency department of a public teaching hospital. Although as of 1900 there were about 100 dispensaries in the United States, by 1918 their numbers had expanded by hundreds more—ultimately accounting for the care of 4 million patients annually (Davis & Warner, 1918).

The increased demand for dispensary care in the first decades of the 20th century signaled that the nation's reliance on a wholly private fee-based model medicine, augmented by the arbitrary judgments of private medical charity, must come to an end. The forces that led to this dilemma included immigration-driven population growth, industrialization, rising literacy, and a greatly increased level of public confidence in the medical profession. Responding to a growing consensus that some alternative to the wholly private fee-based model of medical care must be found, in 1912 the Progressive Party of Theodore Roosevelt included a call for national health insurance as a part of its platform. After some initial waffling, the AMA ultimately (in 1920) declared its definitive opposition to a plan of compulsory health insurance (Litman, 1991). In fact, opposition to any plan that would involve government health insurance ultimately became the dominant rallying cry for AMA membership for decades to come.

The AMA's progressive era opposition to health insurance had many reasons, two of them dominant. The first involved the genuine belief (and enduring public relations refrain) that the government financing of health care would relentlessly undermine the authority of the physician to practice medicine in a manner consistent with the patient's best interest. The second, less visible to the broad public, was the AMA's conviction that government financing of health care would bring an end to the lucrative rewards of private fee-based medicine. The political strategy of the AMA, then as today, was three pronged: Label publicly sponsored forms of health insurance as radical socialism, emphasize the predatory tendencies of government bureaucrats, and remind the public that the doctor–patient relationship was sacrosanct and never the business of government. In a nutshell, this strategy entailed convincing the voting public that a vote for a plan of national health insurance was a vote against the beneficent wisdom of their family doctors. A curious ally of the AMA during this initial run at a national plan of health insurance was labor patriarch Samuel Gompers, founder and first president of the American Federation of Labor. Although Gompers did not speak for or agree with many other leaders in organized labor on the issue of compulsory health insurance, at the time his was labor's most powerful voice. Gomper's opposition to national health insurance was at once philosophical and strategic; health insurance coverage was emerging as an important bargaining issue and government sponsorship of health insurance represented an infringement upon labor's right to engage in collective bargaining (Litman, 1991).

The temporary Progressive Era alliance between organized labor and the AMA on the issue of health insurance was short-lived,[12] but it came at a critical juncture. As suggested by Starr (1982), with America's entry into World War I, the Progressive Party's capacity to focus the public's attention on domestic economic issues dwindled, as did its political power. By the early 1920s, the most vociferous supporters of national health insurance had become a political fringe movement, and the AMA had by then consolidated its membership around the national health insurance issue and refined its strategy to defeat it. This strategy, which in its various permutations defeated the national health insurance agendas of subsequent presidential administrations (including F.D.R., Truman, and Clinton), continued to play upon the public's distrust of government, notions of creeping socialism, and most of all the idea that doctors (unlike the government) would always act in the best interests of patients.

What was more acceptable to the AMA, though not without some level of internal controversy as to the specifics, was the voluntary model of health insurance. From the standpoint of the AMA, the most ideal financing model for health care would involve private insurance for catastrophic illnesses that required hospital care, private payment of physician's services, and care for the poor as a matter of private charity. To the AMA, the appeal of this model was that hospital care would be affordable and the solvency of hospitals assured, while at the same time physicians would be permitted to engage in medical free enterprise—unencumbered by government regulation or oversight. This model was also supported by the American Hospital Association (AHA), which had been founded in 1899 as a professional association for hospital superintendents. By the 1930s, when the nation had arrived at a crossroads between an AMA model of health care financing and a social insurance model favored by the Franklin D. Roosevelt administration, the AHA had evolved toward a business model of hospital administration that favored the more conservative hospital insurance solution to health care (Litman, 1991; Shi & Singh, 2001). Although the nascent AHA of the 1930s did not have the political clout of the AMA, the convergence of perspectives between the AHA and the AMA on the issue of a voluntary health insurance model versus the social insurance model advocated by the Roosevelt administration ultimately helped the AMA retain the upper hand. Roosevelt's plans to extend the Social Security Act to a universal health insurance entitlement were thus obstructed until the nation's impending entry into World War II dominated the national agenda—a war that Roosevelt did not live to see to its end.

The dominant structures of voluntary health insurance that ultimately evolved were the nonprofit Blue Cross and Blue Shield plans, the former providing hospital insurance coverage and the latter providing insurance coverage for physician services. Notably, both Blue Cross and Blue Shield plans originated as artifacts of a process of innovation and diffusion rather than the outcomes of a comprehensive national health care planning process. In the case of Blue Cross hospital coverage plans, they began as an innovative strategy to create a fund for the hospital care of school teachers at Baylor University Hospital in Dallas, Texas, in 1929 (Litman, 1991; Shi & Singh, 2001). Over time, and ultimately through the coordinative efforts of the AHA, Blue Cross hospital insurance evolved from a single-hospital plan sponsored by independent hospitals to a Blue Cross network of plans, and ultimately to a Blue Cross Association that operated independently of hospitals (Shi & Singh, 2001; Starr, 1982). The first Blue Shield plan appeared in California in 1939, a decade after the original model for Blue Cross hospital insurance was established in Texas (Shi & Singh, 2001). In significant part, the delay reflects the medical profession's reluctance to endorse even voluntary health insurance for physician's services, until it became obvious that it was needed as a strategy to forestall the emergence of publicly sponsored health care insurance. Following the California model, the nonprofit Blue Shield plans were sponsored by state and county level local medical associations, leaving physicians largely in control of the range of benefits offered and the fees paid (Shi & Singh, 2001; Starr, 1982). In fact, these plans were generally structured in ways that allowed individual doctors to maximize their fees in accordance with the income level of their patients (Starr, 1982). Finally, aside from protecting the autonomy of physicians, physician control of the dominant form of health insurance for outpatient care ensured that physicians could continue to exclude competitive providers from the outpatient care market for decades to come.[13]

Ultimately, both the complementary protections of Blue Cross and Blue Shield plans and the rising importance of health insurance benefits as a bargaining tool for labor established the dominant role of employment-based voluntary health insurance in the financing of health care. Notably, both general forms of insurance emerged from the provider side rather than the consumer side of health care—thus also establishing the dominance of provider interests over the public interest in the financing and delivery of health care. Eventually, the health insurance industry itself emerged as an autonomous player in the political economy of health care with its own interests—sometimes aligning on the side of the provider interests in health care (e.g., the AHA, the AMA, and in more recent decades, PhRMA)[14] and other times not. However, the tie that binds them all is the perennial claim (of each) that they represent the public interest in affordable and high-quality health care, juxtaposed with their common opposition to the fundamental reforms in health care financing that would be necessary to accomplish just such an end.

THE HISTORICAL EVOLVEMENT OF THE FEDERAL GOVERNMENT IN HEALTH CARE

The exercise of federal authority in health care at various points in history can be thought of as arising from two kinds of agendas. The first is an overt agenda that is direct and specific with respect to its immediate health care policy goals. The second kind of agenda, which tends to be more latent, involves the framing or reframing of the political philosophy that defines the general purpose and boundaries of the federal role in health care. The earliest example of this dual agenda structure is seen in the first major piece of health legislation passed by the federal government: the act passed by the Fifth Congress in 1798 that taxed the wages of American seamen in order to establish the U.S. Marine Hospital Service. At the overt level, this legislation established the health care infrastructure needed to attend to the health care needs of the nation's maritime labor force. On the level of political philosophy, this act also established the legitimacy of a federal role in the provision of health care where there is compelling national interest—in this earliest case, the protection and enhancement of the seagoing commerce that was the lifeblood of the new republic. In essence, since the viability of the maritime industry was wholly dependent upon the health of the ordinary seamen that manned the ships, the Fifth Congress created what amounted to the first prepaid medical care system in American history. Later examples of federal actions that also were based on what was perceived as a compelling national interest include the

- National Quarantine Act of 1878;
- the 1917 amendments to the War Risk Insurance Act that provided medical care benefits to veterans disabled as a result of military service;
- the Vocational Rehabilitation Act of 1920 that served to put disabled workers back into the industrial labor force; and
- the World War Veteran's Act of 1924 that further extended hospital benefits to disabled veterans (Litman, 1991).

The overt policy agenda that has motivated the array of federal legislation in health care over the past two centuries has served one or more of six very general goals:

- Expansion of the essential components of health care system infrastructure: facilities, technology, and human resources.
- Expansion of health care access.
- Enhancing health care system cost control and cost effectiveness.
- Promotion of public health, public safety, and consumer protection.
- Promotion of research in health and health care.
- Federal program retrenchment and reductions in health care access.

Each of these six general policy goals rose to prominence during different historical periods. For example, the dominant policy goals during the 2 decades following World War II involved significant federal investments in the infrastructure of the health care system, while the decade between 1965 and 1975 reflected a more significant emphasis on the expansion of health care access for the poor, the disabled, and the elderly. Since 1975 the policy goals driving federal health care legislation placed a significant emphasis on cost containment as a counter to rampant health care inflation—albeit with only limited success. As a result of the general failure of policies aimed at health care cost containment, as well the ascendance of political and social conservatism, until the presidency of Barack Obama the dominant federal health care policy goals had swung toward federal program retrenchment and significant reductions in health care access.

In order to provide a general historical overview of the role of federal legislation in the development of the health care system, a series of four tables is provided that show the critical federal health care legislation that was enacted over the different periods composing U.S. post-colonial history. Each of the tables covers a specific historical period, and shows which of the six policy goals are served by each article of federal health care legislation passed. While over 90 specific articles of legislation are shown on these tables, they represent only the more significant articles of federal legislation pertaining to health care enacted over the nation's history. In reviewing the tables, the reader should pay primary attention to differences in trends within each historical period and the broad categories of legislation that have over time defined the federal role in health care. Although it is beyond the scope of this chapter to discuss the specifics of each piece of federal legislation shown, there will be some comment on the most influential or illuminating articles of federal legislation.

Federal Health Care Legislation in Early Nationhood Through the New Deal and World War II

The first period considered, shown in Table 2.1, covers nearly 150 years of the nation's history and reveals a very minimal federal role in health care. Only 23 significant pieces of federal legislation pertaining to health care were enacted, mostly during the period following World War I. The most active arenas for federal activism in health care during this period pertained to policies that were tied to commerce, war, treaty obligations, or threats to public health. Up until the Sheppard–Towner Act's passage in 1921, the population groups that were entitled to even a minimal level of federal support for the direct provision of health care were limited to those serving in the military and some disabled veterans, federal prisoners, Native Americans living on tribal reservations, and American merchant seamen. Examples of federal legislation aimed at the provision of health care for these populations include the establishment of the U.S. Marine Hospital Service in 1798, the creation of the Bureau of Indian Affairs in 1824,[15] the 1917 revisions to the War Risk Insurance

Table 2.1 *Federal Health Care Legislation in Early Nationhood Through the New Deal and World War II*

Federal Legislation	Expansion of Infrastructure	Expansion of Access	Cost Control/ Effectiveness	Public Health/ Safety/ Protection	Health/ Health Care Research	Retrenchment/ Reductions in Access
1798 U.S. Marine Hospital Service	X	X				
1824 Bureau of Indian Affairs (BIA), which ultimately assumes federal responsibility for health care to Native Americans	X	X		X		
1878 National Quarantine Act	X			X		
1902 Public Health and Marine Hospital Service Merger	X			X		
1906 Federal Food and Drugs Act				X		
1912 Children's Bureau Est.				X	X	
1912 Public Health and Marine Hospital Service Renamed to U.S. Public Health Service	X			X	X	
1917 Medical Benefits Added to War Risk Insurance Act		X				
1920 Smith–Fess Vocational Rehabilitation Act		X				
1921 Sheppard–Towner Act	X	X		X		

(continued)

Table 2.1 Federal Health Care Legislation in Early Nationhood Through the New Deal and World War II (continued)

Federal Legislation	Expansion of Infrastructure	Expansion of Access	Cost Control/ Effectiveness	Public Health/ Safety/ Protection	Health/ Health Care Research	Retrenchment/ Reductions in Access
1921 Snyder Act expands federal appropriations and role in Native American Health Care	X	X		X		
1924 World War Veteran's Act	X	X				
1929 Repeal of Sheppard–Towner Act[a]						X
1930 National Institute of Health Est.				X	X	
1933 Federal Emergency Relief Act		X				
1935 Social Security Act		X		X		
1936 Walsh–Healy Act				X		
1937 National Cancer Institute Est.					X	
1938 LaFollette–Bulwinkle Act				X	X	
1938 Food, Drug, and Cosmetic Act				X		
1941 Lantham Act[b]	X					
1941 Nurse Training Act	X					
1944 Public Health Service Act	X			X		

[a]Strictly speaking, the Sheppard–Towner Act was not repealed, but was not reauthorized despite its popularity among women of child bearing age. Opposition to the renewal was a victory for the American Medical Association, which considered Sheppard–Towner a threat to medical free enterprise.
[b]The 1941 Lantham Act (PL-77-137) provided funds for a wide range of public works projects, including the construction of both public and private not-for-profit hospitals (Perlstadt, 1995).

Act that extended medical benefits to disabled soldiers, and the Snyder Act of 1921 that expanded federal appropriations to Native American health care.

There were a variety of reasons for the very limited federal involvement in health care that characterized most of U.S. history. These reasons included the marginal role that the federal government occupied in most peoples lives until the Progressive Era, the very limited benefits that organized medicine could provide in the event of serious illness, and the prevailing belief that the provision of health care was a matter of either medical free enterprise or nongovernmental charity where dictated by individual misfortune (Rosenberg, 1987; Rothstein, 1972; Starr, 1982). Pertaining to the very limited benefits that 19th-century medicine had to offer in the event of serious illness, demographic historian Samuel Preston pointed out that had medicine more to offer, the survival chances of the children of physicians would have been significantly better than the children of those unable to afford medical care—but they were not (Preston & Haines, 1991).

The first major departure from the federal government's very limited and selective involvement in health care did not occur until the second decade of the 20th century, with the passage of the Smith–Fess Vocational Rehabilitation Act in 1920 and the Sheppard–Towner Act of 1921. While the Smith–Fess Act's provision of vocational rehabilitation services to injured workers was certainly a new federal foray into an area that heretofore had been distinctly absent of government involvement at any level, the underlying interest of the federal government in Smith–Fess was tied far more to the promotion of commerce and productivity than to the health and welfare of workers (Litman, 1991). In that sense, the Smith–Fess Vocational Rehabilitation Act was consistent with the rationale that had led to the creation of the U.S. Merchant Hospital Service in 1798. The Sheppard–Towner Act, however, was an altogether radical expansion of the federal role in health care—at least in symbolic terms, if not in dollars allocated.

Early Federal Funding of Maternal Child Health: The Sheppard–Towner Act of 1921

In 1921 the U.S. Congress passed legislation that provided federal funds to states that would enable states to sponsor an array of maternal child health programs. "The Congressional Act for the Promotion of the Welfare and Hygiene of Maternity and Infancy of November 23, 1921," or the Sheppard–Towner Act, as it became generally known, provided a modest $1.2 million dollars per year for states to fund an array of community maternal and child health-promotion programs with the broad aim of reducing infant and child mortality (Almgren, Kemp, & Eisinger, 2000).

The reasons behind the radical departure of the U.S. Congress from its historical reluctance to play a larger role in either the organization or financing of health care are a complex mixture of naive assumptions about the voting behavior of the nation's women, worries about the high levels of infant mortality among the native-born White American population (fears that were rooted in racism and xenophobia), highly effective political activism of the progressive reformers affiliated with the settlement house movement, and the judicious interjection of empirical science to the process of political deliberation. Concerning the first factor, naive assumptions about the voting behavior of women, Sheppard–Towner was passed at the apex of the women's suffrage movement—and it was assumed by the males of Congress that once women won the vote they would continue to vote largely as a block on whatever seemed to be defined as a female political issue. In fact, the primary advocates of the Sheppard–Towner legislation, the Hull House-trained leadership of the federal Children's Bureau, worked closely with their allies in the suffrage movement to make sure that the passage of Sheppard–Towner was of highest priority among the newly enfranchised female voters (Almgren et al., 2000). The leadership of the Children's Bureau also had science on their side. Through what was then a highly innovative series of community studies, the Children's Bureau established a compelling case for the preventative strategies embedded in the Sheppard–Towner Act. For a brief moment in history, just long enough to marshal sufficient support to overcome the vigorous objections of the AMA, an act was funded by Congress that federalized the provision of health care to women and children.

Although states were permitted enormous discretion in the mix of prevention programs funded under Sheppard–Towner, in general they followed a series of health education strategies developed by the federal Children's Bureau on the basis of the evidence garnered from community studies undertaken by that agency in the decade preceding the enactment of Sheppard–Towner. The health education strategies funded under Sheppard–Towner included maternal and child health conferences for physicians and other public health workers, publicly funded maternal and child health clinics, health education classes for women of child-bearing ages and their daughters (who would often act as the prime infant care provider), classes for midwives, and the distribution of maternal and child health promotion literature (Almgren et al., 2000).

In the end, though, the Sheppard–Towner Act was repealed in what became a continuous string of political victories for the medical profession over the interests of public health (Starr, 1982). At the behest of the AMA, the Sheppard–Towner Act was repealed in 1927 with a sunset clause that permitted it to continue through 1929—despite the widespread popularity of its programs among women in rural communities nationwide. The demise of Sheppard–Towner at the hands of social conservatives and the AMA was in large part due to their joint opposition to the establishment of any precedent for publicly funded health care—even one as laudable as basic maternal child health (Lindenmeyer, 1997). In particular, the AMA was eager to preserve the relatively new domain of "well-baby care" as the exclusive province of medical free enterprise. Another reason for Sheppard–Towner's demise was likely the belated discovery by the men of Congress that the women's suffrage movement, as powerful as it was, did not erase the other political and economic divisions among women. Although Sheppard–Towner was initially successful politically because the men of Congress were persuaded by social welfare activists that this legislation was potentially critical to winning and retaining the votes of newly enfranchised women, as the first decade of women's voting rights transpired this strategy gradually unraveled.

In historical appraisal, the rise and fall of Sheppard–Towner had little to do with either its rationale or its effectiveness as a public health program. Although the infant mortality rate plummeted during the years of Sheppard–Towner's existence, recently available historical evidence suggests that the beginning of the decline in infant mortality actually preceded implementation of the Sheppard–Towner Act. However, the historical evidence is consistent with the conclusion that the public health initiatives undertaken by the Children's Bureau and its public health allies, as well as other contextual factors (like the rising literacy rates among women), likely played a significant role in initiating the decline in infant mortality during the decade that immediately preceded the implementation of Sheppard–Towner (Almgren et al., 2000; Lindenmeyer, 1997; Meckel, 1990). Though the public health interventions sponsored by Sheppard–Towner were indeed on target and likely were effective on a small scale, they were never funded on a scale that would reach more than a small fraction of women of child-bearing age (Lindenmeyer, 1997). A final significant critique of the Sheppard–Towner Act was that its programs were largely targeted on the maternal and child health issues of White women living in agrarian communities, rather than either the new urban poor or African American families.

Despite these shortcomings, there remains a greater historical relevance to the Sheppard–Towner Act. First, the structure of Sheppard–Towner and its early political success were outcomes of empirical investigations undertaken by female social scientists and social welfare activists that ultimately emerged as intellectual leaders of the emerging profession of social work.[16] Second, the Sheppard–Towner Act was an early policy application of multi-level theories and methods of prevention that in later decades became known as "prevention science" (Kemp, Almgren, Gilchrist, & Eisinger, 2001). Third and last, Sheppard–Towner served as an early pioneer of what ultimately emerged as an expanded federal role in national public health and federalized health care for the poor, elderly, and disabled during the post-WW II era. In this sense, the advocates of the Sheppard–Towner had the last word over the AMA.

Emergence of the Federal Role in Health and Health Care Research

The medical profession's longstanding opposition to the federal government's involvement in the provision of health care does not extend to federal funding of health and health care research. In fact, with the passage of legislation that funded the National Institute of Health in 1930, Congress established the foundations of an enduring partnership between the hospital and clinics affiliated with American universities, a massive federal research bureaucracy, and medical free enterprise. In benign appraisal, the establishment of the National Institutes of Health (NIH) in 1930 and later legislative acts that expanded the NIH bureaucracy to include such sub-institutes as the National Cancer Institute (1937), the National Heart Institute (1948), and the National Institute of Mental Health (1949) propelled the United States to prominence in the domain of the health sciences research. In more critical perspective, it can be argued that the federal government's investment in health research has also fueled the establishment of an exploitive "medical–industrial complex" that historically has privileged the health care industry, the investor class, and the medical profession over the public interest (Abraham, 1995; Starr, 1982; Wohl, 1984). No matter what lens is employed in historical appraisal of the federal government's leading role in funding health and health care research, with the establishment of the National Institutes of Health in 1930, the Congress elevated the funding of health and health care research to one of the federal government's critical functions.

The New Deal and the Emergence of Federalized Health Care

The fears on the part of the AMA that the provision of health care would one day become federalized nearly materialized in the wake of the Great Depression and the New Deal legislation of the 1930s. Throughout his administration, President Franklin D. Roosevelt had intended that the social and economic guarantees of the federal government would extend to the provision of health care—and had he had his way, the Social Security Act of 1935 would have included the provision of universal health insurance. Although the AMA's strategy of threatening to scuttle the Social Security legislation package as a whole if it included health care insurance was successful at dissuading the Roosevelt administration from this course, the Social Security

Act's (SSA) passage in August of 1935 still managed to establish the precedent whereby economic security became the role of the federal government where market systems failed. This, in fact, was an essential precedent for the later establishment of the Medicare and Medicaid programs enacted in 1965, and the various smaller federal acts in the years between that gradually expanded federal funding of health care for the poor, old, and disabled.

These later acts included amendments to the Social Security Act, permitting state payments to health care providers to the welfare recipients in 1950, and the Kerr–Mills legislation of 1960 that permitted federal grants to states for care of "medically indigent" elderly.[17] Notably, the SSA also managed to include some funds for local and state public health efforts, like those that in prior years had been vigorously opposed by the AMA.[18]

Federal Health Care Legislation in the Post–World War II Era of Prosperity

Much of the health care legislation in the period following World War II reflects the interplay between two general policy agendas. One policy agenda involved a fallback strategy undertaken by the proponents of national health care insurance and their congressional allies to incrementally expand federal funding of health care to eventual universal coverage. The second policy agenda involved expansions of the health care system infrastructure that were broadly supported by the public, the medical profession, and the hospital industry.

With respect to the first agenda, although both the Truman and the Roosevelt administrations favored amendments to the Social Security Act that would have created a program of national health insurance, the fact that neither administration was able to overcome the opposition of the AMA and its allies ultimately left incremental universal coverage as the only strategy to pursue. The ultimate goal of this incremental strategy was not just to eliminate the coverage gaps left by the employer-based health insurance, but to eventually transform health insurance to a federal entitlement. The federal health care legislation that was passed toward this end included the 1950 amendment to Social Security, the act that established the Indian Health Service in 1955, the (Military) Dependents Act of 1956, the Federal Employees Health Benefits Act of 1958, the previously mentioned 1960 Kerr–Mills amendments to the Social Security Act, and, finally, in 1965 the amendments to the Social Security Act that established the Medicaid and Medicare programs. While the incremental coverage was successful in terms of eliminating significant gaps in health insurance coverage for persons poor enough to qualify for public assistance and persons over age

65, as history has shown, the incremental strategy never did achieve universal health insurance coverage or transform to a universal federal entitlement to health care. In fact, in retrospective appraisal it can be argued that the health care insurance programs associated with the incremental coverage strategy in a variety of ways undercut the evolvement of a national health care insurance program—despite their huge beneficial impacts on the poor and elderly that were eligible for these programs.[19]

As Table 2.2 shows, the immediate post-World War II decades were characterized by enormous federal investments in health care system infrastructure—both in human resources and in hospital facilities. The earliest investments, most notably the Hill–Burton Act of 1946 and its later amendments, poured millions of dollars annually into the construction of public and voluntary hospitals in communities nationwide. Later investments, including the 1963 Health Professions Educational Assistance Act and the 1964 Nurse Training Act, helped train a generation of health care professionals. Because of its enormous influence on shaping the institutional structure of the U.S. health care system, the Hill–Burton Act merits particular attention.

The Hospital Survey and Construction Act of 1946 (The Hill–Burton Act)

In very basic terms, this act allocated funds to states for the construction and modernization of hospitals, with the broad goals of improving the hospital capacity of the nation and eliminating disparities between states in hospital resources. Hill–Burton funds were allocated to states according to a formula that considered existent hospital resources and per capita income, and required states to submit a comprehensive hospital facilities development plan. Within states, eligibility for Hill–Burton funds was predicated on a community's ability to raise a significant (as originally written, a two-thirds) proportion of construction funds. During the first 25 years of the Hill–Burton Act's existence, $3.7 billion in federal funds was allocated to hospital construction, accounting for 30% of all hospital construction projects (Starr, 1982).

The origins of the Hill–Burton, named for Senators Lister Hill of Alabama and Harold Burton of Ohio, can in large part be traced to the prewar New Deal legislative agenda to establish a general plan of economic and social security that included a national program of health care for all Americans (Perlstadt, 1995, p. 80).

While the Roosevelt administration was able to incorporate limited provisions for health care into the Social Security Act of 1935 pertaining to maternal child health, as already mentioned, the national health care program component failed to gain the political traction needed to overcome AMA opposition. The AMA was far friendlier to the idea of federal funding

Table 2.2 *Federal Health Care Legislation in the Post–World War II Era of Prosperity*

Federal Legislation	Expansion of Infrastructure	Expansion of Access	Cost Control/ Effectiveness	Public Health/ Health/ Safety/ Protection	Health/ Health Care Research	Retrenchment/ Reductions in Access
1946 National Mental Health Act	X	X		X	X	
1946 Hill–Burton Act	X	X		X		
1946 National Health Act					X	
1949 Hospital Construction Act	X					
1950 SSA Amendments		X				
1950 National Science Foundation Est.					X	
1954 Hill–Burton Act Expansion	X	X				
1955 Polio Vaccination Assistance Act				X		
1955 Indian Health Service Esb.	X	X		X		
1956 SSA Amendments		X				
1956 (Military) Dependents Medical Care Act		X				
1956 Health Amendments Act	X					

(continued)

Table 2.2 *Federal Health Care Legislation in the Post–World War II Era of Prosperity (continued)*

Federal Legislation	Expansion of Infrastructure	Expansion of Access	Cost Control/ Effectiveness	Public Health/ Health/ Safety/ Protection	Health/ Health Care Research	Retrenchment/ Reductions in Access
1956 National Health Survey Act					X	
1958 SBA Loan Program Expansion	X					
1958 Grants in Aid to Schools of Public Health	X			X	X	
1958 Federal Employees Health Benefits Act		X				
1960 Kerr-Mills Amendments to SSA		X				
1961 Community Health Services and Facilties Act	X					

	Col 1	Col 2	Col 3
1962 Health Services for Agricultural Migratory Workers Act	X	X	
1963 Health Professions Educational Assistance Act	X		
1963 Maternal and Child Health and Mental Retardation Planning Amendments	X	X	X
1963 Mental Retardation Facilities Consruction Act/ Community Mental Health Centers Act	X	X	X
1964 Nurse Training Act	X		
1964 Hill–Burton Act Expansion	X		

for hospital construction, just as long as the federal funds did not open the door to a strong federal role in the planning of health services. Another New Deal component to the origins of the Hill–Burton Act had to do with a significant concern on the part of the Roosevelt administration (and subsequently the Truman administration) that to avert a postwar depression, there needed to be significant amount of preemptive federal investment in public works programs to counter the effects of massive demobilization. No politician, conservative or progressive, wanted a repeat of the 1932 Bonus Army occupation of Washington, DC, or the violence and political retribution that followed.[20]

Although historical narratives of the Hill–Burton Act differ on what players and forces occupied the most significant roles in the crafting and passage of this landmark legislation, in Perlstadt's (1995) rigorous analysis of the history of this legislation the main partners were the then fledgling AHA, the U.S. Public Health Service and its allies in the American Public Health Association, and the Senate Subcommittee on Wartime Health and Education chaired by Senator Claude Pepper—a member of the progressive wing of the Democratic party. In its final form, the Hill–Burton Act attended to the central agendas of all three partners. For its part, the AHA got what it wanted in a federal plan that would fund the construction of both voluntary (private not-for-profit) hospitals as well as public hospitals without a commitment to either publicly sponsored health insurance or federal involvement in local hospital management. The Public Health Service, which had advocated the allocation of hospital construction funds on a regional need basis, won provisions in Hill–Burton that would target funding to states with fewer hospital beds relative to the population. The progressives for their part were able to win a victory for health services for the poor in the Hill–Burton Act provisions that (1) obligated hospitals to admit patients without discriminating on the basis of race, creed, or color and (2) required that hospitals furnish a reasonable volume of services for persons unable to pay (Perlstadt, 1995, p. 92).

Despite the fact that the AMA was not a major partner in the negotiations that ultimately yielded the Hill–Burton Act, its political agenda to promote the sovereignty of medicine and protect medical free enterprise from the specter of socialized medicine was very well served by the Hill–Burton Act. First, the Hill–Burton Act further reinforced the incrementalist alternative to the provision of health care for the poor and those without health insurance—as opposed to the progressive approach that would have included universal health insurance as a further extension of the Social Security Act. Second, as Hill–Burton funds were poured into hospital construction, physicians derived enormous direct economic benefits from the opportunities to expand their practices to include hospital care—without significant federal involvement in either hospital service planning or hospital utilization management. Thus, under the provisions of Hill–Burton, physicians were largely free to promote and ultimately affect the kinds of investments in hospital facilities that were most favorable to their economic interests. Often this involved the channeling of Hill–Burton funds into more affluent and less medically needy communities, and toward the kinds of hospital facilities that served the economic interests of medical free enterprise over the interests of public health.

In his historical appraisal of the hospital construction provisions of the Hill–Burton Act, Paul Starr[21] notes that while in principle the provisions of the act were "redistributive" in the formula for allocating funds among states placed a higher priority on those states with lower per capita income, in reality, the allocation of hospital construction funds within states favored more affluent communities (Starr, 1982, p. 350). In large part this outcome was a consequence of provisions in the law, which required that communities pay a large share of hospital construction expenses—in more affluent communities as much as two-thirds (Starr, 1982). A second major deficit of the Hill–Burton Act pertains to the weakness of its antidiscrimination provision, which, until the Supreme Court intervened in 1963, allowed hospitals that had received Hill–Burton funds to refuse admission to African Americans if "separate but equal facilities were available in the area" (Starr, 1982, p. 350). The most significant historical criticism of the Hill–Burton Act, again offered by Starr but echoed by many others since, is that the Hill–Burton program "retarded the integration of the hospital industry," in that the regional planning provisions included the act did not extend to the continued coordination of hospital facilities and service planning once the funds were allocated (Starr, 1982, p. 351). In effect, this permitted uneconomical and marginally competitive hospitals to keep operating and, even more significantly, helped lay the groundwork for the costly "capital-based competition" between hospitals that later ensued in the wake of the Medicare program.[22]

Later Hill–Burton Amendments and the Evolution of the Nursing Home Industry

In 1954, the Hill–Burton Act was extended to the construction and modernization of nonprofit and public nursing homes and ambulatory care facilities, with a dramatic impact on the structure of the long-term care component of the health care system. By the mid-1950s, the combination of such factors as postwar advancements in antibiotic therapies, the effect of Social Security pensions on the capacity of retired elderly to live independently in such places as boarding homes, and the geographic mobility of adult children of the elderly translated to an increased level of demand for residential nursing care of the frail elderly (Almgren, 1990; Vladeck, 1980). In the face of an inadequate supply of voluntary and public sector nursing homes, the lack of community-based long-term care services, and the inadequate and often dangerously constructed former boarding homes that composed the for-profit sector of the nursing home industry, Congress passed a new version of the Hill–Burton legislation that poured millions into the nonprofit institutional long-term care industry. Because the 1954 Hill–Burton provisions demanded hospital-level facility standards to qualify for funding, it in essence created a highly institutionalized model of care for the frail aged that was later extended to the for-profit sector of the industry.

Although the for-profit owners of boarding homes and investors planning to build nursing homes were not eligible for Hill–Burton funds, federal construction subsidies were extended to the proprietary sector of the nursing home industry in the late 1950s in the form of legislation that provided Small Business Administration loans. This legislation, in concert with amendments to the Social Security Act in 1950 and in 1956 that provided federal matching funds for provision of custodial care in proprietary nursing homes, fueled the growth of the for-profit nursing home industry—an industry that over time became dominated by corporate nursing home chains. In contrast to the hospital industry, which historically has had a very small for-profit ownership sector, the nursing home industry evolved to a high proportion of for-profit ownership—today comprising two-thirds of the industry (Kaiser Family Foundation, 2011).

In retrospect, it must be said that while the Hill–Burton Act and its later revisions were enacted with the best of intentions, the structure of the legislation that provided massive federal subsidies for institutional expansion in absence of federal control yielded a variety of unintended consequences. In the hospital component of the health care system, the Hill–Burton Act contributed significantly to geographic disparities in hospital resources and also sowed the seeds of the capital-based competition between hospitals that flourished with the later introduction of Medicare. In the long-term care segment of the health care system, the investments of Hill–Burton funds that favored the development of a quasi-hospital institutional model of care for the frail elderly ultimately created the template for the modern and predominantly for-profit nursing home industry. The road not taken in long-term care until decades later—investments in community-based long-term care—now struggles to compete for public dollars against a deeply entrenched and politically influential investor-driven nursing home industry (Almgren, 1990; Kane, Kane, & Ladd, 1998; Vladeck, 1980). While the Hill–Burton Act provided critical momentum for construction and remodeling of badly needed hospitals nationwide and in many ways expanded access to health care for generations of Americans, the Hill–Burton Act is also saddled with an unfortunate legacy of incrementalism, missed opportunities, and latent inflationary effects on the national cost of health care.

Federal Health Care Legislation Through the Rise and Fall of the Great Society

As Table 2.3 shows, the period between 1965 and the late 1970s is characterized by Congressional actions that favored significant investments in health care system infrastructure, health care access, and health care research. Legislation aimed at curbing the growth of health care inflation did not emerge until the early 1970s, and even then without much political will or measurable effect.

By the mid-1960s, the U.S. health care system had been relentlessly expanding its capacities in facilities, technology, and resources year after year for nearly 2 decades. As a result, the average life expectancy of Americans was accelerating and the principal barriers to health care access had largely shifted from the availability of hospitals and trained staff to the availability of health care insurance. For the majority of Americans, those of working age and their dependents, access to health care was enhanced through the postwar rise in real wages and the increasingly common availability of health insurance coverage as a fringe benefit of employment (Starr, 1982, p. 372). Congressional actions during the prior decade had also yielded expansions in the health care access for veterans, Native Americans, federal employees, and the poor. The most significant segment of the population left out were the nonpoor aged, who nonetheless were threatened by poverty as their individual health care needs escalated year by year. This set the stage for the historically greatest expansions of federal funding of health care, the 1965 amendments to the Social Security Act that established the Medicare and Medicaid entitlements.

The Emergence of the Medicare and Medicaid Compromise

At the point that the Kennedy administration assumed power in 1961, there remained a significant level of public support for amendments to the Social Security Act that would expand its entitlements in universal health insurance. Moreover, such a plan remained on the radar screen of the remnants of New Deal era politicians that remained in Congress. Faced with the very real possibility of a formidable pro-universal health insurance coalition comprised of

Table 2.3 *Federal Health Care Legislation Through the Rise and Fall of the Great Society*

Federal Legislation	Expansion of Infrastructure	Expansion of Access	Cost Control/ Effectiveness	Public Health/ Safety/ Protection	Health/ Health Care Research	Retrenchment/ Reductions in Access
1965 SSA Medicare and Medicaid Amendments	X	X				
1965 Community Mental Health Services and Facilities Act	X	X				
1965 Mental Health Centers Act Amendments	X					
1965 Health Professions Educational Assistance Act Amendments	X					
1965 Heart Disease, Cancer and Stroke Amendments	X					
1965 Older Americans Act	X	X		X		
1966 OEO Neighborhood Health Centers Amendments	X	X		X		
1966 Comprehensive Health Planning and Service Act	X	X				
1966 Allied Health Professions Act	X					
1967 &1968 SSA Nursing Home Amendments	X					
1968 Health Manpower Act	X					

	(1)	(2)	(3)	(4)	(5)
1968 National Science Foundation Expansion					X
1969 Medicaid 75th Percentile Fee Schedule			X		
1970 Community Mental Health Service Act	X	X			
1970 Occupational Safety & Health Act (OSHA)				X	
1970 National Institute of Alcohol Abuse & Alcoholism Esb.	X	X		X	X
1970 National Health Core Esb.	X	X			
1971 Economic Stabilization Act Targets Health Care Inflation			X		
1971 Comprehens ive Health Manpower Act	X				
1972 SSA Amended to Establish Peer Review Organizations			X		
1972 Emergency Medical Services Systems Act	X	X			
1972 SSA Amended to offer Medicare HMO Option			X		

(continued)

Table 2.3 *Federal Health Care Legislation Through the Rise and Fall of the Great Society (continued)*

Federal Legislation	Expansion of Infrastructure	Expansion of Access	Cost Control/ Effectiveness	Public Health/ Safety/ Protection	Health/ Health Care Research	Retrenchment/ Reductions in Access
1973 Health Maintenance Organization Act	X		X			
1974 National Health Planning and Resources Development Act	X		X			
1974 National Institute on Aging Esb.					X	
1976 Indian Health Care Improvement Act[a]	X	X		X	X	
1976 Health Professions Educational Assistance Act	X		X			
1977 Rural Health Clinics Act	X	X				

[a]The 1976 Indian Health Care Improvement Act (IHCIA) was preceded in 1975 by the Indian Self-determination and Education Assistance Act, which established the intent to expand local tribal governance of health care services to Native Americans (Kuschell-Haworth, 1998).

labor, the elderly, the remnants of New Deal era politicians in Congress, and a progressive White House, the AMA and its allies ultimately had to acquiesce to a compromise that would yield *some* ground to further federalization of health insurance. For their part, the liberals also needed to compromise. The AMA's past tactics that played on the public's fears of a creeping socialist agenda and governmental interference in the doctor–patient relationship had been very effective in sidelining attempts to create a universal entitlement to health insurance in the Roosevelt and Truman administrations, and until 1964 the Democratic party lacked the clout in Congress to even approach enacting such an agenda (Starr, 1982). The final compromise contained elements of both liberal and conservative ideology; universal entitlement to health insurance for the elderly recipients of Social Security and for the poor, a means-tested medical care assistance program that left a large share of the cost and much of the eligibility discretion to the states. It might be said that the AMA and liberal camps both held their respective noses and signed on to this legislation, each claiming a partial victory and plotting for the further battles to come. With AMA opposition to the further expansion of federal financing of health care held in abeyance, in 1965 Congress passed the amendments to the Social Security Act that provided medical care for the elderly (Title 18) and grants to states for the funding of medical care for the poor (Title 19) by a final vote of 307 to 116 in the House of Representatives and by a vote of 70 to 24 in the Senate (Litman, 1991).

While there are many distinctions between the Medicare and Medicaid programs, the fundamental one involves the difference between a social insurance model and one dependent on year-to-year appropriations and means-tested eligibility. The former, like the Social Security old-age pension entitlements, enjoys the status of a return on paid investments and brings with it the sense of "entitlement" in the truest sense of the term. Medicare was constructed as just such a program, combining payroll contributions to a hospital insurance trust fund (Medicare Part A) with a second benefit that involved voluntary premium deductions from Social Security pension checks (Medicare Part B).[23] Moreover, eligibility for Medicare is essentially universal for all Americans that reach a minimum age, with rich and poor alike reaping the benefits. Medicaid, on the other hand, is burdened with extreme state-to-state variations in eligibility criteria and coverage, a financial structure that is completely based on general tax revenues, and the stigma of demonstrable poverty as the essential precondition for eligibility. Despite these shortcomings, there is no question that with the implementation of Medicaid those in deepest poverty at last had a level of access to health care that in many respects was comparable to the level of health care access achieved for the middle class—at least in most parts of the country.

Community Mental Health Legislation

The early 1960s was also a watershed period for the expansion of community mental health services, in large part as a legacy of the Kennedy administration's particular commitment to the reformation of the mental health system and serendipitous advancements in psychopharmacology that made deinstitutionalization feasible. President Kennedy's particular commitment to the radical reformation of mental health care is generally believed to have arisen from his family's tragic experience with the then conventional treatment of mental illness. In the early 1940s, Kennedy's younger sister had undergone a lobotomy when she and Kennedy were young adults. Since the mid-1950s there had been a series of breakthroughs in the development and use of psychotropic medications that diminished the prevalence of the most debilitating symptoms of severe and persistent mental illness—thus undercutting the necessity and rationale for the institutional confinement of the severely mentally ill and the abuses that followed. Due to Kennedy's unprecedented direct advocacy of radical reformation of the mental health system to a community mental health service model, in 1963 Congress passed the Community Mental Health Centers Construction Act/Mental Retardation Facilities Construction Act (PL 88-164). This legislation shifted the federal role in mental health from primarily the funding of research to the financing of mental health care infrastructure. In 1965 and then again in 1970, further amendments to the Mental Health Centers Act increased the level of federal funds for facilities construction and created seed grants for mental health centers to increase their staffing levels (The Brookings Institution, 2006). With the availability of SSA Title 19 (Medicaid) matching funds for payment of community mental health services for the many mentally ill that were poor, continued revolutionary advances in psychopharmacology, and a series of judicial decisions that greatly restricted use of involuntary institutionalization, by the early 1970s the dominance of a community-based approach to the care of the mentally ill was firmly entrenched.[24]

Expansions in Health Services for Native Americans

During the 1970s Congress passed two acts that improved upon what heretofore had been a grossly inadequate response to the federal government's treaty obligations pertaining to the health and welfare of Native Americans. The first act, the 1975 Indian Self-Determination and Educational Assistance Act, affirmed that it was the federal government's obligation to promote the maximum level of Native American participation in the governance of federal health, welfare, and education programs serving Native American communities. In essence, this act made Indian Health Service programs accountable to tribal governance. The Indian Health Care Improvement Act (IHCIA), passed in 1976, was largely motivated by public health research findings that highlighted the gross disparities between the health status of Native Americans and the general population (Northwest Portland Area Indian Health Board, 2006). Although the IHCIA provided an array of appropriations pertaining to health programs and services on behalf of Native Americans, the most significant aspect of the IHCIA was its declaration that it was a policy of the United States to achieve of health status parity for Native Americans (Northwest Portland Area Indian Health Board, 2006).

The Emergence of Cost Control in Health Care

By the early 1970s, it was becoming increasingly apparent that some of the critics of the Medicare program had been correct in their prediction that there were aspects of the program that were inherently inflationary. As initially designed, there were two aspects of the Medicare program that were particularly inflationary.

The first inherently inflationary feature of Medicare involved a "costplus" form of reimbursement, similar to the federal government's often infamous payments to defense contractors. In essence, hospitals providing care to Medicare beneficiaries were reimbursed for the services they provided based upon the costs they were able to justify under the most generous of guidelines. Under cost-plus reimbursement, hospitals had no particular incentive to avoid providing unnecessary care, and, in fact, had strong incentives to provide as much care as was conceivably defensible. Indeed, it became a widespread practice in the hospital industry to reward ancillary department heads for their ability to get physicians to order ever higher levels of supplies, tests, and treatments. This feature of Medicare fueled a hospital care culture that "more care was better" and also led hospitals to be less resistant to rising staffing levels and rising wages. Although it was left to physicians to determine the necessity of hospital admissions, the procedures performed, and the length of hospital stay, the structure of Medicare Part B reimbursement ensured that physicians would have strong financial incentives to use hospital services for patients and an absence of financial incentives for early discharge.

The second inherently inflationary aspect of Medicare reimbursement involved the "capital pass-through" provision of Medicare, which in essence allowed (and indeed encouraged) hospitals to invest in new technology and facility upgrades by recovering these expenses through quite generous Medicare cost allowances. In simple terms, Medicare provider payment rules permitted hospitals to include in their allowable costs whatever dollar investments in new technology, equipment, and facilities the hospital deemed necessary for providing care for Medicare beneficiaries. Thus, hospitals had the equivalent of a blank check from Medicare to invest in whatever facility improvements and purchases of technology could be defended as essential to improved patient care. During the 1970s in particular, it appears that hospital administrators and their physician constituents pushed the blank check nature of capital pass-through to its limits, thus fueling health care inflation to *its* limits (Garrison & Wilensky, 1986).

In the interest of fairness, it should be acknowledged that the capital pass-through provisions of Medicare were very deliberately intended to serve as a mechanism through which federal dollars could be infused into the health care system to fund modernization, improvements in capacity, and advancements in health care technology. In fact, it is indeed the case that the enhanced purchasing and investment capacity of hospitals available under the Medicare capital pass-through mechanism played a crucial role in providing incentives for the development of new innovations in health care technology, such as computerized tomography (CT) scanners. Although these policy goals were well served by the capital pass-through provisions of Medicare, an unintended consequence was the fueling of rampant capital-based competition between hospitals.

Capital-based competition between hospitals, described here and elsewhere in this volume as the use of advantages in physical facilities and/or health care technologies to either preserve or expand a hospital's share of the health care market, is a major driver of health care inflation. As a simple example, suppose Hospital A chooses to acquire a linear accelerator[25] for the treatment of a variety of cancers at the cost of roughly $2 million for the base equipment and related facility improvements. Hospital B, concerned that it will lose some of its market share of cancer patients to Hospital A, chooses to invest in a similar upgrade that involves a like purchase of a linear accelerator. There are now two virtually identical multimillion dollar linear accelerators within 10 miles of each other, each being paid for in substantial part by Medicare capital pass-through funds—with no demonstrable net benefit to the survival of cancer patients as a result of having two identical linear accelerators available rather than one. There is however, a substantial local contribution to Medicare cost inflation. Although this might seem like a ludicrous example, it is exactly the kind of capital-based competition that has led to the oversupply of expensive health care technologies in many communities across the United States, in many respects to the ultimate detriment of health care quality and access (Bryce & Cline, 1998).[26]

By the early 1970s, health care inflation was finally recognized as a significant public policy issue, complicating a more general problem of rampant inflation that characterized all sectors of the national economy. While Congress did not deal with the inflationary aspects of the Medicare program directly at that point, it did pass the Economic Stabilization Act in 1970, which permitted the Nixon administration to implement various forms of price control across key sectors of the economy, including health care. Recognizing that direct price controls were at best a short-term solution to health care inflation (as well as antithetical to the laissez-faire sentiments of the Republicans that elected him), in 1971 Nixon urged Congress to promote the provision of health care through Health Maintenance Organizations (HMOs). In a stinging defeat to the AMA, in 1972 Congress both extended Medicare benefits to newly established HMOs and established Professional Standards Review Organizations (PSROs) to monitor the quality and the necessity of care provided to beneficiaries of Medicare, Medicaid, and other government health programs (Litman, 1991; Starr, 1982). In an even larger defeat for the AMA, in 1973 Congress passed the Health Maintenance Organization Act, which provided direct federal subsidies for the establishment and expansion of HMOs (Litman, 1991). Finally, as a restraint to the capital-based competition between hospitals that had fueled problems of oversupply in health care facilities and technology in some geographic areas and under-supply in others, in 1974 Congress passed the National Health Planning and Resource Development Act. This act established a national network of "Health Systems Agencies" (HSAs), which were responsible for the development of annual plans for the improvement of local health resources and oversight of the local "certificate of need" review process (The Brookings Institution, 2006).[27] As a result of these various legislative acts, by the mid-1970s hospitals and other institutional providers were (1) made financially accountable to Medicare and Medicaid for patient care that was either unnecessary or of substandard quality and (2) were largely precluded by making large new investments in technology and facilities without the formal sanction of local health care planning authorities. Although the effects of these restraints on health care inflation ultimately proved negligible in the short run, the actions of Congress during much of the 1970s at least signaled the end of any assumptions by either political party that health care providers could be relied upon to self-regulate or spontaneously act in the public interest.

Federal Health Care Legislation Through the Eras of Managed Care and Health Care Reform

By the close of the 1970s, the health care sector of the domestic economy had nearly doubled since 1960, and was fast approaching the 10% proportion of the GDP. As a result, a 30-year national policy that had been characterized by an emphasis on the expansion of health care infrastructure and access gave way to a policy agenda aimed at cost control (see Table 2.4). Although the federal legislation that established mandatory peer review of hospital care proved successful in curbing the more severe abuses of the Medicare and Medicaid programs and also provided important impetus to the adoption of more cost-effective approaches to patient care, the general trend in health care inflation continued unabated. Similarly, the imposition of a national "certificate of need" process over major new investments in health care facilities and technology proved insufficient to the task. In many parts of the country, politically powerful hospitals and other health care investment groups intent on expansion and the acquisition of new technology found ways to subvert the process. As a result, the certificate of need process to a significant extent fueled rather than restrained the growth of disparities between affluent communities and poor ones in the quality of facilities and the level of technology available.

Emergence of the Prospective Payment and the New Era of Managed Care

In the early 1980's, the primary problem faced by the just-elected Reagan administration and Congress was that the cost accounting and reimbursement structure of the Medicare program, like that of the health care insurance industry as a whole (with the exception of HMOs), financially rewarded both physicians and hospitals for providing more care rather than less. Although by this time it was generally apparent that mandatory peer review and other forms of federal regulatory oversight would not be enough to cure health care inflation as long as financial incentives of health care tilted toward expanding its use remained, neither the health care insurance industry nor Congress was eager to reverse the financial incentives too far toward withholding the provision of health care. In the end though, Congress elected to act boldly and directly in a series of legislative acts that culminated with the restructuring of the Medicare hospital benefit to a *prospective payment system* (PPS) in 1983.[28]

The PPS method of hospital reimbursement pays hospitals for episodes of inpatient care of Medicare beneficiaries in accordance with each hospital episode's assignment to any one of 467 diagnosis-related groups (since expanded to roughly 500; Shi & Singh, 2001). The DRG is determined at discharge and involves a select array of factors that include the patient's discharge diagnosis and other case characteristics that have proved to be predictive of hospital care costs (e.g., patient age, sex, type of surgery, if any, or presence of comorbid conditions). Because this method of reimbursement is based on a standard fee per DRG rather than either the amount of

Table 2.4 *Federal Health Care Legislation Through the Eras of Managed Care and Health Care Reform*

Federal Legislation	Expansion of Infrastructure	Expansion of Access	Cost Control/ Effectiveness	Public Health/ Health/ Safety/ Protection	Health/Health Care Research	Retrenchment/ Reductions in Access
1980 Omnibus Reconciliation Act		X	X			
1981 Elimination of Public Service Hospitals & Free Medical Care to Seamen			X			X
1982 Tax Equity and Fiscal Responsibility Act (TEFRA) Funds Hospice Care & Imposes Hospital Cost Controls	X	X	X			
1982 Health Resources and Services Administration (HRSA) Esb.	X				X	
1983 DRG-Based Prospective Payment System for Medicare Esb.			X			
1985 Consolidated Omnibus Budget Reconciliation Act (COBRA)[a]		X		X		
1986 Medicare reimbursement provisions added for disproportionate share of poor and graduate medical education	X	X				
1986 Medicaid eligibility coverage extended to poor pregnant women, infants, and young children		X				
1987 Omnibus Budget Reconciliation Act (OBRA)[b]	X	X	X	X		
1988 Medcare Catastrophic Coverage Act[c]		X				
1988 Health and Human Services (HSS) Issues Restrictive Rules to Family Planning barring abortion related services						X

(continued)

Table 2.4 *Federal Health Care Legislation Through the Eras of Managed Care and Health Care Reform (continued)*

Federal Legislation	Expansion of Infrastructure	Expansion of Access	Cost Control/ Effectiveness	Public Health/ Safety/ Protection	Health/Health Care Research	Retrenchment/ Reductions in Access
1989 OBRA Esb. Agency for Health Care Policy and Research (AHPR)					X	
1989 Repeal of Catastrophic Coverage Act						X
1990 Americans with Disabilities Act		X				
1992 Reauthorization of the Indian Health Care Improvement Act[d]	X	X		X		
1996 Personal Responsibility and Work Opportunity Reconciliation Act (TANF)						X
1996 Health Insurance Portability and Accountability Act		X		X		
1996 The Veterans' Health Care Eligibility Reform Act[e]		X	X			
1997 SSA Amendments Establishing State Children's Health Insurance Program (SCHIP)		X				
1997 Balanced Budget Act creates Medicare Part "C" Benefit Options, Expands Mandatory Enrollment in Medicaid Managed Care and Critical Access Hospital Provisions	X	X	X	X		
2003 SSA Amendments establishing Medicare Part D–Prescription Drug Benefit[f]		X				X

2005 Deficit Reduction Act Introduces Unprecedented Cuts in Medicaid[g]				X
2010 Patient Protection and Affordable Care Act/Health Care and Education Reconciliation Act of 2010[h]	X	X	X	

[a]COBRA 1985 was a sweeping piece of legislation that contained several significant health care system provisions, including making hospice a permanent part of Medicare, allowing states the option to provide a Medicaid hospice benefit, allowing employees and their dependents to continue employer-based health insurance despite disruptions in employment, and regulations that sanctioned hospitals for "patient dumping," i.e. transferring patients to other hospitals for the specific purpose of avoiding uncompensated care costs.

[b]OBRA 1987 also included several key health care provisions: further expansion of Medicaid that required states to extend eligibility to poor women and young children; encouraged expansion of Medicaid clinics to the homeless; extensive regulatory upgrading of the nursing home industry, including significant staffing upgrades; nursing home pre-admission screening standards, and Medicaid funding for community based services for aged persons at high risk for nursing home care.

[c]Although the Catastrophic Coverage Act provided prescription drug coverage, expansion of nursing home care coverage and additional health care service coverage—this legislation also imposed increased premium charges that were means tested. Despite the significant benefits to the health care and financial security of seniors, the overwhelming majority of seniors viewed this legislation as an unfair financial burden on the elderly and a retreat from the federal commitment to affordable health care for older Americans.

[d]Since its initial authorization in 1976, the Indian Health Care Improvement Act (IHCIA) has been reauthorized numerous times. However, the 1992 reauthorization explicitly reinserted key language from the original (1976) authorization that identified the achievement of health status parity between Native Americans and the general U.S. population as a fundamental obligation to Native peoples and a central goal of federal policy (Kuschell-Haworth, 1998; Northwest Portland Area Indian Health Board, 2006).

[e]The Veterans' Health Care Eligibility Reform Act of 1996 restructured the Veterans Affairs health care system from a population-based system, and realigned eligibility standards to a system of eight priority groups that included eligibility criteria-based on financial need and non-service connected disablement. This is seen as a critical acknowledgment of the VA health care system's commitment to all low-income and disabled veterans, not just those disabled as a direct result of military s ervice.

[f]Although the rationale and centerpiece of 2003 revisions to Medicare was the addition of the prescription drug benefit that will add billions to the cost of the Medicare program, it also contained provisions that place a higher financial burden of the poorest and sickest of the elderly by raising their out-of-pocket costs. Thus, this legislation can be said to have expanded access to health care for some elderly while reducing access for others.

[g]According to Congressional Budget Office estimates, this legislation will cut Medicaid by a total of 26.4 billion dollars over a ten year period, with significant reductions in access to health care for the poor (Congressional Budget Office, 2006).

[h]The Patient Protection and Affordable Care Act and certain provisions of the Health Care and Education Reconciliation Act of 2010 togther comprise the Obama administration's health care reform package. The former was signed into law March 23, 2010 and the latter on March 30, 2010.

hospital services provided or the length of hospital stay involved, neither hospitals nor physicians are financially rewarded for the ordering of unnecessary
tests and procedures, providing unnecessary treatments, or keeping the
patient in the hospital longer than is essential. Under PPS, hospitals may
lose money on some episodes of care and make money on others, but in
general the profits and losses offset each other if the hospital puts into place
effective mechanisms of cost control and quality assurance. During the first
year of its implementation, Medicare PPS reduced the average length of hospital stay for Medicare beneficiaries from 10.0 days to 9.1 days and proved
quite effective at restraining the growth in Medicare program hospital utilization (Morrisey, Sloan, & Valvona, 1988; Sheingold, 1989).

The early success of the Medicare PPS system in placing constraints on
hospital costs and forcing hospitals to put into place strong mechanisms of
cost control ushered in the new era of managed care. Parallel developments
in the health care insurance market such as the rapid shift from the
community-rated insurance products to employer-based insurance pricing
and the emergence of preferred provider hospital contracts ultimately saw
hospitals bidding against one another to retain their market share of privately
insured patients. Beginning with Medicare PPS and ultimately diffusing over
the next decade throughout the private insurance market, the primary risk of
health insurance abuse turned 180° from the provision of unnecessary care to
the withholding of it. It was this worry,[29] validated in some instances and
overblown in others, that ultimately led to the retreat of managed care in
the later half of the 1990s.

Other Congressional Efforts at Cost Control

Even though the Omnibus Budget Reconciliation Act of 1987 sought in a
variety of ways to improve the quality of care in the nursing home industry
and further expansions of Medicaid program eligibility for children, it also
authorized funds for states to develop community-based long-term care services for persons who would otherwise be at risk for nursing home placement
(Litman, 1991). Because the largest financial burden for nursing home care is
assumed in roughly equal share by states and the federal government through
the Medicaid program, both states and Congress had a strong incentive
to develop community-based long-term care programs as a cost effective
alternative to nursing home care.[30]

In order to deal with the rising demands of the Veterans Affairs health
care system and move away from the antiquated hospital-based structure of
the VA system, in 1996 Congress passed the Veterans' Health Care Eligibility
Reform Act. In effect, this legislation transformed the Veterans Affairs health

care system from a hospital-based system to a population-based system that allocates care by an explicit set of eligibility priorities.

The Balanced Budget Act of 1997 (1997 BBA) expanded the criteria for mandatory enrollment in Medicaid managed care programs, created Medicare "Part C" benefit options, and provided special Medicare financing subsidies for rural hospitals that were qualified for "Critical Access Hospital" designation. Under Medicare Part C (also called Medicare + Choice), beneficiaries who participate in Medicare Part A and Part B were given the option of enrolling in a Medicare approved managed care plan (HMO or PPO) that would provide expanded benefits,[31] or for a limited number of people enrolling in a medical savings account (MSA) program (Shi & Singh, 2001). Although Congress had hoped to retard the growth in Medicare expenditures by providing incentives for beneficiaries to move to managed care alternatives, the first years of the program were replete with an array of setbacks in implementation.

The Critical Access Hospital provisions of the 1997 BBA created a flexible cost-based funding mechanism that enables small rural hospitals to survive financially despite high levels of uncompensated care and erratic fluctuations in demands for services. In addition to providing a range of acute care inpatient services, Critical Access Hospitals are also required to provide 24-hour emergency care (CMS, 2011). Absent the Critical Access Hospital provisions of the 1997 BBA, the nation's network of rural hospitals would have collapsed completely, leaving millions of Americans hours of travel from lifesaving medical intervention.

Selective Expansions in Access/Infrastructure

The health care cost control theme that characterized the political agenda of Congress during the last 2 decades of the 1900s did not preclude some instances of expansion in either access or infrastructure—though by the standards of the 1950s and 1960s they were quite modest. First, the previously mentioned 1982 TEFRA legislation funded a Medicare hospice benefit, which has since been expanded in scope and also extended to Medicaid. In addition, Congressional actions in 1986 and 1997 witnessed important eligibility expansions in Medicaid, the most critical of which involved the Social Security Act amendments establishing the State Children's Health Insurance Program (SCHIP).[32] Although the SCHIP program significantly expanded Medicaid eligibility for children of all ages in low-income families, it also came in the wake of another "near miss" in the establishment of a federalized universal health program—the so-called Clinton plan. In this sense, the SCHIP expansions of Medicaid eligibility were consistent with Congress's long record of preferring an incremental response to disparities in health care. In particular, the kinds of incremental solutions that would not run counter to the preferences of the health care establishment, that is, the nonpublic hospital industry, the conservative sectors of the medical profession, the health insurance industry, and the pharmaceutical industry.

Two other acts of Congress during this period addressed significant public health crises affecting particular segments of the U.S. population. The 1990 Ryan White Comprehensive AIDS Resources Emergency (CARE) Act provided funds for an array of community-based social and health care services to persons suffering from HIV disease and AIDS. The Ryan White CARE Act was amended and reauthorized in 1996 and 2000, and as of 2006 serves over 500,000 persons per year (HRSA HIV/AIDS Bureau, 2006). The 1992 Reauthorization of the Indian Health Care Improvement Act addressed the lingering health disparities suffered by Native Americans. In addition to authorizing funds for the expansion of access and infrastructure, the language of this legislation established the achievement of health status parity for Native Americans as an obligation of the federal government and as a central policy goal. Despite the continued gap between the level of federal funding and the magnitude of health and health care disparities between the general U.S. population and Native Americans, this legislation represented an important advancement in the cause of Native American health.

Although considered civil rights legislation rather than health care legislation, the 1990 Americans with Disabilities Act (PL 101-336) carried with it an array of provisions that in effect expanded access to health care for persons with disabilities. This is because the Americans with Disabilities Act (ADA) prohibits disability-based discrimination and upholds equal opportunity in an array of spheres that affect health care access, such as employment, government services, public accommodations, transportation, and commercial facilities. Because of the ADA, a disabled person is more likely to be eligible for employment-based health insurance, is more likely to have the transportation accommodations needed to access medical care, and is less likely to be discriminated against by health care providers who prefer not to treat persons with some stigmatizing disabilities. Although employers and health care providers have successfully used the courts to narrow the definition of disablement subject to ADA protections, in its 1998 Bragdon decision (*Bragdon v. Abbott*, 118 S Ct 2196) the U.S. Supreme Court both extended ADA protections to persons with HIV seeking health care and left the door open to other health conditions (Gostin, Feldblum, & Webber, 1999).[33] Of equal importance, the courts have interpreted the definition of "public accommodations" to extend to hospitals, clinics, and the offices of health professionals.

The largest and most controversial expansion in the federal role in health care during this period was the passage of amendments to the Social Security Act in 2003 that established Medicare Part D, generally referred to as the "Medicare Drug Benefit." This was not the first time that the Congress had passed legislation extending Medicare benefits to outpatient prescription drug coverage. The earlier attempt by Congress to expand Medicare benefits to drug coverage occurred with the passage of the Catastrophic Coverage Act of 1987. Although this legislation provided expanded nursing home coverage and home health care benefits in addition to prescription drug coverage, it also involved the imposition of increased Medicare premium charges that were means tested. In response to widespread outrage among Medicare program beneficiaries, Congress repealed the Catastrophic Coverage Act in 1989. In stark contrast to the rhetoric of the GOP-dominated Congress and the George W. Bush administration about the critical need to rein in entitlement spending, in the summer of 2003, Congress, by the narrowest of margins, passed the largest expansion of Medicare program's entitlements since 1965. In political terms, the Medicare Modernization Act of 2003 was crafted to serve two masters: the large voting block of Medicare beneficiaries seeking federal help with the ever-increasing costs of their prescription drugs, and a pharmaceutical industry eager to see an expansion of the purchasing power of Medicare beneficiaries without the threat of federal price controls. The predictable result was a fiscally irresponsible and politically deceptive compromise that in the end is estimated to add $400 billion to federal Medicare program spending from 2004 through year 2013 (Congressional Budget Office, 2004). Despite the enormous burden that the expanded Medicare entitlements added to the federal budget deficit, the complexity of the program baffled consumers and retail pharmacists alike, and still left many Medicare beneficiaries at risk for catastrophic personal expenditures. Those least served by this legislation, aside from federal tax payers, were the many Medicare beneficiaries living in poverty who were forced to assume an increased share of their pharmaceutical expenses as a result of this legislation (Steinberg, 2005).[34]

Reductions and Retrenchments Affecting Access to Health Care

Congress opened the 1980s with an act (in 1981) that eliminated the U.S. Public Hospital system, which its critics had long claimed was redundant, expensive, and inefficient. The systems facilities were in fact largely antiquated and operationally inefficient, but the closure of U.S. Public Hospitals also signaled a further devolvement of the national health care safety net—just at the point when the voluntary sector of the hospital was becoming less willing and able to absorb its share of the costs of uncompensated care.[35] A second major reduction in access to health care, specific to women seeking family planning services, occurred when the Department of Health and Human Services adopted rules that blocked federal funds to family planning clinics that engaged in any actions that facilitated women's access to abortions (Litman, 1991). Because the family planning clinics affected provided low-income women with an array of reproductive health care services that were unrelated to abortion, the failure of Congress to counter this action by the Reagan administration represented a significant retreat from the federal commitment to women's health.[36]

In limited but important ways, the 1996 amendment to the Social Security Act that eliminated traditional Aids to Families with Dependent Children (AFDC) in favor of the Temporary Assistance to Needy Families (TANF) also represented a retreat from access to health care for poor families, though its negative effects depended on the SCHIP and TANF eligibility criteria specific to each state. In some states, involuntary termination from TANF also terminated Medicaid benefits to poor families (Center for Public Policy Priorities, 2003).

The most severe retreat from access to health care in the last decade was the 2005 Deficit Reduction Act. According to Congressional Budget Office estimates, the provisions of the Deficit Reduction Act (DRA) was expected to trim more than 26 billion dollars from Medicaid over the next decade and result in large-scale reductions in Medicaid benefits and eligibility, thus affecting millions of the working poor and their health care providers (Congressional Budget Office, 2006). The centerpiece of this act involves provisions that permit states to impose health care cost-sharing requirements on Medicaid recipients, and other provisions that are clearly intended to discourage otherwise eligible persons from applying for Medicaid, such as increasing proof-of-citizenship requirements. While some aspects of the DRA may be more defensible,[37] on the whole the DRA represented an historically unprecedented blow to the federal health care safety net for the poorest of Americans.[38]

The DRA perfectly illustrates the dual agenda nature of federal health care legislation explained at the beginning of this section. The overt policy agenda, as identified in the title of the DRA, is "deficit reduction" at the federal level and the curbing of growth in the Medicaid program that imposes a particular burden in state budgets. The latent agenda of the DRA, which involves the framing of the political philosophy that defines the general purpose and boundaries of the federal role in health care, further reflected the triumph of a political philosophy that seeks to diminish the role of the federal government as the ultimate guardian of access to health care for America's poor families. However, this was a short-lived victory. By 2008, a new presidential administration was elected to office by a largest margin in recent history, based in significant part on a policy platform that embraced universal access to health care.

The Resurgence of Health Care Reform

At the point that Barack Obama was elected to the presidency in November of 2008, there were 45 million Americans without any form of health insurance (private or public), and more middle-class households were losing their health insurance coverage than any time in history (U.S. Census. 2011). In 2009, as the recession that began in the final years of the Bush administration deepened and long-term unemployment became a risk for earners at all levels of income, the ranks of the uninsured swelled to nearly 50 million (U.S. Census, 2011). Further making the public case for fundamental health care reform were nationally publicized narratives of formally middle-income householders being bankrupted by medical bills, often despite some level of commercial health insurance coverage. Aside from this advantageous public opinion context, President Obama (a Democrat) enjoyed a democratic party majority in both the House of Representatives and the Senate. In sum, the time was ripe for fundamental health care reform that would realize the heretofore unrealized goal of universal health insurance coverage for all citizens.

Despite this unprecedented opportunity and the depth of his personal commitment to a plan that would bring about universal health insurance coverage, Obama was wary of repeating the strategic errors of the Clinton administration—in particular, devising a plan of health care reform in absence of public visibility and not giving congress significant ownership of the specific approach taken.[39] Although Obama was criticized by many of his supporters for deferring too much to congressional negotiations and not taking full advantage of the presidential bully pulpit to advocate for more radical reform (in particular, a public insurance option), in the end, by March of 2010 a health insurance package was signed into law that, if fully implemented, by the year 2019 will cover an additional 32 million Americans with health insurance (Kaiser Family Foundation, 2012a). In effect, this would mean that well over 90% of Americans would be covered by health insurance—by any measure, a historically unprecedented policy accomplishment.

Ironically, despite the fact that the mixed public and private approach to near universal health insurance undertaken by the Obama administration mirrors that previously advocated by the moderate wing of the Republican Party and implemented by Republican presidential contender Mitt Romney while he was governor of Massachusetts—the Obama reform plan was quickly characterized by the Republican party as a "government takeover of health care." Although much of the vitriol in opposition to the Obama administration's health care reform package (the Patient Protection and Affordable Care Act, or P.L. 111-148) can be attributed to the bitter partisan politics that has dominated the American political discourse over the last decade, the law's requirement that households would require some form of basic health insurance (aka as the "individual mandate") also provoked a strong ideological backlash among Americans that believe the federal government was exceeding its Constitutional authority in requiring the purchase of health insurance. Despite the popularity of some specific provisions of the Patient Protection and Affordable Care Act (PPACA) (such as the elimination of the ability of health insurance industry to deny coverage for preexisting conditions, and the elimination of maximum insurance coverage caps), by the time the PPACA had completed its second full year of implementation (in January of 2012), public opinion was evenly divided between those that held favorable views on health care reform and those who held unfavorable views (Kaiser Family Foundation, 2012b).[40] In addition, the individual mandate provision and the Medicaid expansions of the PPACA became the target of litigation that made its way to the U.S. Supreme Court by March of 2012 (*National Federation of Independent Business v. Sebelius* and *Florida v. Department of Health and Human Services*). Finally, the PPACA faced the very real possibilities that the November 2012 elections would bring Republican party majorities in both the U.S. House of Representatives and the Senate that would enact that party's vow to repeal the PPACA.[41]

CONCLUDING COMMENTS: PROSPECTS FOR ACHIEVING HEALTH CARE REFORM

The last century of federal health care legislation was in large part characterized by a continuous struggle between incrementalism and fundamental structural reform, framed by a persistent belief by a strong majority of Americans that the assurance of health care access for all Americans should be the central goal of federal health care policy (Blendon & Benson, 2001; Roberts, 2010). During the past decade, the struggle between incrementalism and fundamental reform of health care has been framed by a third issue—the American public's very real worries about the size of government, the ever-increasing size of the federal budget deficit, and unsustainable public entitlement programs. While evidence from other wealthy democracies have shown it is possible to both restrain health care costs and achieve universal health care coverage through a variety of financing pathways (mixed public/private, completely public, and completely private), an informed national discourse on these alternatives has been consistently obscured by vitriolic partisan electoral politics—often aided and abetted by an avalanche of media dollars from an array of stakeholder groups invested in the status quo. In this sense, the passage and gradual implementation of the PPACA has been both a historical anomaly and somewhat of a political miracle. Even so, the prospects for the PPACA's version of health care reform survival to full implementation are at best uncertain—a crucial topic that will be explored in depth in the final chapter of the book dedicated to the principles and politics of health care reform.[42] No matter what the ultimate fate of the PPACA or any of its specific provisions, the next chapters of the book should convince the reader that fundamental health care reform is not only essential, but also inevitable.

NOTES

1. The term voluntary organization derives from the notion of a voluntary association or gathering of citizens for some shared purpose, generally civic, political, charitable, or religious in nature. Thus, the term voluntary hospital, which throughout this book is used interchangeably with the term private not-for-profit.
2. Rosenberg, C. (1987). *The Care of Strangers: The Rise of America's Hospital System.* New York: Basic Books.
3. This chapter provides what amounts to a synopsis of key observations and arguments of Starr's history, even then painted in very broad strokes. Interested readers are urged to read the original work, along with a set of retrospective critical essays published in the 29th volume (August–October, 2004) of *The Journal of Health Politics, Policy and Law.*
4. This passage in quoted from an essay of Daniel Drake (1785–1852) titled *The Selection and Preparatory Education of Pupils,* published in a book that was a collected set of Drake's essays in 1832. Drake was a prolific author of publications devoted to medicine and medical education, and a legendary figure in early American medicine. The source for Drake's essay is a reprint of the original version, published by medical historian GertBrieger in *Medical America in the Nineteenth Century* (1972: Johns Hopkins University Press).
5. Eclectics, like homeopaths, were a sect of physicians that had managed to develop to the point where eclectic medicine had its own medical schools. Eclectic medicine, which had its roots in botanical medicine, had no coherent theory of physiology and disease so much as it had a range of medical ideas on illness and therapeutics drawn from multiple traditions (Rothstein, 1972).
6. Also ironically, Nightingale herself wholly rejected germ theory's central premise that disease was attributable to microscopic contagions. To Nightingale, the sources of disease were seen and smelled in the filth and disorder that

characterized European and American hospital wards through most of the 19th century (Cope, 1958).

7. Nightingale was not at all a feminist in the contemporary use of the term. In fact, she believed that medicine and surgery were best left to men, whereas the hospital ward and the sickroom were clearly the dominion of women (Hobbs, 1997).

8. The enormous gains made in the status of nursing as a profession made over the past half-century have not been dependent upon the transformation of medicine, but have come from within through formidable nurse-driven advancements in nursing research, clinical practice, and education. However, it seems reasonable to conclude that as long as men dominate the ranks of the medical profession, either in numbers or in prestigious specializations, the interaction between gender privilege and occupational status will remain a burdening factor in the ascendance of the nursing profession.

9. In this brief history, the origins of the gender balance in the medical profession are not explored. Suffice it to say that as late as 1940 only 6% of the students in U.S. medical schools were women and that the AMA did not extend membership to women until 1915 (Cassedy, 1991). In part, this could be readily attributed to general subordinate status of women that was quite literally written into the U.S. Constitution until the triumph of the Women's Suffrage Movement in 1920. However, it can also be argued that exclusion of women from the medical profession served an instrumental purpose. That is, the large presence of women (as the subordinate gender) in the medical profession would have undermined the profession's struggles to achieve professional sovereignty.

10. Although individual acts of charity in the form of free medical care by physicians has always been an important source of health care for those unable to afford it, it has also been perennially arbitrary and inadequate to the need.

11. The term dispensary is derived from the initial function of the first dispensary as it was founded in London in 1696, the dispensing of medicines to the poor.

12. This was not so much of a formal alliance as it was a temporary convergence of interests.

13. Ultimately, as health insurance benefits assumed a larger share of the total compensation of workers, the labor movement began to assert more control over structure of Blue Cross plan benefits through collective bargaining. This offset the power of physicians until the labor movement itself began to decline in the 1970s, at which point health care inflation and consumerism emerged as another source of constraint on the power of physicians.

14. The Pharmaceutical Research and Manufacturers of America.

15. In creating the Bureau of Indian Affairs (BIA), Congress established the bureaucracy through which the federal government was supposed to have channeled its treaty obligations to Native Americans—including obligations pertaining to the health and welfare of tribal members. However, most of what the BIA did over its history was to the (often deliberate) detriment of Native Americans.

16. Julia Lathrop, a pioneer of empirical methodology in social policy, and Grace Abbott, who later wrote the *Child and the State* and became the longtime editor of *Social Service Review*.

17. The term "medically indigent" applies to persons who are unable to afford payment for essential health care.

18. Title V (Part I) of the Social Security Act of 1935 included provisions for the federal funding of material and child health programs that were administrated by states and subject to the approval of the federal Children's Bureau—very much like the Sheppard–Towner Act that the AMA had ultimately defeated a decade earlier.

19. The most compelling arguments concerning the ways in which programs associated with the incremental strategy undercut the evolvement of universal health care coverage involve the inflationary structure of the Medicare program and helping to sustain the political viability of the employer-based system of health care insurance coverage.

20. The "Bonus Army," as it was called, was comprised of roughly 20,000 unemployed World War I veterans and their dependents who marched on Washington in the spring of 1932. Their central demand involved early dispersal of war service bonuses that had been voted on by a (then) grateful Congress in 1924. The marchers were dispersed after General Douglas MacArthur, in defiance of orders from President Hoover, commanded his troops to burn their encampments. Hoover and the Republican party, and not MacArthur, paid the political price as public outrage over the incident helped fuel the election of Roosevelt and the congressional Democrats the following November (Zinn, 1999).

21. Throughout this chapter and others, multiple references are made to Paul Starr's observations and arguments concerning the history and organization of the U.S. health care system, as published in his landmark *The Social Transformation of American Medicine* (Basic Books, 1982). This is arguably the most authoritative and controversial history and critique of the U.S. health care system and the medical profession written.

22. Capital-based competition, as described elsewhere in this book, involves investments in medical technology and facilities that are aimed at gaining or preserving a hospital's market share of patient referrals. Frequently (and more often), these investments are made to attract referring physicians. Capital-based competition is distinct from price- or outcome-based competition, both of which have greater potential to reduce health care costs. Capital-based competition may or may not be tied to better health care outcomes depending upon a large array of contextual factors. However, it is inherently inflationary and in historical perspective has proved exceedingly detrimental to equitable access to essential health care.

23. While the costs of Medicare Part B are federally subsidized, the fact that enrollment in Part B is voluntary and involves premium cost sharing on the part of program participants seems to remove the stigma that is usually associated with other forms of government subsidy.

24. Although the community mental health approach was generally attractive to state politicians on humanitarian grounds and ultimately mandated by the judicial branch of government, the main incentives were always financial. By the accounts of its many critics, over time the community mental health movement devolved to an abrogation of public responsibility for the mentally ill and a principal factor in the growth of the homeless population.

25. A linear accelerator is a device that precisely focuses a stream of fast-moving subatomic particles. As applied to cancer therapy, it can be employed to destroy or at least retard the growth of some types of cancerous tumors.

26. The capital pass-through mechanism was not unique to Medicare, but also was embedded in the hospital pricing practices for the health insurance industry as a

whole during this period. During the 1970s this was a nonissue, because insurance companies were able to pass these costs onto the purchasers of health insurances by increasing the health insurance premium prices.

27. A "certificate of need" process involves a public review and approval process for the purchase of highly expensive health care technologies or health care facility construction projects in excess of a given amount. Prior to the 1974 National Health Planning and Resource Development Act, this process was carried out individually by a minority of states. Without the issuance of a "certificate of need" that sanctioned specific investments in new technologies or facility upgrades, hospitals would not be able to bill Medicare and Medicaid for their use.

28. The 1983 amendments to the Social Security Act that established the prospective payment system were preceded by the 1982 Tax Equity and Fiscal Responsibility Act (TEFRA), which implemented a hospital reimbursement system that was based on a cost per discharge that was weighted by each hospital's case mix (distribution of cases by severity and related costs). This gave hospitals several months to adapt their utilization review systems to identify ways to eliminate sources of unnecessary patient care expenditures and realign their array of hospital services toward those that were economically viable.

29. Combined with incredible bureaucratic excess.

30. There is an ongoing debate as to whether community-based long-term care systems yield net savings, but in passing these provisions Congress at least gave the benefit of the doubt to this argument.

31. Medicare + Choice has since been renamed Medicare Advantage.

32. See Chapter 3 in this book on health care finance for a more detailed description.

33. Bragdon, a dentist, had refused to fill the tooth cavity of a woman who had disclosed she was HIV positive unless the services were performed in a hospital at significant extra expenses to the patient. In a 5 to 4 split decision, the Supreme Court held that a person with HIV fell under the impairment provisions of the ADA and that the refusal to provide services due to risk to the health care provider must be based on convincing scientific evidence.

34. Under the provisions of the Medicare Modernization Act of 2003, low-income elderly who qualify for Medicaid assistance for prescription drug coverage are transferred to a federally approved prescription drug plan in 2006. As a result, most will be required to pay a co-pay fee of up to $5 on every prescription. For the poorest and sickest of elderly, this may mean the choice between food and pharmaceuticals.

35. The capacity of the voluntary (private not-for-profit) hospitals to absorb the costs of uncompensated care (bad debt and charity care) has always been dependent upon the ability of hospitals to "cost-shift," that is, recover their losses through higher charges to insured patients. By the early 1980s, the health insurance market was shifting toward more competitive provider contracts with hospitals that reduced the ability of hospitals to cost shift—thus reducing their capacity to provide uncompensated care.

36. The failure of Congress to counter these HHS rule changes is consistent with the Congressional record beginning with the Hyde Amendment of 1976, which in its various updates has restricted the federal part of Medicaid funding for abortions to pregnancies that result from rape or incest, or endanger the life of the mother (National Abortion Federation, 2006).

37. The DRA imposed more restricted limits on the transfer of assets in order to qualify for Medicaid nursing home care funding. The pre-DRA generous allowances for nursing home care-related asset transfers were of greatest benefit to the middle and upper class families.
38. The DRA also introduced changes to the Medicare program aimed at reducing costs by $6 billion over the 5-year period beginning with 2006. However, the changes proposed did not represent a significant retreat from program benefits.
39. The Clinton administration had developed their managed competition model of health care reform through a lengthy process that featured a sequestered panel of experts chaired by Hillary Clinton. By the time the plan for health care reform was unveiled, much of the political momentum for health care reform had been lost and the already fragile coalition of pro-reform advocates and stakeholders had begun to unravel. There were other factors, of course; in particular, a ferocious and protracted budget battle.
40. Findings from a nationally representative poll of 1201 adults over age 18 conducted by Kaiser Family Foundation researchers, conducted by landline telephone and cell phone, between February 29 and March 5, 2012. The poll finds 40% believing the PPACA should be repealed, another 41% in favor of either keeping the PPACA or expanding it, and 19% unsure/undecided. These findings are basically the same as those conducted in an identical poll 2 years previously, at the point the PPACA had been signed into law.
41. While it is unlikely that the Republican Party would have a large enough majority to override a veto of the PPACA repeal by President Obama, the election of a Republican president in November of 2012 would all but assure the demise of the PPACA.
42. As discussed in the Preface, the final chapter will consider both the principles of health care reform that would be suggested by alternative approaches to social justice, and the extent to which they are reflected in the specific provisions of the PPACA. In addition, the final chapter will more fully examine PPACA's prospects for either partial or complete implementation.

REFERENCES

Abraham, J. (1995). The production and reception of scientific papers in the academic–industrial complex: The clinical evaluation of a new medicine. *The British Journal of Sociology, 46*(2), 167–190.

AHA. (2010). *Fast facts on U.S. hospitals from AHA hospital statistics.* Retrieved March 17, 2011, from http://www.aha.org/aha/content/2010/pdf/101207fastfacts.pdf

Almgren, G. (1990). *Artificial nutrition and hydration practices and the American nursing home: Currents of social change and adaptation by an industry in transition.* Unpublished doctoral dissertation, University of Washington, Seattle.

Almgren, G., Kemp, S., & Eisinger, A. (2000).The legacy of Hull House and the Children's Bureau in the American mortality transition. *Social Service Review, 74*(1), 1–19.

Blendon, R. J., & Benson, J. M. (2001). Americans' views on health policy: A fifty-year historical perspective. *Health Affairs, 20*(2), 33–46.

Brieger, G. (Ed.) . (1972). *Medical America in the nineteenth century.* Baltimore: The Johns Hopkins Press.

The Brookings Institution. (2006). *Government's 50 greatest endeavors: Enhance the nation's health care infrastructure.* Washington, DC: The Brookings Institution Governance Studies Program.

Bryce, C. L., & Cline, K. E. (1998). The supply and use of selected medical technologies. *Health Affairs, 17*(1), 213–224.

Cassedy, J. (1991). *Medicine in America: A short history.* Baltimore: Johns Hopkins University Press.

Center for Public Policy Priorities. (2003). *Comments on proposed DHS rules regarding TANF and Medicaid.* Retrieved March 14, 2006, from http://www.cppp.org/research.php?aid=320

CMS. (2011). *Critical access hospital rural health fact sheet series.* Retrieved March 16, 2012, from https://www.cms.gov/MLNProducts/downloads/CritAccessHospfctsht.pdf

Congressional Budget Office. (2004). *A detailed description of CBO's cost estimate for the Medicare prescription drug benefit.* Washington, DC: Congress of the United States.

Congressional Budget Office. (2006). *Congressional Budget Office cost estimate: S. 1932 Deficit Reduction Act of 2005.* Washington, DC: United States Congress.

Cope, Z. (1958). *Florence Nightingale and the doctors.* London: Museum Press.

Davis, M., & Warner, A. (1918). *Dispensaries: Their management and development.* New York: Macmillan.

Garrison, L. P., Jr., & Wilensky, G. R. (1986). Cost containment and incentives for technology. *Health Affairs, 5*(2), 46–58.

Gostin, L., Feldblum, C., & Webber, D. (1999). Disability discrimination in America: HIV/AIDS and other health conditions. *Journal of the American Medical Association, 281,* 745–752.

Hobbs, C. (1997). *Florence Nightingale.* New York: Twayne.

HRSA HIV/AIDS Bureau. (2006). *Ryan White CARE Act: Purpose of the CARE Act.* Retrieved March 15, 2006, from http://hab.hrsa.gov/history/purpose.htm

Kaiser Family Foundation. (2011). *State health facts: Distribution of nursing care facilities by ownership type, 2009.* Retrieved March 13, 2011, from http://statehealthfacts.org

Kaiser Family Foundation. (2012a). *Focus on reform: Summary of Health Reform Law.* Retrieved March 17, 2012 from http://www.kff.org/healthreform/upload/8061.pdf

Kaiser Family Foundation. (2012b). *Health tracking poll: Exploring the Public's views on the Affordable Care Act (ACA).* Retrieved March 17, 2012, from http://healthreform.kff.org/public-opinion.aspx

Kane, R., Kane, R., & Ladd, R. (1998). *The heart of long term care.* New York: Oxford University Press.

Kemp, S., Almgren, G., Gilchrist, L., & Eisinger, A. (2001). Serving "the Whole Child": Prevention practice and the U.S. Children's Bureau. *Smith College Studies in Social Work, 71*(3), 475–477, 499.

Lindenmeyer, K. (1997). *A right to childhood: The U.S. Children's Bureau and child welfare, 1912–1946.* Urbana: University of Illinois Press.

Litman, T. (1991). Appendix: Chronology and capsule highlights of the major historical and political milestones in the evolutionary involvement of government in health care in the United States. In T. Litman, & L. Robins (Eds.), *Health politics and policy* (2nd ed.). Albany, NY: Delmar.

Meckel, R. (1990). *Save the babies: American public health reform and the prevention of infant mortality, 1850–1929.* Baltimore: Johns Hopkins University Press.

Morrisey, M. A., Sloan, F. A., & Valvona, J. (1988). Shifting Medicare patients out of the hospital. *Health Affairs, 7*(5), 52–64.

National Abortion Federation. (2006). *Public funding for abortion: Medicaid and the Hyde Amendment.* Retrieved March 14, 2006, from http://www.prochoice.org/about abortion/facts/public funding.html

Northwest Portland Area Indian Health Board. (2006). *Legislative history of the Indian Health Care Improvement Act.* Retrieved February 28, 2006, from http://www.npaihb.org

Perlstadt, H. (1995). The development of the Hill-Burton legislation: Interests, issues and compromises. *Journal of Health and Social Policy, 6*(3), 77–96.

Preston, S., & Haines, M. (1991). *Fatal years: Child mortality in the late nineteenth century America.* Princeton, NJ: Princeton University Press.

Roberts, R. (2010). *The politics of health reform.* CBS Opinion: Summary of CBS/ New York Times Poll, June 14, 2010. Retrieved March 19, 2012. from http://www.cbsnews.com/2100-500160_162-2528357.html

Rosenberg, C. (1987). *The care of strangers: The rise of America's hospital system.* New York: Basic Books.

Rothstein, W. (1972). *American physicians in the nineteenth century: From sects to science.* Baltimore: Johns Hopkins University Press.

Sheingold, S. H. (1989). The first three years of PPS: Impact on Medicare costs. *Health Affairs, 8*(3), 191–204.

Shi, L., & Singh, D. (2001). *Delivering health care in America* (2nd ed.). Gaithersburg, MD: Aspen.

Starr, P. (1982). *The social transformation of American medicine.* New York: Basic Books.

Steinberg, M. (2005). *Trouble brewing? New Medicare drug law puts low-income people at risk.* Washington, DC: Families USA.

Twiss, J. (1960). Medical practice in colonial America. *Bulletin of the New York Academy of Medicine, 36,* 538–551.

U.S. Census Bureau. (1972). *Statistical abstract of the United States, 1972.* Washington, DC: Author.

U.S. Census Bureau. (2011). *Income, poverty, and health insurance coverage in the United States: 2010.* Retrieved March 16, 2012, from http://www.census.gov/prod/2011pubs/p60-239.pdf

Vladeck, B. (1980). *Unloving care: The nursing home tragedy.* New York: Basic Books.

Wohl, S. (1984). *The medical industrial complex.* New York: Harmony Books.

Zinn, H. (1999). *A people's history of the United States* (Twentieth Anniversary ed.). New York: HarperCollins.

CHAPTER THREE

THE CONTEMPORARY ORGANIZATION OF HEALTH CARE: HEALTH CARE FINANCE

There is no paradox that equals that found in the system of health care finance in the United States. According to estimates released in 2010, the United States spends about $2.6 trillion on health care, annually, or an average of about $8,402 per year for every person residing in the United States (Martin, Lassman, Washington, & Catlin, 2012). In relative expenditures per capita, the United States spends over 2 times the average of per capita expenses for Canada, Germany, Sweden, and France (OECD, 2012). Although the United States spends more dollars per capita than any other OECD (Organisation for Economic Co-operation and Development) member nation, the United States ranks among the lowest among OECD countries in the proportion of its citizens having some form of public or private insurance for routine health care. In fact, among OECD members, only Mexico and Chile have a smaller proportion of their population covered by either public or private health insurance (OECD, 2012).[1] The purpose of this chapter is to provide the reader with a general understanding of the dynamics of this paradox, its origins, and the ways in which it is sustained.

To accomplish this, the chapter will review the system of health care finance in the United States, both in terms of its current organization and in the evolvement of its unique structure. The topics will include the magnitude and distribution of health care expenditures in the United States, the relative contributions of government and private sector forms of insurance, the fundamentals of risk and insurance, alternative models of health insurance finance and provider structures, and a detailed description of Medicare, Medicaid, and more recent policy initiatives in the public financing of health care (e.g., SCHIP, the Medicare Prescription Drug Improvement and Modernization Act, and the Patient Protection and Affordable Care Act of 2010). The central aim is to provide the foundation necessary for an informed assessment of the current approach to health care system reform undertaken by the Patient Protection and Affordable Care Act, and other health care reform alternatives—the issues that are the principal focus of the book's final chapter. The logical place to begin is a basic review of how the United States spends its health care dollars.

HEALTH CARE EXPENDITURES

The United States currently spends about 18% of its GDP (gross domestic product) on health care. Further, relative to the other OECD countries, the United States spends about two times as much of its GDP on health care (OECD, 2012). The brunt of the $2.6 trillion in U.S. health care expenditures (80% of all health care dollars) are allocated (in this order) to hospital care, physician services, retail prescription drugs, nursing home care, and administrative costs. It should be noted that the $176.1 billion spent on administrative costs that are shown on the first panel of Table 3.1 are an underestimate, in that they do not capture the administrative component of prices charged for hospital care, physician services, and other health care services. Estimates that include the administrative component of health care services suggest that the administrative component of U.S. health care expenditures may be as high as 31% (Woolhandler, Campbell, & Himmelstein, 2003).

To gain an understanding of the principle payment sources of the nation's $2.6 trillion in health care expenditures, the second panel of Table 3.1 provides a breakdown of the health care expenditures by payment source. First, it should be noticed that Americans pay 47% of their health care costs either in the form of out-of-pocket expenditures (12.3%) or in the form of private health insurance (34.7%). It should be recognized that private health insurance premiums are either paid directly by workers, or by employers in the form of benefits that are substituted for higher wages. The primary sources of the public share of health care expenditures are through two programs, Medicare (the federal health insurance program for persons aged 65 years and older) and Medicaid, a state and federally funded means-tested program targeted at the poor and medically indigent.[2] While Medicare and Medicaid are the largest public funding programs of health care (together paying 37.9% of health care costs), there are several smaller public health care programs that when added together comprise another 3.9% of the nation's health care costs—these include State Children's Health Insurance Program (SCHIP) and also the Veterans Administration

Table 3.1 *Distribution of Health Expenditures by Type and Payment Sources in 2010*

	$Billion	Percent of Total
Panel 1 Distribution of Health Care Expenditures		
Hospital care	814.0	31.4
Physician's services	515.5	19.9
Dental care	104.8	4.0
Nursing home care/Continuing care commun.	143.1	5.5
Home health care	70.2	2.7
Retail prescription drugs	259.1	10.0
Government public health activites	82.5	3.2
All other health services	279.4	10.8
Administrative costs[a]	176.1	6.8
Total national health consumption expenditures	2444.7	94.3
Investment	149.0	5.7
Total national health expenditures	2593.6	100.0
Panel 2 Health Care Consumption Expenditures by Source		
Private share		**47.0**
Private health insurance	848.7	34.7
Out of pocket	299.7	12.3
Public share		**41.8**
Medicare	524.6	21.5
Medicaid	401.4	16.4
SCHIP, Dept. of Defense, Veterans Administration	96.1	3.9
Other public and private[b]	274.1	**11.2**
Total health consumption expenditures	2444.6	100.0

[a]Includes government administrative expenditures ($30.1 billion) and administrative costs for private health insurance ($146 billion), which are calculated as the difference between premium expenditures and health care benefit expenditures.
[b]Includes private sector revenues, worksite health programs, Indian Health Service, workers compensation, and other state and Federal programs.
Data Source: Martin A, Lassman D, Washington B, and Catlin A. (2012). Growth in US Health Expenditures Remained Slow in 2010; Health Share of Gross Domestic Product Was Unchanged From 2009. *Health Affairs*, 31(1):208–219; Exhibit 1 National Health Care Expenditures, Aggregate and Per Capita Amounts and Share of Gross Domestic Products, Selected Calendar Years, 1980–2010 and Exhibit 3 National Health Expenditures (NHE), Amounts and Average Annual Growth from Previous Years Shown, By Source of Funds, Selected Calendar Years 1980–2010.

health care system. When all private and publically funded health care sources are considered, there is a nearly even split between those health expenditures that come from private sources (such as commercial health insurance and out-of-pocket payments) and those that come from publicly funded entitlements and programs.[3]

Comparing the American Approach to Health Care Financing to Other Industrialized Democracies

Health Care Expenditures

Throughout this book, the 34 nations that (along with the United States) comprise the Organisation for Economic Co-operation Development (OECD) are used in making comparisons between the United States and other countries. This is because the OECD member states, like the United States, are constitutional democracies with a market economy. In addition, the member states of the OECD, also like the United States, have achieved an industrialized state of development. While the United States has a per capita income that exceeds most OECD member states and it spends more of its national income on health care, it lags many OECD members in a variety of critical population health indicators. In fact, no matter what measure of population health is employed, the U.S. health care system achieves less in health per dollar of health care expenditure than any of it OECD counterparts. While the reasons for this discrepancy between U.S. health care investment and U.S. health care achievement originate a variety of burdens on population health that lie outside of the health care system,[4] the United States is also unique among other OECD member states in the extent to which it relies on the marketplace for health care financing and delivery.[5]

To highlight this point, Figure 3.1 compares the private and public expenditures per capita on health care in the United States relative to a sample of OECD countries and also the OECD average. First, it can be seen that relative to the sample of countries shown as well as the OECD average, the United States spends in excess of 2 times as much per capita on health care. That is, for the year for which the most recent comparative data was available (2008) this amounted to $7719 per year per person relative to an OECD average of $3233. Perhaps surprising to many readers, the public expenditures per capita in the United States exceed the OECD per capita average of *total* health care expenditures. Stated another way, the United States spends roughly two dollars on health care per capita for every one dollar that the typical modern democracy spends on health care, one dollar through public expenditures that are supported by taxes, and then a second

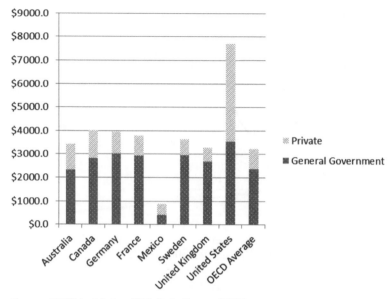

Source: *OECD health data 2011*. Paris, France: OECD.

Figure 3.1 *Public, private and total health care expenditures in U.S. dollars: United States relative to selected OECD countries and OECD average, 2008* **(OECD, 2011).**

dollar from private dollars (either in the form of out-of-pocket expenses or in private health insurance benefits) that one way or another represent a deduction from household income.[6]

Finally, it can be seen that, in contrast to the United States, almost all other OECD countries shown (as well as the OECD average), the United States finances its health care system through a roughly even balance of public and private funds. In all but a few OECD countries, health care is funded primarily through public programs (the OECD public funding average is about 73% of all health care expenditures).

Also in contrast to other member states of the OECD, the United States has over the past half-century sustained a much higher rate of annual health care inflation. As shown in Figure 3.2, while the United States *has always* spent more of its GDP[7] on health care than the other modern democracies comprising the OECD, the relative *rate* of growth in health care expenditures began to exceed that of other OECD member states in the 1970s. In general, over most of the 50-year period shown in Figure 3.2, the growth of health care expenditures has exceeded the growth in the nation's general economy by about 2% per year. While this does not seem like much, over time it has led the

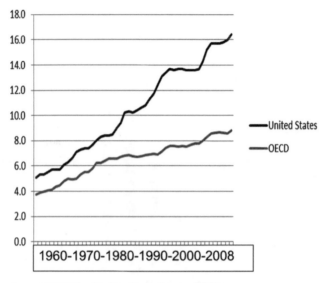

Source: *OECD health data*. Paris, France: OECD.

Figure 3.2 *Growth in health care expenditures as a proportion of the GDP, the United States relative to the OECD average, 1960–2008.*

United States into a situation where health care expenditures are consuming almost nearly one-fifth of the nation's overall domestic production. This level of health care inflation has a variety of undesirable impacts that have reverberated throughout the national economy, as well as in the daily lives of everyday Americans. With respect to the national economy, it should be kept in mind that dollars that are allocated to health care in excess of what is required to achieve desirable population health outcomes are dollars that might otherwise be allocated to education, investments in national infrastructure (e.g., roads and bridges), and in programs for the alleviation of unemployment and poverty. At the household level, a high level of health care inflation has made health insurance and out-of-pocket health care expenditures increasingly unaffordable. Finally, sustained health care inflation has functioned as a significant barrier to the achievement of universal health insurance coverage.

Figure 3.2 shows that there were only two periods over the past 50 years when the growth of health care expenditures flattened to near zero. The first was the early 1980s, when both an economic recession and a fundamental restructuring of the Medicare program combined to briefly halt health care inflation,[8] and the second was in the 1990s when the managed care programs where aggressively implemented in the commercial health insurance industry. More recent estimates of U.S. health care expenditures (not shown in Figure 3.2) indicate we have encountered a third pause on the growth of health care expenditures, which has been attributed to the sustained recession that emerged in 2008 (Martin et al., 2012).

Comparing the Relative Yield of Health Care Expenditures: Essential Resources and Essential Health Outcomes

Perhaps simplistically, we might expect that since the United States spends about twice as much per capita on health care as countries such as France, Germany, Australia, Canada, and the United Kingdom, we should expect to find evidence of superior achievements in health care infrastructure and also health care outcomes. This proves not to be the case. Taking achievements in health care infrastructure as our first comparative criterion, we can examine whether the 2:1 U.S. health care expenditures have provided Americans with more hospitals and doctors. Although there are a range of health care infrastructure investments that might be considered other than doctors and hospitals, the building of hospitals and the training of physicians are among the most expensive and essential. As shown in Figure 3.3, the roughly 2:1 ratio of U.S. health care expenditures has not produced a health care system with more doctors and hospitals per capita—but actually fewer.[9]

Although there are many health outcome measures that might be employed to compare the performance of the U.S. health care system relative

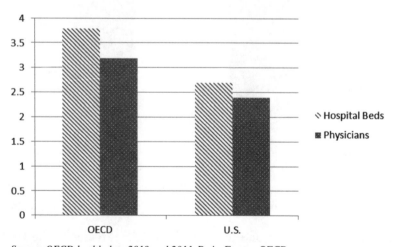

Source: OECD health data 2010 and 2011. Paris, France: OECD.

Figure 3.3 *Acute hospital beds and physicians per thousand persons, The U.S. vs. OECD Average (2007–2009).*

to the OECD average, a commonly favored measure for these kinds of comparisons is *potential years of life lost* per 100,000 persons, because it focuses on the prevalence of premature mortality in a national population—that is, the deaths that in large part can be prevented by timely access to appropriate health care and critical investments in public health programs.

As Figure 3.4 shows, according to the most recent data available, the United States lags significantly on this measure of premature mortality relative to the general average of OECD countries, despite the fact that the United States is among the most affluent in per capita income and spends 2:1 on per capita health care. Presumably, the United States should do at least as well as the average, given its national wealth and level of investment in health care—but it does not. The question as to why the U.S. health care system so dramatically "underperforms" relative to its affluence and investments in health care is among the most crucial policy issues of our day— and the answers extend to factors that go well beyond the organization and financing of our health care system. In fact, this question is the primary

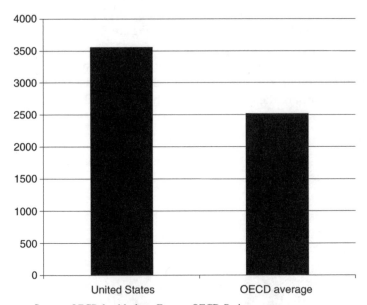

Source: OECD health data. France: OECD Paris.

Figure 3.4 *Potential years of life lost, United States vs. OECD average, 2007.*
Note: **Data are calculated on the most recent comparisons to the United States available, which includes 26 of 34 OECD member states. Potential years of life lost are defined as the number of years of life lost per 100,000 persons, based on the deaths that occur before age 70.**

focus of two later chapters in this book, which interrogate the prevalence and determinants of disparities in health care and in health. For the purposes of this chapter, we must satisfy ourselves with the conclusion that beyond a certain level of investment in essential health care resources, dollars invested in health care and advancements in health care technology by themselves do not translate improvements in national health.

So, if roughly 50% of the per capita spending on health care in the United States goes for naught, why or for what purpose are these dollars spent?

In simple terms, there are three general answers to this question: either Americans utilize more health care than citizens of other modern democracies, or Americans spend more for the health care that they use, or they do some combination of both. In order to determine which of these possibilities is true, a group of health care policy researchers from Johns Hopkins University School of Public Health and the Woodrow Wilson School of Public Policy at Princeton used OECD data to compare health care expenditures and utilization of health care services between the U.S. residents and those of other OECD countries (Anderson, Reinhardt, Hussey, & Petrosyan, 2003). The logic of the researchers' analysis was straightforward: essentially, if the level of health care utilization relative to other OECD countries matched its higher levels of expenditures, then it would be safe to conclude that the explanation of expenditure difference between the United States and the lower OECD average lies on the demand side of the health care economy equation—in essence, Americans spend more on health care because they use more health care. If, on the other hand, the level of health care utilization among Americans is not higher than the OECD average, then the excess in U.S. expenditures is really embedded in the supply side of the equation, that is, the costs of the services delivered. Their analysis of health care service utilization was focused on three broad indicators of health care utilization: the median number visits to physicians per person per year, the median number of hospital admissions, and the median length of hospital stays (in days) per hospital admission. Although a number of other health care utilization indicators might have been used, physician visits and hospital care are the two primary sources of per capital health care expenditures, with pharmaceutical expenditures still a distant third.

The results of the investigators' analysis are both surprising and illuminating. As it happened, relative to the OECD median, Americans were shown to have almost exactly the same number of physician visits per capita per year. Even more surprisingly, population rates of hospital admission and average lengths of hospital stays were found to be *lower* than the OECD median. In terms of these key measures of health care utilization, the authors of this landmark study find that Americans appear to be paying more for less; or stated in another way, differences in expenditures between the United States and other OECD member states really are about prices (G. F. Anderson et al., 2003). Although it can be argued that differences in price can and often do reflect differences in quality, any differences in the relative quality of health care between the United States and other OECD countries are not reflected in an array of population health indicators (OECD, 2012). The authors of this study speculate that a significant source of the price differential in health care between the United States and rest of the OECD community is embedded in the "highly fragmented and complex U.S. payment system" (Anderson et al., 2003, p. 98), something that is obvious to almost anyone seeking health care in the United States. This leads us to the primary task of this chapter—a general review of the system of health care finance in the United States.

AN OVERVIEW OF HEALTH CARE SYSTEM FINANCE— EMPLOYMENT-BASED HEALTH INSURANCE

Payment for health care in the United States comes from five general sources: out-of-pocket expenditures, employment-based private health insurance, Medicare, Medicaid, and public finance programs other than Medicare and Medicaid—most notably the Veterans Administration. As Table 3.1 makes obvious, the single dominant source of payment for health care is the private health insurance market. In fact, recent estimates show that the private insurance market covers 34.7% of all domestic health care expenditures, whereas the *combined share* of health care expenditures covered by the two largest public health care finance programs (Medicare and Medicaid) *account for 37.9% of health care consumption expenditures.*

Understanding how the private health care insurance market works is essential to understanding the system of health care finance in the United States, not only because of the private health care insurance market's dominance as a payment source for health care, but also because the key principles that govern the private insurance market also extend to various aspects of public health care finance. Specifically, these principles pertain to the dynamics of "risk and insurance"—in the most basic sense, not unlike those governing the automobile, homeowner, and life insurance markets. Although there are critical differences between the incentives governing the health insurance market and the markets for other forms of insurance that have huge health care policy implications, the underlying principles of insurance apply to all.

Basic Principles of Risk and Insurance

Insurance markets exist because individuals are "averse" to large expenditures for events that *might* occur over some given period, but in the individual case have a low probability of occurrence—again over this given period. Thus, many of us carry renter's or homeowner's insurance against the possibility of a break-in and burglary, because we are strongly averse (e.g., feel we cannot afford) the loss of material things that are costly for us to replace. If the price of the break-in and burglary insurance seems more affordable to us than cost of the loss should a break-in occur, we are inclined to purchase insurance. In fact, under these circumstances purchasing break-in insurance is a prudent and rational thing to do. This kind of scenario works for both the consumer and the insurance company because:

1. The risk of the insured event (a break-in and burglary) is low over the period of coverage (in the case of homeowner's or renter's insurance, generally either 6 months or 1 year).
2. The consumer views the actual cost of the event as prohibitive and therefore is strongly averse to assuming the risk of loss (i.e., self-insuring).
3. The "fair actuarial" insurance premium (or the main part of the insurance price) that is determined from a calculation of the risk of the event occurring and the cost of the loss, should it occur, is low—in fact, low enough not to create a disincentive against the purchase of insurance.

It should be noted that while the risk of a break-in and burglary might be very high over the entire period one owns or rents a home, over each period of insurance coverage the risk is quite low. Thus, insurance products of this sort are purchased and sold over specified periods.

Embedded in this example are several key principles of insurance markets. The first concerns the actual price of the insurance, or as identified in point 3, the "fair actuarial premium" or FAP. In simple algebraic terms, the $FAP = P_iC_i$, where P_i is the estimated probability of event i occurring and C_i is the estimated cost of event i should it occur—again, as calculated over a specified period of insurance coverage.

Let us say the FAP for a break-in and burglary in a given low-crime middle-class neighborhood is about $4 per month or, more precisely, $47.70 over the 1-year period of coverage—not an unreasonable estimate in a low-crime middle-class neighborhood. In our hypothetical neighborhood, while the average cost of a break-in and burglary is $4500, the probability of a break-in and burglary estimated from local crime rates and prior insurance claims is .0106 (thus FAP = .0106*4500, or $47.70). Note that the low FAP reflects both the low probability of a break-in and burglary occurring and the modest average level of loss when one occurs—few people in our hypothetical neighborhood keep large stashes of money or own expensive jewelry.

A second principle embedded in this example concerns the risk of *moral hazard*. In the parlance of insurance theory, a problem of "moral hazard" arises when the state of being insured for a given event leads the insured to being less averse to the event occurring—thus altering their risk-related behavior. In the context of this example, a "moral hazard" problem would arise if, as a result of being insured against burglary, the homeowner or renter worried less about leaving the front door locked because the insurance company covers the cost of stolen property. In this simple example, the moral hazard is minimal because for a variety of reasons besides theft, people generally do not like the idea of uninvited strangers walking into their homes and will still lock their doors. That is, people tend to remain equally "risk averse" to unauthorized home entry despite the fact that they are insured against theft. People also tend to be risk averse to car accidents, fires, and events involving personal injury or death despite being insured for these things—but what about health care? For reasons that will shortly be explained in more detail, the moral hazard problem in health care insurance is far more complex than for most other forms of insurance. Suffice it to say at this point that, under a variety of circumstances, individuals are not necessarily averse to an event that leads to an episode of health care and, further, that many kinds of health behavior are influenced by having health care coverage.

A third principle of insurance that can be drawn from the example of household insurance concerns the problem of *adverse selection*. In very basic terms, when an insurance company markets a specific insurance product (in this example, household insurance in the event of break-in and burglary), they assume that each person sold the insurance product has a level of insured risk and cost that is consistent with that used to calculate the fair actuarial premium or FAP. Of course, insurance companies do not have perfect information on each purchaser, but the FAP is based on the average risk and cost as pooled across large number of insurance purchasers that share common predictive characteristics (e.g., being of a certain age, living in a low-crime location, and having no prior criminal history involving insurance fraud or property theft). Adverse selection occurs when individual purchasers actually have a level of insurance risk that is significantly in excess of the risk and cost assumed in the FAP calculation. Normally, individual instances of adverse selection are offset by comparable instances of favorable selection due to the mathematics of random chance. However, if there is some systematic and unfavorable selection bias in either the nature of the insurance product or the way that it is advertised, the insurance company is headed for significant financial loss. In the example of householders' insurance, the insurance company may try to avoid adverse selection by avoiding the marketing of their lower cost insurance product in neighborhoods with rising rates of property crime. In the higher crime neighborhoods, the insurance company may attempt to market an insurance product with a higher FAP and a higher deductible that better reflects the local level of burglary risk—in effect, creating a separate *insurance pool* for the purchasers living in the higher crime neighborhood. Specifically, an *insurance pool* refers to a set of insured individuals sharing the same estimated level of risk and cost as that used to calculate their common FAP price, with the FAP applied to offset the costs of any instances of an insured event occurring to any member of the insurance pool.

In sum, insurance companies are viable financial entities to the extent that they have capacity to: (1) accurately assess the risks and the costs of an array of events people are averse to having occur, (2) define and market insurance products that will attract people into appropriately priced insurance pools, and (3) accurately assess and pay the costs of claims for which they are legally liable. The actual price of an insurance premium is in excess of the FAP, because the FAP does not incorporate the costs of administrative overhead and profit. However, most forms of insurance function in highly competitive markets and the non-FAP portion of the insurance premium is typically a small fraction of the total premium price.

Risk and Insurance in the Context of Health Care Insurance

In a variety of ways, health care insurance violates a number of assumptions that are viable for other forms of insurance. As noted previously, unlike other forms of insurance, individuals who possess health care insurance are not always averse to the insured event—an episode of health care. While few people genuinely enjoy being ill (there are exceptions to everything, of course), there are often aspects of receiving health care that if not enjoyable, are at least reassuring. Any parent of a sick child, even when the illness appears routine and probably self-resolving, can attest to the anxiety experienced and the desire to have a doctor present to dispel very normal, albeit unrealistic, fears. If mom or dad is more disposed toward a visit to the ER for what is likely a nonthreatening childhood illness *because the visit is substantially covered by their health care insurance*, this constitutes an instance of moral hazard. There are also aspects of health care that are either pleasurable or self-reinforcing that have no basis for the diagnosis given for an episode of care, such as visiting a clinic to dispel loneliness and isolation. Again, the moral hazard issue arises where, due to the fact of health care insurance coverage, the patient is at least less averse to receiving care. Although the problem of moral hazard is conceptualized as an issue pertaining to the motivation and behavior of the insured patient rather than the health care provider, health care providers are also significantly influenced in their treatment decisions and interventions by the extent of health insurance coverage (Fuchs, 2004).[10] In fact, the fundamental dilemma of health care insurance is that both the insured and the provider often have very strong incentives to promote the use of health care, while at the same time both are protected from the true costs (Starr, 1992).

The problem of adverse selection is also a significant dilemma in health care, the dynamic here being that health insurance products that are designed to attract one type of consumer at a given level of risk often attract higher risk consumers. This is a particular problem in health care policies that are marketed to individuals rather than groups, because for a variety of reasons persons who are not eligible for coverage under group insurance plans have higher levels of illness, injury, and disability and on average have higher rates of health care utilization (Harrington & Miller, 2002). It is also true that when individuals are paying the costs of their own health care insurance premiums, as is typically the case with individual plans, they are more likely to drop the insurance when healthy and seek insurance health care coverage when ill or injured. This, of course, becomes the definition of adverse selection. Less healthy workers are more likely to work in low-end jobs as a function of their poor health, jobs that do not offer affordable health insurance—thus leaving them to the vicissitudes of the individual insurance plan market. In many insurance markets, even healthy individuals find the costs of health insurance to be prohibitive because of the impact of problems with adverse selection. Finally, for reasons that are explained in more detail in the discussion that follows, small employers employ a disproportionate share of the risk burden that is a function of the linkage between social class and health. Things were not always so grim for individuals seeking health care insurance. Until the 1970s, the U.S. insurance market was dominated by health insurance plans that utilized *community rating* systems of premium pricing. Under the community rating scheme of health insurance pricing, "risk pool" for purposes of insurance pricing was defined as the community of residence—for historical reasons, typically the county of residence. For most communities, this meant the calculations of health care risks and costs were based upon a large pool of heterogeneous individuals that differed by education, occupation, and, in effect, overall state of health. However, as health inflation escalated over the 1970s, employers began to balk at the rising costs of community-rated health care plans and a market for *employer-based rating* systems of health insurance gradually became dominant. As a parallel trend, many of the largest employers began to *self-insure,* in essence placing the health care benefit portion of labor costs in a fund earmarked to pay the cost of employee health insurance claims—with the role of health insurance company limited to claims processing and reinsurance.[11] In essence, employer-based rating systems worked well for those employers with more skilled, more educated, and, ergo, generally healthier workers because such employers were able to shed the higher costs of the less skilled, less educated, and less healthy workers (and their dependents) that they had previously subsidized through the community-rated health care plan. Because the labor market has become increasingly segmented by social class since the 1970s (Scott, Berger, & Black, 1989), lower-skilled and less-educated workers are ever less likely to work for the kinds of employers that offer health care benefits and are ever less likely to be able to afford the costs of their relatively higher health care risks. In simple terms, prior to 1970, health insurance access and pricing was, to a significant degree, a buffering mechanism that mitigated the effects of social class on health through the nearly universal mechanism of community rating-based health insurance. In the decades since the 1970s, the private health insurance market has devolved to an employer-based rating system that serves to *enlarge* the linkages between social class and health.[12]

Forms of Risk and Payment of Claims

Hopefully, it has been clear to this point that health care insurance does not insure against illness, but rather it assumes some specified level of risk for the costs of health care services. There are multiple ways to do this, but the dominant forms of health care insurance risk assumption are *indemnity* based, *benefit* based, and *capitation* based. In the case of indemnity insurance, the health care insurance product assumes the cost of care for a given claim up to a set amount that is explicitly stated in the insurance contract—no matter what the provider's fee or the ultimate cost. In contrast, benefit-based plans pay for a specified range of health care services or health care products without stipulating the dollar amount of the costs covered—thus leaving the insured largely out of any pricing negotiations between the provider and the insurance company. The third form of insurance risk assumption, capitation, is best conceptualized as insuring not the specific costs for episodes of care, but rather agreeing to provide the totality of health care that the insurance carrier deems is prudent and/or necessary to sustain health and treat illness over the agreed-upon period of coverage. The latter form of health care risk assumption is the foundation of health maintenance organiz-ations. In truth, these forms of insurance risk assumption no longer tend to exist as pure types; most health care insurance carriers combine different fea-tures of each in the complex array of insurance products that serve the prefer-ences of different purchasers. However, it is also true that of these general forms of risk assumption (the once popular indemnity-based plans are the exception) largely as a function of rising health care costs, managed care, and preferred provider networks.

Payments made to providers of health care take any one of five general forms: *fee-for-service, per diem payment, prospective payment, cost plus reimburse-ment,* and *capitation* payment. All five forms of payment have played promi-nent roles in the structure of health care finance at different points in the history of the U.S. health care system. It is also the case that different forms of insurance payment arrangements offer very different incentives for health care providers and insurers, with related effects on the accessibility, quantity, and quality of health care delivered. Throughout most of the history of the health insurance industry, fee-for-service forms of payment have been both dominant and the preferred form of payment—consistent with the dominant ideal of medical free enterprise in American medicine (Starr, 1982). In essence, the provider either sets or negotiates a fee for a given diagnostic or treatment procedure, and the provider's income is deter-mined by the profit margin, service mix, and the overall volume of services provided. When claims are paid on a per diem basis, the health care provider is reimbursed at a daily rate for care that is a fixed amount for all health care services and products/procedures provided over the course of each day the patient is under the care of the provider. The prospective payment method of claims payment involves a set amount paid to the provider for a given episode of care that is typically defined in terms of a diagnosis or a combi-nation of diagnosis and procedure. Finally, cost plus reimbursement guaran-tees the provider a small margin for profit or return on equity after the provider has justified the costs of providing care to the insurance carrier.

Obviously, each form of claims payment offers a different set of risks and incentives for the health care provider that ultimately affects the nature of the care provided. In fact, there is a large health care policy literature on the effects of alternative systems mechanisms of insurance payment on clinical decision making by physicians, clinics, and hospitals. Figure 3.5 provides a simple illustration of the provider incentives to encourage more or fewer episodes of care (e.g., hospital admissions or physician visits) and higher or lower levels of care intensity under different regimes of insurance payment. The term "care intensity" is deliberately chosen to represent the quantity of care provided during a given episode of care without inferring anything about

	Episodes of Care	
	More	**Fewer**
High Care Intensity	Fee-for-Service Cost Plus Reimbursement	-------------------------
Low Care Intensity	Per Diem Prospective Payment	Capitation

Figure 3.5 *Provider incentives under alternative payment mechanisms.*

quality—the point being that more procedures, tests, and medications are not in and of themselves suggestive of higher quality (Anderson & Poullier, 1999). It should also be noted that the incentives shown in Figure 3.5 are assumed to operate where the knowledge pertaining to what constitutes "best practices" is in dispute or ambiguous, as is often the case in clinical decision making.[13]

As Figure 3.5 shows, both fee-for-service and cost plus mechanisms of insurance payment are the most inflationary, in the sense that providers have an economic incentive to both promote episodes of care and provide a more intensive level of care within each episode. The textbook example of this was the hospital reimbursement mechanism during the first decades of Medicare (between 1965 and 1982), when hospitals were reimbursed on a cost plus basis for every procedure, item of supply, and hospital day utilized by each episode of care. Equally, under a fee-for-service regime of insurance payment, it is in the economic interest of the care provider to provide as much care as can be defended as "medically necessary." It is easy to see why these two forms of reimbursement functioned as the engines of the health care inflation growth that occurred as public and private health care insurance coverage dramatically expanded during the 1960s and 1970s. Per diem reimbursement and prospective payment regimes have similar "mixed" incentives in many respects, because providers have strong incentives to promote episodes of care, but then to reduce as much as possible the utilization of test, procedures, and supplies that contribute to the costs of care. This is because the dollars reimbursed for care are fixed on the basis of either a given amount paid for each day of care or a given amount based on the diagnostic/procedure code assigned to the episode of care. Both forms of reimbursement are extensively used by insurance carriers to control health care claims expenditures. The prospective payment approach has been a major form of inpatient hospital reimbursement mechanism since the early 1980s—a payment regime that yielded dramatic reductions in the growth of hospital care expenditures. Notably, the capitation-based system of insurance reimbursement offers providers the fewest incentives to provide care; in fact, in contrast to the other forms of insurance payment, the capitation system creates a strong *disincentive* to provide care—typically in the absence of any clear long- or short-term benefits to health. This is because under the capitation system the provider is paid a fixed amount per person in the insurance plan pool, whether or not health care is provided during the period of coverage. In the parlance of Health Maintenance Organization, "lives" or person-years of health care expenditures are covered rather than specific episodes of health care.

How Private Health Insurance Operates

The conventional private health care market (as previously explained in Chapter 2—"The Historical Evolvement of the U.S. Health Care System") emerged as a partnership between local (typically county level) hospitals, physicians, employers, and labor unions. In all respects it has been an employment-based system, with either the labor union or the employer acting as a sponsor of group health insurance plans. During roughly the first four decades of private insurance, employers would typically contract with the county-level Blue Cross and Blue Shield insurance plans, which as mentioned earlier functioned on the basis of community rating systems. This made contracting very straightforward, because health care benefits were a much smaller proportion of overall labor costs and health insurance premium prices were consistent across employers for whatever array of benefits were either offered by the employer or negotiated through collective bargaining. During this earlier period, health insurance premium prices were subject to a multiyear *insurance cycle* that permitted the insurance health care plan to both keep prices low and avoid irrecoverable losses. During the first period of the cycle, premium prices for a health insurance plan were based upon an actuarial estimate of the anticipated expenditures in claims. Because it takes time to properly process claims data and assess the claims expenditures for a given year of coverage, the second period of recalibration of premium prices to take account of true expenditures and recover losses occurred 2 to 3 years after the initial first year of premium pricing. In effect, this created a fairly consistent fluctuation of profits and loss that typically encompassed six calendar years (Doran, Dobson, & Harris, 2001).

As mentioned previously in this chapter, by the early 1980s a decade of rampant health care inflation and ineffective cost controls pushed employers to seek more competitively priced health care plans that were based upon the employer's rather than the community's actuarial risk. This in turn spawned expansion in the insurance brokerage industry and various attempts by employers to pool their risk and purchasing power. As the private insurance market functions currently, how employers purchase health insurance is very much a function of the size of the employer's labor force and the industry sector in which the employer is located (e.g., manufacturing, mining, retail, service). Both labor force size and industry sector are key attributes of a "segmented labor market" (Dickens & Lang, 1992), meaning in essence that the labor market is comprised of distinct parts, each with different rules for the determination of wages and employment policies, and with different levels of employment opportunity (Dickens & Lang, 1992, p. 7). Although size and industrial sector both affect the dynamics of health insurance availability and costs, the first attribute to be considered is employer size—in particular, the distinction between the health insurance markets for small and large employers.

Small employers typically rely on an insurance broker, a function analogous to real estate that brings together the buyers and the sellers and charges the seller a commission—in the case of group health insurance, typically 2% to 8% of the premium price (Conwell, 2002). Medium-sized employers, those with a labor force of 100 to 500 employees, tend to involve both brokers and health care benefits consultants (Marquis & Long, 2000). Large employers who do not self-insure tend to use a combination of insurance brokers and external benefits consultants, while self-insured large employers tend to rely more upon a combination of benefits consultants and third-party administrators—the latter being a firm that contracts with the employer to act as the administrator of employee health care benefits (Marquis & Long, 2000).

An important consideration in the operation of health insurance markets is the extent to which the insurance broker acts as an agent of the employer seeking the affordable group health care coverage or the health insurance company seeking to find the "lowest risk" employers—in essence, employers that have employees who are the least likely to introduce an adverse selection problem. It is not uncommon in some health insurance markets for insurance carriers to use financial incentives that discourage brokers from bringing them higher risk business, sometimes in violation of state and federal laws that govern the health insurance market (Conwell, 2002).[14] The situation is akin to the problem of racial discrimination in housing, where real estate agents are given incentives by developers and lenders to "steer" minority home buyers away from desirable neighborhoods. While extensive regulations have been promulgated to promote small employer access to reasonably priced health insurance, there is a significant debate as to whether these reform efforts are effective or even counterproductive (Xirasagar et al., 2004). Ironically, other federal regulations contained in the Employee Retirement Income Security Act of 1974 (ERISA) do not appear to prohibit employers from engaging in various forms of risk selection, including finding ways to push higher risk employees out of their labor force (U.S. Court of Appeals Third Circuit, 2000; U.S. Court of Appeals Eleventh Circuit, 1993).[15] In fact, ERISA protects self-insuring employers who engage in risk selection practices from state level laws banning such activities.

Employer Effects on Insurance Coverage and Costs

Ninety percent of the nonelderly Americans who have health insurance coverage receive it through an employer-sponsored health insurance plan, which are typically heavily subsidized by the employer as a benefit in lieu of higher wages (AHIP Center for Policy and Research, 2009). As discussed in the previous chapter, the U.S. approach to health care insurance evolved over decades as a mixed incremental strategy that would eventually achieve near universal health insurance coverage through a combination of social insurance for retired citizens (Medicare), a means tested health insurance entitlement for the poor (Medicaid), and employer-based health insurance for workers and their dependents. However, this health care policy approach was predicated on two assumptions that history has shown to be flawed. The first erroneous assumption was that the private health insurance would be more effective at restraining rising health insurance costs than government health care insurance programs (see Figure 3.2 for clear evidence to the contrary), and the second faulty assumption was that over time the number of Americans covered by employer-based health insurance would expand. With respect to the second assumption, over the past decade health insurance coverage of nonelderly Americans has declined from 69% to 59% and the numbers of uninsured have increased from 36 million to 49 million (Holahan & Chen, 2011).

For the millions of Americans that receive health care coverage through employment, the price they pay for their health insurance coverage, the extent to which they have coverage for both ordinary and financially catastrophic expenditures, and whether or not they have a choice over specific benefits and health care providers is primarily determined by three factors:

1. The size of their employer
2. The number of hours they work
3. Whether their specific position is a high-wage or low-wage occupation

While there are other factors that influence the quality of employer-based coverage, such as region of the country and employment sector of the economy, the size of the employer, full-time vs. part-time employment status, and high vs. low wage are the most determinant.

Generally speaking, large employers (those with more than 200 employees) offer a more generous range of benefits and also pay a larger share of the costs of the workers, health care benefits, as well as that of their dependents. Table 3.2 provides a basic comparison of the premium coverage costs by employer size (firms of over 200 workers vs. firms with less than 200 workers) based on a recent national survey of employer health benefits and coverage (Kaiser Family Foundation, 2011a). Large employers purchase more expensive benefit plans, both for employees and their dependents, and then pay a larger share of the costs for these plans. Small employers, in contrast to large employers, are also more likely to drop employee insurance coverage or dependent coverage as costs continue to escalate and/or in difficult economic times. During the last decade, the percentage of very small employers (3–9 employees) offering employee health insurance has declined from 55% to 48% (Kaiser Family Foundation, 2011a). Among the firms that employ a large number of low-wage workers (35% of firm employees earn less than $23,000/year), by 2011 only 28% continue to offer employee health insurance. With respect to part-time workers (those working less than 35 hours per week), only 16% of employers offer benefits to part-time workers.

Considered as a whole, the prospects for the continued affordability of health insurance for both employers and workers are increasingly dubious— at least in absence of the implementation of health care reform. Despite an economy that dipped into a sustained recession with declining middle-class incomes between 2005 and 2010, the costs of health insurance paid by workers increased by 47% against an employer share of health insurance cost increase of 20% (Kaiser Family Foundation, 2010). While the most recent estimates of the overall health care inflation rate appear to have taken a pause in response to the recession, health insurance premiums have continued to rise.

Managed Care and Other Forms of Cost Control

Thus far, the brunt of the discussion pertaining to employment-based health insurance has concerned the problem of adverse selection and its effects on equity of health insurance access. However, the original dynamic that propelled the private health insurance market toward employer-based insurance pricing (from the community rating system) was the *moral hazard* problem discussed previously—the problem that arises when the effect of having

Table 3.2 *Annual Health Insurance Premium Costs by Employer Size*

	Large Employer (200+ Employees)		Small Employer (3–199 Employees)		Large Employer	
	($)	(%)	($)	(%)	Cost Difference ($)	Percent Difference
Individual Worker Annual Premium Cost	5477		5328		149	
Worker part	996	18	762	14	234	4
Employer part	4481	82	4566	86	– 85	– 4
Family Coverage Annual Premium Cost	15,520		14,098		1422	
Worker part	3755	24	4946	35	–1191	–11
Employer part	11,765	76	9152	65	2613	11

Source: Kaiser/HRET Survey of Employer Sponsored Health Benefits, 2011, Kaiser Family Foundation, http://ehbs.kff.org/pdf/2011/8225.pdf

insurance alters the risk behavior of the insured. To repeat a point made earlier in the chapter, under a variety of conditions, individuals are more disposed toward seeking health care because they have health care insurance than they otherwise would be. To compound the problem, the availability of health insurance has fueled technological innovation in nearly every sphere of health care (e.g., drugs, diagnostic equipment) that lends its own inflationary pressures. Finally, providers have strong incentives to provide more health care at higher prices to the extent that insurance is available to assure them a profitable return for their services.[16]

In contrast to the incentives of the other three actors (the patient, the provider, and the technology innovator), employers and health insurance carriers have strong incentives to reduce health care utilization and the prices paid for health care. Further, in contrast to the interests of health care providers and the health care innovators, the employer and the insurance carrier have joint incentives to reduce the prices of health care products and services. There are five very basic ways for them to do this:

1. Lower the level of health risk among the insured pool of health care consumers.
2. Make health care consumers more risk averse to seeking health care, in essence, impose penalties for health care utilization.
3. Reduce or reverse the incentives on the part of providers to provide care.
4. Reduce the prices/costs of health care services and products provided.[17]
5. Reduce utilization of care that falls outside explicit standards of efficacy and/or cost efficiency.

The first way to control the escalation of health care expenditures generally involves various recruitment and retention strategies by the employer to develop a healthier pool of employees. Also, some employers pursue a range of health promotion strategies in the work place, particularly large employers who self-insure. Prominent among health promotion strategies are employer campaigns to eliminate smoking and other forms of tobacco addiction, although other avenues of employer-sponsored health promotion include weight loss campaigns, exercise programs, stress management, and education about the effective use of health care services. The evidence suggests that such efforts pay a return to employers in the reduced use of sick leave and avoidable health care expenditures that are 3 to 4 times their cost (Fries et al., 1993).

The remaining four strategies to reduce health care utilization and costs fall under the broad rubric of *managed care*. Although "managed care" is defined in multiple ways, it commonly encompasses various activities by health care underwriters to control health care costs, quality, and access (Baily, 2003). In contrast to the passive stance of traditional insurance companies that merely estimate risk, set insurance premium prices, and then process the payment of claims, managed care organizations engage in a variety of activities aimed at influencing the process of health care decision making—both by the providers and the consumers of health care (Baily, 2003, p. 36). Managed care can also be thought of as referring to *provider structures* (i.e., specific forms of organizational arrangements between the providers and underwriters of health care), and a repertoire of tactics pertaining to the control of health care utilization and pricing. Because all managed care provider structures, to a greater or less extent, rely upon a similar set of utilization and pricing tactics, it makes sense to describe the main types of provider structures first.

Although there are multiple variations within each type, employment-based health care plans rely on three main kinds of managed care organization provider structures: HMOs, PPOs, and POS providers (Robinson, 1999). In contrast to other provider structures, HMOs (Health Maintenance Organizations) combine the functions of health care underwriting and health care provision within a single organization through the mechanism of capitated financing. As explained earlier in this chapter, instead of insuring against the costs for specific services and episodes of care, capitation insures against the costs of totality of health care that the insurance carrier (HMO) deems is prudent and/or necessary to sustain health and treat illness over the agreed-upon period of coverage. The term "capitation" is derived from the idea that the insurance financing on a per member–per month (or per capita) basis rather than on the basis of episodes of care, or services/products furnished. Among HMOs, a distinction is made between HMOs that provide health care services through a network of provider contracts such as with Independent Practice Associations (IPAs)[18] and HMOs that principally provide care through health care professionals they employ and facilities that they own and operate. Preferred provider organizations (PPOs) are networks of providers (e.g., physician groups, hospitals, pharmacies) that contract with health insurance underwriters to furnish an array of health care services and products at a discounted price. Providers that are a part of a PPO network are also generally required to follow procedures set by the insurance underwriter that serve to monitor and control health care utilization and quality, and they often must meet specified benchmarks in each to avoid financial penalties. Finally, point-of-service (POS) provider structures are a particular form of the preferred provider arrangement that permits the health care consumer to choose their own primary care provider, who then functions as the "gate-keeper" for other health care services—or more benevolently, as the provider responsible for coordinating all other aspects of the consumer's health care. Many consumers prefer the POS provider structure because they perceive that they are able to exercise more personal choice in the health care they utilize, including referral to specialists (Forrest et al., 2001). It should be noted that POS arrangements are often included as a higher cost option within HMO health plans, and that such "hybrid" provider structures have become increasingly common as consumers have sought alternatives to more rigid forms of managed care (Mechanic, 2004).

According to the Henry J. Kaiser Foundation national survey of employer health benefits, only about 1% of workers who are covered by health insurance are enrolled in health care plans that do not have a managed care provider structure (Kaiser Foundation, 2011a). Of the remaining 99% of workers, 17% are enrolled in HMOs, 55% in PPOs, and 10% in POS plans (Kaiser, 2011a). Table 3.3 provides a general overview of how each type of managed care organization provider structure employs various methods that serve the four previously discussed "managed care" strategies for the reduction of health care utilization and cost. The strategies and methods that are shown are those that tend to be more prevalent within each type of organizational structure.

Many of the cost containment mechanisms displayed in Table 3.3 are generally familiar and do not require special explanation. Others may be less familiar and require brief explanation. Under the first column, selective wait-listing refers to imposing longer waits on some forms of care where urgent attention is not critical. Gatekeeping triage refers to information and referral processes that have as a central goal diversion of the patient from clinical services that are deemed nonessential, such as requiring primary care visits be scheduled through a clinic nurse. High co-pays for use of non-PPO providers require the patient to pay more out of pocket if the patient selects the use of a health care provider that is outside the PPO provider network.

Under the second column, "utilization review" refers to the auditing of clinic records for the purposes of identifying care delivery by providers that fails to meet explicit standards of care established by the insurance underwriter, and "sanctioning of outliers" refers to actions by the insurance carrier that have negative consequences for the provider—including, at the extreme, terminating the contract with the provider, and identifying providers who deliver care outside of the established practice. The positive incentive method identified in the second column involves the mechanisms of profit sharing or higher provider reimbursements for meeting patient risk pool-based outcomes, such as achieving a benchmark for a reduced incidence of hospital admissions among the pool of the HMO members assigned to the HMO physician's practice.

Table 3.3 *Managed Care Cost Containment Methods by MCO Provider Structure*

Managed Care Organization Structure	Managed Care Cost Containment Strategy I *Make health care consumers more risk averse to seeking health care, in essence, impose penalties for health care utilization*	Managed Care Cost Containment Strategy II *Reduce or reverse the incentives on the part of providers to provide care*	Managed Care Cost Containment Strategy III *Reduce the prices and costs of health care services and products provided*	Managed Care Cost Containment Strategy IV *Reduce utilization of care that falls outside explicit standards of efficacy and/or cost efficiency*
HMO	Modest co-pays for selected services Selective wait-listing Gatekeeping triage	Salaried providers Utilization review and sanctioning of provider outliers Risk pool-based incentives/profit sharing	Bulk purchasing and competitive bidding Selective outsourcing/carve-outs Selective case management Discounted contracts for outside providers	Utilization review and care process improvement Selective pre-review Selective case management Widespread use of clinical protocols
PPO	Significant to modest co-pays for broad range of services Significant deductibles High co-pays for use of non-PPO providers	Utilization review and sanctioning of outliers Payment denial for services deemed unnecessary	Bulk purchasing and competitive bidding Selective case management	Utilization review and care process improvement Selective pre-review Selective case management Widespread use of clinical protocols
POS	Significant to modest co-pays for broad range of services Significant deductibles High co-pays for referrals to specialists	Close monitoring of utilization of services, sanctioning of provider outliers Payment denial for services deemed unnecessary	Discounted provider fees Referral within PPO network Primary care gatekeeping	Utilization review and care process improvement Selective pre-review Primary care case management Widespread use of clinical protocols

The cost-reducing method of "selective outsourcing/carve outs" shown in the third column involves the selective use of either subcontracting the management and provision of a segment of the benefits package to a specialty provider or making some benefits available on a discounted fee-for-service basis through an external provider contract. These kinds of arrangements are made where the HMO determines it is less able to manage a certain type of benefit on a capitation basis and contracting with an external provider is more cost efficient—the typical example being the carve-out of benefit obligations for mental health care. Also under the price and cost control strategy (the third column) is selective case management. Case management has a variety of definitions and approaches, but for the purposes here it means assignment of a care coordination specialist to a patient with a difficult-to-manage disease profile or one that involves high utilization of resources, such as a patient dually diagnosed with Type 1 diabetes and bipolar disorder. Depending on a variety of factors, the case manager may be a clinical nurse specialist, social worker, or a licensed physician's assistant.[19]

Under the fourth column, the strategy to reduce utilization of care that falls outside explicit standards of efficacy and/or cost efficiency, key methods include selective pre-review for some categories of health care service, and utilization review for care process improvement. The former is familiar to most patients having employer-based insurance that have needed either surgery, an expensive diagnostic procedure, or specialized treatment—and it involves review by an agent of the insurer (typically a nurse specialist or physician) and preapproval as a condition of insurance coverage. The justification usually entails criteria related to clinical necessity and cost efficiency, though many patients and providers view and have experienced this method as a bureaucratic obstacle that serves a penalty function (per Cost Containment Strategy I). Utilization review for purposes of process improvement involves retrospective review of clinical practice processes to discover opportunities for improvement either in cost savings, clinical outcomes, or both. It is often the case that more efficient care is also care that yields direct clinical benefits to the patient: unnecessary care is often not only costly but also detrimental—the classic example being the risks to the patient imposed by needlessly prolonged hospital stays.[20]

The final method shown in column four that is worthy of highlighting, widespread use of clinical protocols, refers to the delivery of care in accordance to pre-established standards of care for a given profile of disease symptoms, stage of disease, and/or patient characteristics in combination with a given diagnosis. In simple terms, clinical protocols generally involve doing what the evidence suggests is most effective and cost efficient for a given type of case—in some situations, substituting the clinical practitioner's and/or the patient's independent judgment or preference concerning what is best or most effective in the individual situation.[21]

Although the strategies and methods shown in Table 3.3 fall far short of an exhaustive review of the full range of managed care strategies and methods for the control of health care utilization and costs, those shown encompass the prevalent approaches. Aggressively pursued, most have proved very effective as mechanisms of cost reduction and control under a variety of contexts. In fact, managed care utilization mechanisms employed by insurance companies as well as by the federal government largely accounted for the temporary plunge in health care cost inflation that occurred during the first half of the 1990s decade (Altman & Levitt, 2002). It is also clear that the insurance market has shifted away from aggressive forms of managed care over the most recent years—much to the detriment of health care cost containment. According to the widely accepted narrative of medical sociologist David Mechanic,[22] the use of many of these utilization and cost control mechanisms have been on the wane in the face of a widespread "managed care backlash" that gained momentum as the insurance industry consolidated and a larger share of middle-class Americans experienced reduced exercise of preferences and access to health care firsthand (Mechanic, 2004). However, even in Mechanic's analysis, there are many promising aspects of managed care that will remain in the U.S. health care system to the extent that they contribute to better management of chronic diseases and to health care quality rather than solely to reductions in utilization or cost (Mechanic, 2004, p. 82).

Given the short life of the more aggressive forms of managed care, the employer-based health insurance system has more recently turned to other avenues of cost containment, specifically reductions in employee coverage, *health savings accounts* (HSAs), and *defined contribution plans*. Each of these forms of cost containment will be discussed in depth in a later chapter on health care reform. However, a brief explanation of each is in order at this point to round out the understanding of the private insurance market. As noted previously, reductions in employer-based coverage have primarily shown up in the reduced tendency of many (particularly small) employers to offer dependent coverage and the simultaneous decline in the proportion of employers providing health insurance as a benefit (Kaiser Foundation, 2011a). Health savings account plans have two parts, a conventional health insurance plan with a high deductible and a tax-sheltered savings account that is dedicated to an array of Internal Revenue Service (IRS) approved health care expenditures. This insurance approach works as a mechanism of utilization and cost containment because the worker has a financial incentive to avoid unnecessary health care expenditures: under IRS rules, funds not spent for health care in qualified HSA accounts are retained by the worker. While this approach has some distinct advantages with respect to the management of moral hazard as well as exercise of individual preferences for health care, it also introduces a significant adverse selection problem to the extent that healthier employees abandon conventional health insurance plans for HSAs.[23]

The third "non-managed care" approach to health insurance cost containment, defined contribution plans (DCPs), vary in structure but commonly limit upfront the employer's overall contribution to the cost of employee health insurance by either (a) specifying a set contribution toward the purchase of an array of employer-approved health insurance plans or (b) setting up an employer-sponsored HSA that is linked to a high deductible policy (Christianson, Parente, & Taylor, 2002). Currently, about 17% of workers with health insurance coverage are enrolled in plans that are of the HSA/high deductible type, whereas less than 5% of covered workers were enrolled in such plans 5 years prior (Kaiser Family Foundation, 2011a).

Regulation of the Employment-Based System

Extensive regulation of the employer-based health insurance system takes place at both the state and the federal level. At the federal level, regulation largely comes through the tax code and three omnibus acts of legislation, the Employee Retirement and Income Security Act of 1974 (ERISA), the Consolidated Omnibus Budget Reconciliation Act of 1985 (COBRA), and the Health Insurance Portability and Accountability Act of 1996 (HIPAA). At the state level, regulation occurs through the oversight of state insurance commissioners and state laws that govern insurance industry practices. State insurance commissioners serve as advocates for insurance consumers, and to some extent as mediators between the interests of the public and the interests of the insurance industry. Insurance commissioners also function as the state government's official expert on various insurance markets within their respective states. Although state legislatures vary greatly in the extent to which they aggressively regulate the health insurance industry and pursue reform (Xirasagar et al., 2004), they play a central role in setting the basic conditions for participation of insurers in the state insurance market; conditions that generally include the array of required benefits, requirements of disclosure of costs and limitations in coverage, and procedures for the adjudication of insurance claim disputes. However, states do not have carte blanche in the governance of the local health insurance industry. In fact, there are very key limitations imposed by the federal government through ERISA that have been used to "eviscerate state attempts to regulate both health care financing and health care delivery" (Chirba-Martin & Brennan, 1994, p. 152).[24]

As originally conceived, the Employee Retirement and Income Security Act of 1974 (ERISA) was intended to protect employee pension and benefit plans from abuses by employers and pension benefit plans administrators and fiscal managers (Chirba-Martin & Brennan, 1994). As pointed out previously, ERISA was also designed to protect workers from employer discrimination on the basis of benefit utilization. In order to assure that workers in different states enjoyed uniform protections against pension and benefit plan abuses and pension and benefit plan underwriters could operate across state lines without encountering different rules pertaining to the protection of workers or management of benefits, ERISA was passed with provisions that preclude states from imposing regulations on pension and benefit plans that fall under ERISA regulation—a preclusion that extends to self-insured health care benefit plans. In effect, these provisions of ERISA undermine the capacity of states to reform their local employer-based health insurance markets and, moreover, promote segmentation of employer-based health insurance coverage and benefits. Although the details are complex, employers can avoid a wide array of state regulations aimed at enhancing or even protecting minimum health insurance coverage protections because self-insured plans are sheltered under ERISA from state-level health care reforms. Because of the favorable treatment of self-insuring employers under ERISA, employers that are in the best position to self-insure (in essence, large employers with a healthier work force) exit the conventional health insurance market—thus deepening the adverse selection problem among small employers. ERISA has also been used by opponents of state-level health care reform efforts to block the implantation of employer mandates, the development of state-sponsored strategies to cross-subsidize the benefit costs of workers confined to high-risk insurance pools, and even regulate key aspects of the way HMOs and PPOs do business (Chirba-Martin & Brennan, 1994, p. 152). Under ERISA, the segment of the health insurance market comprised of larger self-insuring employers is sheltered from the central features of state-level health insurance regulation (consumer protection, coverage provisions, and minimum benefits) that applies to all other health care benefit plans—without the reciprocal oversight of equally relevant federal regulations (Hall, 2000). Thus, the Patient Protection and Affordable Care Act contains some provisions that impose stronger regulatory provisions on large employer self-insured plans (Temchine, 2010).

In contrast to ERISA, the health insurance regulations spelled out in the Health Insurance Portability and Accountability Act of 1996 (HIPAA) primarily affect the segments of the health insurance markets that are unable or unwilling to self-insure (Hall, 2000). The insurance regulation provisions of HIPAA added a new title to the Public Health Service Act that essentially complemented and made more uniform various insurance market reforms that had been undertaken at the state level in the early 1990s (Hall, 2000). Included in these reform provisions are guarantees of the availability of coverage for small employers, the ability to renew coverage for both small and large employer groups, limitations on preexisting condition exclusion periods, and prohibitions against discrimination against individual insurance participants based on health status (CMS, 2004).

Like most budget bills, the Consolidated Omnibus Budget Reconciliation Act of 1985 (COBRA) contains a wide array of provisions affecting multiple sectors of the government and economy. The health care provisions in COBRA[25] that directly affect the health care insurance market provide protection for workers and dependents against losing health care insurance coverage through events such as loss of employment, divorce, bankruptcy, and even reduction in work hours below the maximum required for inclusion in employment coverage (Cabral, 2003). Under COBRA regulations, the worker or dependent that loses eligibility for coverage under the group plan of a private or public employer is allowed the option of continuing the coverage for a specified period (that ranges from 18 to 36 months depending on a variety of specifics) at a cost that is no more than 102% of the full premium cost.[26] The critical protection that COBRA provides is the ability of the worker or affected dependent to extend the advantages of the group insurance rate for a period that is often sufficient to gain other health insurance coverage, such as through reemployment.

AN OVERVIEW OF HEALTH CARE SYSTEM FINANCE—PUBLIC FINANCING OF HEALTH CARE

As emphasized earlier in this chapter, when all public programs are considered together, almost half the health care expenditures in the United States are publicly funded. As also explained at the beginning of the chapter, the largest proportion of public funding of health care is through two programs: Medicare (21.5% of all expenditures) and Medicaid (16.4% of all expenditures; Martin et al., 2012). In addition, a large share of public health care expenditures occur through the Veterans Administration health care system—estimated to be $52 billion for 2011 (Congressional Budget Office, 2010). Of all public programs, Medicare has by far been the most influential in building the infrastructure of the health care system and currently enjoys the most political support. As noted in Chapter 2 on the history of the U.S. health care system, Medicare has also been the most inflationary of all public health care programs. For all of these reasons, Medicare will be the first of the three major public finance programs to be described.

The Basics of Medicare

Medicare and Medicaid were jointly enacted by the U.S. Congress in 1965, with Medicare designed as a health insurance program for persons aged 65 and above and Medicaid designed as a state and federal partnership to fund health care for the poor. The enactment of Medicare was seen by many advocates and opponents of a federally sponsored system of universal health insurance as an intermediate step toward a system of universal entitlement to health care, and on that basis the profession of medicine vigorously resisted Medicare's creation (Starr, 1982). In order to counter this resistance, the Medicare program as originally structured lacked any mechanisms of cost control, and left the discretion of what was medically necessary to the judgment of medical providers that were being paid on a noncompetitive, fee-for-service basis. Although effective cost control mechanisms were introduced in the early 1980s that for a time reined in runaway hospital care expenditures,[27] the fee-for-service system of reimbursement for physician providers remains the cornerstone of Medicare's approach to medical provider reimbursement.

As of 2010, 47.5 million people were covered by Medicare: 39.6 million were aged 65 and above, and 7.9 million qualified on the basis of long-term disability (Medicare Board of Trustees, 2011). Due to the aging of the population and the transition of the "baby-boom" generation to Medicare eligibility in the coming decade, Medicare enrollment is expected to increase by 35% to 64 million beneficiaries by the year 2020 (Medicare Board of Trustees, 2011). This growth trend in enrollment in combination with health care inflation is projected to place the Medicare Hospital Insurance Trust Fund (Medicare Part A) in financial insolvency by the year 2024 (Medicare Board of Trustees, 2011), an occurrence that precedes by many years the projected insolvency of the Social Security retirement trust fund. The second major component of the Medicare program that covers physician services (Medicare Part B) is also presenting a major fiscal challenge because of its ever-increasing bite on general tax revenues. It should also be noted that the current projections for the fiscal insolvency of the Medicare program's Hospital Insurance Trust Fund assume that the cost reduction components of the Patient Protection and Affordable Care Act (PPACA) will be implemented as originally signed into law. Absent the implementation of the PPCA's myriad cost reduction provisions, the Hospital Insurance Trust Fund is likely to become solvent prior to the end of the current decade (Medicare Board of Trustees, 2011).

There are a number of proposals on the table averting this financial crisis, including transforming Medicare from a defined benefit program to a defined contribution program or imposing an annual global budget with mandatory spending caps similar to the cost control policies of other OECD countries with universal health insurance programs (Marmor & Oberlander, 1998). These issues are discussed in more depth at a later point in this chapter.[28]

Medicare is a highly complex program that links together different parts (A, B, C, and D) with various levels of coverage for hospital care, physician's services, outpatient diagnostic and therapy services, nursing home care, home health care, and, since 2006, outpatient prescription drugs. In place of a tedious narrative, Table 3.4 provides a general overview of the essentials. Although Table 3.4 serves well as a general reference for the Medicare program's main features, it is not an exhaustive guide to all current benefits and eligibility criteria.

What Medicare Doesn't Cover: Gaps in Coverage and the Role of Supplemental Insurance

Even with the addition of limited coverage for prescription drugs in 2006, it should be apparent from Table 3.4 that the out-of-pocket hospital deductibles and coinsurance requirements under Part A and the high levels of coinsurance under Part B leave any Medicare beneficiary with a severe acute illness or chronic illness in serious financial jeopardy, even leaving aside such uncovered services as dental care. In fact, relative to the households of working-age adults, the households of elderly Medicare beneficiaries spend three times as much of their income on health care (Kaiser Family Foundation, 2011b). Among the 48 million Medicare beneficiaries, about 9 million meet the low-income limits for dual eligibility for both Medicaid and Medicare (Kaiser Family Foundation, 2011c).

Supplemental insurance for Medicare (the so-called Medigap insurance) varies substantially in premium prices and in coverage. Since the reforms enacted by the Omnibus Budget Reconciliation Act (OBRA) of 1990, Medigap insurance policies that are sold to Medicare recipients are required to conform to any one of 10 standardized benefit packages and (in contrast to the abusive insurance industry practices prior to OBRA 1990) insurance companies are not permitted to sell duplicate policies or engage in a variety of other unethical marketing practices.

The Medicare Funding Crisis and Alternatives to Medicare Reform

Since 2008, the expenditures of the Medicare Hospital Insurance Trust fund (Medicare Part A) were above revenues, leading a trend of deficits that are projected to exhaust the trust fund's assets by the year 2024 (Medicare

Table 3.4 *Overview of Medicare Program Services, Coverage, and Eligibility Criteria*

Medicare Part A: The Hospital Insurance Program

Financing: Provider's payments and expenditures are drawn from a trust fund created by a 2.9% tax on earnings, paid in equal parts by employer and employee.

Program Eligibility Criteria: Persons aged 65 and older who are otherwise eligible for Social Security Old-Age and Survivors Insurance (OASI) benefits, persons under age 65 who have received Social Security Disability Insurance payments for 2 years, and persons with end-stage renal disease.

The applicable coverage period for Part A benefits is defined as a "spell of illness," which begins at the point the beneficiary enters hospital care and ends at the point the person has been out of the hospital or skilled nursing facility for 60 days.[a]

Services	Scope of Coverage[b]	Coverage Eligibility Criteria
Hospital Care	100% after a $1132 deductible hospital stays of 1–60 days. All but $283 per day in days 61–90 of a hospital stay. All but $566 per day for days 91–150 of a hospital stay.	Hospital admissions certified by the hospital utilization review committee as "medically necessary" under Medicare program criteria for acute care.
Skilled Nursing Facility Care	Nothing for the first 20 days. $114 per day for days 21–100.	Care in Medicare certified skilled nursing facility that is certified as skilled, "noncustodial" care.[c]
Home Health Care	100% of "part-time or intermittent skilled nursing or home health aide services" and/or specific therapies (physical, occupational, or speech). 20% of the Medicare-approved amount for durable medical equipment.	Plan of care signed by physician. Beneficiary must be "home-bound," meaning unable to leave home without considerable effort and assistance. Need for intermittent skilled nursing care or specific therapies (physical, occupational, or speech).

142

Hospice Care	In general, 100% of in-home hospice services and in-patient hospice services where determined medically necessary or for purposes of caregiver respite. There is a $5 co-payment for outpatient prescription drugs.	Physician certification that the beneficiary is suffering from a terminal illness (with a prognosis of 6 months or less) and the beneficiary's acceptance of palliative (comfort) vs. cure-oriented care.

Medicare Part B: The Medical Insurance Program

Financing: 25% of the estimated Part B insurance premium actuarial cost is deducted from the OASI recipient's Social Security benefit ($99.90 to a maximum of $319.70 for 2012, depending on income level), and the balance is financed from general tax revenues.

Program Eligibility Criteria: Predicated on eligibility for Medicare Part A plus voluntary enrollment in the Part B premium cost deduction option.

Services	Scope of Coverage	Coverage Eligibility Criteria
Physician Services	80% of approved charges after $100 deductable for Part B services and supplies.	Based on physician order.
Rehabilitative Therapies[d]	As above	As above
Diagnostic Tests/Procedures	As above	As above
Durable Medical Equipment	Varies by type of equipment	As above
Preventative Care	80%–100% of approved charges	As above, some exceptions

(continued)

Table 3.4 *Overview of Medicare Program Services, Coverage, and Eligibility Criteria (continued)*

Medicare Part C: Medicare Advantage Plans

Financing: Medicare "Advantage Plans" (prior to 2005 referred to Medicare + Choice options) combine the funds from Medicare Parts A and B into an array of coverage alternatives to the traditional Medicare fee-for-service program. These options include Medicare-sponsored HMOs, Preferred Provider Organizations (PPOs), Provider Sponsored Organizations (PSOs), alternative private fee-for-service (PFFS) plans, Medical Savings Account (MSAs), and Special Needs Plans (chronic disease management plans). Medicare Advantage plans are essentially local (county and regional level) health care plans that contract with the Medicare program (CMS) on a capitated basis to provide the equivalent of Medicare Parts A and B services to enrolled beneficiaries. Differences between Medicare payments to such plans and the costs of services provided are returned to the plan enrollees in the form of additional benefits, lower Part B premiums, and/or lower co-payments.

Program Eligibility Criteria: Predicated on eligibility for Medicare Part A, plus voluntary enrollment in the Part B premium cost deduction option, plus voluntary enrollment in a locally available Medicare Advantage plan.[e]

Services	Scope of Coverage	Coverage Eligibility Criteria
At minimum, the equivalent of Medicare Parts A and B	Typically, at minimum, the equivalent of Parts A and B, with enhanced coverage (e.g., outpatient prescription drugs or reduced co-payments) a component of some plans.	Medicare Part C plans that are managed care plans (HMOs, PPOs, PSOs, and SNPs) have similar eligibility criteria to traditional fee-for-service Medicare, but constrain the beneficiary's choice of providers to those within the plan network. In addition, such plans (like most managed care plans) impose restrictions on access to specialty care and services.

Medicare Part D: Outpatient Drug Benefit

Financing: Medicare Part D is financed through a combination of drug-coverage premiums paid directly by Medicare program beneficiaries to prescription drug insurance plans, premium subsidies from general tax revenues, and fund transfers from states for coverage costs of former Medicaid program enrollees.[f] Medicare beneficiaries either pay premiums to private plans that are certified by Medicare (CMS) to provide the Part D prescription drug benefit, or they are able to enroll in Medicare Part C (Medicare Advantage) plans that are enhanced with a prescription drug benefit.

Program Eligibility Criteria: Predicted on eligibility for Part A, plus voluntary enrollment in Medicare Part D program.

Services	Scope of Coverage (Standard Plan, 2012)	Coverage Eligibility Criteria
Outpatient prescription drug restrictions through subsidized and Medicare-approved private sector insurance plans. Approved plans can employ formularies and tiered cost sharing, but must provide at least two drugs within each therapeutic class of drugs.	75% annual prescription drug costs after a $320 deductible, to a cap of $2930. Annual prescription drug costs in excess of $2930 are excluded from coverage, until out-of-pocket costs reach $4700. When out-of-pocket costs reach $4700 in any year, 95% of prescription drug costs for the balance of the calendar year.	Enrollment is required when first eligible for Medicare, and thereafter during specified annual enrollment periods. Enrolled beneficiaries will be required to pay a monthly premium (estimated average of $39.62 for 2012).

[a] It is possible for Medicare beneficiaries to exhaust their benefits during a single spell of illness and not be eligible again unless and until their care has been able to be sustained outside of a hospital or skilled nursing facility for at least 60 days. Such instances are rare but they do occur, for example, a case of severe burns and multiple skin grafting surgeries that requires more than 150 continuous days of hospital care.

[b] The deductible amounts and benefit coverage limits are those that were in effect for 2012, recent updates can be obtained at the CMS website: www.medicare.gov/publications.

[c] Medicare does not provide coverage for ordinary or custodial nursing home care. This is a limitation that is often confusing to consumers because state licensing regulations can identify nursing homes as "skilled nursing facilities," despite the "custodial" level of care being provided under Medicare program criteria.

[d] Including but not limited to physical therapy, occupational therapy, and speech therapy, although coverage can vary by the type of rehabilitative therapy.

[e] The past 15 years have seen an enormous volatility in the demand for alternatives to traditional Medicare among beneficiaries, the availability of nontraditional Medicare options in various parts of the country, and the solvency of plans.

[f] These are cost estimates for the CMS standard plan, Medicare Part D enrollees may choose from a range of CMS-approved plans that have different deductibles, co-pays and coverage gap protections and also premium costs. The estimated average premium, estimated by Q1 Medicare.com, http://www.q1medicare.com/PartD-MedicarePartDPlanStatisticsState.php

Board of Trustees, 2011)). In addition, the other major Medicare benefit programs, both the voluntary Supplementary Medical Insurance Program (Medicare Part B) that pays for physician services and outpatient diagnostic services and pharmaceutical benefit (Medicare Part D) are projected to require substantial increases over time. There are a variety of factors that converged to create this crisis, but most are tied to health care inflationary pressures arising from both advancements in health care technology and the growing population of Medicare beneficiaries—especially those in the medically intensive advanced years of aging. For literally decades, Congress and successive presidential administrations have delayed taking more than incremental actions on the so-called "impending Medicare funding crisis" for years, and now the word "impending" must in all honesty be dropped from the phrase. The Medicare funding crisis has arrived.

Medicare Reform Options. At this point, there are seven general policy alternatives that have either been implemented to a limited extent or at least seriously debated. These policy alternatives include:

1. Creating incentives to move Medicare beneficiaries out of the inherently inflationary traditional fee-for-service program to Medicare benefit options that either entail managed care or health savings account plans that encourage selective use of health care;
2. Unilaterally reducing payments to physicians and hospitals;
3. Raising beneficiary age of eligibility, co-payments, premiums, or some combination thereof;
4. Reducing the scope of Medicare program coverage;
5. Raising Medicare Trust Fund payroll taxes;
6. Transforming Medicare from a defined benefit to a defined contribution program.
7. Fundamental transformation of the health care delivery system.

Despite the political appeal of incentives that would move Medicare beneficiaries over time from traditional fee-for-service plans to either managed care or health savings account options (policy alternative 1), these Medicare options plans have been plagued with enrollment difficulties and unintended policy consequences, including the excessive complexity of plan options and the confusion created among the elderly; the tendency of Medicare private plans to attract healthier, lower-cost beneficiaries; extreme geographic variations in plan options; and significant instabilities in benefits, out-of-pocket costs, and provider participation (Biles, Dallek, & Nicholas, 2004).

Both alternatives (3) and (4) thus far have proved equally politically unviable, particularly in the current highly polarized Congress where each party vies to be viewed as the true guardian of Medicare entitlements. Alternative (5), raising Medicare payroll taxes, is equally alienating to the under-50 age group of wage earners and would run counter to the national economic recovery strategy undertaken by the Obama administration (with a rare degree of bi-partisan support). Alternative (6), although it fundamentally alters the nature of the Medicare social contract (from benefit entitlement to a defined contribution) and encounters a politically formidable coalition of elderly and progressive-wing Democrats, has gained significant support among Republican politicians as the conservative alternative to the Medicare reform measures embedded in the PPACA. In contrast, the PPACA approach to Medicare reform has embraced a combination of alternatives 2 and 7—that is, a combination of reductions in Medicare payments to providers and fundamental reform of the health care delivery system.[29]

Even though it is difficult to discern which approach or combination of approaches to Medicare reform will ultimately gain traction, as the insolvency of the Medicare Hospital Insurance Trust Fund looms, economic realities are transforming what were once deemed unshakable political ones. Within just a few years (likely no more than 5) the executive branch and Congress will be compelled to converge on a Medicare reform compromise that the various key stakeholders in Medicare (beneficiaries, wage-earners, providers) will have to live with. The specific directions this might take will be examined more closely in the final chapter of the book, which focuses on health care reform.

The Basics of Medicaid

As originally designed, Medicaid was a state and federal partnership to meet the costs incurred in providing health care for the poor. Essentially, Medicaid functions as a federal program that is administered by states under a strict set of rules pertaining to state participation in funding, eligible recipients, and covered services. Depending on the state's per capita income, the federal share of Medicaid program expenditures range from a statutory minimum of 50% to a maximum of 83%. However, in times of economic hardship, Congress may enact temporary increases in the federal share of Medicaid funding, as happened in 2009. Thus, in 2010, the federal share of Medicaid expenditures was 67% while the states' share was 33% (Martin, Lassman, Washington, & Catlin, 2011; National Health Policy Forum, 2011). At the time that Medicaid was enacted into law (1965), other sources for funding health care for the poor existed through such sources as the Hill–Burton program[30] and widespread use of cost-shifting mechanisms that allowed hospitals to recover uncompensated care costs through higher prices to privately insured patients. In the decades since, Medicaid has evolved to a program that is the principal source of care for both the low-income recipients and also the largest single source of funding for the elderly in need of nursing home care.

Although various modifications and expansions of Medicaid program coverage have occurred over nearly 50 years of its existence, the key expansions in recent years have targeted low-income children. For example, the Omnibus Budget Reconciliation Act of 1990, expanded mandatory coverage to children under age 5 in families with an income at or below 133% of the federal poverty level and to older children living in families with income at or below 100% of the poverty level. More recently, the Patient Protection and Affordable Care Act of 2010 (PPACA) expands Medicaid eligibility standards for low-income adults. Beginning 2014, individuals under 65 years of age with income below 133% of the federal poverty level (FPL) will be eligible for Medicaid. In addition, low-income adults without children will be guaranteed coverage through Medicaid in every state without need for a waiver, and parents of children will be eligible at a uniform income level across all states (CMS, 2012). This was one of the many aspects of the PPACA that was vigorously opposed by congressional conservatives, because it was viewed as an unwarranted expansion of the federal government entitlements and a move that would further undermine employment-based health insurance. Among its proponents, this expansion was seen as an essential response to the failures of the employment-based health insurance system to provide for low-income working families.

SCHIP. To expand Medicaid eligibility further plus allow states some flexible alternatives to the funding of health care for children, in 1997 Congress enacted the State Children's Health Insurance Program (SCHIP). SCHIP is essentially a block grant program that provides an enhanced federal match to state expenditures on Medicaid and other forms of state-subsidized health insurance coverage for children. The most important feature of the SCHIP program is the capacity of states to expand Medicaid and other vehicles for publicly subsidized health insurance to children in families with income in excess of 200% of the federal poverty level. Under the provisions of the PPACA, states will have an increase in the SCHIP federal matching rate beginning in 2015 (CMS, 2012). In contrast to the Medicaid program as a whole, the SCHIP program has generally enjoyed significant bipartisan support at both the state and federal levels, and most states appear to look for ways to expand SCHIP's enrollment as yearly economic circumstances allow (Hill, Courtot, & Sullivan, 2005). However, a significant barrier to SCHIPs enrollment of many eligible children in low-income families appears to be related to the stigma the program inherits through its close association with conventional Medicaid. However, as more and more lower income families enroll in SCHIP in response to the ever shrinking coverage available through employment-based insurance, it may be that the stigma once associated with SCHIP will fade away. This, in fact, is a major concern among many conservative opponents, who believe that the stigma associated with public programs is an essential impediment to government dependency and "creeping socialism."[31]

Contrasting Medicaid and Medicare

Unlike Medicare, Medicaid is a means-based program rather than a social insurance program that includes all gradients of wealth. In that sense, the distinction between Medicaid and Medicare mirrors the differences between public assistance (Temporary Assistance to Needy Families) and Social Security. That is, Medicaid is politically a much less popular program and its recipients are burdened with program-based stigma.[32] Among health care providers, Medicaid recipients are generally regarded as dependents, whereas Medicare program participants are seen as beneficiaries. Despite these negative aspects of Medicaid, many of the provisions of Medicaid are significantly more expansive than Medicare.

Figure 3.6 provides a general overview of Medicaid program eligibility criteria and services that are universal among states, and examples of optional eligibility criteria and services that states may add at their discretion. However, states must absorb as much as 50% of whatever Medicaid expenditures are incurred by more generous eligibility criteria and services—thus, Medicaid programs differ widely from one state to the next depending on local economic resources and the prevailing political context.

There are abundant policy questions that surround the Medicaid program, most pertaining in one way or another to its sustainability, as limited state resources are increasingly strained by competing demands and the costs of the Medicaid program escalate. Clearly, though, Medicaid plays dual crucial roles in providing funds for health care to the most vulnerable segments of society, in particular, children in poverty and the most fragile of the aged and disabled (see Figure 3.7). Further, Medicaid has been called upon to subsidize the failures of the employer-based insurance system to a degree that was never anticipated at the inception of the program in 1965. For example, in 2009, over 28 million children were enrolled in Medicaid, either on the basis of their low family income or their status as children in foster care. By 2010, nearly one-third (29%) of the nation's children receive health care coverage through either traditional Medicaid or SCHIP, while

Mandatory Medicaid Services, Applicable to All States as a Condition of Medicaid Program Participation:

- Inpatient hospital services
- Outpatient hospital services
- Early and periodic screening, diagnostic, and treatment (EPSDT) services
- Nursing facility services
- Home health services
- Physician services
- Rural health clinic services
- Federally qualified health center services
- Laboratory and X-ray services
- Family planning services
- Nurse Midwife services
- Certified Pediatric and Family Nurse Practitioner services
- Freestanding Birth Center services (when licensed or otherwise recognized by the state)
- Transportation to medical care
- Tobacco cessation counseling for pregnant women
- Tobacco cessation

Optional Medicaid Services, Determined by States but Qualified for the Federal Share of Medicaid Expenditures

- Prescription drugs
- Clinic services
- Physical therapy
- Occupational therapy
- Speech, hearing, and language disorder services
- Respiratory care services
- Other diagnostic, screening, preventive, and rehabilitative services
- Podiatry services
- Optometry services
- Dental services
- Dentures
- Prosthetics
- Eyeglasses
- Chiropractic services
- Other practitioner services
- Private duty nursing services
- Personal care
- Hospice
- Case management
- Services for individuals age 65 or older in an institution for mental disease (IMD)
- Services in an intermediate care facility for the mentally retarded
- State Plan Home and Community Based Services–1915(i)
- Self-Directed Personal Assistance Services–1915(j)
- Community First Choice Option–1915(k)
- Other services approved by the Secretary

Source: CMS (2012) Medicaid.gov: Medicaid Benefits:
http://www.medicaid.gov/Medicaid-CHIP-Program-Information/By-Topics/Benefits/Medicaid-Benefits.html

Figure 3.6 *Medicaid mandatory and optional services.*

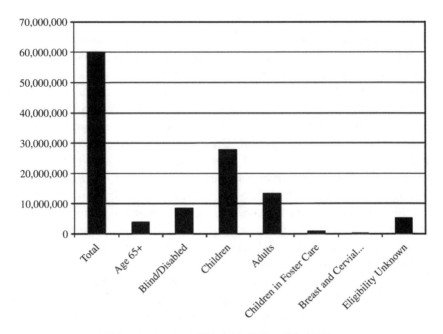

Source: National MSIS tables by state—2009, Table 09 Fiscal Year 2009
Medicaid Beneficiaries by Basis of Eligobility (BOE). CMS 2012 MSIS
Tables, http://www/cms.gov/MedicaidDataSourcesGenInfo/MSIS

Figure 3.7 *Number of Medicaid beneficiaries by general eligibility status:
FY 2009.*

only about half (55%) of the nation's children continued to be covered by the
employment-based insurance of their parents (Holahan & Chen, 2011). While
the insurance market reforms and health insurance purchasing subsidies to
low-income families that are part of the PPACA may halt the deterioration
of employment-based insurance coverage for children, it seems more likely
that a near 50/50 split between employment-based insurance for children
and public program coverage will be necessary to achieve universal health
care coverage for children—a policy goal all but the most recalcitrant ideolo-
gues agree is in the national interest.

The Department of Veterans Affairs Health Care System

The Department of Veterans Affairs (VA) health care system has its roots in
the special obligations of the U.S. government has historically assumed on
behalf of its military veterans, beginning with those of the Revolutionary
War. At various points in national history and typically at the conclusion of
major wars, Congress has extended and enlarged upon special provisions

and compensations created on behalf of the nation's veterans, including homes for aged and disabled veterans, veteran's pensions, survivor's benefits, special loan programs, educational benefits, and the provision of health care. The VA health care system's beginning can be traced to an action by Congress in 1917 that amended the War Risk Insurance Act to include medical benefits to veterans with service-connected disabilities. In the World War Veterans Act of 1924, Congress expanded benefits to include hospital services to all war veterans. During this same period, Congress also enacted laws that transferred several hospitals that had been a part of the U.S. Public Health Service to the Veterans Bureau—the early predecessor to the VA (Kizer, Demakis, & Feussner, 2000). Through various reorganizations and expansions, the VA health care system encompasses 153 medical centers, 882 ambulatory care and community-based outpatient clinics, 207 Vet Centers, 136 nursing homes, 45 residential rehabilitation treatment programs, and 92 comprehensive home-based care programs (CBO, 2007).

Throughout most of its history, the VA health care system operated as a hospital-based system with a highly centralized and rigid bureaucracy. Since 1997, however, the VA system has been radically transformed from a hospital-based system with utilization-based financing to an enrollment-based system of 22 regional networks financed principally by capitation (Ashton et al., 2003). As such, the VA health care system exists as the only federally sponsored and operated system of comprehensive capitation-based care. Unlike the Medicare and Medicaid programs, both of which are primarily fee-based programs, the VA has the capacity to directly negotiate favorable pricing of drugs with the pharmaceutical industry.[33]

Although all veterans are eligible for enrollment in the VA health care system, eligibility for care in the system is determined by the year-by-year balance between utilization and congressional appropriations, and the veteran's standing in a system of prioritized eligibility criteria. The only veterans that are automatically eligible for VA system care are those that have an established service-connected disability that is rated as at least 50% disabling, or veterans that have been recently discharged from military service with a service-connected disability that has not as yet been rated. Other higher priority groups for VA care include veterans with service-connected disabilities that are rated as 30% or 40% disabling, former POWs, and recipients of the Purple Heart. The VA health care system's eligibility criteria also include a means-based qualifier for low-income veterans that do not have a service-connected disability—as it happens, an eligibility criterion that has proved critical to countless veterans.

Aside from the VA health care system's central mission to provide health care to disabled veterans and its role as a health care safety net for low-income veterans, the VA health care system supports an extensive array of medical school residency programs and has long been on the cutting edge of research on trauma, substance abuse, mental illness, and aging. More recently, the VA has made significant inroads in the development of health care system quality assessment and improvement methods that are both innovative and applicable to the improvement of health care quality among nongovernmental health care systems (Kizer et al., 2000). Although evidence of the benefits of military service on lifetime earnings and education is mixed and appears to differ significantly by historical period (Teachman, 2005), there is little question that the VA health care system plays a critical role as the health care safety net for low-income veterans. According to the Congressional Budget Office, in 2009, low-income veterans without qualifying service connected disabilities accounted for 28% of all VA health care system enrollees (CBO, 2010).

Federally Funded Community Health Centers

Although small relative to Medicare, Medicaid, and the VA health care system, federally funded Community Health Centers (CHCs) serve as a critical safety net provider in low-income communities. CHCs are a diverse group of not-for-profit and public health care clinics that are federally funded under provisions of the Public Health Service Act to provide an array of primary health care services to low-income and medically underserved communities.[34] The essential elements that are required of all CHCs as a condition of federal funding include location in a high-need community, the provision of comprehensive primary care services, availability of transportation and language translation services that promote access to health care, a community- and consumer-based governance structure, and fees that are adjusted for patients' ability to pay (HRSA, 2005). Despite an infinitesimal annual budget (by federal standards) of $2.5 billion, during fiscal year 2010 about 19.5 million uninsured and underserved patients received primary care through 1124 CHCs (HRSA, 2012; Medicare Payment Advisory Commission, 2011).

CONCLUDING COMMENTS: THE LARGE PRESENCE OF PUBLIC DOLLARS IN THE FINANCING OF HEALTH CARE

The public role in the financing and provision of health care is not limited to direct care. For example, in 2010, the National Institutes of Health and its subordinate agencies (e.g., the National Institute of Mental Health, National

Institute on Drug Abuse, the National Institute on Aging) were appropriated $30.1 billion—most of these funds for basic and applied research on health and health care (NIH, 2011). During the same recent fiscal year, the Centers for Disease Control and Prevention, another key destination of public health expenditures, was appropriated $10.1 billion (CDC, 2012). These expenditures underscore further the reality that the U.S. health care system, at least in its system of finance, is as much a public system of health care as a private one. The next chapter, which addresses the organization of health care services, will further illustrate the private/public interdependence that characterizes the U.S. health care system.

NOTES

1. The OECD refers to the *Organisation for Economic Co-operation and Development*, an international organization of 30 democratic countries that espouse the common goal of promoting world economic progress, democratic forms of governance, and market economies. The origins of the OECD are in the post–World War II reconstruction of Europe sponsored by the United States and Canada through the Marshall Plan. The OECD is used extensively here as a comparative frame of reference for U.S. health care policies since OECD countries share the common characteristics of democratic government, mature industrial development, and a market economy. However, within the OECD there is significant variation with respect to the government's role in the provision of health care, the distribution of wealth and income, and structure of the social welfare system.
2. The term "medically indigent" refers to persons who encounter catastrophic medical expenditures in the absence of either health insurance or substantial private funds.
3. As is shown in Table 3.1, the major categories of private funding of health care account for 47% of health care consumption expenditures, while the major public programs account for about 42% of health care consumption expenditures. The remainder of health expenditures are covered by a mixture of smaller but very essential private sector and public sector programs, such as the Indian Health Service, worksite health programs sponsored by employers, school-based health care programs, and federally and locally funded maternal and child health programs.
4. We examine the principal reasons for the United States being a laggard in population health relative to its health care expenditures in Chapter 7.
5. While a few other OECD member states (such as Chile, Brazil, Mexico, and South Africa) employ a similar balance between private and public expenditures for health care, they invest far less per capita than the United States in both private and public health care expenditures.
6. The point is made here, as well as in other chapters, that health insurance benefits are purchased either directly from households through insurance premium payments or as a substitute for wages and salary. While there are tax advantages to employer health benefits, they primarily represent a substitute for higher wages.

7. The gross domestic product, or GDP, is defined as the monetary value of all of the goods and services produced within a country over a defined period, typically 1 year. It is employed primarily as a monetary measure of the size of an economy.

8. In 1983 the Medicare hospital payment system changed from a fee-for-service reimbursement system to a "prospective payment system" (PPS), where hospitals were paid based on the DRG (diagnosis-related group) assigned to a patient at the point of hospital discharge in accordance with a set of specified patient diagnostic characteristics. Among other things, this method of payment dramatically reduced the financial incentives of hospitals to provide unnecessary care and services.

9. Individual country comparisons of hospital and physician resources per capita are shown in the chapter that follows, in Table 4.1.

10. Often this is either benign or benevolent, because the physician wants to provide optimal treatment irrespective of cost to the patient. There are of course a variety of economic incentives to providing more rather than less health care, having little to do with what constitutes optimal care.

11. Reinsurance, also a form of stop-loss, refers to an insurance policy that applies to health care expenditures that significantly exceed those anticipated. Employers who self-insure typically allocate only the health care benefit funds that they expect to spend, and then purchase an insurance policy that covers the cost of health care claims that significantly exceed the funds set aside.

12. There will be an extensive discussion on the socioeconomic gradient in health in chapters that follow. Briefly, individual socioeconomic characteristics (education, employment, occupation, and income) are all strongly linked to health through multiple pathways, for example, higher levels of exposure to illness in childhood, poorer nutrition, access to health care, and by some accounts the deleterious effects of discrimination and lower social status. Because lower socioeconomic status (SES) increases the risk of poorer health and lower SES is linked to the likelihood of employment in the small employer sector of the economy, small employers face a significant disadvantage in the insurance market due to the dynamics of adverse selection.

13. This assumption takes into account that patient care decisions typically involve subjective and objective components, and that provider economic incentives hold more sway where the level of subjectivity is high. This is a very benevolent assumption, of course, but a fair one with respect to the far majority of health care providers.

14. For example, the Federal Health Insurance Portability and Accountability Act of 1996 (HIPAA) contains provisions against small employer discrimination. The origins of HIPAA and its sweeping impacts on health care insurance markets and patient care delivery will be discussed at a later point in this chapter.

15. The first of these referenced cases, *Owens v. Storehouse*, involved a $25,000 cap placed on care for AIDS for all employees. The second, *DiFederico v. Rolm Company*, involved allegations of wrongful discharge by an employee who contended that her employment termination was based upon her employer's desire to avoid health and disability insurance benefit obligations. In both of these cases, federal courts established legal precedent for a significant burden on the employee to establish a clear link between the employer's actions and selective abrogation of health care coverage obligations. The specifics of ERISA will be discussed in more detail at a later point in the chapter.

16. The term "profit" is used broadly to refer to the difference between the costs of providing a service and the price paid. Not-for-profit organizations refer to this difference as a return on equity.

17. The terms "prices" and "costs" are both used here, to note the distinction between prices that are paid by an insurance underwriter to a given provider and the costs of providing care if the care is provided by the insuring organization—as in the case of an HMO.

18. An Independent Practice Association (IPA) is an association of providers, most typically physicians, who contract with the HMOs and other managed care organizations to provide care for managed care plan members. The contracts typically involve some level of "risk sharing" by the IPA, meaning that the IPA agrees to furnish some level of care on a capitated basis rather than a fee-for-service basis. Obviously, if the IPA provides care that exceeds that covered by the capitation rate, the IPA membership assumes the financial loss. IPAs permit a member physician to maintain ownership and control over his or her individual practices while providing the physician with the advantages of a corporate structure for the negotiation and administration of managed care contracts (Grumbach, Coffman, Vranizan, Blick, & O'Neil, 1998).

19. Case managers are in some cases selected from other disciplines, as well, but for the purposes stated here, the three disciplines identified are more prevalent.

20. There is an extensive literature pertaining to the iatrogenic risks (risks arising from medical treatment rather than underlying disease processes) of hospital care. See in particular the Institute of Medicine report *To Err Is Human: Building a Safer Health Care System*, issued in 1999 and available through the National Academy Press, Washington, DC.

21. In the pejorative sense, this can be seen or referred to as "assembly line medicine" that discounts the unique nature of each clinical encounter and the autonomous exercise of informed clinical judgment. On the benevolent side, use of clinical protocols reduces the incidence of arbitrary decision making and biased preferences by individual practitioners that ultimately reduce the quality of care. Clinical protocols often entail explicit cost justifications for the probability of achieving a given clinical outcome, which can be viewed as good or bad depending upon the ethical framework of the practitioner.

22. Aptly titled "The Rise and Fall of Managed Care," published in the *Journal of Health and Social Behavior* 2004 (Vol. 45).

23. It should be intuitively clear that HSAs have high potential to "cream off" or favorably select healthier workers, thus raising the average level of insurance risk and costs to workers left in other plans. Since health is highly correlated with SES, it is widely believed that over time the increased prevalence of HSAs will contribute further to the social stratification of health care.

24. This is harsh language, but I believe more accurate than not.

25. COBRA also has provisions that impose serious sanctions on health care facilities that transfer indigent or underinsured patients for reasons that appear to be financial. In hospital jargon, this is referred to as "patient dumping."

26. The full premium cost under COBRA refers to the sum of both the employer and the employee contribution.

27. The central feature of this cost control legislation was the Prospective Payment System (PPS) to hospitals, which changed hospitals from an inherently inflationary

fee-for-service form of reimbursement to a system of reimbursement based on a patient's assignment to any one of roughly 450 Diagnosis Related Groups (DRGs). DRGs are categories of patient characteristics that include such factors as discharge, diagnosis, sex, age, complicating conditions, and procedures performed. The fact that reimbursement is based on a DRG rather than the number of days of hospital care provided, procedures performed, or services used reduces the incentives of doctors and hospitals to provide unnecessary or unbeneficial care.

28. The leading contenders among Medicare reform alternatives will be discussed in greater depth in a later chapter devoted to the general topic of health care system reform.

29. The PPACA approach to Medicare reform will be described and critiqued in detail in the final chapter of the book, which is dedicated to the alternatives and prospects for health care reform.

30. The Hill–Burton Act, previously discussed in Chapter 2 on the history of the U.S. health care system, is a federal program that requires "obligated facilities" (health care facilities including hospitals) that have used federal money for facility reconstruction or modernization to provide free or low-cost health care services to local medically indigent patients.

31. It should be borne in mind, however, that SCHIP emerged in response to the failures of the labor market to secure health insurance benefits for low-income workers and their dependents, as opposed to a triumph of either liberal or socialist ideology.

32. Some of this stigma is introduced directly through the means-based nature of Medicaid, but Medicaid also brings with it the twin disincentives of bureaucracy and low fees to providers—thus adding further impetus to the stigma experienced by Medicaid patients.

33. At the behest of the powerful pharmaceutical industry lobby, the "Medicare Prescription Drug, Improvement and Modernization Act," passed by Congress in 2003, precludes the Medicare program using purchasing power to negotiate more favorable drug pricing.[33] A complete listing of the VA system's eight-level priority system can be accessed at http://www.va.gov/healtheligibility/eligibility.

34. Section 330 of the Public Health Service (PHS) Act, as amended by the Health Centers Consolidated Act of 1996 (P.L. 104–299) and the Safety Net Amendments of 2002.

REFERENCES

AHIP Center for Policy and Research. (2009). *Individual health insurance 2009: A comprehensive survey of premiums, availability and benefits*. Retrieved January 23, 2012, from http://www.ahipresearch.org/pdfs/2009IndividualMarketSurveyFinalReport.pdf

Altman, D. E., & Levitt, L. (2002). The sad history of health care cost containment as told in one chart. *Health Affairs, (W-2)*, 83.

Anderson, G., & Poullier, J. (1999). Health spending, access, and outcomes: Trends in industrialized countries. *Health Affairs, 18*(3), 178–192.

Anderson, G. F., Reinhardt, U. E., Hussey, P. S., & Petrosyan, V. (2003). It's the prices, stupid: Why the United States is so different from other countries. *Health Affairs, 22*(1), 90–105.

Ashton, C. M., Souchek, J., Petersen, N. J., Menke, T. J., Collins, T. C., Kizer, K. W. et al. (2003). Hospital use and survival among veterans affairs beneficiaries. *New England Journal of Medicine, 349*(17), 1637–1646.

Baily, M. A. (2003). Managed care organizations and the rationing problem. *The Hastings Center Report, 33*(1), 34–42.

Biles, B., Dallek, G., & Nicholas, L. H. (2004). Medicare advantage: Dejá Vu all over again? *Health Affairs, (W-4),* 586–697.

Cabral, A. B. (2003). COBRA for state and local governmental plans. *Employee Benefits Journal, 28*(4), 34–38.

CBO. (2007). *The health care system for veterans: An interim report.* Retrieved January 26, 2012, from http://www.cbo.gov/ftpdocs/88xx/doc8892/12-21-VA_Healthcare.pdf

CBO. (2010). *Potential costs of veterans' healthcare.* Retrieved January 26, 2012, from http://www.cbo.gov/ftpdocs/118xx/doc11811/2010_10_7_VAHealthcare.pdf

CDC. (2012). *State of budget and workforce.* Retrieved January 26, 2012, from http://www.cdc.gov/about/stateofcdc/html/budget-workforce.htm

Chirba-Martin, M. A., & Brennan, T. A. (1994). The critical role of ERISA in state health reform. *Health Affairs, 13*(2), 142–156.

Christianson, J. B., Parente, S. T., & Taylor, R. (2002). Defined-contribution health insurance products: Development and prospects. *Health Affairs, 21*(1), 49–64.

CMS. (2004). *Requirements for the group health insurance market; non-federal governmental plans exempt from HIPAA Title I requirements. Final rule.* Washington, DC: Centers for Medicare & Medicaid Services (CMS), HHS.

CMS. (2012). *Medicaid.gov: Eligibility.* Retrieved January 26, 2012, from http://www.medicaid.gov/AffordableCareAct/Provisions/Eligibility.html

Congressional Budget Office. (2010). *Potential costs of Veteran's health care.* Retrieved January 24, 2012, from http://www.cbo.gov/ftpdocs/118xx/doc11811/2010_10_7_VAHealthcare_Summary.pdf

Conwell, L. J. (2002). *The role of health insurance brokers: Providing small employers with a helping hand (no. 57).* Washington, tDC: Center for Studying Health Policy Change.

Dickens, W. T., & Lang, K. (1992). *Labor market segmentation theory: Reconsidering the evidence.* Unpublished manuscript, Cambridge, MA.

Doran, P. A., Dobson, R. H., & Harris, R. G. (2001). *Financial management of health insurance: Forecasting, monitoring and analyzing health plan experience.* Milliman, Tampa, FL.

Forrest, C. B., Weiner, J. P., Fowles, J., Vogeli, C., Frick, K. D., Lemke, K. W. et al. (2001). Self-referral in point-of-service health plans. *JAMA, 285*(17), 2223–2231.

Fries, J. F., Koop, C. E., Beadle, C. E., Cooper, P. P., England, M. J., Greaves, R. F. et al. (1993). Reducing health care costs by reducing the need and demand for medical services. *N. Engl. J. Med., 329*(5), 321–325.

Fuchs, V. R. (2004). Perspective: More variation in use of care, more flat-of-the-curve medicine. *Health Affairs,* var. 104.

Grumbach, K., Coffman, J., Vranizan, K., Blick, N., & O'Neil, E. H. (1998). Independent practice association physician groups in California. *Health Affairs, 17*(3), 227–237.

Hall, M. A. (2000). The geography of health insurance regulation. *Health Affairs, 19*(2), 173–184.

Harrington, S., & Miller, T. (2002). Perspective: Competitive markets for individual health insurance. *Health Affairs,* w2.359.

Hill, I., Courtot, B., & Sullivan, J. (2005). *Ebbing and flowing: Some gains, some losses as SCHIP responds to third year of budget pressure* (Series A, No. A-68). Washington, DC: The Urban Institute.

Holahan, J., & Chen, V. (2011). *Changes in health insurance coverage in the great recession, 2007–2010.* Washington, DC: Kaiser Commission on Medicaid and the Uninsured. Retrieved January 23, 2012, from http://www.kff.org/uninsured/upload/8264.pdf

HRSA. (2005). *Bureau of primary care: Community health centers.* Retrieved July 1, 2005, from http://bphc.hrsa.gov/chc/

HRSA. (2012). *Health center data.* Retrieved January 26, 2012, from http://bphc.hrsa.gov/healthcenterdatastatistics/index.html

Kaiser Family Foundation. (2010). *Kaiser/HRET survey of employer sponsored health benefits.* Retrieved January 23, 2012, from http://facts.kff.org/results.aspx?view=slides&topic=3

Kaiser Family Foundation. (2011a). *Kaiser/HRET survey of employer sponsored health benefits.* Retrieved January 23, 2012, from http://kff.org/pdf/2011/8225.pdf

Kaiser Family Foundation. (2011b). *Health care on a budget: The financial burden of health spending by medicare households an updated analysis of health care spending as a share of total household spending.* Retrieved January 25, 2012, from http://www.kff.org/medicare/upload/8171.pdf

Kaiser Family Foundation. (2011c). *Dual eligibles: Medicaid's role for low-income medicare beneficiaries.* Retrieved January 25, 2012, from http://www.kff.org/medicaid/upload/4091-08.pdf

Kizer, K., Demakis, J., & Feussner, J. (2000). Reinventing VA health care: Systematizing quality improvement and quality innovation [VA's Quality Enhancement Research Initiative]. *Medical Care, 38*(6 (Special Supp)), 7–16.

Marmor, T., & Oberlander, J. (1998). Rethinking medicare reform. *Health Affairs, 17*(1), 52–68.

Martin, A., Lassman, D., Washington, B., & Catlin, A. (2012). Growth in US health expenditures remained slow in 2010; Health share of gross domestic product was unchanged from 2009. *Health Affairs, 31*(1), 208–219.

Marquis, M. S., & Long, S. H. (2000). Who helps employers design their health insurance benefits? *Health Affairs, 19*(1), 133–138.

Mechanic, D. (2004). The rise and fall of managed care. *Journal of Health and Social Behavior, 45*(1), 76–86.

Medicare Board of Trustees. (2011). *2011 Annual report of the board of trustees of the federal hospital insurance and federal supplementary medical insurance trust funds.* Retrieved January 25, 2012, from https://www.cms.gov/ReportsTrustFunds/downloads/tr2011.pdf

Medicare Payment Advisory Commission. (2011). *Report to the congress: Medicare and the health care delivery system (Chapter 6, Federally Qualified Health Centers).* Retrieved January 26, 2012, from http://www.medpac.gov/chapters/Jun11_Ch06.pdf

NIH. (2011). *NIH budget request: Overview by institute.* Retrieved January 26, 2012, from http://www.nih.gov/about/director/budgetrequest/NIH_BIB_020911.pdf

National Health Policy Forum. (2011). *The basics: Medicaid financing.* Retrieved January 26, 2012, from http://www.nhpf.org/library/the-basics/Basics_ MedicaidFinancing_02-04-11.pdf

OECD. (2011). *Health at a glance: 2011 indicators.* Retrieved January 18, 2012, from http://www.oecd.org/dataoecd/24/8/49084488.pdf

OECD. (2012). *Health at a glance 2011.* Figure 7.1.1 Total health expenditure per capita, public and private, 2009 (or nearest year). Retrieved January 11, 2012, from http:// www.oecd-ilibrary.org/docserver/download/fulltext/8111101ec060.pdf?expires= 1326318062&id=id&accname=guest&checksum=682ACEB99B0F9CFCE97C626CE AFA3F03

Robinson, J. C. (1999). The future of managed care organization. *Health Affairs, 18*(2), 7–24.

Scott, F. A., Berger, M. C., & Black, D. A. (1989). Effects of the tax treatment of fringe benefits on labor market segmentation. *Industrial and Labor Relations Review, 42*(2), 216–229.

Starr, P. (1982). *The social transformation of American medicine.* New York: Basic Books.

Starr, P. (1992). *The logic of health care reform.* Knoxville, TN: Whittle Direct Books.

Teachman, J. (2005). Military service in the Vietnam era and educational attainment. *Sociology of Education, 78*(1), 50–69.

Temchine, D. (2010). *The impact of the Patient Protection and Affordable Care Act on self-insured ERISA health and welfare benefit plans: A guide for administrators of self-insured plans.* Retrieved January 23, 2012, from http://www.ebglaw.com/files/40532_ Temchine-PPACA-WHITE-PAPER-ADMINISTRATORS.pdf

U. S. Court of Appeals Third Circuit. (2000). *DiFederico v. Rolm Company, 201 F.3d 200.*

U.S. Court of Appeals Eleventh Circuit. (1993). *Owens v. Storehouse, Inc.*

Woolhandler, S., Campbell, T., & Himmelstein, D. (2003). Costs of health care administration in the United States and Canada. *New England Journal of Medicine, 349,* 768–775.

Xirasagar, S., Samuels, M., Stoskopf, C., Shrader, W., Hussey, J., Saunders, R. et al. (2004). Small group health insurance: Ranking the states on the depth of reform, 1999. *Journal of Health and Social Policy, 19*(1), 1–35.

CHAPTER FOUR

THE CONTEMPORARY ORGANIZATION OF HEALTH CARE: HEALTH CARE SERVICES AND UTILIZATION

THE MIXED PUBLIC/PRIVATE STRUCTURE OF THE U.S. HEALTH CARE SYSTEM

*T*he U.S. health care system is a highly complex and often volatile mixture of free enterprise, philanthropy, and public sector health care. It is also the most expensive health care system in the world both in per capita dollars spent and in the proportion of national economic output spent on health care. The purpose of this chapter is to provide a general overview of the organizational structure of the U.S. health care system, in particular, what the dollars allocated to health care purchase in terms of the facilities, services, technologies, and human resources that comprise the resources of the health care system. Significant attention will also be devoted to the structure of the health care "safety net"—generally defined as the clinics, hospitals, and individual health care providers that care for a disproportionate share of the poor, the uninsured, those afflicted by stigmatizing health conditions, and persons otherwise isolated from the mainstream health care system.

A good beginning point to a general grasp of the organization of the U.S. health care system is a brief comparison between the U.S. health care system and the health care systems of other democracies with market economies. Undertaking even a very basic comparison yields some surprising findings. For example, although it is widely known that the United States allocates more of its economic output to health care than all other countries, the United States is significantly below the OECD[1] average in the hospital and physician resources available to provide health care to its citizens (see the first and final two columns of Table 4.1).

Table 4.1 *Brief Comparative Overview of Expenditures and Resources: The United States vs Other OECD Countries*[a]

OECD Country	Health Care as Percent of GDP	Percent Expenditures Publicly Financed	Health Expenditures Per Capita USD PPP	Percent Expenditures for Pharmaceuticals	Acute Care Hospital Beds/ 1000 Persons	Practicing Physicians/ 1000 Persons
United States	16.0	48.0	7538	12.5	2.7	2.4
France	11.2	77.8	3696	16.9	3.5	3.3
Belgium	11.1	75.0	3995	16.4	4.3	3.0
Switzerland	10.7	59.1	4627	10.3	3.3	3.8
Germany	10.5	76.8	3737	15.6	5.7	3.6
Austria	10.5	76.9	3970	14.1	5.6	4.6
Canada	10.4	70.2	4079	18.1	3.3	2.4
New Zealand	9.9	80.4	2685	9.6	2.2	2.5
Netherlands	9.9	85.0	4063	9.6	2.9	2.9
Sweden	9.4	81.9	3470	13.9	2.8	3.7
OECD Member Average	11.3	72.1	4291	14.2	3.8	3.2

Source: OECD Health Data 2010 and 2011, *Tables of health, spending and resources and health at a glance.* Paris: OECD.
[a]The countries shown are the 10 that spend the highest proportion of their gross domestic product (GDP) on health care. Statistics shown encompass estimates for the years 2007–2009.

Another nonintuitive finding from the OECD comparisons pertains to pharmaceutical expenditures. Despite the escalating controversy that surrounds rising prescription drug prices in the United States and the pricing practices of the pharmaceutical industry, relative to all other OECD countries, the *share* of the health care dollar spent on prescription drugs is actually below that of the OECD average. However, this comparison does not adjust for the large difference in the total dollars spent per capita on health care by U.S. citizens relative to all other OECD countries. When this is considered it is indeed the case that U.S. citizens *spend more dollars* on prescription drugs than citizens from the other OECD countries. This example illustrates the point that when considering how a health care system is organized, both the total amount of expenditures allocated to different parts of the health care system and the distribution of those expenditures should be taken into account.

More consistent with common perceptions of the U.S. health care system is the magnitude of the gap between the share of health care costs that are publicly financed in the United States and the publicly financed share in other countries. That is, only about 48 cents of the U.S. health care dollar comes from government programs such as Medicare, Medicaid, and health care benefits for veterans, while the OECD average is 72 cents of every dollar. Among the OECD member states, only the United States and Mexico have less than half of health care expenditures funded by public dollars (OECD, 2011). In the case of the United States, the larger share of health care system expenditures is assumed by a combination of the private health care insurance market (30.2%) and out-of-pocket expenditures by health care consumers (9.6%).[2]

An additional distinctive feature of the U.S. health care system is that, in contrast to the general pattern among OECD member states, the United States does not ensure health care coverage for all of its citizens. Although several OECD member states have a mixture of public and private insurance funds for the coverage of health care, the United States is one of the few OECD countries that does not provide access to publicly funded health care for all persons that lack other sources of health insurance. The other exceptions among OECD member states are countries that are considerably less affluent than the United States.

One consequence of the lack of universal health insurance coverage is the reinforcement of a *two-tiered* system of health care in the United States; one system for the segment of the population with adequate health care insurance coverage and another for those dependent upon either inadequate public subsidies for health care or "charity care" from the limited number of health care providers willing to provide it.[3] Although almost all countries have some semblance of a two-tiered health care system that privileges the more affluent and influential, in the United States, the two-tiered structure of the health care system is particularly pronounced.

THE RESOURCES OF THE U.S. SYSTEM: FACILITIES, TECHNOLOGY, AND HUMAN RESOURCES

Facilities

Hospitals and Hospital Systems

As mentioned in the previous chapter, the American hospital and hospital system industry[4] (HHSI) is divided into three distinct ownership sectors: the public sector, the voluntary sector, and the proprietary sector. Public hospitals are those that are owned and operated by local, state, and federal government agencies. They include hospital and hospital systems operated by the county and municipal governments, state universities, state and federal prison hospitals, the Veterans Administration (VA), the various branches of the military, and the Indian Health Service (2005). The voluntary sector of the HHSI is comprised of hospitals and hospital systems that are owned and operated as not-for-profit organizations by religious, civic, and philanthropic organizations for the broad purpose of providing benefits to the community. The proprietary sector of the HHSI operates its facilities to make profit that is returned to investors, which may be a small group of investors or a publicly traded corporation.

Statistics on Hospital Ownership

Of the 5795 hospitals in the United States in 2009, there were 211 hospitals operated by the federal government (AHA, 2010). Most of the remaining hospitals (5008) are classified as *community hospitals*, that is, nonfederal, short-term general and specialty hospitals that provide services to the general public (Shi & Singh, 2001).

As Figure 4.1 shows, the voluntary sector of the hospital industry in the United States dominates the industry, despite growth over the past two decades in the proportion of hospitals owned by the proprietary sector. The state and local government sector, although only about a fifth of the hospital industry, is crucial because local and state government hospitals serve a much higher relative proportion of the poor and uninsured than either the voluntary or the proprietary sectors of the hospital industry (GAO, 2005b).

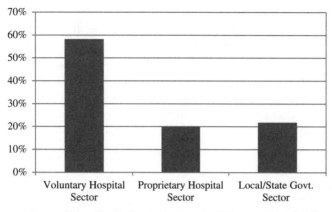

Source: Kaiser Family Foundation, statehealthfacts.org, Hospitals by Ownership Type, 2009.

Figure 4.1 *Proportion of U.S. hospitals by ownership category, 2009.*

The for-profit sector of the hospital industry is the smallest nationally, however, in some parts of the United States investor-owned hospitals and hospital systems have a large market share. This tends to be a regional phenomenon among states in the South and Southwest. The state with the highest proportion of investor-owned hospitals is Florida, where 49.1% of hospitals belong to the proprietary sector (Kaiser Family Foundation, 2011c). Although many Americans are strongly opposed to the idea that hospitals should exist for the purpose of generating profits to investors, there is no question that in large parts of the country the idea is firmly entrenched. It is also the case, when it comes to dollars returned in the form of tangible community benefits like uncompensated care for the poor and uninsured, that the not-for-profit hospitals in the voluntary sector do not behave in ways that appear to clearly justify their tax-exempt status. For example, in an analysis of the relationship between hospital ownership and the proportion of operating expenses allocated to uncompensated care in five representative states, the U.S. Government Accountability Office (GAO) found that there was a relatively small difference between the voluntary and the proprietary sector in the dollars contributed to care for the poor and the uninsured (GAO, 2005b). In fact, a large number of lawsuits have been filed against not-for-profit hospitals, contending that they have failed to fulfill their charitable obligations (Horowitz, 2005).

TYPES OF HOSPITALS. Hospitals can be classified and made distinct from one another in a variety of ways, but the most common classifications applied pertain to acute short-term versus long-term care, acute specialty care versus acute general service hospitals, the level of care provided (secondary versus tertiary care hospitals), teaching versus nonteaching hospitals, number of licensed beds, and urban versus rural location. Of the specialty care hospitals, the most common are psychiatric hospitals (according to the American Hospital Association's 2009 survey, there are 444 nonfederal psychiatric hospitals nationwide (AHA, 2010). Nonpsychiatric long-term care hospitals tend to provide care that is too complex and intensive for custodial long-term care facilities such as nursing homes; for example, hospitals that provide care for patients that are dependent upon artificial respirators. General service hospitals are the most common type, and these hospitals provide medical and surgical services that include an array of highly utilized surgical specializations, internal medicine subspecialties (e.g., gastroenterology, cardiology, and pulmonary medicine), obstetrics and gynecology, and emergency medicine. Not all general service hospitals provide the full array of medical and surgical services. In fact, what any hospital provides is determined by such factors as market demand for particular services, local competition among hospitals, and the decisions of state and community health planning authorities.

Hospitals are also differentiated by the *level* of care provided. Most community hospitals in the United States provide what is termed *primary care* and *secondary care*, and a minority of hospitals provides what is termed *tertiary* care. Primary care, broadly speaking, refers to the routine care that is provided for the common health care needs that make up the brunt of clinical encounters between doctor and patient. Examples include short-term respiratory infections, small injuries, well-baby care, and control of hypertensive disease. Secondary care refers generally to the health services provided by a specialist and the use of more advanced diagnostic and treatment technologies. However, secondary care also typically involves the diagnosis and treatment of a relatively common array of both serious (life threatening or disabling) and ordinarily nonserious health conditions or events (e.g., childbirth, tonsillectomy). Tertiary care, on the other hand, typically involves diagnosis and treatment of more rare and complex diseases or injuries that require highly specialized practitioners and technologies (e.g., neonatal intensive care, organ transplantation).[5]

Hospital Systems

Over the past three decades the hospital industry in the United States has been in a consolidation trend that favored the emergence of multihospital systems over the survival of independently operated hospitals. The definition of a multihospital system employed by the American Hospital Association involves provider relationships where "two or more hospitals are owned, leased, sponsored, or contractually managed by a central organization" (Shi & Singh, 2001, p. 290). Historically, most multihospital systems have existed in either the government or not-for-profit sectors of the industry. It is also the case that, in the last decade, most of the consolidation of the hospital industry has taken place in the not-for-profit sector. This is not to suggest that for-profit hospital corporations are not large players among hospital systems—they are. For example, the Tenet Healthcare Corporation operates 49 acute care hospitals with 31,428 licensed beds in 11 states and Healthcare Corporation of America operates 164 hospitals in 20 states (Hospital Corporation of America, 2011; Tenet Healthcare Corporation, 2011).

Historically, the earliest hospital systems were created primarily through expansion into communities that did not have hospitals, an example being the Sisters of Providence hospital system on the West Coast that emerged in the latter half of the 19th century. In more recent decades, hospital systems developed through mergers and acquisitions (Cuellar & Gertler, 2003). Mergers are transactions in which separate hospitals come together under a shared license, whereas acquisitions involve the acquired hospitals' retention of their individual licenses under a common governing body (Cuellar & Gertler, 2003, p. 77). The hospitals that merge into a multihospital system generally involve facilities within the same community. Hospitals merge with each other to pursue survival and competitive advantage through such mechanisms as consolidation of purchasing power, reductions in duplication, and the pooling of capital essential to modernization. Hospitals that are acquired may become a part of an existent local hospital system, or they may be acquired by an outside multihospital system that is seeking expansion into a new health care market (Cuellar & Gertler, 2003). Although it is too soon to sound the death knell of the independent community hospital, in the most recent decade, independent hospitals have become a minority (Cuellar & Gertler, 2003, p. 79).

For a variety or reasons, it seems safe to assume that the consolidation trend toward multihospital systems will continue. Aside from the reasons just cited, multihospital systems have the advantage of "vertical integration"—providing the complete array of health care services from prevention to chronic illness management and long-term care under a single organizational umbrella. Aside from the competitive advantages gained in purchasing of supplies, equipment, and services, multihospital services are also in a better position than solo hospitals in the negotiation of favorable contracts with the insurance plans and employer groups that are primary purchasers of their services. Finally, larger multihospital systems also have better capacity to accommodate or even play a direct role in sponsoring an array of health insurance products capable of capturing different segments of the health insurance market.

RECENT TRENDS IN HOSPITAL RESOURCES. Table 4.2 provides a general overview of the hospital facility resources over the most recent 10-year period for which federal data on hospitals are available (National Center for Health Statistics, 2011). As Table 4.2 shows, there is a general downward trend in the number of hospitals and the number of hospital beds in the United States, and also occupancy rates. These trends reflect a broad shrinkage of the hospital industry that has occurred over the past 30 years due to two major, highly interactive factors: advances in medicine and the advances in systems of managed care. In simplified terms, advances in medicine permitted more of health care to be provided on an outpatient basis, and the evolvement of managed care provided the health care information systems and financial incentives that were the essential preconditions and impetus necessary for such widespread institutional change. It should also be appreciated that advances in medicine and the evolvement of managed care are interactive. In essence, advances in managed care information and financing create knowledge and incentives for advancements in medicine, which in turn lead to further adaptation in systems of managed care.

Although the inpatient care side of the hospital industry has contracted significantly over the past three decades (a 19% reduction in hospitals and a 35% reduction in the number of hospital beds), there are some areas of growth. For example, over this same period, the for-profit sector of the hospital industry has grown by 27% in the number of hospitals and by 65% in the number of hospital beds (National Center for Health Statistics, 2011).

Another trend over most of the past decade has been a gradual rise in hospital occupancy rates after a long period of significant decline. The rise in occupancy rates among hospitals in the for-profit sector has been particularly vigorous, underscoring the observation from hospital industry analysts that the for-profit sector is better able to hone its marketing strategies to

Table 4.2 *Hospitals, Hospital Beds, and Occupancy Rates: 1975–2008*

	1975	1980	1990	2000	2008
Hospitals	7156	6965	6649	5810	5815
Hospital beds	1,465,828	1,364,516	1,213,327	983,628	951,045
Occupancy rate	76.7	77.7	69.5	66.1	68.2

Source: Table 113. *Health, United States, 2010.* Table 113, Hospitals, beds, and size of hospital: United States, selected years 1975–2008. National Center for Health Statistics. Hyattsville, MD. 2011.

profitable use of resources (Horowitz, 2005). Although there was a dramatic decline in the occupancy rates of federal hospitals in recent decades, which in part reflected a significant shift toward ambulatory health care management of both acute and chronic diseases among the VA system, since the beginning of the Iraq War in 2003 there has been a 20% increase in the number of VA hospital admissions (Department of Veterans Affairs, 2012).[6]

GEOGRAPHIC DISTRIBUTION OF HOSPITAL RESOURCES. The conventional statistic for describing the distribution of hospital resources is the number of community hospital beds per 1000 persons in a given geographic entity, such as cities, metropolitan areas, counties, states, and sovereign nations. Within the United States, there is wide variation in the number of hospital beds per thousand persons no matter what geographic unit is considered. In large part, the hospital resources in a given geographic area are as much a matter of local history, politics, and the socioeconomic distribution as they are a matter of population characteristics that are more predictive of the need for hospital care—such as the age distribution and prevalence of disease. Other factors that have influenced geographic variation in the number of hospital beds/1000 persons are geographic variations in the diffusion of alternatives to hospital care (e.g., outpatient diagnostic and surgical centers) and variations in standards of medical practice that impact hospital utilization.

In order to offer a general idea of the degree to which there are significant geographic variations in hospital resources and utilization of hospital services, Table 4.3 shows state-by-state variations for 10 selected states. For example, the state with the highest number of beds/1000 is South Dakota (5.1 beds/1000) and the state with the fewest is Washington (1.7/1000). Differences in average length of stay among states are also quite dramatic, ranging from a high of 9.8 days per hospital stay in South Dakota to a low of 4.4 days in Oregon. In general, the trend nationally over the past couple of decades has been a dramatic decline in the average length of hospital stays, which in turn has contributed to the decline in the number of hospitals and hospital beds shown previously in Table 4.2.

For the most part, these trends in the decline of hospital resources reflect advancements in the delivery of health care. However, in many parts of the United States, communities with the highest level of population morbidity (disease and injury) have the fewest hospital beds/1000 persons available. This problem has long been known to be common to low-income rural communities, but analysis by Andrulis and Duchon (2005) highlights this issue among low-income suburban areas. As Figure 4.2 shows, the distribution of hospital utilization and resources is very much a function of a given suburban

Table 4.3 *Average Length of Hospital Stays and Hospital Beds/1000 Persons, by Selected States, 2009*

State	Average Length of Stay	Beds/1000 Persons
Oregon	4.4	1.8
Washington	4.5	1.7
Illinois	5.0	2.7
Ohio	5.1	2.9
Michigan	5.2	2.5
Virginia	5.5	2.3
Alaska	5.9	2.3
Georgia	6.3	2.6
New York	6.9	3.2
South Dakota	9.8	5.1
Average for United States	**5.7**	**2.9**

Note: Data pertain only to community hospitals.
Sources: Data from AHA 2009 Annual Servey of Hospitals (2009). State Comparisons: Average Length of Stay in Community Hospital Units by State-2008 and Kaiser Family Foundation. (2009). Statehealthfacts.org. Beds per Thousand Population 2008.

area's poverty level. Were the number of hospital visits, admissions, and staffed beds an exact function of the size of the local population, all of the bars shown in Figure 4.2 for the utilization and resource percentages would be in perfect alignment with the population percentages living in low- and high-poverty suburbs. Instead, what the pattern reveals is a strongly disproportionate representation of hospital visits, hospital admissions, and hospital beds in the suburbs that have low levels of poverty.

Specific to hospital resources, the suburbs with the lowest poverty levels contain 26% of the population but account for 42% of the hospital beds and 44% of hospital admissions. Generally, similar patterns are shown for hospital emergency department visits and outpatient visits. Given the well-documented higher prevalence of disease and premature death among the poor, it is hard to escape the conclusion that, to a large extent, the distribution of hospital resources in the United States is a matter of population wealth rather than population health.

HOSPITAL UTILIZATION. Nationwide, there are 118 hospital admissions per 1000 persons annually to community hospitals (Kaiser Family Foundation, 2011b). However, admission rates vary dramatically by geographic location due to a number of factors, all of which can be considered either demand side factors or supply side factors. On the demand side are population

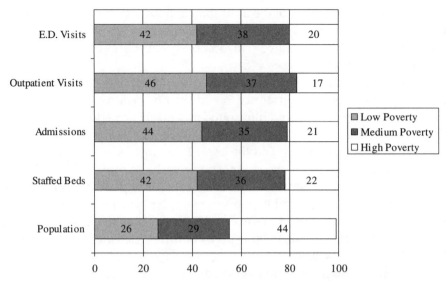

Source: Data from Andrulis, D. P., & Duchon, L. M. (2005). *Hospital care in the 100 largest cities and their suburbs, 1996–2002: Implications for the future of the hospital safety net in metropolitan America.* New York, NY: SUNY Downstate Medical Center. Chart 4: Suburbs of 100 Largest Cities by Poverty Level: Distribution of 2000 Population Compared with Distribution of Hospital Beds and Utilization, 2002.

Figure 4.2 *Percentage distribution of hospital visits, admissions, and staffed beds in suburbs of 100 largest cities by suburban poverty level, 2002.*

health factors including the age distribution, socioeconomic status distribution, the prevalence and distribution of disease, health insurance coverage, and cultural norms that influence the demand for health care. On the supply side are such factors as hospital beds and related staffing resources, physicians who specialize in hospital care, and diagnostic and treatment technology capable of yielding health benefits. Notably, a significant component of hospital utilization pertains to local area standards of practice pertaining to the diagnosis and management of injury and disease. Among the states, the rates of hospital admission vary from a low of 82.7/1000 persons annually in Vermont, to a high of 156/1000 persons in West Virginia (Kaiser Family Foundation, 2011b). Patterns of hospital utilization are also reported and analyzed in a variety of ways, including by discharge diagnosis, by procedure(s) performed, by year, and by demographic characteristics such as age, sex, race, and nativity.

As implied by the decline in hospital beds over the past decade shown previously in Table 4.2, hospital utilization rates have also declined over the same period. One way of accounting for the reasons for the decline is to examine changes over time in the utilization of hospital diagnostic and surgical procedures. Shown in Table 4.4 are the changes in relatively common diagnostic and surgical procedures that occurred in U.S. hospitals during the recent two decades.

As Table 4.4 shows, the annual rates of hospitalizations for all diagnostic and surgical procedures performed on adults declined by 10.9%, with the largest declines in CT scan and ultrasound diagnostic procedures. In contrast, there was a dramatic rise in the rate (per 10,000 persons) in hospital stays for joint replacements of the hip and the knee. To a large extent, the downward trend in hospital stays for the diagnostic procedures represent the shift of these technologies over time to ambulatory care settings. On the other hand, the rise in hospital stays for hip and knee joint replacements suggests more prevalent use of these procedures to counter the degenerative effects of aging.

To a significant extent, the prospects for future increases or decreases in hospital utilization will be an outcome of two opposing trends: the rise in the general demand for health care that accompanies the aging of the population and a countertrend that is driven by innovations in health care technology and other advances in medicine that reduce the demand for hospital care. Possibly of even more significance might be changes in the Medicare program in response to either the Patient Protection and Affordable Care Act or other health reform actions by congress may propel the Medicare program toward a significant transformation of the program's benefits and risk structure. Given the large role of Medicare as a payment source for hospital care, any broad changes in this program will in one way or the other significantly influence hospital utilization.[7]

AMBULATORY CARE FACILITIES. The largest sector of the U.S. health care system is that committed to various forms of ambulatory care. Ambulatory care is health care that is delivered to persons who are classified as outpatients (not confined to a hospital or classified as an inpatient) at the time care is provided. As such, ambulatory services include the offices of such licensed health care practitioners as physicians, dentists, physical therapists, chiropractors, optometrists, and various kinds of mental health care professionals (e.g., psychologists, social workers, and psychiatric nurse practitioners). The ambulatory care sector of the health care industry also includes diagnostic laboratories, diagnostic imaging centers (e.g., CT and MRI scanners), radiation therapy centers, family planning clinics, and the entire home health care industry. Although the term "ambulatory" implies the capacity to move about rather than being bedridden, as applied to the organization of the health care industry, "ambulatory care" refers to care other than that

Table 4.4 Discharges With at Least One Procedure in Nonfederal Short-Stay Hospitals, Persons 18 and Over: United States, Selected Years 1990 through 2009 (Per 10,000 Persons)

	1990[a]	2009	Percent Change
Hospital discharges with at least one procedure, age adjusted[b,c]	1,020.1	908.8	−10.9%
Hospital discharges with at least one procedure, crude[b]	1,006.4	920.0	−8.6%
Operations on vessels of heart	28.3	36.0	27.2%
Coronary angioplasty or arthrectomy	14.0	25.6	82.9%
Coronary artery bypass graft (CABG)	14.1	10.5	−25.5%
Cardiac catheterization	52.1	46.1	−11.5%
Pacemaker	8.6	9.2	7.0%
Carotid (neck arteries) endarterectomy	3.6	4.0	11.1%
Endoscopy of small intestine	40.8	45.7	12.0%
Endoscopy of large intestine	27.9	21.9	−21.5%
Gall bladder removal.	27.9	18.4	−34.1%
Treatment of intra-abdominal scar tissue	17.0	15.1	−11.2%
Reduction of fracture	27.6	22.8	−17.4%
Excision of intervertebral disc and spinal fusion	18.7	22.3	19.3%

(continued)

TABLE 4.4 *Discharges With at Least One Procedure in Nonfederal Short-Stay Hospitals, Persons 18 and Over: United States, Selected Years 1990 through 2009 (Per 10,000 Persons)* *(continued)*

	1990[a]	2009	Percent Change
Total hip replacement	6.4	13.8	115.6%
Partial hip replacement	4.8	13.3	177.1%
Total knee replacement	6.7	28.0	317.9%
CAT scan	68.4	*17.1	−75.0%
Arteriography and angiocardiography with contrast	59.7	56.4	−5.5%
Diagnostic ultrasound	72.3	34.7	−52.0%
Magnetic resonance imaging	9.5	*10.1	6.3%
Mechanical ventilation	17.6	32.9	86.9%

*Estimates are considered unreliable. Data preceded by an asterisk have a relative standard error (RSE) of 20%–30%. Data not shown have an RSE of greater than 30%.

[a]Starting with 2008 data, the sample of nonfederal short-stay hospitals was cut in half. This smaller sample size has increased standard errors. Therefore, caution should be exercised in interpreting trends in these data. See Appendix I, National Hospital Discharge Survey (NHDS).

[b]Includes discharges for procedures not shown separately.

[c]Estimates are age-adjusted to the year 2000 standard population using five age groups: 18–44 years, 45–54 years, 55–64 years, 65–74 years, and 75 years and over.

Source: Health, United States 2010, Table 103. Discharges with at least one procedure in nonfederal short-stay hospitals, by sex, age, and selected procedures: United States, selected years 1990 through 2008–2009. Centers for Disease Control and Prevention 1600 Clifton Rd. Atlanta, GA.

provided to inpatients of institutions such as hospitals, nursing homes, and inpatient hospices.

Table 4.5 provides a general overview of the ambulatory care sector of the U.S. health care system. The table delineates the facilities and annual revenue by six major areas: physicians' offices, nonphysician provider offices, outpatient care centers, medical laboratories and diagnostic imaging centers, and a general category for all other health care services (e.g., ambulance services, blood banks). While the physicians' offices are the dominant component of the ambulatory care sector of the health care industry, it should be noted that physicians' offices typically employ large numbers of staff in the allied health professions (e.g., registered nurses, physician assistants, physical and occupational therapists, medical technologists, and social workers) as well as support staff (e.g., medical assistants, medical record technicians). The trend for physicians' offices to be ever larger employers of nonphysician health care workers reflects the evolvement of medical practice in the United States from the traditional independent medical free enterprise model to multispecialty group practices that provide a broad array of diagnostic and therapeutic services.

NURSING HOMES AND OTHER LONG-TERM CARE FACILITIES. Although the hospital and ambulatory care components of the U.S. health care system provide services to the chronically ill and disabled populations, for the most part hospital and ambulatory health care resources remain organized around an acute care paradigm. In essence, this means that the organization of the hospital and ambulatory services sectors of the health care system is dominated by an implicit assumption that the diagnostic and treatment process is immediate problem-focused and short term. In contrast, the long-term care component of the health care system is organized around the provision of health care over a sustained period of time for health conditions that are chronic and disabling in nature (Kane, Kane, & Ladd, 1998). In addition, long-term facilities, services, and funding mechanisms are primarily focused on optimal functioning and quality of life as opposed to cure.

For a variety of historical reasons, the dominant mode of provision of long-term care services has been institutional care. That is, over much of U.S. history care for persons with functional limitations that strain the resources of family and community (or significantly challenge prevailing notions of acceptable appearance and behavior) has been the province of long-term psychiatric hospitals (asylums), nursing homes, and residential care facilities. Despite the progress that has been made over the past 50 years in the "de-institutionalization" of long-term care services, nursing homes and other types of residential care facilities remain central to the provision of long-term care in

Table 4.5 *Ambulatory Care Sector of the Health Care System: Facilities, Annual Revenue, and Paid Employees (Year 2007)*

Ambulatory Health Care Services	Employers	Annual Revenue (in thousands)
Offices of Physicians	**406,887**	**$352,531,923**
Offices of physicians (mental health specialists)	358,527	$345,720,419
Offices of physicians (nonmental health specialists)	48,360	$6,811,504
Offices of Nonphysician Practitioners	**650,887**	**$161,690,417**
Offices of dentists	166,512	$96,819,951
Offices of chiropractors	62,267	$11,428,127
Offices of optometrists	32,619	$11,205,807
Offices of mental health practitioners (except physicians)	111,575	$9,181,008
Offices of physical, occupational, and speech therapists and audiologists	94,986	$20,222,120
Offices all other health practitioners	182,928	$12,833,404
Outpatient Care Centers	**29,776**	**$74,091,852**
Family planning centers	2275	$1,796,743
Outpatient mental health and substance abuse centers	8848	$12,066,788
HMO medical centers	521	$5,362,234
Kidney dialysis centers	4278	$12,359,206
Freestanding ambulatory surgical and emergency centers	4896	$15,420,096
All other outpatient care centers	8958	$27,086,785
Medical Laboratories and Diagnostic Imaging Centers	**33,196**	**$41,296,277**
Home Health Care Services	**23,070**	**$47,617,015**
Other Ambulatory Health Care Services	**9358**	**$26,136,069**
Ambulance services	4490	$9,951,022
Blood and organ banks	1267	$8,913,726
All other miscellaneous ambulatory health care services	3601	$7,271,321

Source: Data extracted from U.S. Census Bureau. 2007 Economic Census; Ambulatory Health Care Services NAICS 62199

the United States and a significant component of the U.S. health care system. For example, of the most recent (2009) estimates, the number of certified nursing facilities by the Henry J. Kaiser Family Foundation places the number of these facilities in the United States at 15,568, and the number of their residents at 1.4 million (Kaiser Family Foundation, 2012).[8] The far majority of the residents of these facilities are elderly adults, about 4% of the population of Americans age 65+. It should be noted, however, that throughout most of the United States, the criteria for admission to these facilities are the level of functional disablement and need for nursing assistance as opposed specifically to age—thus, certified nursing facilities also provide care for persons that are disabled primarily by injury, chronic disease, retardation, or mental illness.

Compared with hospitals, the other institutional component of the health care system, the nursing home and residential care component has a much higher proportion of its facilities owned and operated by for-profit partnerships and corporations. This is particularly the case for nursing homes and retirement homes (the latter shown in Table 4.6 as "homes for the elderly"). Of all the nursing homes in the United States, approximately two-thirds are owned and operated as for-profit entities (Kaiser Family Foundation, 2011a).

A brief statistical summary of the resources allocated to the nursing home and residential care component of the health care system is shown in Table 4.6. Community care facilities account for the largest share of the institutional long-term care services shown in the table ($109 billion in revenue), followed by the dollars spent on nursing care facilities for the elderly ~($26.6 billion). This is in contrast to the prior (2002) Economic Census report, when nursing care facilities had been the dominant institutional care provider. This change reflects a long-term care industry evolvement toward less "medicalized" residential settings for the institutional care of the nation's elderly as alternative to the traditional nursing home.

Technology

Health care technology can be broadly defined as the practical application of knowledge gained from shared experience and scientific research to the delivery of health care (Shi & Singh, 2001, p. 155).[9] Thought of in this way, health care technology encompasses both "hard technologies" in the form of material devices such as CT scanners, laser knives, and kidney dialysis machines, and "soft technologies" in the form of procedures, protocols, and ways of organizing, disseminating, and applying large volumes of complex information to the delivery of health care. Although not completely inclusive, one way to conceptualize health care technology is to delineate the forms

Table 4.6 *Nursing Home and Residential Care Sector of the Health Care System: Facilities, Annual Revenue, and Paid Employees (Year 2007)*

	Facilities	Revenue (in thousands)	Paid Employees
Nursing and residential care facilities	76,395	$169,059,857	3,070,693
Nursing care facilities	16,320	$92,516,564	1,591,190
Residential mental retardation, mental health, and substance abuse facilities	33,113	$26,966,946	594,679
Residential mental retardation facilities	26,273	$18,274,946	445,950
Residential mental health and substance abuse facilities	6840	$8,692,000	148,729
Community care facilities for the elderly	59,591	$109,078,943	2,037,492
Continuing care retirement communities	5939	$26,029,696	442,219
Residential care facilities for the elderly	20,831	$41,237,824	732,560
Homes for the elderly	14,892	$15,208,128	290,341

Source: Data extracted from U.S. Census Bureau. (2011). *2007 Economic Census: Homes for the Elderly* -NAICS 623312. Washington DC: U.S. Department of Commerce.

that it takes by information systems, diagnostic technology, and treatment technology.

Information Systems

Health care information systems involve the procedures and devices that are employed to collect, organize, store, analyze, and disseminate health care information. Although there has been a historic distinction between health care information systems that have been dedicated to administrative management information and those dedicated to clinical information, these lines have become increasingly blurred as health care providers assume an ever larger share of the financial risk for health care that is costly relative to its clinical benefits. Moreover, there is a central trend in the health care industry toward consolidation into large multihospital provider systems that integrate traditionally independent components of the health care system—which in turn demands a high level of information system integration. The hardware and software components of health care information system technology are essential to the ultimate accomplishment of three forms health care provider system integration: *functional integration*, *physician–system integration,* and *clinical integration* (Conrad & Shortell, 1996). Functional integration refers to the extent to which key support functions and activities are efficiently coordinated across different parts of the provider system. Physician–system integration brings physicians into an increased level of engagement with the provider system in terms of exclusive utilization and system governance. Finally, clinical integration involves the coordination of health care decision-making and services across providers, functions, and settings within the system to maximize patient benefits relative to cost (Conrad & Shortell, 1996, pp. 5–6). A short list of the information system technologies that this level of integration involves includes electronic medical records, hardware networks that link diagnostic labs and imaging services with physician clinics, and software that links clinical decision makers with utilization management and quality improvement data.

As important as these information system technologies have been, the most significant source of technological innovation in health care information systems in recent years has been the Internet (Shi & Singh, 2001). In addition to shrinking the information gap between the health care consumer and health care providers, the Internet is assuming an ever larger part of the patient care management infrastructure of health care provider systems and serving as an important source of information for clinical decision making, for example, through connections between physicians' offices and the information databases of medical libraries located at top research universities.

Diagnostic Technology

Diagnostic technology primarily refers to the devices and procedures employed to detect and differentially diagnose disease processes and injuries. As such, diagnostic technology includes such things as the equipment used in clinical laboratories to process body fluid and tissue samples and diagnostic imaging devices like ultrasound machines, computerized tomography (CT) scanners, magnetic resonance imaging (MRI) scanners, and positron emission tomography (PET) scanners. The three latter devices are examples of extremely sophisticated and expensive technologies that, while they represent significant advancements in the application of physics and computer science technology to health care, also require enormous investments by the hospitals/hospital systems that seek to acquire them—and thus retain their competitiveness as a health care provider.

Treatment Technology

In contrast to diagnostic technology, the definition of treatment technology encompasses devices and procedures that have been developed for the purposes of curing injury and disease, promoting optimal independence, functioning in the face of chronic illness and disability, alleviating suffering, and preventing disease. A partial list of treatment technologies includes pharmaceutical products, auxiliary devices like pacemakers and hearing aids, "big ticket" devices such as linear accelerators, the full range of surgical procedures from the routine to the highly technical (e.g., hernia repair vs. organ transplant), clinical protocols for the treatment of specific diseases (e.g., adjuvant chemo and radiation therapy for treatment of breast cancer), and specialized facilities such as neonatal intensive care units. Some treatment technologies, just like diagnostic technologies, require similarly enormous investments by the hospitals/health care systems motivated to acquire them. Also like highly expensive diagnostic technologies, expensive and sophisticated treatment technologies also serve as fodder for "capital-based competition" among different hospitals, hospital systems, and provider groups.[10]

Diffusion of Health Care Technology

The broad-scale diffusion and utilization of very expensive health care technology (whether categorized as diagnostic or treatment technology) is a point of significant distinction between the organization of health care in the United States and that found elsewhere. In the United States, much of increased investment in highly sophisticated and expensive technology is driven by the phenomenon of "capital-based competition" between hospitals and hospital systems vying against one another to attract and retain a limited pool of insured patients. This is very distinct from either price-based competition or outcome-based competition, where the consumer chooses the provider based on either lower price or a higher likelihood of delivering a desirable outcome. In most other OECD countries, where the health care technology is pitted much more directly against other kinds of public dollar expenditures, the diffusion of technology is driven far more by a cost–benefit orientation. The result, from a system-wide standpoint, is less investment in the most sophisticated and expensive health care technologies and more selective utilization.

An illustrative example is the contrast between the system of health care technology assessment and acquisition in France and the general process of technology assessment acquisition in the United States offered by Rosenau (2000). The process of technology assessment is in essence a process for determining the benefits, applications, and costs of new innovations in health care technology for the purpose of guiding decisions pertaining to technology acquisition, distribution, and appropriate utilization. Although the federal government is the largest single purchaser of health care (principally as a function of the Medicare and Medicaid programs), the technology assessment functions of the federal government are quite weak relative to the power of the medical technology industry in the United States. Several federal agencies assume important technology assessment functions (e.g., the National Institutes of Health, the Centers for Medicaid and Medicare Services, and the Agency for Health Care Research and Quality), but no particular agency either coordinates the health care technology assessment process or assumes a lead role in making specific recommendations pertaining to the best use of public dollars (Rosenau, 2000). This not just an example of government inefficiency, but rather a sustained pattern of political decisions reflecting an entrenched and erroneous belief among many American politicians and policy makers that the free market functions as the most efficient mechanism for identifying the optimally efficacious health care technologies.

In France, where the national government both directly regulates various health care insurance funds and assures universal coverage, health care technology assessment is a highly centralized function that involves a nonprofit agency sanctioned and funded by the French government to both carry out the technology assessment function and guide appropriate use. Of equal importance, the French government plays a very direct role in determining the geographic distribution of medical technology in accordance with such factors as population need and disparities in access (Rosenau, 2000). As stated by Rosenau (p. 625), health care technology is generally regarded as public good rather than a commodity.

The results of these two different approaches, predictably enough, are that in the United States there is a significant pattern of overinvestment in very expensive health care technologies relative to France. Using MRI units as an illustrative example, the OECD health statistic estimates for 2009 put the number of MRI units in France at 6.4 MRI units per million persons, while in the United States the OECD estimated there were 25.9 MRI units per million persons (OECD, 2012a). Although some might take issue with the notion that such differences represent an example of overinvestment, the population health indicators in the United States relative to France fail to make the case that there is a discernible population health benefit yielded by having four times as many MRI units per capita. For example, life expectancy in France exceeds that of the United States by nearly 2 years, despite spending only half the dollars per capita on health care (OECD, 2012b). Aside from spending less dollars per capita, France has emphasized investments in universal health care access over costly health care technology.

Human Resources

According to the U.S. Department of Labor (Bureau of Labor Statistics, 2011), there were over 14 million Americans employed in health care in the United States in 2008, a figure expected to grow by 22.5% over the next decade. Table 4.7 provides a general overview of the distribution of the health care labor force by health care occupation, along with a forecast of employment growth within each occupation over the next decade. Several of the health care labor force statistics on Table 4.7 are worthy of comment. First, it can be seen that physicians and registered nurses, generally considered the core health occupations, actually comprise less than a fifth of the health care labor force (19.9%). Second, it is evident that the areas of greatest expansion in the health care labor force over the next several years involve occupations that provide services that are extension of roles and tasks that at one time were largely the exclusive province of physicians. A third interesting observation is that the growth across all professional health care occupations is in the double digits. This level of growth will require significant near-term investments in health care labor force development, which the Patient Protection and Affordable Care Act of 2010 endeavors to address through a range of public health and workforce development provisions (Congressional Research Service, 2010).

As the baby boom generation joins the ranks of the nation's aged population, it will exacerbate further an already significant gap between the demands of an aging population and the human resources essential to the

Table 4.7 Employment of Workers in Health Services by Occupation, 2008 and Projected Change, 2008–2018. (Employment in Thousands)

Occupation	Number	Percent	Percent Change: 2008–2018
Total, all occupations	14,336	100	22.5
Management, business, and financial occupations	614.6	4.3	16.8
Professional and related occupations	**6283.00**	**43.8**	**22.5**
Counselors	171.3	1.2	22.6
Social workers	206.7	1.4	19.5
Dietitians and nutritionists	35.5	0.3	9.8
Pharmacists	67.5	0.5	14.0
Physicians and surgeons	512.5	3.6	26.0
Physician assistants	66.2	0.5	41.3
Registered nurses	2192.40	15.3	23.4
Clinical laboratory technologists and technicians	278.8	1.9	14.0
Emergency medical technicians and paramedics	122	0.9	27.8
Licensed practical and licensed vocational nurses	586	4.5	14.2
Office and administrative support occupations	**2540.30**	**17.7**	**19.7**
Billing and posting clerks and machine operators	194.8	1.4	19.7
Receptionists and information clerks	386.3	2.7	16.1
Medical secretaries	770.7	5.4	26.5

Source: Bureau of Labor Statistics, U.S. Department of Labor, Career Guide to Industries, 2010–11 Edition, Healthcare, on the Internet at http://www.bls.gov.offcampus.lib.washington.edu/cg/oco/cg/cgs035.htm (visited March 24, 2011).

183

provision of adequate health care. Within the service occupation sector of the health care industry (home care aides, nurses aides, and orderlies), it is highly likely that the adequacy of the human resource pool over the next decade will in large part be determined by immigration policy—given the skewed age distribution of the native U.S. population. Within the professional sector of the health care industry, the human resource pool will likely be determined by the interplay between immigration policy and the level of domestic investment by professional schools in the health sciences and in their affiliated clinical training sites (e.g., teaching hospitals and community clinics). While human resource issues loom across a broad range of health care occupations in the coming decade, those pertaining to the supply of physicians and nurses will be highlighted. In the case of both professions, issues emerge in both overall labor supply and in specialization.

Physicians

As previously shown in Table 4.1, the United States has about 2.4 practicing physicians per thousand persons, considerably below the OECD average of 3.2 practicing physicians per thousand. Although at various points over the past 50 years policy makers have identified either an oversupply or under-supply of physicians, the number of physicians in the United States has historically increased as a nearly perfect linear function of the nation's gross domestic product (GDP; Cooper, Getzen, McKee, & Laud, 2002). That is, as the economy has produced more across all sectors, demand for health care services from physicians has also expanded—and for the most part the supply of physicians has increased sufficiently to accommodate it. This simple demand model of physician supply does not in and of itself suggest what mechanisms are employed to accommodate the demand, but in reality only three options are available: expanding the number of medical school slots, recruiting graduates of foreign medical schools, and preventing the attrition of trained physicians (e.g., delaying retirement). In a departure from earlier projections of a physician oversupply, in 2005 the Council on Graduate Medical Education (COGME) predicted the emergence of a significant undersupply of physicians by the year 2020. Among the factors that the COGME cites is the aging of the population, changes in the lifestyle preferences of physicians toward fewer hours of work, and continued growth in the GDP (Council on Graduate Medical Education, 2005). More recent analysis has placed a particular emphasis on the shortage of adult care generalists, in the order of 35–44 thousand adult primary care physicians by 2025 (Colwill, Cultice, & Kruse, 2008). In the wake of the passage of the Patient Protection and Affordable Care Act, it is widely speculated that the shortage will greatly exceed earlier projections, as historically uninsured populations will have increased access to health care.

Supply of Specialists

Relative to other countries with advanced health care systems, the United States has a higher proportion of its physician labor force allocated to specializations in medicine, namely physicians who are trained to diagnose and treat a defined subset of health conditions that generally are specific to a system of the body. Examples include endocrinology, orthopedic medicine, cardiology, and pulmonary medicine. In contrast, primary care physicians are trained to treat a wide range of routine health conditions and attend to the patient's overall health needs. The dominant primary care domains of medicine include family practice, pediatrics, general internal medicine, and obstetrics/gynecology. Where health care by a specialist tends to be shorter term and disease focused, care by a primary care physician is by nature longer term and holistic (Shi & Singh, 2001, p. 122).

In the United States, the ratio between specialists and primary care physicians is about 2:1, whereas in Canada the ratio between specialists and primary care physicians is almost exactly 1:1 (Bodenheimer & Grumbach, 2002; Canadian Labour and Business Centre, 2003). Fifty years ago, the specialist–primary care ratio in the United States was essentially the same as that observed in Canada today, but the combined forces of a specialist-oriented culture in U.S. medical schools and a health care finance system that provides superior income opportunities for specialists ultimately yielded a physician labor force that is dominated by specialists (Bodenheimer & Grumbach 2002, p. 196). Although it might appear that a physician labor force that is dominated by specialists with in-depth expertise in a wide range of debilitating and deadly health conditions should yield better population health outcomes, there are reasons to suggest that the opposite is true. For example, the more extensive training requirements of specialists take dollars out of the health care system that might have been spent on prevention or the direct provision of health care and, further, retain already highly trained physicians in training settings for a longer period (Grumbach, 2002). In fact, there is evidence that, to the extent that an emphasis on the training of specialists decreases the supply of primary care physicians, both population mortality levels and health disparities may increase (Starfield, Shi, Grover, & Macinko, 2005).

At this point, it is difficult to predict what direction the trend in the specialist–primary care mix will take over the next decade. Forces that are pushing toward a sustained emphasis on specialization include the aging of the population, and the retreat from the aggressive growth of managed care that characterized the 1990s. On the other hand, the reemergence of significant health care inflation throughout most of the current decade and the implementation of health care reform provisions that include increased emphasis on primary care may signal a shift toward health care financing solutions that are less favorable to specialists.

Registered Nurses

One person out of every seven that is employed in the health care industry is a registered nurse (see Table 4.7). Nationally, there are 8.6 registered nurses for every 1,000 persons, although there is wide geographic variation in the supply of registered nurses relative to the population (Kaiser Family Foundation, 2011d). The basic level of credentialing for a Registered Nurse is completion of either a 2-year community college nursing program, or 4-year baccalaureate degree from an accredited school of nursing, followed by qualification for state licensure via passage of a state-sanctioned written examination. Registered nurses are also credentialed in a wide range of advanced clinical specializations, including pulmonary care, intensive care, geriatrics, psychosocial nursing, and obstetrics—to name a few. In recent decades there has been enormous growth in the training and employment opportunities for nurse practitioners, generally defined as nurses with an advanced academic degree (e.g., a DNP/Doctor in Nursing Practice) and the requisite clinical experience to diagnose and manage a wide range of common health conditions and chronic diseases. In most parts of the country nurse practitioners are sanctioned to practice as primary care providers. That is, they may diagnose disease, order diagnostic tests, prescribe medications, and otherwise fulfill all other essential functions of a primary care provider.

The first edition of this book, published in 2007, placed significant emphasis on a rigorous and compelling analysis of nursing labor force trends conducted by Buerhaus, Staiger, and Auerbach (2000) that suggested the supply of registered nurses in the labor force would fall as much as 20% short of demand by the year 2020. In this new edition of the book, our discussion of nursing labor force trends is largely based on an updated study of nursing labor force trends by these same authors that, in contrast to their previous findings, now suggests that it is quite possible that the supply of registered nurses in the labor force will be sufficient to meet demand at least through the year 2030 (Auerbach, Buerhaus, & Staiger, 2011). What explains this dramatic turnaround? The authors identified the reversal of the much anticipated nursing shortage crisis (shown in Figure 4.3) to two unanticipated changes. First, it seems that more recent cohorts of young adults are taking

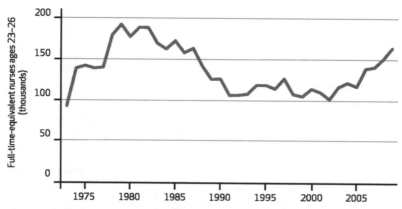

Source: Auerbach, D., Buerhaus, P., & Staiger, D. (2011). Exhibit 3 trend in the number of full-time equivalent registered nurses age 23–26, 2009. *Health Affairs, 30*(12). Used with permission.

Figure 4.3 *Trend in the number of full-time equivalent registered nurses aged 23–26, 2009.*

advantage of the employment opportunities in nursing than the young adults of a decade ago. Second, the profession of nursing is now attracting adults in their late 20s and 30s, whereas a decade previously this was not the case (Auerbach et al., 2011).

While the dramatic surge over recent years in nursing as the career choice of young adults is encouraging, we are still left to ponder the cause. Auerbach et al. (2011) suggest that both innovations in nursing education programs (such as accelerated degree programs) and increased federal investments in nursing education funding (Title III Nursing Workforce Development programs) have been particularly crucial factors in the resurgence of nursing as a career choice. It is also possible that the earlier cohort of young female adults, raised in the context of the Women's Liberation Movement, may have been more socialized to consider careers that had been historically resistant to women (e.g., law, medicine, and finance). In contrast, the young adult women of the new century may feel they can choose nursing as a career without the sense that it represents an engendered career constraint. That said, nursing remains a profession that is predominantly comprised of females. Though the ratio of female nurses to male nurses has shifted slightly downward over the last decade, it is still the case that just over 90% of early career registered nurses are women (HRSA, 2010). Finally, as also suggested by Auerbach et al. (2011), it may be that both the expanded range of career opportunities in nursing and the prospect of entering a field where labor shortages are projected long into the future have favored the selection of nursing as a career choice among more recent cohorts of young adults.

Despite the dramatic resurgence of the number of registered nurses in the most recent decade (see Figure 4.3), it is still very plausible that a significant nursing shortage will emerge over the next several years. There are several reasons for this, including in particular the possibility that the Patient Protection and Affordable Care Act will meet its policy objective of increasing health care access to millions of Americans that currently lack health insurance. In addition, there remains what Auerbach et al. (2011) describe as a worrisome "bottleneck" in the nursing education pipeline that continues to result in the rejection of thousands of qualified school of nursing applicants. Finally, the future balance between supply and demand in the professional nursing labor force is contingent both upon the continuation of the current upward growth trend in the number of young adults entering the nursing profession and selection of fields within nursing that are specific to the health care needs of an aging population and the projected expansions of the primary care sector of the U.S. health care system (Auerbach et al., 2011).

For all of these reasons, it seems crucial that both the legislative branch of the federal government as well as its key health care agencies (in particular the Health Resources and Services Administration and the Institute of Medicine) keep in place the research and policy initiatives that were prompted by the previously worrisome projections of a significant shortage of registered nurses in the coming decades.[11]

THE HEALTH CARE SYSTEM SAFETY NET

The health care safety net is conventionally defined as the health care providers that care for those without health insurance, those on Medicaid, and populations that face "special conditions"; such as those with tuberculosis, AIDS, or serious and persistent mental illness (Hegner, 2001; IOM, 2000). As noted by the Institute of Medicine's comprehensive assessment of the nation's health care safety net published in 2000,[12] health care safety net providers can be distinguished from other providers of health care by two features: (1) either by mission or by legal mandate they are committed to the acceptance of any and all patients regardless of the patient's ability to pay and (2) their patient base is largely comprised of the uninsured, those on Medicaid, and those who have the special illnesses and conditions that often carry the burden of stigma and marginalization (IOM, 2000, pp. 3–4). This latter feature of safety net providers is particularly critical, because by definition it acknowledges that the burden of care for the poor and the marginalized in the U.S. health care system is not distributed uniformly across providers—but rather that safety net providers absorb a disproportionate share of care for the poor and the stigmatized. Put another way, the very existence of the health care safety net establishes the two-tiered nature of health care in the United States: one system for those having the ability to pay and another system for those relying on various forms of government-subsidized programs. As will be shown in the discussion that follows, the magnitude of the burden of publicly financed and uncompensated care on the health care safety net reflects the extent to which the U.S. health care system is both segregated and hierarchical along lines of race and social class.

The Provider Composition of the Health Care Safety Net

Generally speaking, health care safety net providers include public and private not-for-profit community hospitals, publicly funded community health clinics, local health departments, and individual physicians and other providers that for various reasons have a high level of commitment to caring for a disproportionate share of the poor and medically indigent.[13] Due to the mandates of the Emergency Medical Treatment and Labor Act (EMTALA) of 1986, a significant part of the health care safety net includes hospital emergency departments, since the provisions of EMTALA require that hospitals with emergency departments provide a medical screening examination for any individual who comes to the hospital and requests such an examination, regardless of ability to pay.[14] In practical terms, this means that hospital-based emergency departments function not only as the primary provider of emergency care for the poor and medically indigent, but also as the provider of care for ordinary illnesses and minor injuries for those millions of Americans who for a variety of reasons do not have a regular source of medical care.

A remarkable feature of the health care safety net is its existence as a loosely knit and in general ad hoc system of care—despite its crucial role as the care provider of last and only resort for many of the nation's poor, uninsured, and otherwise marginalized. As noted by the Institute of Medicine's (IOM) *America's Health Care Safety Net: Intact but Endangered* report (IOM, 2000), the safety net is at best a "patchwork of institutions, financing and programs that vary dramatically across the country as a result of a broad range of economic, political, and structural factors" (IOM, 2000, p. 4). These factors include the local tax base, each state's particular eligibility rules for Medicaid, and each community's historical commitment to the adequate provision of health care to the poor.

Since the patchwork nature of the safety net system precludes an accurate and simple description that includes all of the nation's safety net providers, the approach taken here will involve a systematic description of the safety net's core providers—as identified by the Institute of Medicine. These core providers of the safety net include public hospitals, community health centers, local health departments, community hospitals, teaching hospitals, some categories of private providers (for example, rural physicians, rural pharmacists, inner-city minority physicians), school-based clinics, Veterans Administration hospitals and clinics, and the Indian Health Service.

Public Hospitals

Excluding federal hospitals and hospitals serving special categories of illness and disability, as of 2009 there are 5008 hospitals in the United States, of which 21.8% are owned by state and local governments (Kaiser Family Foundation, 2011c). The remainder of the industry is divided between nonprofit hospital ownership (58.3%) and for-profit ownership (19.9%). Although public hospitals have a relatively small share of the health care market, they carry the largest share of the burden for care that is broadly classified as "uncompensated"—that is, care that is either classified as charity care or bad debt. The graph shown in Figure 4.4, extracted from a research report prepared by the GAO (2005b), illustrates the pattern of uncompensated care by hospital ownership in five states that were selected as a representative sample of the United States. With the exception of Indiana, where nonprofit hospitals provide a slightly higher proportion of uncompensated care, the public hospitals function provide two to three times the uncompensated care than is provided by either the not-for-profit sector or the proprietary (for profit) sector of the hospital industry. In the states sampled by the GAO in this report, the for-profit sector of the industry devotes an average of 4.0% its patient care expenses to uncompensated care, while the public sector average level of commitment to uncompensated care is 11.7%. This difference represents the very different patient populations of public and for-profit hospitals, as well as their quite opposite fiduciary mandates. The fiduciary mandate of public hospitals pertains to the accessibility of essential health care for all, while the boards and administrators of for-profit hospitals are obligated to place the interests of the hospital's investors ahead of the interest of the public. From this perspective, the gap in relative dollars devoted to uncompensated care between public hospitals and private ones is pretty much as one might expect.

However, what is less intuitive is the low level of commitment to charitable care on the part of not-for-profit hospitals, which on average have only a marginally higher proportion of their patient care dollars devoted to

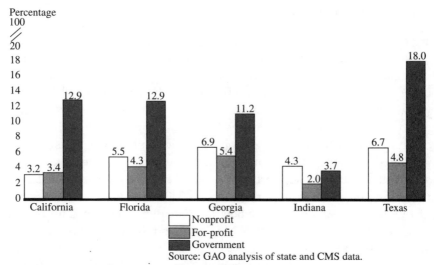

Source: GAO analysis of state and CMS data.

Source: "Testimony before the committee on ways and means, U.S. house of representatives-nonprofit, for-profit, and government hospitals: Uncompensated care and other community benefits. Figure 4.2 average percent of operating expenses devoted to uncompensated care, by hospital ownership type, 2003. Washington, DC: General Accounting Office.

Figure 4.4 *Operating expenses devoted to uncompensated care by hospital ownership type.*
Notes: The average percent of patient operating expenses devoted to uncompensated care for a hospital ownership group is calculated by dividing the sum of uncompensated care costs for hospitals in that group by the sum of the group's total patient operating expenses. Hospitals include nonfederal, short-term, acute care general hospitals.

uncompensated care than for-profit hospitals (5.4% on average as opposed to 4.0% in the for-profit ownership sector). As noted by the GAO in the narrative that accompanies Figure 4.4, there are no clear standards to hold not-for-profit hospitals accountable for providing community benefits that are commensurate with the favored tax benefits of being a not-for-profit entity (GAO, 2005b, p. 19). Thus, for the most part, nonprofit and for-profit hospitals behave very much like each other in terms of the kinds of patients each competes to serve—and competes not to serve.

The public hospitals that comprise the core of the health care safety net, although they represent only 2% of U.S. hospitals, provide 20% of the nation's uncompensated care (NAPH, 2012). These hospitals and health care systems represent such names as the Cook County Hospital system in Chicago,[15] Bellevue Hospital in New York, the Los Angeles County Hospital system, and Charity Hospital in New Orleans—the latter totally destroyed in the wake of Hurricane Katrina in 2005.

Community Health Centers

Originally founded during the Lyndon Johnson administration as a partial measure to counter Medicare and Medicaid's inability to close the universal coverage gap (Hegner, 2001), community health centers and clinics provide primary care and preventative health services in communities characterized by high rates of poverty, low rates of health care insurance coverage, and limited access to health care services (IOM, 2000, pp. 59–60). Although local government financing, charitable support, and in-kind contributions are important sources of support for community health centers, federal funds are a large and essential source of support for the many community health centers that qualify for federally funding under Section 330 of the Public Health Services Act (IOM, 2000). As noted elsewhere (see Chapter 3, Health Care Finance), though small relative to Medicare, Medicaid, and the VA health care system, federally funded Community Health Centers (CHCs) serve as a critical safety net providers in low-income communities. As a condition of federal funding, CHCs must be located in a high-need community, provide comprehensive primary care services, must ensure availability of transportation and language translation services, must have a community- and consumer-based governance structure, and, finally, must adjust fees in accordance with patients' ability to pay (HRSA, 2005a). Other common characteristics of CHCs include more extensive use of physician's assistants, midwives, and allied health professionals like social workers than is typically found in private sector primary health care practices, as well significant commitments to teaching, training, and entry-level employment opportunities for community residents (Waitzkin, 2005). The Health Resources and Services Administration estimates that 1124 federally supported CHCs served 19.3 million patients during 2010, with 93% of those served being below the federal poverty level (HRSA, 2012).

Local Health Departments

As noted by the Institute of Medicine (2000), more than 3,000 local city and county health departments are an essential source of health care for those that are the least advantaged and often the most at risk for disease and death from preventable causes, such as homeless persons, immigrants, the working poor, and those without health insurance or a regular source of medical care (IOM, 2000, p. 64). Even so, local health departments function under an ongoing historical tension between the provision of those services that are critical to disease prevention and preventable mortality and ongoing close scrutiny from the politically dominant private practice sector of medicine—the primary concern being the incursion of public medicine into areas that are potentially profitable for the private practitioner (Starr,

1982). Thus, there is a significant discrepancy between what the federal government defines as the core public health functions of local health departments (e.g., population health status monitoring, health regulation enforcement, birth and death registration, and public health education) and a broader agenda endorsed by the far majority of Local Health Department (LHD) directors that extends to the provision of direct health care services to vulnerable populations (IOM, 2000). In addition to such direct services as maternal and child health care, screening and treatment for sexually transmitted diseases, tuberculosis, and immunizations; LHDs often venture into a broader scope of direct primary care for populations that are poorly served and of little interest to private sector medicine (Shi & Singh, 2001). Although the rise of Medicaid-managed care programs and the shifting of some Medicaid-mandated services to conventional health care providers during the last decade reduced the direct health care role of many LHDs, it appears that the most progressive LHDs can continue to provide some essential specialized services that are less likely to be directly provided by conventional managed care organizations (IOM, 2000).

Teaching Hospitals

Although many teaching hospitals are also public hospitals with a mandated role as a safety net provider, many teaching hospitals that fall within either the private not-for-profit sector or the private for-profit sector also provide health care to the poor, the uninsured, and the chronically ill and disabled by default. This occurs for several reasons, of which two are primary. The first is a historical relationship between clinical training and health services for the poor, where those unable to afford access to needed health care through private providers resort to teaching hospitals and affiliated clinics that have some willingness to provide free or heavily subsidized care in return for the patient's illness and treatment serving as an exemplar for teaching (Starr, 1982). Although on its face this appears (and sometimes is) an exploitive relationship, it is also the case that teaching hospitals often offer superior care. A second reason is that teaching hospitals are often the sole community or even regional providers of highly specialized and technologically advanced health care, such as trauma care, burn units, organ transplants, rare infectious diseases, and spinal cord injury (IOM, 2000). The patients that are in need of these specialized services are often without adequate health care insurance coverage, are made poor through the effects of their health conditions on their employment and savings, or are at higher risk for these conditions as a function of poverty (e.g., as in the relationship between housing conditions and severely burned children). An important source of funding for the care of the poor in teaching hospitals comes from both Disproportionate Share (DSH) and Indirect Medical Education (IME) payment adjustments through the Medicaid and Medicare programs.

Community Hospitals

Despite the disproportionate burden of care for the uninsured assumed by large public hospitals, it also is the case that not-for-profit community hospitals and their affiliated clinics furnish the brunt of uncompensated care (IOM, 2000). Even though community hospitals typically provide a much smaller individual share of uncompensated care relative to public hospitals, they are by far the largest sector of the hospital industry in the number of hospitals and thus have a very large collective contribution. Community hospitals are generally defined as hospitals that are nonfederal and whose services are open to the general public (Shi & Singh, 2001), and they typically provide a broad array of the most commonly needed acute care medical and surgical services. The prevalent origins of community hospitals include establishment by religious organizations and ethnic communities, and through the joint efforts of civic leaders, local medical societies, and local philanthropists. However, by far the largest source of development and growth for community hospitals originated with the federal government's Hill–Burton Act of 1946,[16] which provided funding for the largest expansion of hospitals and hospital bed capacity in U.S. history. Because funding from the Hill–Burton Act carried with it the obligation to make an annual repayment of the federal debt in the form of uncompensated care, throughout most of the latter half of the 20th century the term "community hospital" implied a significant commitment to provision of uncompensated care to the poor and the uninsured. Another reason that community hospitals play such a key role in the health care safety net, aside from the faith-based commitments or the long-term impact of Hill–Burton funding obligations, is that they are often the sole local provider of hospital and emergency services—thus necessitating a certain burden of care to the poor and uninsured that cannot be shifted elsewhere. In rural communities in particular, this poses a significant burden on the financial solvency of small community hospitals (Stensland & Milet, 2002).

The VA System

The VA System has long served as the core provider of health care services to disabled veterans, and historically as the health care provider of last resort for veterans who were unable to afford health care through the conventional employer-based insurance market. In the recent decade, as more working Americans lack health insurance and as states have imposed greater restrictions on access to Medicaid for low-income adults, the VA system has become an even more essential source of health care for low-income veterans. Aside from those veterans receiving care from the VA for service-connected disabilities and in particular the surge of casualties from the Iraq and Afghanistan wars, the VA health care system identifies the provision of health care to low-income veterans as a specific priority. As discussed in Chapter 3 (Health Care Finance), beginning in 1997 the VA system has gone through a radical transformation from primarily an inpatient-based system with a centralized bureaucracy to a more outpatient intensive system of 22 regional networks with independent budgets that are based on capitation (Ashton et al., 2003). Under the current system of organization, the VA is accessible to veterans on the basis of an ordered set of eight priorities, of which low-income status is ranked fifth. Under the current scheme, the extent to which any of the VA health care system's regional networks is able to serve as a safety net for low-income veterans appears in large part to be a function of the local proportion of veterans who are among the ranks of the uninsured.[17]

The Indian Health Service

The Indian Health Service (IHS) is an agency within the U.S. Department of Health and Human Services responsible for the provision of health services to American Indians and Alaska Natives. Thus, the IHS is supposed to serve as the principal health care safety net for the indigenous peoples of the lower 48 states and Alaska. According to the most recent IHS estimates, the IHS serves approximately 2 million American Indians and Alaska Natives residing on or near reservations (IHS, 2012). The Native Americans and Alaska Natives receiving health care services from the IHS are members of one of 556 tribes in 35 different states (IHS, 2012), so from that perspective it must be acknowledged that the IHS has limited geographic coverage as a safety net. For the tribal members that the IHS is able to serve, it acts as not only a primary care provider but also as the principal public health agency for indigenous peoples. Prevention and treatment initiatives undertaken by the IHS address (among other priorities) the disproportionate rates of injury, alcoholism, diabetes, and mental health problems among Native Americans (Shi & Singh, 2001). Nationally, the IHS is divided into 12 geographic area offices responsible for program operations that generally deliver direct health care services through IHS-funded hospitals, health centers, and health stations (GAO, 2005a). As the Government Accountability Office points out, the Native Americans and Alaska Natives dependent upon the IHS for health care encounter a variety of barriers to adequate access to primary health care services. These barriers include waiting periods in some clinics of between 2 and 6 months, limited access to transportation, and endemic shortages in staff, equipment, and contract care funds for services INS hospitals and clinics could not provide directly (GAO, 2005a). Although the Indian Health Care Improvement Act of 1976 had as its central goal a systematic effort to raise the level of Native Americans to parity with the U.S. general population (Shi & Singh, 2001), it is clear that the agency has never been funded to achieve anything like parity in health care services—let alone parity in population health.[18] However, the IHS, to its credit, continues to pursue an aggressive and often innovative public health and health care safety net agenda despite limited fiscal resources relative to the massive population challenges the IHS confronts.

Other Safety Net Providers

Other safety net providers highlighted by the IOM report include school-based health clinics, some private health care practitioners, and in particular some groups of private health care practitioners. While it is the case that some private physicians and other allied health care providers such as dentists, psychologists, and social workers in private practice often discount or provide uncompensated health care, it is difficult to quantify their contributions or identify their criteria for determining the recipients of uncompensated care. However, the IOM report identifies three practitioner groups that tend to provide a disproportionate share of care to the poor, disabled, and/or the uninsured. These are physicians that practice in rural communities, rural pharmacists, and minority physicians serving inner-city populations.

Federal Support for the Health Care Safety Net

Federal support for the health care safety net comes in two primary forms. The first form of support is legislation that requires some health providers to ensure essential care for an array of medical emergencies, health conditions, and special populations with or without adequate reimbursement. One example of federal supportive legislation is the previously mentioned Emergency Medical Treatment and Labor Act of 1986 (EMTALA), which requires that hospitals with emergency departments provide a medical screening examination for any individual who comes to the hospital and requests such an examination, regardless of ability to pay. A second example is the Consolidated Omnibus Reconciliation Act of 1985 (COBRA), which precludes hospitals from "patient dumping," that is, transferring patients in need of care to other less appropriate facilities for financial reasons. The third example and most crucial of support for the health care safety net is funding through Medicaid direct care programs that fund health care for low-income children and adults living in poverty, and indirect supports like Medicaid and Medicare Disproportionate Share payment adjustments that provide limited subsidy to providers with a large share of poor patients. In addition, there are important tax benefits to not-for-profit private sector providers that provide the brunt of safety net health care—although there is some debate as to whether the tax benefits are given their full value in charity care and other community benefits. Finally, there is the federal funding allocated to community health care clinics in low-income communities, and systems of health care for populations—most notably the VA system and the Indian Health Service.

Assessing the Future of the Nation's Health Care Safety Net

Owing to both its patchwork nature and the year-to-year financial solvency problems of its core providers, the health care safety net in America has long existed in a state of ongoing jeopardy. Absent the implantation of health care reform measures that will reverse the trend toward ever greater numbers of uninsured, it is difficult to avoid the conclusion that the fiscally threadbare hospitals and community clinics that comprise the health care safety net will be one-by-one be overwhelmed by the rising tide of the uninsured. An object lesson that underscores the possibility of this bleak future is Miami's Jackson Memorial Hospital, which on the eve of the Patient Protection and Affordable Care Act being signed into law in early 2010 confronted a $230 million budget deficit as a result of its continued commitment to it mission as a provider of health care to Dade County's poor and uninsured (Almgren & Lindhorst, 2012).

However, even with the full implantation of the Patient Protection and Affordable Care Act, the fiscal future of the hospitals and community clinics that comprise the nation's health care safety net is fraught with jeopardy. For example, Andrulis and Siddiqui (2011) point out that while some aspects of the Patient Protection and Affordable Care Act may strengthen the viability of safety net health care providers (notably the additional $11 billion allocated to community health centers for capacity building), other provisions (in particular, the reduction of $18 million in federal disproportionate share funding to safety net hospitals) pose a worrisome challenge.[19] In addition, there is also the concern that increased access to health care for heretofore uninsured populations will have unintended consequences, such as the introduction to increased numbers of poor with neglected and complicated health conditions in already strained systems, and the possibility that safety net hospitals will be at a disadvantage in their ability to retain highly trained staff in the face of a health care labor shortage (Redlener & Grant, 2009).[20]

Devolution of the Safety Net Infrastructure: The Case of Charity Hospital in New Orleans

In the immediate wake of Hurricane Katrina on September 2, 2005, President Bush assured Senator Trent Lott (R-Mississippi) that his mansion that had been destroyed by Katrina would be rebuilt.[21] In defense of what many saw as an elitist remark that ignored the plight of those thousands of poor who had lost either family members or what little they possessed to Katrina, President Bush's staunchest defenders were quick to point out that the President meant his comment as a metaphor for his commitment to rebuild and restore the homes and communities that were equally reduced to rubble by Katrina. In fact, probably no better test for the Bush administration's commitment to such rebuilding existed than Charity Hospital, the safety net hospital that became for a time the focus of national scandal when its patients and staff were left un-evacuated and essentially abandoned for days without clean water, electricity, food, and even the most basic emergency medical supplies (Berggren, 2005).

Known locally as "Big Charity," Charity Hospital of New Orleans was the second oldest hospital in the United States, opening its doors in 1736, just weeks after the first patients were admitted to Bellevue Hospital in New York. At the time Katrina hit New Orleans in August of 2005, Charity Hospital occupied a building that was constructed in 1939 to accommodate 2680 inpatients (Medical Center of Louisiana at New Orleans, 2003). Although Charity's aged facility had been reduced to 565 staffed beds in more recent years, it remained among the busiest safety net hospitals in the United States. For example, in 2003, Charity Hospital provided 146,178 annual inpatient days of care and accounted for nearly 3000 births (NAPH, 2005). Of equal importance and more typical to critical safety net providers of comparable size, Charity Hospital of New Orleans also served as a regional trauma center and teaching hospital. Finally, Charity Hospital was Louisiana's and New Orleans' principal provider of hospital care for the poor—deriving 85% of its revenues from Medicaid (NAPH, 2005).

Although both local and national authorities were quick to concede the floodwaters unleashed by Katrina had made the already decrepit hospital building unsalvageable, it was also apparent that there was nothing to replace the role Charity Hospital had long served as the hospital of last and only resort for the city's poor (Gesensway, 1999). Several years after Hurricane Katrina's destruction of Charity Hospital, the rebuilding of Charity Hospital has remained mired in conflict and uncertainty. While the Bush administration pushed for a plan that would divert health care safety net funds (specifically DSH funds) essential for the rebuilding of Charity Hospital to subsidies for the purchase of health insurance coverage for the poor,[22] the most influential local authorities were committed to a plan that would use federal disaster recovery funds and DSH funds to build a modernized version of Charity Hospital that would be linked to a new VA facility (Clark, 2010). Even though the local authorities that favored the rebuilding of a modernized Charity Hospital were ultimately able to circumvent the opposition of the Bush administration and pursue a plan to rebuild, objections to the rebuilding of Charity Hospital from local private for-profit and private nonprofit hospitals then emerged and imposed additional political obstacles to overcome (Clark, 2010). Adding to the uncertain prospects for the rebuilding of Charity Hospital is the 2010 passage and gradual implantation of the Patient Protection and Affordable Care Act—which while it may create a larger pool of insured patients also has provisions that will reduce the DSH funds that are essential to the funding of a rebuilt Charity Hospital.

The case of Charity Hospital provides two lessons concerning the devolution of the health care safety net. The first is that Charity's decrepit condition preceding its final destruction reflected a longstanding failure to reinvest in the buildings and equipment needed to sustain an adequate safety net—either directly through state-level capital construction funds or indirectly through Medicaid and Medicare payment mechanisms. Although discussions in recent years among local health care planners had identified the replacement of the 65-year-old Charity Hospital building and related infrastructure as a critical need, the pre-Katrina cash-strapped state of Louisiana was in no position to allocate the funds necessary to either refurbish the aging institution or provide the resources to enable the Charity Hospital system to adapt to a changing health care market (Gesensway, 1999). The second lesson is that, absent a major overhaul of the health care finance system for the poor and those without access to health insurance, other safety net providers like Charity Hospital will ultimately collapse under the burden of uncompensated and undercompensated health care costs. For example, in a survey of its member institutions, the National Association of Public Hospitals and Health Systems found that, in the years preceding the destruction of Charity Hospital, the average operating margins among the core safety net hospitals sank to .5%—though a 2% operating margin is considered the minimum that is essential for the long-term survival of both private and public sector hospitals (NAPH, 2005). While the recent average operating margins of the public hospital safety net are slightly above the critical 2% range, any significant reductions in DSH funds will place most public hospitals into operating at a loss (NAPH, 2009b).[23]

CONCLUDING COMMENTS: THE PARADOXICAL UNDERACHIEVEMENT OF THE U.S. HEALTH CARE SYSTEM

For decades the health care reform debate has been framed by the assumption that primary deficits in the U.S. health care system pertain to its failure to provide universal access to health care. However, the evidence continues to mount that the U.S. health care system, despite its being the most expensive in the world, fails to achieve the population health outcomes of nations that spend far less per capita on health care. While many of the factors that influence population health are only peripherally affected by the organization of the health care system, the prevalence of the diseases that contribute the most to disability and early death are also a function of the adequacy of the health care system. The United Kingdom, a nation with a rigid social class structure that spends less than 50% per capita on health care relative to the United States, has an adult population that is in remarkably superior health *at all levels of the social class gradient* (Banks, Marmot, Oldfield, & Smith, 2006). Rich, middle income, or poor, British adults in middle age have dramatically lower prevalence rates of diabetes, hypertension, heart disease, and cancer than U.S. citizens of the same socioeconomic status (Banks et al., 2006, p. 2039). Because these disadvantages in relative health affect affluent Americans as much as Americans in poverty, it cannot be claimed that the primary deficits of the U.S. health care system are attributable to the health insurance gap. What else could be wrong?

In truth, there is no clear answer or scientifically unequivocal explanation to this paradoxical underachievement of the U.S. health care system. By some accounts, the disconnect between the dollars and resources spent on health care in the United States and deficits in population health lies almost entirely outside of the health care system, through such mechanisms as poverty, racism, social isolation, and rising levels of income inequality (Phelan, Link, Diez-Roux, Kawachi, & Levin, 2004; Wilkinson, 1996). A second take, from a more Marxist perspective, is that the health care system paradox is nothing more and nothing less than a reflection of the system's success at achieving its latent function: the reinforcement of class structure and the expansion of opportunities for capital class exploitation. A third account suggests that the paradox arises from the U.S. health care system's orientation toward disease treatment and symptom management rather than the key factors that shape individual health behaviors and use of health services (Fuchs, 2004). Although there are strains of truth in each of these explanations (as well as a range of other accounts not mentioned), the common thread is that flaws in the organization of the health care system are complex, endemic, and deeply embedded in other aspects of social structure. In the chapters that follow, many of these interconnections will be illuminated—as well as some of the key implications for health care system reform.

NOTES

1. The Organisation for Economic Co-operation and Development.
2. See Keehan et al. (2011). National health spending projections through 2020: Economic recovery and reform drive faster spending growth. *Health Affairs*, 30(8), 1594–1605.
3. Charity care is generally defined as care that is provided both without payment and without obligation to pay for persons unable to afford it. This is distinct from the other form of uncompensated care, bad debt, which represents a provider's decision to write off fees for health care that are deemed uncollectible. Both forms of uncompensated care compose a significant source of the financing for health care delivered to the poor and the uninsured.
4. The term "hospital and hospital system industry" is used to denote the fact that hospitals may be owned and operated as independent institutions, or as a component of an integrated health care system comprised of multiple hospitals and clinics.
5. Sometimes the term "quaternary care" is used to denote an even higher level of care than tertiary. However, the term "tertiary care" is more typically used to refer to the highest level of hospital care.
6. This shift toward ambulatory care in the VA system reflects a recent restructuring of the system to a population-based model of health care, as opposed to the VA system's traditional hospital-based system for caring of veterans. (See Chapter 3 on Health Care Finance).
7. Medicare financing and reform issues are discussed at length in later chapters.
8. The term "certified nursing facility" applies to nursing homes and other residential care facilities that are licensed by states to provide nursing care, and in most cases qualify for either Medicare or Medicaid funding for services.
9. Shi and Singh's (2001) definition of medical technology refers more narrowly to the "application of the scientific body of knowledge produced by biomedical research." The more broad definition here takes into account the nonscientific sources of information that contribute to the accepted body of knowledge in health care, for example, the diffusion of conventions in diagnosis and treatment that, when closely examined, have no scientific basis.
10. Capital-based competition refers to the use of competitive advantages in physical facilities and/or health care technologies to either preserve or expand a health care provider's market share. In contrast to price-based competition, capital-based competition is inherently inflationary.

11. In this regard, the Initiative on the "Future of Nursing" partnership between the Institute of Medicine and the Robert Wood Johnson Foundation, launched in 2008, is a particularly good example of the policy initiatives that are crucial to the sustainment of an adequate labor supply of registered nurses trained in the needed competencies of the immediate future. See http://www.iom.edu/Activities/Workforce/Nursing.aspx.

12. *Americas Health Care Safety Net: Intact but Endangered*, full citation in list of references.

13. The term "medically indigent" generally refers to those that lack sufficient insurance, income, or savings to pay for essential health care. Although medically indigent persons are more often either unemployed or in low-wage jobs, under a variety of circumstances the medically indigent can include persons of middle and even high income.

14. Sanctions for violations of EMTALA are quite severe, and can include both direct fines and even the termination of the hospital's status as a provider of care to federally funded patients—which for almost all hospitals would result in financial ruin.

15. Since 2002, the John H. Stroger, Jr. Hospital.

16. Also known by its official title as the Hospital Survey and Reconstruction Act of 1946 (see Chapter 2 on the history of the U.S. Health Care System).

17. The VA health care system is currently operating with 21 regional networks.

18. It should be emphasized here, as it is elsewhere in this volume, that population health is only partially a function of public health interventions and optimal access to high-quality health care services. The disproportionate incidence of infant mortality, adult-onset diabetes, injuries, suicides, pneumonia, and renal disease among Native Americans is a function of historic and contemporary racial oppression, poverty, and enduring sources of structural disadvantage that cannot be overcome by even radical improvements in the health services available to native peoples.

19. In making this dramatic $18 million reduction in disproportionate funding (DSF) a provision of the Patient Protection and Affordable Care Act (PPACA), the architects of this legislation assume that these reductions will be offset by gains in health insurance revenue as the ranks of the uninsured diminish. However, the PPACA excludes undocumented immigrants from health insurance coverage, and it is unlikely that some other groups that depend upon safety net hospitals will acquire either Medicaid or commercial health insurance coverage (e.g., the homeless and chronically mentally ill).

20. In the state of Massachusetts, as health care coverage was dramatically expanded in the wake of state-level health care reform, significant shortages in primary care providers ensued (NAPH, 2009a).

21. "Out of the rubble of Trent Lott's house—he lost his entire house—there's going to be a fantastic house. And I'm looking forward to sitting on the porch" (Milbank, 2005).

22. It argued that the Bush administration's pressure on Louisiana to allocate DSH funds to subsidize health insurance for the poor, instead of using these funds to rebuild Charity Hospital, "was part of a larger strategy to convince states to swap DSH allotments for insurance programs extending direct assistance to the poor while shielding the federal budget from growing uncompensated care costs" (Clark, 2010, p. 760).

23. As mentioned at an earlier point in this chapter, the architects of the PPACA assume that the reductions in Disproportionate Share Hospital payments to safety net hospitals will be off-set by increased revenues from newly insured patients. Although if fully implemented there would be some off-set expected from PPACA, it seems unlikely that these off-sets will be sufficient to overcome the losses that safety net hospitals will still incur in the provision of uncompensated care to the remaining uninsured that PPACA coverage expansions will not include (e.g., undocumented immigrant workers).

REFERENCES

AHA. (2010, December 7). *Fast facts on U.S. hospitals from AHA Hospital Statistics*. Retrieved March 17, 2011, from http://www.aha.org/aha/content/2010/pdf/101207fastfacts.pdf

Almgren, G., & Lindhorst, T. (2012). *The safety-net health care system: Health care at the margins*. New York: Springer Publishing Co.

Andrulis, D. P., & Duchon, L. M. (2005). *Hospital care in the 100 largest cities and their suburbs, 1996–2002: Implications for the future of the hospital safety net in metropolitan America*. New York: SUNY Downstate Medical Center.

Andrulis, D., & Siddiqui, N. (2011). Health reform holds both risks and rewards for safety-net providers and racially and ethnically diverse patients. *Health Affairs, 30*(10),1830–1836.

Ashton, C. M., Souchek, J., Petersen, N. J., Menke, T. J., Collins, T. C., Kizer, K. W. et al. (2003). Hospital use and survival among Veterans Affairs beneficiaries. *New England Journal of Medicine, 349*(17), 1637–1646.

Auerbach, D., Buerhaus, P., & Staiger, D. (2011). Registered nurse supply grows faster than projected amid surge in new entrants ages 23–26. *Health Affairs, 30*(12), 2286–2292.

Banks, J., Marmot, M., Oldfield, Z., & Smith, J. P. (2006). Disease and disadvantage in the United States and in England. *Journal of the American Medical Association, 295*(17), 2037–2045.

Berggren, R. (2005). Unexpected necessities—Inside Charity Hospital. *New England Journal of Medicine, 353*(15), 1550–1553.

Bodenheimer, T., & Grumbach, K. (2002). *Understanding health policy: A clinical approach* (3rd ed.). New York: Lange Medical Books/McGraw-Hill.

Buerhaus, P. I., Staiger, D. O., & Auerbach, D. I. (2000). Implications of an aging registered nurse workforce. *JAMA, 283*(22), 2948–2954.

Bureau of Labor Statistics. (2011). *Career guide to industries*. Table 2 Employment of wage and salary workers in health care, 2008 and projected change, 2008–2018. Washington, DC: U.S. Department of Labor.

Canadian Labour and Business Centre. (2003). *Physician workforce in Canada: Literature review and gap analysis*. Ottawa, Canada: Canadian Medical Forum.

Clark, M. (2010). Rebuilding the past: Health care reform in post-Katrina Louisiana. *Journal of Health Politics, Policy and Law, 35*(5), 743–769.

Colwill, J., Cultice, J., & Kruse, R. (2008) Will generalist physician supply meet demands of an increasing and aging population? *Health Affairs, 27*(3), w232–w241.

Congressional Research Service. (2010). *Public health, workforce, quality, and related pro-visions in the Patient Protection and Affordable Care Act (P.L. 111–148)*. Retrieved January 11, 2012, from http://www.idsociety.org/uploadedFiles/IDSA/Policy_and_Advocacy/Current_Topics_and_Issues/Workforce_and_Training/Related_Links/Public%20Health%20Workforce%20Quality%20and%20Related%20Pro-visions%20in%20PPACA%20P.L.%20111-148%20032510.pdf

Conrad, D., & Shortell, S. (1996). Integrated health systems: Promise and performance. *Frontiers of Health Services Management, 13*(1), 3–40.

Cooper, R. A., Getzen, T. E., McKee, H. J., & Laud, P. (2002). Economic and demo-graphic trends signal an impending physician shortage. *Health Affairs, 21*(1), 140–154.

Council on Graduate Medical Education. (2005). *Physician workforce policy guidelines for the United States, 2000–2020*. Rockville, MD: Health Resources and Services Administration, Department of Health and Human Services.

Cuellar, A. E., & Gertler, P. J. (2003). Trends in hospital consolidation: The formation of local systems. *Health Affairs, 22*(6), 77–87.

Department of Veterans Affairs. (2012). *Selected Veterans Health Administration Charac-teristics: FY2003 to FY2010*. Retrieved January 9, 2012, from http://www.va.gov/vetdata/Utilization.asp

Fuchs, V. R. (2004). Perspective: More variation in use of care, more flat-of-the curve medicine. *Health Affairs, 104*.

GAO. (2005a). *Indian Health Service: Health care services are not always available to Native Americans (No. GAO-05-789)*. Washington, DC: U.S. Government Accountability Office.

GAO. (2005b). *Testimony before the Committee on Ways and Means, U.S. House of Represen-tatives—Nonprofit, for-profit, and government hospitals: Uncompensated care and other community benefits*. Washington, DC: General Accounting Office.

Gesensway, D. (1999). *How a legendary New Orleans hospital is struggling to finally change its ways*. Retrieved January, 2006, from http://www.acponline.org/journals/news/apr99/orleans.htm

Grumbach, K. (2002). Perspective: The ramifications of specialty-dominated medicine. *Health Affairs, 21*(1), 155–157.

Hegner, R. (2001). *The health care safety net in a time of fiscal pressures*. Washington, DC: National Health Policy Forum.

Horowitz, J. (2005). Making profits and providing care: Comparing nonprofit, for-profit, and Government Hospitals. *Health Affairs, 24*(3), 790–801.

Hospital Corporation of America. (2011). Retrieved March 18, 2011, from http://www.hcahealthcare.com/news/press-kit.dot

HRSA. (2005a). *Bureau of primary care: Community health centers*. Retrieved July 1, 2005, from http://bphc.hrsa.gov/chc/

HRSA. (2010). *The registered nurse population findings from the 2008 National Sample Survey of Registered Nurses*. Retrieved January 13, 2012, from http://bhpr.hrsa.gov/healthworkforce/rnsurveys/rnsurveyfinal.pdf

HRSA. (2012). *Health center data: Reporting highlights*. Retrieved January 13, 2012, from http://bphc.hrsa.gov/healthcenterdatastatistics/index.html

IHS. (2005). *Indian health service introduction*. Retrieved January 24, 2006, from http://www.ihs.gov/PublicInfo/PublicAffairs/Welcome Info/ IHSintro.asp

IHS. (2012). *IHS fact sheets: IHS year 2012 profile.* Retrieved January 13, 2012, from http://www.ihs.gov/PublicAffairs/IHSBrochure/Profile.asp

IOM. (2000). *Institute of Medicine—America's health care safety net: Intact but endangered.* Washington, DC: National Academy Press.

Kaiser Family Foundation. (2011a). *Statehealthfacts: Distribution of nursing care facilities by ownership type, 2009.* Retrieved March 13, 2011, from http://statehealthfacts.org

Kaiser Family Foundation. (2011b). *Statehealthfacts: Hospital admission per 1,000 persons 2008.* Retrieved March 24, 2011, from http://statehealthfacts.org

Kaiser Family Foundation. (2011c). *Statehealthfacts: Hospitals by ownership 2008.* Retrieved March 16, 2011, from http://statehealthfacts.org

Kaiser Family Foundation. (2011d). *Statehealthfacts: Registered nurses per 10,000 population, 2009.* Retrieved March 18, 2011, from http://statehealthfacts.org

Kaiser Family Foundation. (2012). *Statehealthfacts: Total number of certified nursing facilities, 2009.* Retrieved January 11, 2012, from http://statehealthfacts.org

Kane, R., Kane, R., & Ladd, R. (1998). *The heart of long term care.* New York: Oxford University Press.

Medical Center of Louisiana at New Orleans. (2003, January 31, 2006). *The beginnings of Charity Hospital.* Retrieved January 31, 2006, from http://www.mclno.org/

Milbank, D. (2005, September 3). A day of contradictions. *The Washington Post,* p. A15.

NAPH. (2005). *America's public hospitals and health care systems: Results of the annual NAPH hospital characteristics survey.* Washington, DC: National Association of Public Hospitals and Health Systems.

NAPH. (2009a). The health care reform dialogue: Key questions about coverage and access. *Issue Brief, March 2009.* Retrieved January 13, 2012, from http://www.naph.org/Publications/Dialogue.aspx

NAPH. (2009b). *America's public hospitals and health systems, 2009 results of the annual NAPH hospital characteristics survey.* Retrieved January 16, 2012, from http://www.naph.org/Main-Menu-Category/Publications/Safety-Net-Financing/2009-Public-Hospital-Financial-Characteristics-.aspx?FT=.pdf

NAPH. (2012). *Hospital characteristics report.* Retrieved January 13, 2012, from http://www.naph.org/Main-Menu-Category/Our-Work/Safety-Net-Financing/Characteristics-Report.aspx

National Center for Health Statistics. (2011). *Health, United States, 2010.* Hyattsville, MD: Centers for Disease Control and Prevention, U.S. Department of Health and Human Services.

OECD. (2010c). *OECD health data 2010.* Retrieved March 18, 2011, from http://www.oecd-ilibrary.org/social-issues-migration-health/data/oecd-health-statistics/oecd-health-data_data-00350-en?isPartOf=/content/datacollection/health-data-en

OECD. (2011), Public expenditure on health. *Health: Key tables from OECD,* No. 3. doi: 10.1787/hlthxp-pub-table-2011-1-en

OECD. (2012a), *Health at a glance 2011,* Figure 4.2: MRI units, 2009 (or nearest year). Retrieved January 11, 2012, from http://www.oecd-ilibrary.org/docserver/download/fulltext/8111101ec030.pdf?expires=1326316326&id=id&accname=guest&checksum=FFB6515404D9C42BCE8393EA9CDEA326

OECD. (2012b). *Health at a glance 2011,* Figure 7.1.1 Total health expenditure per capita, public and private, 2009 (or nearest year). Retrieved January 11, 2012, from http://www.oecd-ilibrary.org/docserver/download/fulltext/8111101ec060.pdf?

expires=1326318062&id=id&accname=guest&checksum=682ACEB99B0F9CF-CE97C62 6CEAFA3F03

Phelan, J. C., Link, B. G., Diez-Roux, A., Kawachi, I., & Levin, B. (2004). "Fundamental causes" of social inequalities in mortality: A test of the theory. *Journal of Health Society and Behavior, 45*(3), 265–285.

Redlener, & Grant, (2009). America's safety net and health care reform—What lies ahead? *New England Journal of Medicine, 361*(23),2201–2204.

Rosenau, P. V. (2000). Managing medical technology: Lessons for the United States from Quebec and France. *International Journal of Health Services, 30*(3), 617–639.

Shi, L., & Singh, D. (2001). *Delivering health care in America* (2nd ed.). Gaithersburg, MD: Aspen Publishers.

Starfield, B., Shi, L., Grover, A., & Macinko, J. (2005). The effects of specialist supply on populations' health: Assessing the Evidence. *Health Affairs, hlthaff.w5.97.*

Starr, P. (1982). *The social transformation of American medicine*. New York: Basic Books.

Stensland, J., & Milet, M. (2002). The variance of rural small-town hospitals' financial performance. *Policy Anal Brief W Series, 5*(3), 1–4.

Tenet Healthcare Corporation. (2011). *Corporate website*. Retrieved March 9, 2011, from http://www.tenethealth.com

Waitzkin, H. (2005). Commentary—The history and contradictions of the health care safety net. *Health Services Research, 40*(3), 923–940.

Wilkinson, R. G. (1996). *Unhealthy societies: The afflictions of inequality*. London: Routledge.

CHAPTER FIVE

LONG-TERM CARE OF THE AGED AND DISABLED

*L*ong-term care involves the financing and delivery of an array of health and social services to the aged and disabled. In contrast to acute care, which is disease based and curative in orientation, the orientation of long-term care is inherently holistic and function based. The conventional definition of *long-term care*, provided by Kane, Kane, and Ladd's (1998) authoritative analysis of U.S. long-term care policy and services, is the "[h]ealth, personal care, and related social services provided over a sustained period of time to people who have lost or never developed certain measurable functional abilities" (p. 314). The scope of long-term care policies and services thus encompasses the aged, the developmentally disabled, the chronically ill, and persons disabled by trauma. Although there are many specific health care services and episodes of care that are typically defined and financed as a part of the acute care system, long-term care has a distinct identity in its own right (Kane et al., 1998). Ordinary acute care services are typically episodic in delivery, oriented toward curative interventions, and are often experienced as a disruptive event in people's everyday lives. In contrast, the prolonged and holistic nature of long-term care leads to its becoming integral to people's lives (Kane et al., 1998, p. 4). Also in contrast to ordinary acute care, where there are formal boundaries between health care services, social services, and the supports provided through family, friendship networks, and the community, long-term care's boundaries are far more informal and permeable.

Although the public discourse pertaining to long-term care policy and services has generally been focused on the elderly, in reality, 42% of the people receiving long-term care services are under age 65 (Kaiser Commission on Medicaid Facts, 2011). The nonelderly long-term care users include the developmentally disabled, the mentally ill, persons with chemical dependencies, persons with chronic disabling illness (e.g., multiple sclerosis) and persons disabled through injury (Kane et al., 1998; Spector, Fleishman,

Pezzin, & Spillman, 2000). Obtaining a precise estimate of the number of persons receiving long-term care services is relatively straightforward for those residing in institutional long-term care settings such as nursing homes and long-term psychiatric hospitals, because counts of residents of these facilities are routinely reported to state and federal regulatory agencies. However, for the far majority of persons receiving community-based long-term care services, precise estimates are much more difficult to obtain. Through a methodology that combines household-level survey data on the use of long-term care assistance and institutional data, the Agency for Healthcare Research and Quality (AHRQ) estimates that approximately 2.2% of adults aged between 18 and 64 (4 million) are long-term care recipients, while for those aged 65+, about 16.7% (6 million) are long-term care recipients (Spector et al., 2000; U.S. Census Bureau, 2005a). It should be noted that while these estimates provide some idea of the number of long-term care users, like other health care utilization statistics, they underestimate the number of persons actually in need of care.

THE LONG-TERM CARE SERVICES SYSTEM

The very broad definition of long-term care as encompassing "health, personal care, and related social services provided over a sustained period of time" (Kane et al., 1998, p. 314) suggests that it can be thought about in a number of ways. The approach taken by the AHPR distinguishes three general types of long-term care: formal care provided in the community setting, informal care provided in the community setting, and institutional care. Because formal care refers to care that is provided by paid persons as opposed to care that is provided by family, friends, and volunteers, institutional care is inherently formal (Spector et al., 2000). Although there is great local variation in the relative balance between the three general types of long-term care, the AHRQ (2001) *Characteristics of Long-Term Care Users* provides a glimpse of the national picture:

- Only about 4% of the nonelderly recipients of long-term care (those aged 18–64) are institutionalized, while 27% of the elderly long-term care recipients (those aged 65+) receive their care in institutional settings.[1]
- For the nonelderly population of long-term care recipients living in the community, most (about 70%) rely exclusively on informal supports. For the elderly long-term care recipients living in the community, it is more common to rely on a mixture of formal and informal supports.

- About 30% of long-term informal caregivers of the elderly are themselves elderly, and most (63.1%) are women. By far, the most common category of informal caregivers are adult daughters (27%).[2]

Taken together, these trends portray a long-term care system that has a signifi-cant institutional bias with respect to the elderly, and a system of care that is also enormously dependent upon the social norms that define women as the prime caregivers of the elderly. Though the three general types of long-term care (informal community-based care, formal community-based care, and institutional care) are structurally distinct, they address the same array of long-term care needs—generally defined as forms of assistance with either ADL (activities of daily living) or IADL (instrumental activities of daily living). ADL refer to tasks of everyday self-care that are basic or essential: getting in and out of bed, dressing, eating, toileting, and bathing. IADL refer to the more complex tasks of everyday living that draw upon more highly developed capacities in cognition, communication, physical dexterity, and stamina: cooking, doing laundry, driving a car, paying bills, and buying groceries. In contrast to acute care, where the prevalent kinds of health ser-vices attend to sophisticated things untrained people are unable to do for themselves, in long-term care the prevalent kinds of service attend to ordinary things people have either lost or been unable to develop the capacity to do.

Community-Based Long-Term Care Services

Community-based long-term care services, as the name implies, provide ser-vices to the elderly and otherwise disabled who are able to live in the commu-nity. Although the bases of many community-based long-term care services were developed as a specific alternative to institutional care or as a way to reduce the risk for institutionalization, much if not most of their value pertains to their ability to enhance the range of functional capacity and improve quality of life. While some forms of community-based long-term care are designed to be rehabilitative and others designed to maintain functioning, in reality there is a continuum of both design and true effect. Sometimes rehabilitative ser-vices do little more than maintain functioning and sometimes the so-called custodial forms of long-term care that are guided by a strong philosophy of optimism and capacity maximization promote incremental recovery. Another significant contrast between acute care health services and long-term care services is that, while the target of intervention in acute care is the so-called primary patient, long-term care services tend to be structured around the impaired person's caregiving network. For example, participation in an adult day care center generally benefits the functioning of the participating older adult and promotes the resilience of the elder's informal caregiver through the provision of emotional support and respite. The major components of community-based long-term care services typically include in-home services (skilled nursing, restorative therapies, personal care, companions, and chore services), residential care (adult foster homes, group homes, assisted living facilities), voluntary multiservice agencies, senior centers, adult day health centers, hospices, public social and health service agencies, and case management services from any number of sources.

In-Home Services

Although Medicare provides payment for a limited array of professional home care services that are specific to an episode of illness, the in-home services that more typically fall under the definition of long-term care involve long-term assistance with ADL and IADL. Because ongoing skilled nursing services are prohibitively expensive, individuals requiring that level of care for protracted periods tend to become institutionalized. For most persons in need of in-home long-term care services, the specific services needed typically entail personal care (assistance with getting in and out of bed, dressing, eating), companions (persons able to provide supervision and socialization), and chore services (housekeeping, laundry, shopping). These services are either paid for privately, through long-term care insurance, or funded by Medicaid. In-home services are the most likely services that would be provided by an able and willing family member, and they are also the services that are the most critical in terms of preventing institutionalization. For this reason, states are often strongly motivated to fund these services for the poor and more severely disabled, aside from the judicial imperatives to do so that extend from the Olmstead decision.[3]

Residential Care

Residential care encompasses a variety of living arrangements that have the common feature of providing group living in a community environment. Adult family homes (also referred to as adult foster homes) typically provide shelter, supervision, and assistance with ADL and IADL to the extent necessary, for from two to six residents. Adult Family Homes are licensed by states and provide residential care for the mentally ill, the developmentally disabled, and the elderly. While they have the advantage of providing a range of supports to their residents and in many states have prevented further expansions of the nursing home industry, the lack of professional staff and the low costs of entry into the market have also attracted a minority of unscrupulous operators. Group homes are basically larger versions of adult family homes, serving a larger number of residents. They are often operated by voluntary agencies. Unlike adult family homes, they serve the mentally ill and developmentally disabled more than they do the elderly. Assisted living centers are large congregate care homes that are akin to retirement homes, except that they offer some limited in-house or contracted nursing and personal support services to their (typically elderly) residents. More than nursing homes and adult family homes, they tend to attract middle-class and more affluent elderly and have a large presence of for-profit corporate ownership.

Multiservice Agencies

For many of the elderly and nonelderly disabled, their ability to retain optimal independence is contingent upon an array of social services that include information and referral, advocacy, skills training, counseling, transportation, and contracted case management services (which will be defined later). They are voluntary local agencies organized to serve specific populations of the disabled (e.g., the developmentally disabled, the severely visually impaired, the mentally ill, and the elderly) and are funded by a mixture of public and local private funds. Many qualify for federal funding as designated centers for independent living, a federally funded program established under the Rehabilitation Act of 1973 to serve broad classes of the disabled (Kane et al., 1998).

Senior Centers

Strictly speaking, as originally conceived, senior centers were not organized as long-term care service providers so much as they were social and recreational organizations for older adults. However, in recent decades they have evolved to places where older adults can obtain meals, be offered nutrition and health education services, and obtain a limited array of important social and health care services, such as flu shots, health screening, counseling, and assistance with health insurance (Shi & Singh, 2001). For many fragile elders, the local senior center plays a central role in their lives and offers the critical supports needed to sustain independent living.

Adult Day Centers

Like senior centers, adult day centers (ADCs) are oriented toward seniors and provide an array of supportive services. Unlike senior centers, ADCs function as a carefully structured and protective environment for elderly adults with substantial cognitive and physical impairments. ADCs have been organized by voluntary community groups, as extensions of community hospital programs, and even by for-profit providers as an alternative to nursing home care. As noted by Shi and Singh (2001), ADCs often serve as a means of respite to caregivers of elders. Akin to conventional day care centers, ADC's generally operate during hours that permit other members of the elder's family to work normal day jobs. Although ADCs vary in their relative emphasis on rehabilitation, health maintenance, and social–psychological support, in general they all provide a socio-medical milieu that permits very fragile elders to "age-in-place" as opposed to being segregated in institutions (Cutchin, 2003; Shi & Singh, 2001). While in many respects the long-term care support needs of modestly impaired residents of Assisted Living Centers and modestly impaired participants in ADCs are identical, there is a tendency for ADCs to serve lower income elders unable to afford the costs of living in an assisted living center (Cutchin, 2003). These trends not only reflect the disadvantages of social class accrued over the life course, but also state and federal policies that have favored the for-profit nursing home industry as the long-term care solution for the aged poor. This issue will be revisited in the next section of this chapter.

Hospice and Palliative Care Programs

Even though hospice care in the United States originated as an extension of the acute health care benefits of Medicare and private insurance, the history of the hospice concept and the nature of hospice care (as an integrated array of social and medical care services delivered over a sustained and often indefinite period) makes hospice care and hospice agencies an integral part of the long-term care system. The hospice concept originated in England with the pioneering work in the care of the dying by British physician Cecily Saunders. Although the beginnings of the U.S. hospice movement can be traced to a visit Saunders made to Yale University in 1963, hospice care in the United States did not become a conventional approach for care of the dying until after Congress made hospice care a permanent feature of the Medicare benefit package and an optional component of state Medicaid programs in 1986 (NHPCO, 2006). Despite widespread support for hospice care among the public and across the health professions, in many communities the growth of hospice care has been constrained by curative biases within the local medical community and the political economy of private medical practice. The specific benefits of hospice vary by the form of insurance coverage, but in general hospice benefits follow the Medicare model, which includes physicians' services and provides intermittent home nursing care, medical supplies, outpatient drugs, home health aide services, social work, professional therapies (physical, occupational, and speech), short-term inpatient care for respite/symptom management, and spiritual counseling. The caveats are that the hospice recipient must be diagnosed by a physician as terminally ill within a specified period (conventionally 6 months), and must voluntarily accept hospice care benefits as an alternative to standard Medicare benefits. *By definition,* the hospice benefits provided are for comfort care as opposed to curative care. While the receipt of hospice care does not preclude a recipient from pursuing a cure, either through a decision to withdraw from hospice care or to pay for curative health care services out of pocket, the far majority of hospice patients have made the transition from the pursuit of cure to an emphasis on optimal quality of remaining life.

In contrast to hospice care, "palliative care does not rigidly dichotomize the choice between curative and supportive care, and normalizes the coexistence of potentially fatal disease processes with hope and uncertainty" (Almgren 2009, pp. 2–3). The World Health Organization's definition of palliative care describes it as a holistic approach to care that both helps patients live as actively as possible until death and also "can be provided in conjunction with other therapies that are intended to prolong life" (World Health Organization, 2011). Palliative care, unlike hospice care, acknowledges that people can live a very long time in the penumbra between the pursuit of curative or at least ameliorative treatment and the acceptance of death. Palliative care is particularly a crucial alternative for persons of advanced age that are burdened with multiple chronic and potentially fatal conditions with largely indeterminate trajectories (Almgren, 2009, p. 3). Unfortunately, health care financing policy in the United States remains enmired in a dichotomized approach to end-of-life care that offers either aggressive curative treatment or conventional hospice care. In contrast, many other countries (e.g., Australia, Canada, New Zealand, and the United Kingdom) approach palliative care as more of a holistic continuum with permeable boundaries between curative and purely supportive care.

Public Social and Health Service Agencies

As mentioned previously, the long-term care population is comprised of the aged, the developmentally disabled, and also poor persons who have become disabled by injury or chronic illness at some point in their lives. Obviously, all of these characteristics are nonexclusive and are frequently overlapping. For the mentally ill, the developmentally disabled, and the aged there are generally local (county and municipal) public agencies that both provide an array of publicly funded social and health services and at least help mediate the benefits of other public programs. The origins of these agencies are either major federal programs aligned with major deinstitutionalization initiatives at different points in history, or policy initiatives more generally designed to enhance the well-being and quality of life for a specific group. An example of the former is the *1963 Community Mental Health Centers Construction Act/Mental Retardation Facilities Construction Act (PL 88-164)*, which funded the construction of comprehensive community centers for the community-based care of the developmentally disabled and the mentally ill. An example of the latter is the *1965 Older Americans Act (Pl 89-73)*, which established grants to states for community planning and services programs for older adults and ultimately a network of more than 600 local "Area Agencies on Aging" to both plan and contract services for older adults (Kane et al., 1998).[4] For nonelderly persons who are disabled through injury or illness, their entry into long-term care services is via the local branch of the state agency charged with attending to the needs of the so-called "worthy" poor, that is, those with a legitimized reason for not being employable. In contrast to the local public agencies with a mandate to advocate on behalf of a specific population (the developmentally disabled, the mentally ill, and the elderly), state agencies with a more general scope of responsibility for the poor are more known for creating bureaucratic barriers to program benefits and services. Thus, persons who are disabled and in need of community-based long-term care services due to injury or chronic illness are more often seen through the lens of poverty and character deficits rather than through their status as a disabled person.

Case Management

Case management is at once a particular kind of service and a major structural component of community-based long-term care. Some also claim it as a distinct profession. Although case management is applied to a wide variety of client-centered activities, in general there are two general kinds of case management—both of which are relevant and essential to community-based long-term care. Managed care approaches to case management entail an organized approach to social and health care needs assessment, the acquisition of appropriate services through the most cost-effective setting and providers, coordinating service delivery, and monitoring the ongoing delivery and quality of services (Kane et al., 1998, p. 46; Shi & Singh, 2001, p. 582). Although the managed care model of case management can involve a health professional with a distinct set of individual ethical and legal obligations toward the client, case managers that work within the managed care model are often paraprofessionals with a bureaucratic orientation and agenda. In contrast, clinical case management is delivered by health care professionals (physicians, nurses, social workers) who are accountable to a distinct set of professionally prescribed ethical obligations that transcend organizational interests and requirements. While most of the activities will look similar (assessment, planning, care coordination, and service monitoring), clinical case management also involves careful attention to the engagement of the client in the care planning process, consultation with the client's family and system of natural supports, collaboration with other involved clinical professionals, and crisis intervention (Kanter, 1989). In truth, well functioning community-based long-term systems rely on both models of case management, because managed care organizations and health care professionals bring different structural benefits to an integrated system of long-term care.

The Institutional Component of Long-Term Care: The American Nursing Home Industry

The institutional component of long-term care is comprised of long-term psychiatric hospitals, state institutions for the developmentally disabled, long-term rehabilitation facilities, prisons, and nursing homes.[5] The primary distinction between institutional long-term care and community-based long-term care involves institutional segregation from the nondisabled population and a related emphasis on protective confinement. Other common features include the "medicalization" of ordinary needs and services, extensive restrictions on personal autonomy, and the prevalence of a medical model pathology-based interpretation of disablement. It is for these reasons that over 50 years of long-term care policy have placed an emphasis on deinstitutionalization. As a general trend, the legislation and litigation that have defined the deinstitutionalization movement have been dramatically successful in reducing the populations of state institutions—a trend that has favored the developmentally disabled and the mentally ill far more than it has the aged. Care for the aged disabled still retains a strong institutional emphasis, for a variety of reasons that include changes in family structure and role expectations, labor force trends and policies, a longstanding federal policy bias toward nursing home care, formidable challenges in creating an integrated network of community-based long-term care, the acute care orientation of health care financing, the historic medicalization of the aging process, and an entrenched for-profit nursing home industry.

Nursing Home Utilization

Only a very small proportion of the elderly reside in nursing homes at any one time, about 2% of persons aged 65+ (Houser, 2007). However, the risk of nursing home residency increases as the old grow older, such that among persons aged 85 and older about 14% reside in nursing homes (Houser, 2007). The most recent estimates available place the nursing home population at about 1.4 million persons (Kaiser Family Foundation, 2009a). Although the elderly (those over age 65) comprise the largest share of the nursing home population (about 66%), in recent decades the proportion of the older adults residing in nursing home care has declined significantly (Houser, 2007). This decline in large part is attributable to the growth in community-based long-term care programs for older adults, the addition of more retirement homes communities with assisted living supports, and also the growth of the adult family home industry. That said, a large proportion of older adults will still have some exposure to at least short-term nursing home care (Merlis, 1999). Generally speaking, nursing home spells of less than 1 year are comprised of two populations, those that go into nursing home care to convalesce after a debilitating spell of illness or in order to recover from surgery, and those for whom entrance into nursing home care presages death. Concerning the latter category, this is often an inevitable event in the dying process. However, in many cases, entry into nursing home care is a shock event that itself precipitates death.

There has long been an extensive literature on the role of race, ethnicity, and cultural variation in nursing home utilization (Almgren, 1990). For example, African Americans are far less likely to end their days in a nursing home than either non-Hispanic Whites or Hispanics, even where the confounding effects of age, sex, income, education, and cause of death are accounted for (Iwashyna & Chang, 2002). As the share of older adults residing in nursing homes declines, it may be that racial and ethnic composition of nursing home residents will change. One possibility is that social class, as opposed to race and ethnicity, may emerge as a stronger predictor of long-term nursing home care as the more affluent elderly exercise their ability to better afford noninstitutional long-term care alternatives.

The Structure of the Nursing Home Industry

Of the 16,500 certified nursing facilities nationwide, two-thirds (67%) have for-profit ownership. The remaining nursing homes are divided between nonprofit nursing homes (26%) and the small fraction (6%) of nursing homes that have government ownership (Kaiser Family Foundation, 2009a). Very large corporate nursing home chains account for a significant share of the for-profit sector of the nursing home industry and, by definition, the industry as a whole (U.S. Census Bureau, 2004). The domination of the American nursing home industry by for-profit corporations stands in stark contrast to the hospital industry, which (as discussed in Chapter 4) is dominated by not-for-profit forms of ownership.

Until the late 1970s, the nursing home industry was largely comprised of independent proprietary facilities, akin to other kinds of small businesses owned and operated by a local investor. However, by 1985, approximately 70% of for-profit homes had become a part of a nursing home chain (Almgren, 1990). Like the hospital industry, there is great statewide variation in the extent to which the for-profit sector of the industry is dominant. For example, in Texas, over 80% of all nursing homes are for-profit, while in states with a more established tradition of not-for-profit nursing home care, like Minnesota and the Dakotas, the for-profit sector of the industry accounts for less than a third of ownership (Kaiser Family Foundation, 2010a).

There are enduring policy questions in nursing home research pertaining to whether the form of ownership makes a difference in the quality of nursing home care, and whether different forms of ownership serve different segments of the population. With respect to the question on ownership and quality of care, the prevailing belief among the broad public and health care professionals is that nonprofit nursing homes are inherently of higher quality because they have a fundamentally different reason for being in business and because they are mandated to reinvest their profits into their facilities and services. As intuitive as this might seem, the evidence is actually quite equivocal (Almgren, 1990; O'Brien, 1988; O'Brien, Saxberg, & Smith, 1983; Spector, Seldon, & Cohen, 1998). In large part this is because many studies fail to control for confounding effects or use measures of quality that pertain to clinical outcomes. However, a particularly rigorous study that employed a range of critical outcome measures (e.g., mortality, hospitalizations, and clinical conditions pertaining directly to quality of care) found no significant differences in clinical care outcomes—other than fewer hospitalizations among patients in nonprofit homes (Spector et al., 1998).[6]

With respect to the second question, whether different forms of nursing home ownership serve different segments of the population, it is indeed the case that the nonprofit sector of the nursing home caters to the more socially advantaged (Almgren, 1990; O'Brien, 1988; Spector et al., 1998). Both Almgren (1990) and O'Brien (1988) concur that nonprofit nursing homes, because they tend to have a higher level of public confidence, are better able to support selective admissions policies aimed at avoiding the medically indigent. Another dimension of segmentation in the nursing home industry, aside from the form of ownership, is the division between the relatively small number of nursing homes that carry a very high proportion of Medicaid patients, and those nursing homes that have a higher mix of private and publicly financed residents. According to Mor, Zinn, Angelleli, Teno, and Miller (2004) the former class of nursing homes comprise roughly 15% of the industry, tend to be disproportionately located in poor areas, and tend to have a higher representation of African American residents. These nursing homes also have lower levels of staffing, a higher number of citations for deficiencies, and are more likely to be terminated from the Medicaid/Medicare program—thus, in effect, forcing their closure (Mor et al., 2004). While closure of these medicalized almshouses might be seen as a positive action, their disappearance will not affect the likelihood that impoverished frail elderly will then be able to access the higher quality tiers of the nursing home industry.

The Origins of the Nursing Home Industry

In contrast to other modern democracies, the United States has placed a particular emphasis on an institutional solution for the care of the aged (Kane et al., 1998). While there are many reasons cited for this, including the dominance of a highly individualistic perspective and an overzealous faith in market solutions to most problems, much of the reason has to do with the development of an entrenched proprietary (private for-profit) nursing home industry that has adapted well to the mixed private and public model of health care financing. The primary origins of the proprietary nursing home actually can be traced to the Social Security Act of 1935.

CARE OF THE AGED BEFORE 1935. A common myth about earlier generations of Americans is that they took care of their frail elderly, largely through the mechanisms of the multigenerational household and extensive kinship ties. While it is true that throughout most of U.S. history there were few homes for the aged and no nursing homes, in fact, an early precursor to the modern nursing home was the almshouse. Were it true that frail elders were at one time well attended by children and kin, it would be expected that the population of early 20th-century almshouses would be dominantly comprised of children and working age adults. However, as shown in Figure 5.1, that is hardly the case. Indeed, the most common age category for those entering almshouses at the turn of the century were elderly aged between 60 and 69, which, given the 49-year life expectancy of 1900, was very old age (Almgren, 1990). This was also the age category at which the elderly of the working class were likely to become unemployable due to diminished physical capacities. Given the lack of a national old-age pension program before 1935, the early 60s would be the peak age to be at risk for

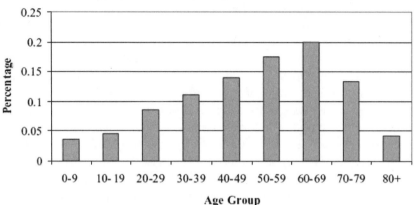

Age at Admission, Paupers in Almhouses 1904

Source: Adapted from Table XX, Census of 1904 Special Report, Paupers in Almshouses. U.S. Census Bureau, Washington, DC.

Figure 5.1 *Age distribution of almshouse entrants from 1904 Census.*

destitution for working class elders. The drop off of admissions to the alms-house after age 70 likely represents the reality that those who were both old and impoverished did not tend to survive to very old age. Although progress-ive era social reformers embarked on a national campaign to eliminate the almshouse as the method for providing for the poor, this movement favored women and children more than it did the elderly. As late as 1923, more than 70% of those that remained in the diminishing number of alms-houses were persons over age 65 (Vladeck, 1980).

The other precursor to the nursing home was the mental institution, typi-cally a state asylum. In the early 1900s, about 2% of all persons aged 65+ were in some kind of institutional setting. Of these institutionalized elderly, the almshouses accounted for about 57%, while the remaining 43% were confined to mental institutions (Almgren, 1990; Manard, Kart, & Gils, 1975). Although it is likely that cognitive deficits were the largest factor in determining whether an impoverished and abandoned elder ended up in a mental insti-tution as opposed to an almshouse, the major drivers to institutionalization were age, poverty, the lack of informal social supports, and the lack of any fed-eralized safety net for the aged poor.

THE SOCIAL SECURITY ACT OF 1935 AND THE BEGINNINGS OF THE FOR-PROFIT SECTOR OF NURSING HOME INDUSTRY. There were two provisions of the Social Security Act of 1935 that in many respects were specifically intended to empty the nation's poorhouses of their elderly. The first was the

Old Age Assistance (OAA) program itself, which established the monthly Social Security pension check that remains an essential buffer between old age and poverty. The second provision precluded from eligibility the aged residents of public and private institutions that could be classified as custodial, correctional, or curative in nature (Thomas, 1969). Although the intent of the latter provision was in effect an attempt to deinstitutionalize the elderly, in a classic paradox of unintended policy consequences, it became the founding cornerstone of the modern proprietary nursing home industry. The basis of the paradox involves a specific *disadvantage* this provision of the Social Security Act extended to the nonprofit sector of the nursing home industry, formally known as "homes for the aged."

Prior to the availability of the OAA pension program, churches, fraternal organizations, and immigrant self-help organizations throughout the country were erecting nonprofit "Homes for the Aged" as a benign and enlightened alternative to the almshouse. Though established from diverse sources, these nonprofit old-age homes established within a few decades the voluntary sector of the nursing home industry, which accounts for 26% of the nursing home industry. Although a far superior alternative to the poorhouse and in many respects a model of care for the frail aged, the OAA pension program provisions aimed at eliminating the institutionalization of elderly in almshouses and mental institutions tarred these nonprofit homes with the same brush. Vladeck (1980) attributes this tragic error of public policy to the domination of new immigrant groups in sponsoring these voluntary homes for the aged rather than middle-class reformers. Whatever the underlying motivations, the effect of this policy ultimately provided the impetus for the establishment of the private sector of the nursing home industry.

Even the meager purchasing power granted by the OAA monthly pension enabled the aged without family resources to either live totally independently or to make their living arrangements in a boarding home. As a result, cities and towns throughout the United States had a burgeoning private boarding home industry that catered to the new social class of elderly pensioners. Most of these homes were large, old multistory family structures with several rooms available to accommodate boarders (Gruber, 1967). As would be expected, those elders that elected to live in a boarding home were more likely to have functional impairments. There is also evidence to suggest that some boarding homes provided nursing care to gain a competitive edge over others (Dunlop, 1979). While some proprietary nursing homes were founded as such, with the passage of time, many of the larger homes that had their beginnings as room and board enterprises gradually transformed to nursing homes. Key to this process of transformation was several pieces of enabling federal legislation, beginning with amendments to the Social

Security Act that followed the first National Conference on Aging in 1950[7] (Almgren, 1990).

By 1953, Congress passed various amendments to the Social Security Act that provided direct payments to providers of nursing home care, enabled residents of voluntary and public homes for the aged to receive OAA pensions, and required states to establish licensing and inspection programs for nursing homes as a condition for receiving federal matching funds for nursing home care. Collectively, these provisions established the essential structural basis for federal financing and oversight of nursing home care in both the voluntary and proprietary sectors of the nursing home industry. Between 1954 and 1959, Congress followed up with a massive infusion of federal dollars into all three sectors of the growing nursing home industry (private, voluntary, and public) via funding programs for nursing home construction and upgrades. In 1954, the Hill–Burton Act was extended to provide construction and upgrade funds for the voluntary and public parts of the nursing home industry. Largely as a result of pressure from the newly formed proprietary nursing home lobby (American Nursing Home Association), in 1956 and 1959 Congress amended both the Small Business Administration Loan Program and the Federal Housing Administration Mortgage Insurance Program to similarly support the proprietary sector of the nursing home industry (Dunlop, 1979; Pegals, 1981). Thus it can be said that by the end of the 1950s federal policy had been thoroughly committed to an institutionalized approach to long-term care—one that privileged the further growth of private sector institutions.

MEDICAID/MEDICARE AND THE ESTABLISHMENT OF THE MODERN NURSING HOME INDUSTRY. While the 1950s had witnessed the entrenchment of institutional solutions to aging and long-term care policy issues, there remained critical gaps in financing, licensure, and quality assurance. In particular, there were no uniform standards in the definition of what constituted a nursing home or uniform standards pertaining to facility construction and operation. All began to change with the passage of the 1960 Kerr–Mills Medical Assistance to the Aged Program, which committed the federal government to the funding of skilled nursing services for the medically indigent and introduced a categorical in-kind assistance program to the nursing home industry. This legislation presaged the Social Security Act Amendments of 1965, which through the financial clout of the Medicare and Medicaid program dollars enabled the federal government to impose uniform definitions of nursing home care, uniform standards for nursing home construction and operation, and uniform requirements for facility inspection. Later amendments (in 1967 and 1972) went even further in expanding nursing home care benefits as well as uniform standards of services, cost, and utilization review (Almgren, 1990). In sum effect, these policies increased the purchasing power of families who might be in the market for the nursing home placement of an elder, assuaged their concerns about nursing home quality, and reinforced the perception of a dichotomous choice between family-based solutions to long-term care and institutional solutions.

THE GROWTH IN NURSING HOME UTILIZATION. Between 1960 and 1970, the nursing home utilization rate for the population aged 65+ increased by a phenomenal 74% (Dunlop, 1979). There is a general consensus that much of this increase is attributable to the massive infusion of public subsidies to the nursing home industry that characterized the long-term care policies of the 1960s (Dunlop, 1979; Kane et al., 1998; Manard et al., 1975; Morony & Kurtz, 1975; Vladeck, 1980). This argument is further reinforced by the fact that in the immediate 9-year period following the introduction of the Medicaid and Medicare subsidies, the annual rate of nursing home beds increased by an average 19% (Almgren, 1990). However, the enduring state-by-state variations in nursing home utilization suggest there are other factors at work. From the demand side of nursing home utilization, the factors that are most plausible include advancements in medical care that increased the survival rates of the elderly in advanced stages of frailty (Chiswick, 1976; Crimmons, Saito, & Ingegneri, 1989), increased rates of internal migration with geographic separation of parents and children (Rabin & Stockton, 1987), an increase in the *old age dependency ratio*[8] arising from increased old-age survivor-ship (Chiswick, 1976), growth in the survival disparities between men and women in old age (Chiswick, 1976), a decrease in the number of multigenerational households (Almgren, 1990; Treas, 1977), and the growth in female labor force participation that characterized the 1960s (Almgren, 1990).

In particular, it is likely that the interaction between an increase in the old age dependency (i.e., the population size of the elderly relative to the population size of potential caregivers) and the increase in the number of women employed outside the home during the 1960–1970 period accounted for a large share of the increased demand for institutional care of the aged. During the period in question, it was well established that women acted as the primary caregivers of the elderly and that women (more than men) believed that dependent elderly should reside with their children (Seelbach & Sauer, 1977; Select Committee on Aging, 1987).[9] As the 1960s unfolded, both the increase in the average number of hours women worked outside the home and the growth of the elderly population collided in ways that, for many families, made nursing home care seem the only realistic alternative.

While it may have seemed like prudent public policy to provide various forms of subsidies for families that would better enable them to provide care for their elders, Congress favored subsidies to the nursing home industry instead as a part of a larger agenda to invest in the infrastructure of the health care system.

POLICY INITIATIVES TO REDUCE NURSING HOME UTILIZATION. In all likelihood, there will never be a consensus on the relative merits of supply side factors versus demand side factors behind the dramatic 1960–1970 growth in nursing home care. In an attempt to develop an effective policy response to the demand side of nursing home utilization, during the 1970s and early 1980s there were several federally funded community-based care demonstration projects aimed at decreasing the necessity of nursing home placement. The common premise of these demonstration projects was that through public investments in the right mixture of community-based care services to elders and their informal care networks, a net savings in tax dollars could be realized through a decrease in the use of nursing home care. It was also hoped that the results from these projects would pave the way to the most cost-efficient benefit structures for the private long-term insurance market. In a widely disputed (but nonetheless influential) analysis of these demonstration projects published in *Health Services Research*, William Weissert[10] concluded that "Community care rarely reduces nursing home or hospital use; it provides only limited outcome benefits; and to this point, it has usually raised overall use of health services as well as total expenditures" (Weissert, 1985, p. 424). In fact, his study concluded that the sickest and most dependent patients may be more cheaply served in a nursing home. As Weissert saw it, the evidence from these projects suggested that the principal benefits to community-based care were not in net cost savings or the even marginal reductions in nursing home care, but in making life somewhat better for the elderly and their caregivers (Weissert, 1985). Although it is convincingly argued that Weissert's findings failed to take into account the favorable effect of community-based care on nursing home care utilization over time (see Kane et al., 1998, p. 71), there is no question that Weissert's conclusions caused policy makers to take a more skeptical view of the potential of community-based care as a cost-effective substitute for nursing home care—thus turning policy attention back toward the supply side.

One very straightforward approach to reducing the growth in nursing home utilization is to simply reduce the growth in the supply of nursing home beds. One argument for this approach is transparent: by constraining the supply of nursing home beds over time, the proportion of the population of elderly in institutional care will decline as the population of elderly increases. The other argument for constraints on the supply side of nursing home care is based on something commonly known in the health services research field as "Roemer's Law." In a nutshell, Roemer's Law holds that *supply tends to induce its own demand where a third party guarantees reimbursement of use* (Roemer, 1961).[11] In the context of institutional care like hospitals and nursing homes, this predicts that to the extent that public funds are available to subsidize the costs of care, a market dynamic of "build the beds and they will come" emerges. Applied more directly to the nursing home industry, Roemer's law suggests that to the extent that more nursing home beds are built and financial subsidies for nursing home care are made available, more of the elderly will become institutionalized.

In fact, beginning in the 1980s many states adopted very restrictive policies aimed at constraining the supply of nursing home beds, including outright moratoriums on new nursing home construction (Kane et al., 1998). The central mechanism for enabling states to do this was the so-called certificate-of-need legislation, which enables states to deny licensure and reimbursement to health care facilities that have not been granted a "certificate need" through the state's health care planning agency.[12] Other supply-side state-level initiatives involve the restriction of access to Medicaid subsidies for nursing home care through such mechanisms as a mandatory preadmission comprehensive functional assessment—an approach that is generally linked with assessment and referral to community-based care alternatives that in effect reduce the demand for nursing home care. Despite some level of skepticism among many policy makers concerning the ability of community-based long-term care services to be a cost-effective alternative to nursing home care, for a variety of reasons most states opted to invest in subsidies to community-based care in combination with efforts to restrict the growth of nursing home bed supply. Between 1992 and 1997, Medicaid waivers to allow subsidy of community-based long-term care services spending grew by almost 260% (The Urban Institute, 2001).

In the Balanced Budget Act of 1997, Congress established the Medicare PACE Program (Program of All-Inclusive Care for the Elderly), which integrates Medicare and Medicaid financing in order to provide a comprehensive array of medical and community-based long-term care services to at-risk elderly. In order to qualify for enrollment, the applicant must be over age 55 and be certified by the cooperating state agency to be eligible for nursing home placement. The PACE program is modeled on the On Lok Social Health Maintenance Organization (S/HOM) demonstration project in San Francisco, California—broadly recognized as a highly successful Health Care Financing Administration demonstration project.[13]

As a result of these supply-side and demand-side efforts to constrain nursing home utilization, the proportion of nursing home beds to the population of persons over age 65 stabilized at about 5% nationwide for several years and more recently has declined to 4% (Kaiser Family Foundation, 2010a; Kane et al., 1998). While this is an encouraging trend, national long-term care policy remains burdened by the unintended policy consequences of the past—and quite belated in its response to the formidable challenges of the immediate future.

THE SUSTAINABILITY OF RESOURCES FOR LONG-TERM CARE: CAREGIVING LABOR AND PUBLIC/PRIVATE FINANCING

There are a set of givens to long-term care policy that should guide policy makers at all levels: (1) the population of the oldest old (those 85+) will have expanded nearly fivefold between the census of 2000 and 2050 (U.S. Census Bureau, 2005b); (2) the newest generation of aged (like those of the past) favor "aging in place" to institutional care; (3) the newest generation of aged (like those of the past) are also ill-prepared to pay for the "aging in place" community support services that have proved an essential adjunct to informal supports from family and friends; (4) the next waves of aged have fewer children available as a resource for informal care than previous generations; and (5) the country is already too deeply in debt to greatly expand public entitlements to long-term care services in the absence of a radical restructuring of both the Medicare and Medicaid programs. As summarized by the Government Accountability Office's report on long-term care to Congress (GAO, 2005), the primary policy challenges facing both state legislatures and Congress that pertain to the financing of long-term care include:

- Determining societal responsibilities
- Considering the potential role of social insurance in financing
- Encouraging personal preparedness
- Recognizing the benefits, burdens, and costs of informal caregiving
- Assessing the balance of state and federal responsibilities to ensure adequate and equitable satisfaction of needs
- Adopting effective and efficient implementation and administration of reforms
- Developing financially sustainable public commitments (GAO, 2005, p. 3)

In the discussion that follows we will consider all of these policy challenges, but each is more or less subsumed within two fundamental policy paradoxes, the first having to do with resources for caregiving labor and the second pertaining to public and private financial resources for long-term care.

The Caregiving Paradox: Reconciling the Public and Private Spheres of Dependency and Caregiving

The crucial debates about long-term care policy are largely predicated on two highly influential but nonetheless erroneous assumptions. The first erroneous assumption is that independence is somehow both the "natural and optimal" state of human existence, when in fact the human condition throughout the life course is characterized by interdependence—economically, socially, and functionally (Fraser & Gordon, 1994). We thus tend to dichotomize people and families into a simple category of either "dependent" or "independent," or in economic terms as either "productive" or "nonproductive." The second erroneous assumption that underpins much of the policy discourse in long-term care policy is the idea that much of caregiving labor (the so-called informal caregiving), because it arises out of quasi-voluntary familial or communal obligations, is not "real work" in the sense of a social contribution that is as essential as growing food, constructing highways, teaching children, or serving in the nation's military (Glenn, 2010). While familial and communal caregivers of the disabled and chronically ill are often praised for their selflessness and loyalty, the reification of the "selfless caregiver" provides one way through which we as a society can deny that much of seemingly voluntary and altruistic caregiving is in reality coerced—through a variety of cultural and economic mechanisms that makes the disproportionate share of unremunerated caregiving by women (in particular, women of color) seem like the natural and appropriate state of affairs.

Evelyn Nakano Glenn (2010), in her historical analysis of the coercive aspects of informal and low-wage caregiving by women and certain racial and ethnic groups, identifies the ways in which public policy over time has been built upon and replicates (through a range of institutional arrangements) deeply embedded racial and gender hierarchies. Glenn notes that caregiving labor has been dichotomized into separate spheres, one private and primarily familial and the other public. In the private sphere, where caregiving takes place in the context of familial and communal relationships, caregiving labor is largely provided by women in response to a "status obligation" that women from most cultural groups are socialized from birth to accept and internalize. Status obligations are in essence institutionalized functions that one is expected to perform as the result of possessing a particular social status (e.g., soldier, doctor, mother, or daughter). The powerful expectations that are embedded within status obligations have both internal and external components. Internally, one feels compelled to perform a function for one or more of the following reasons: out of a deeply felt personal sense of duty, as an expression of love and loyalty, as an affirmation of one's sense of self and social identity, and often out of a sense of personal powerlessness. Externally, failure to perform a function that is considered obligatory to one's social status brings condemnation, as in the soldier that flees from combat, the mother that neglects her child, or the daughter that declines assistance to an aging and needy parent. Women's caregiving, as conformity to deeply internalized and externally sanctioned expectations, may be loving, respectful, admirable, and even noble—but in the truest senses of the term it is not wholly voluntary.

In the public sphere, caregiving labor (in nursing homes, day care centers, and in the home health care industry) is also dominated by women—largely in low-wage occupational categories. Although it may seem that the low wages of women in caregiving occupations is a function of the "unskilled" nature of the work in these occupations and the low levels of formal education required, Glenn (2010) makes the point that the historically low-wage caregiving occupations are in large part a function of their falling within the status obligations of women in society to serve in caregiving roles as a matter of duty. Glenn's analysis of the public sphere of caregiving offers a parallel argument concerning the status obligations of formally enslaved and functionally coerced workers of color, who historically have been seen as the "natural" caregivers and attendants of the dependent members of the dominant white segment of society. As one visible and enduring legacy of these parallel and intersecting status obligations, caregiving laborers and their occupational categories have largely been excluded from the federal labor market protections afforded other categories of workers (Glenn, 2010).

The most dramatic recent case of this selective exclusion paid caregivers was the late Evelyn Coke, an African American single grandmother who had for decades worked as a low-wage in-home caregiver of the elderly, chronically ill, and disabled. Although her responsibilities would often entail 24-hour care, her employer (a proprietary home care agency) contended that the federal Fair Labor Standards Act provisions requiring employers to pay minimum wage and overtime pay did not apply to employees classified as home care aides. At the point that Evelyn Coke was in her mid-60s and herself too disabled to work, on the advice of an attorney who had reviewed her employment records, she sued her employer for back wages that were owed to her based on the massive hours of overtime she accrued (Martin, 2009). Her case, because it raised crucial questions pertaining to Congressional legislative intent vs. the undisputed authority of the U.S. Labor

Department's interpretation of the applicability of the Fair Labor Standards Act in accordance with the prevailing policy preferences of the executive branch, was heard and decided by the U.S. Supreme Court in 2007 (Legal Information Institute, 2010). The case of *Long Island Care at Home, Ltd., et al. v. Coke*, because it also involved the minimum wage and overtime protection of millions of low-wage caregivers employed by private agencies that were often reimbursed by public (Medicaid) dollars, attracted friend-of-the-court briefings from state and industry interests arguing for the continued exclusion of low-wage caregivers like Evelyn Coke from the minimum wage and overtime protections under the Fair Labor Standards Act granted to other workers (Martin, 2009). Two years after the Supreme Court ruled in favor of the continued exclusion of Evelyn Coke and other low-wage caregivers from the Fair Labor Standards Act, Evelyn Coke succumbed to kidney failure—a condition that was diagnosed at the point when she finally became age-eligible for health insurance under Medicare. At an earlier point in her life, when causes of her kidney disease would likely have been diagnosed and treated, Evelyn Coke (like millions of other uninsured low-wage caregivers) could not afford a doctor. Despite the incredible injustices she endured, Evelyn Coke was reported to have said about her working life as a low-wage caregiver: "I don't regret taking care of old people" (as cited by Martin, 2009, p. 2). As highlighted by Glenn (2010), in ruling that the minimum wage and overtime protections of the Fair Labor Standards Act do not extend to home-care workers, in effect, "the Court decreed that the burden of providing 'affordable care' for vulnerable members of society would continue to be borne not by state or federal governments or corporations but by the poorest and most disadvantaged members of the work force" (p. 146). By most disadvantaged Glenn means poor women of color, in particular, immigrants.

Immigration and Intergenerational Resources for Caregiving Labor

In fact, we are crucially dependent on current and future waves of immigrants both for their labor as caregivers of our nation's disabled and elderly, and also their tax contributions to the two social insurance trust funds that keep most of the nation's older adults largely out of poverty. Demographers refer to this twofold intergenerational dependency in terms of a critical statistic—the "old-age dependency ratio." This ratio represents the size of the population that is aged (either 65+ or 85+), relative to the size of the population that is in the age range of the labor force—conventionally expressed as the 15–64 age range.

The magnitude of the old-age dependency ratio has enormous implications for social welfare policy, because this ratio represents both the relative
balance between the entitlement claims of the aged and the taxes placed on the
labor market earnings of the younger working age generations. Within the
context of long-term care policy, the old-age dependency ratio represents
the balance between the demands for formal and informal care posed by a
large aged population and the formal and informal labor resources available
from younger generations. From the standpoint of informal caregiving within
a typical family system, a rise in the old-age dependency ratio represents the
increased strains that occur as there are more older adults in advanced age
relative to the number of children and grandchildren available to provide
informal care. Creating even more strain is the enormous growth in paid
employment outside of the home for women over the past several decades
that limits their availability for informal caregiving in the family system.
From a general labor market perspective, a rise in the old-age dependency
ratio represents a smaller labor pool of available low-wage caregivers relative
to the number of persons in the oldest age ranges in need of care. Under the
basic principle of supply and demand, such an imbalance (scarcity of labor
relative to demand for labor) would ordinarily lead to higher wages and
benefits for workers. However, in the context of a global economy with
fairly permeable borders, wages and benefits for paid caregivers are kept
low by immigration—both legal and illegal. As it happens, the U.S. Census
Bureau provides three projections for the future growth in the old-age dependency ratio (high, middle, and low), based in large part on different estimates
of long-term immigration trends. In the Census Bureau's middle-case projection (which estimates a modest level of continued immigration) the old
age dependency ratio is projected to increase (relative to its year 2000
level) by 58% by the year 2025 and then by 77% by the year 2050 (Almgren,
2008). This projection is shown by the top line in Figure 5.2. Should a U.S.
immigration policy be implemented and enforced to where immigration
over the next few decades slows to a trickle, there would be an even more
dramatic increase in the old age dependency ratio for the first half of the
current century, and then a substantial further increase during the later half
of the century (Shrestha 2006).

Current Long-Term Care Expenditures and Future Projections

As of 2009, long-term care expenditures for older adults and younger populations with disabilities reached $203.2 billion, the majority of which were
public dollars through federal and state contributions to the Medicaid

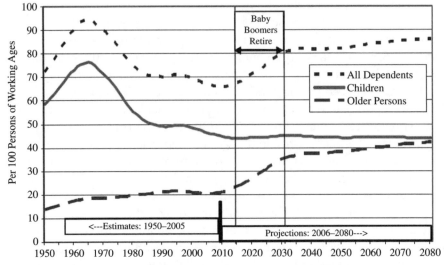

Source: Shrestha, L. Age dependency ratio and social security solvency:
CRS Report for Congress, Oct. 27, 2006: Figure 5.1. Dependency ratios:
Number of dependents per 100 persons of working age, United States:
1950–2080.

Figure 5.2 *Dependency ratios: Number of dependents per 100 persons of working age, United States: 1950–2080.*

program (National Health Policy Forum, 2011). This compares to the $183 billion that were spent in 2003, an increase of over $20 billion in just 6 years (CBO, 2005). As shown in Figure 5.3, just over 60% of national long-term care expenditures occur through the Medicaid program, with out-of-pocket expenditures accounting for only about 20% of the total. "Other Private" sources of funds for long-term care expenditure include payments from private long-term care insurance plans—though it should be noted that despite three decades of government and private sector promotion of long-term care insurance, there are only about 6 to 7 million long-term care insurance policies in full force (National Health Policy Forum, 2011). While Medicare is said to account for only a very small share of long-term care expenditures, it should be borne in mind that billions of Medicare dollars that are labeled as "acute care expenditures" are in reality spent in the management of an array of chronic diseases and various complications from permanent disabilities.

There has long been a consensus among state and federal policymakers that the current growth in public long-term care expenditures is unsustainable. Medicaid, as the primary source of long-term care expenditures (see Figure 5.3), draws precious state tax dollars away from investments in

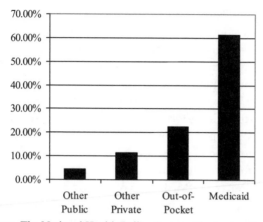

Source: The National Health Policy Forum. *The basics: Long term services and supports*. Washington, DC, March 15, 2011. Based on data from Figure 5.1, LTSS expenditures by source, 2009.

Figure 5.3 *Long-term care service and support expenditures by source, 2009.*

public education, health care for children, public assistance for poor families, and any number of other essential local government functions. At the federal level, funding for Medicaid competes with funding for not only national defense, but also investments in infrastructure essential for commerce, scientific research, housing and urban development, and higher education opportunities for low-income students. It should be kept in mind that Medicaid, in contrast to Medicare and Social Security, is not a social insurance program that is financed through a trust fund—but is financed instead directly through general tax revenues. This places Medicaid long-term care health expenditures in continuous head-to-head competition with other needs and priorities in every state and federal budget legislated. Throughout the most recent two decades, the annual growth in Medicaid expenditures have averaged at about 9%, against an average growth in the economy (as measured by the GDP) of slightly less than 2% over the past decade (Kaiser Family Foundation, 2010b; OECD 2010).

The prime driver of future long-term care expenditures, whether public or private, is not age per se but a complex interaction between the growth of the aged population, the prevalence of disability in the aged population, and the availability of informal supports. The magnitude of public expenditures is further affected by the distribution of income, wealth, and long-term care insurance coverage among the disabled aged—as well as federal and state policies that determine the eligibility criteria for public long-term care subsidies. All of these factors (plus several that have not been introduced) makes the forecasting of public expenditures for long-term care exceedingly uncertain. While the Government Accountability Office has predicted that long-term care expenditures could increase more than two-and-a-half times between 2000 and 2040, another prediction by the Urban institute suggests that long-term care expenditures could quadruple (GAO, 2005; Urban Institute, 2001). Even should public subsidies for long-term care expenditures keep pace with this explosive growth in long-term care expenditures, individuals and families still pay about one-third of long-term care costs (see Figure 5.3). Such a growth in private expenditures for long-term care would make it exceedingly difficult for most families to invest in higher education for their children and grandchildren or afford to save for retirement and other contingencies, and certainly make home ownership even more elusive for working class families than it is today. Given these grim prospects, what are the alternatives?

DIRECTIONS FOR LONG-TERM FINANCING POLICY

As noted by the Government Accountability Office's (2005) testimony to Congress on financing of long-term care, the actual growth in expenditures for long-term care is determined by the interaction between several crucial factors in particular: the increase in the number of persons in need of long-term care services, the types of long-term care services used, and availability of public and private sources for the payment of long-term care (GAO, 2005, p. 13), These factors are in turn influenced by a large array of other factors, including future trends in old-age longevity and relative health, trends in family composition that determine the availability of resources for familial caregiving, technological innovations that may enhance the adaptive capacities of the elderly and disabled, innovations in long-term care delivery systems, and (as highlighted previously) immigration and labor market policies. It is impossible to precisely predict which, if any, of these factors will do the most to shape the future of long-term care financing policies, yet, the central policy question that pertains to long-term care financing is itself easily identified; in essence, as the balance between public and private responsibilities in financing of each individual's future long-term care needs.

While the current system of financing catastrophic long-term care expenditures through Medicaid has been largely successful in shielding middle-class families from poverty, it is not sustainable in the face of ever-escalating Medicaid expenditures for long-term care. In response to this dilemma, policymakers have debated and experimented with the merits of two basic long-term care financing strategies. One strategy, favored by conservatives and to some extent progressives, as well, has been to encourage the development of private long-term care insurance market and consumer (particularly middle-class consumer) incentives to purchase long-term care insurance. The second strategy, far more popular among progressives, favors the creation of a federally administered compulsory social insurance fund for long-term care expenditures—typically as an enhanced version of Medicare. After discussing the viability of each of these approaches, in turn, the long-term care approach incorporated into the Patient Protection and Affordable Care Act will be considered—which, should it have been implemented instead of discarded, might have dramatically reshaped the financing of long-term care for at least the next generations of Americans transitioning to old age.

The Viability of Private Long-Term Care Insurance as a Solution to Long-Term Care Financing

Decades ago it was established that catastrophic long-term care expenditures for nursing home care met the criteria for an insurable event under the prevailing assumptions of insurance markets. That is, nursing home care is a financially burdensome event with a known probability of risk, people are averse to nursing home care, and the probability of extended periods of nursing home care relative to its costs is sufficiently low. In the 1980s, a large share of policy planners and administrators believed that the development of a mature long-term care insurance market would ultimately curtail the growth of public long-term care expenditures. For a variety of reasons, this has turned out not to be the case. Early generation long-term care policies were written in ways that excluded the highest risk conditions from coverage, many elderly believed that their Medicare and Medigap policy benefits would provide adequate coverage for nursing home care and other long-term care services, most elders and their families regarded nursing home care as something they would never accept, and, in particular, those who were most at risk for the need for nursing home care tended not to purchase long-term care insurance (Wilson & Weissert, 1989). Although long-term care insurance carriers have greatly improved their products and their marketing strategies, at this point, long-term care insurance still covers only a small proportion of the more affluent elderly. Only about 10% of the population of elderly aged 75+ have private long-term care insurance, and the group that purchases long-term care insurance over-represents those with the higher income and assets (Johnson & Uccello, 2005; The Urban Institute, 2001). Those at highest risk for catastrophic long-term care expenditures, low-income elderly with significant functional impairments, are far less likely to be able to afford or be eligible for private long-term care insurance coverage.

The Viability of Compulsory Social Insurance for Long-Term Care as a Solution for Long-Term Care Financing

The United States has two federalized compulsory social insurance entitlements that were designed as antipoverty programs for older Americans, Social Security, and Medicare. Both programs impose a compulsory tax on earnings during the working years, in return for a modest income in old age and health insurance protections from catastrophic medical expenditures in old age. Both Social Security and Medicare were eventually signed into law despite formidable opposition from political conservatives, and both compulsory social insurance programs are deemed today as politically unassailable—not only because of the vested interests of older adult voters but also the far majority of younger generations of voters as well. Based on the wildly successful political history of both of these compulsory social insurance programs, progressive policy advocates argued that a social insurance benefit for catastrophic long-term care expenditures should be added to the Medicare program. According to their logic, if Medicare exists as a safety net for older adults with catastrophic health expenditures, that safety net should encompass the other threat to financial security in old age long-term care expenditures. Eventually, in 1988, Congress passed legislation that added some limited subsidies for nursing home care and other insurance protections as an incremental step toward a long-term care Medicare benefit. However, this legislation (the Catastrophic Coverage Act of 1988) was quickly repealed when older adults voiced their unified outrage at the addition of a tax on their incomes for what they perceived as limited and little understood supplemental benefits. Although the Catastrophic Coverage Act did not ascribe to the social insurance financing model of either Social Security or traditional Medicare, congressional resistance to the idea of added compulsory taxation for added Medicare benefits was thereafter hardened by this debacle. A parallel political barrier to the addition of a Medicare long-term care benefit has been the political resistance to any increase in the Medicare payroll tax by those still in the active workforce. The last general Medicare payroll tax increase that was politically viable occurred in 1986, with express purpose of stabilizing the solvency of the Hospital Insurance Trust Fund. Even as the Hospital Insurance Trust Fund has again trended toward insolvency, an increase in the Medicare payroll tax is not considered politically feasible or perhaps even economically prudent. Thus it must be said that the prospects for a compulsory social insurance fund for long-term care are somewhat bleaker than dismal.

The Rise and Fall of the Community Living Assistance Services and Supports (CLASS) Act as a Solution for Long-Term Care Financing

Deeply embedded in the original version of the Patient Protection and Affordable Care Act (PPACA) was the establishment of a quasi-voluntary social insurance trust fund for long-term care expenditures that extended long-term care social insurance coverage to all persons aged 18 and over—the so-called CLASS Act. The term "quasi-voluntary" is used to describe this program because the long-term care trust fund established by the CLASS was to be financed through the monthly premiums of adults who were automatically enrolled in the social insurance plan by their employers—unless they took the deliberate action of opting out. It was anticipated by advocates of this approach that most workers would not make a specific choice to opt out of a program that would be arguably beneficial to them and their dependents, while it is more difficult to get people to voluntarily enroll in program that reduces their paycheck. Persons who would be covered under the CLASS insurance plan become eligible for daily cash allowance of up to either $50 or $100 (depending on their level of disablement) that could be used to defray the costs of an array of long-term care services and supports at the point they were determined to have a functional disability that requires assistance for two or more activities of daily living; for example, eating, bathing, dressing, transferring from a bed to a chair or toilet. Cognitive disablements of equivalent magnitude would also have been considered to be a basis for eligibility (Kaiser Family Foundation, 2009b; National Council on Aging, 2009). Notably, the long-term care insurance benefits created under the CLASS Act would have applied to adults over the age of 18 who met general program criteria, not just older adults.

Had the CLASS long-term care social insurance plan worked as intended, it would not only have provided disabled individuals and their families with significant protections against catastrophic long-term care expenditures and helped them to afford services essential to remaining optimally independent—but it also would have greatly reduced public expenditures for long-term care services. In fact, the Congressional Budget Office (CBO) had estimated that the program's net effect reduced the federal budget by 58 billion dollars during the first decade of its implementation (CBO, 2009).[14] However, the CBO had also cautioned that the CLASS long-term care insurance plan's potential to sustain reductions on federal spending were contingent upon retaining a premium payment structure relative to benefit outlays that would be self-sustaining—meaning, in essence, that the costs of the quasi-voluntary premium would have needed to keep pace both with inflation and also increases in utilization.

In the optimistic scenario envisioned by the CLASS program's proponents, three crucial policy assumptions needed to hold: (1) a large share of healthy working age adults would be willing to enroll in the program and pay its premium cost in return for the insurance benefits offered to them and their dependents,[15] (2) the availability of insurance subsidies for long-term care would not create strong disincentives for family members and other unpaid informal caregivers from continuing to shoulder the larger part of the long-term care burden, and (3) rising premiums in response to increases in CLASS program benefit expenditures would not be such that workers would choose to disenroll from the program in large numbers. As it happened, in October of 2011, 19 months after the PPACA was signed into law, the Obama administration conceded that both the first and the third of these crucial policy assumptions were in fact flawed. That is, in order to provide long-term benefits that would have met the requirements and purposes of the legislation, the Obama administration concluded that the costs of the premiums would eventually rise to the point where healthier workers would either not enroll or drop out (HHS, 2011). Thus, the CLASS long-term care social insurance program became the PPACA's first significant casualty of the implementation process.

LESSONS LEARNED FROM THE DEMISE OF THE CLASS LONG-TERM CARE INITIATIVE. While the decision to include publically financed long-term care as a component of health care reform was both bold and responsive to the demographic realities of an aging population, in design it rested on the premise that a large share of the labor force would be sufficiently concerned about future long-term care expenditures to sacrifice a modest share of today's paycheck in return for the assurance of affordable long-term care services in a distant and uncertain tomorrow. There is little evidence to suggest that the risks of catastrophic long-term illness and disablement are all that apparent to most working age Americans, even though these risks are quite evident to social policy researchers and policy administrators at all levels of government. It must also be recognized that future concerns, as compelling as they might be, must also compete with the influences of a market economy that is yielding diminishing prospects for a middle-class income and lifestyle. In the end, the growth in publicly financed long-term care expenditures will force some kind of political solution. Even with innovations in the management of chronic disease and disability that might stretch limited long-term care dollars, absent radical long-term care financing reform we are left with solutions that entail either a significant rise in the private cost-sharing of long-term care expenditures for earners able to afford private long-term care insurance, catastrophic reductions in long-term care services for the poorest and most disabled of our citizens, or some combination of both.

CONCLUDING COMMENTS: A SOCIAL JUSTICE PERSPECTIVE ON THE FINANCING OF LONG-TERM CARE

As discussed in other chapters (see in particular Chapter 1 on theories of social justice and Chapter 8 on health care system reform), it seems very clear that both Rawls's theory of justice and the Human Capabilities approach advocated by Sen and Nussbaum encompass a positive right to health care. Within the Rawlsian framework, the primary basis for this conclusion is health care's social function as an essential determinant of fair equality of opportunity, whereas in Human Capabilities theory the positive right to health care is based on a political system's central purpose—the promotion of human capabilities and flourishing (Ruger, 2007). However, among the several constraints to an *unlimited* positive right to health care are conflicts between young and old over limited resources (Daniels, 2002). In the last available formulation of his Theory of Justice (*Justice as Fairness: A Restatement*, 2001: Harvard University Press), Rawls acknowledged that special problems arose when considering more extreme health care needs, as in the case of the severely handicapped (and presumably those disabled by age as well). As Rawls saw it, the primary problem involved determining the limit of duties toward disabled citizens when the weight of such duties competes with other basic claims, as in the case of funds for long-term care versus funds for basic education (Rawls, 2001). As a reflection of the complexity of the problem, Rawls himself was uncertain as to whether his theory of justice could be extended to provide a satisfactory resolution to this fundamental conflict: "At some point, then, we must see whether justice as fairness can be extended to provide guidelines for these cases; and if not, whether it must be rejected rather than supplanted with some other conception" (Rawls, 2001, p. 176, n59). At the time Rawls wrote this, he was beyond a doubt well aware of the dilemmas facing the nation as a consequence of population aging—thus his reluctance to give a clear ruling on the issue must also give us pause.

However, there are three basic ideas from Rawls's theory (whether or not Rawls would agree with their application) that seem particularly relevant to the formulation of a just approach to the financing of long-term care. The first is the positive right to health care, the second is that there are limits to that right that involve competing commitments to the provision of other primary goods (like an adequate scheme of basic education), and the third is Rawls's emphasis on the principle of reciprocity as a cornerstone to his conception of justice (Rawls, 2001, p. 77). Reciprocity comes into play as one thinks about the obligations that flow between generations as pertains to Social Security: thus far each generation of workers funds a large share of the retirement for the next. Conversely, it seems incumbent on each generation not to place an undue burden on the opportunity structure of the next—thus limiting each generation's claim to the extent of public entitlements in old age. This, of course, would extend to publicly financed long-term care entitlements. Although this perspective is offered as a plausible application of Rawls's theory of justice, this perspective is also a fairly common point of view. This point of view would also seem to be consistent with the emphasis that Sen and Nussbaum's Human Capabilities theory places upon social arrangements that prohibit the advancement of the privileges of one segment of society to the detriment of another.

Whatever the policy final direction, it is likely that the public discourse about intergenerational obligations will become more pronounced as the newest generation of retirees takes full advantage of the social insurance fund set aside by the generation of their grandparents, and encounters the blessings and burdens of old age.

NOTES

1. See Spector et al. (2000) Table 10. Characteristics of Long-Term Care (LTC) Users by Age and Setting, 1994 and 1996.
2. See Spector et al. (2000) Table 9. Characteristics of Active Family Caregivers: Spouses and Children of Elderly Long-Term Care (LTC) Users, 1994.
3. In 1999, the U.S. Supreme Court in a 6–3 decision interpreted the ADA as affirming the right of individuals with disabilities to live in their community and required states to place persons with mental disabilities in community settings rather than in institutions. States are required to make community-based long-term care available, where treatment professionals determine that community placement is appropriate, it is not opposed by the affected individual, and where such arrangements can reasonably be accommodated. See Olmstead V. L. C. (98-536) 527 U.S. 581 (1999).
4. Later amendments to the Older Americans Act funded such key services to older adults as community nutrition programs, meals to the homebound, services targeted at low-income minority elders and to Native American elders, health promotion programs, and advocacy services.
5. Prison populations include a large number of persons who are disabled by mental illness and diminished intellectual capacities. Critics of the deinstitutionalization movement often cite this fact.

6. There was some limited evidence to suggest that nonprofit nursing homes also reduced adverse outcomes relative to for-profit homes. See Spector et al. (1998, pp. 649–650).
7. This became the precedent for later national conferences on aging that beginning in 1961 were designated as a "White House Conference on Aging."
8. The old-age dependency ratio is defined as the number of persons aged 65+/ number of persons aged 15 to 64, and refers to the number of persons at risk for old-age dependency relative to the number of persons available for caregiving or economic support. There are many ways to adjust the composition of this ratio to account for different subgroups of aged and subgroups of caregivers.
9. As discussed earlier in this chapter, the caregiving of elders remains largely in the hands of women.
10. At the time a professor of Health Policy and Administration at the School of Public Health, University of North Carolina at Chapel Hill.
11. Roemer's Law is named for Milton Roemer (d. 2001), formerly Professor of Health Services at UCLA. The findings and arguments of Roemer were highly influential among legislators and health policy administrators.
12. In 1972, the Social Security Act was amended to require states to review capital expenditures for health care facilities and equipment in excess of $100,000 as a condition of receiving reimbursement for capital expenditures. Over time this legislation was very effective in enabling states to restrict the further expansion of nursing home bed capacity.
13. A Social Health Maintenance Organization (S/HMO) is a comprehensive community-based care program that integrates medical care and social supports under a model of capitated financing. Typical S/HMO benefits include case management, personal in-home support services, adult day care, respite care (including short-term nursing home care), and coverage for pharmaceuticals. Although it was hoped that the S/HMO model would quickly evolve as a substitute for nursing home care, the mixed outcomes of the early S/HMO projects retarded the widespread adoption of the S/HMO approach to long-term care.
14. In their analyses of the CLASS long-term care insurance program, the Kaiser Family Foundation (2009b) cites a Congressional Budget Office deficit reduction estimate of 74 billion between 2010 and 2019. However, the source of this larger estimate is an unpublished e-mail correspondence from a congressional staff member as opposed to a formal published document.
15. The average premium of the CLASS long-term care insurance program would have been $65/month in 2011 and thereafter indexed annually for inflation (CBO, 2009).

REFERENCES

AHRQ (2001). *The Characteristics of Long-term Care Users*. AHRQ Research Report. AHRQ Publication No. 00-0049, January 2001. Agency for Healthcare Research and Quality, Rockville, MD. http://www.ahrq.gov/research/ltcusers/

Almgren, G. (1990). *Artificial nutrition and hydration practices and the American nursing home: Currents of social change and adaptation by an industry in transition.* Unpublished doctoral dissertation, University of Washington, Seattle.

Almgren, G. (2008). Demographics: An overview. *Encyclopedia of social work* (20th ed.). New York: Oxford University Press and NASW.

Almgren, G. (2009). *Section 3: Policy issues related to aging and palliative care, in palliative care with older adults.* CSWE Gero-Ed Health Resource Reviews. Retrieved March 13, 2011 from: http://www.cswe.org/File.aspx?id=24178

CBO. (2005). *The cost and financing of long term care services; testimony before the Subcommittee on Health Committee on Energy and Commerce, U.S. House of Representatives, April 27 2005.* Washington DC: Congressional Budget Office.

CBO. (2009). Letter to Senator Kay R. Hagan, from Douglas W. Elmendorf, Director of the Congressional Budget Office, July 6, 2009.

Chiswick, B. (1976). The demand for nursing home care: An analysis of institutional and noninstitutional care. *Journal of Human Resources, 9,* 295–315.

Crimmons, E., Saito, Y., & Ingegneri, D. (1989). Changes in life expectancy and disability-free life expectancy in the United States. *Population and Development Review, 15*(2), 229–254.

Cutchin, M. P. (2003). The process of mediated aging-in-place: A theoretically and empirically based model. *Social Science & Medicine, 57*(6), 1077–1090.

Daniels, N. (2002). Justice, health and health care. In R. Rhodes, M. Battin, & A. Silvers (Eds.), *Medicine and social justice.* New York: Oxford University Press.

Dunlop, B . (1979). *The growth of nursing home care.* Lexington, MA: Lexington Books.

Fraser, N., & Gordon, L. (1994). A geneology of dependency: Tracing a keyword in the U.S. welfare state. *Signs: Journal of Women and Culture in American Society, 19*(2), 309–336.

GAO. (2005). *Testimony before the subcommittee on health, committee on energy and commerce, House of Representatives: Long-term care financing: Growing demand and cost of services are straining federal and state budgets.* Washington, DC: United States Government Accountability Office.

Glenn, E. N. (2010) *Forced to care: Coercion and caregiving in America.* Cambridge, MA: Harvard University Press.

Gruber, H. (1967). In the American Medical Association: Department of Hospitals and Medical Facilities (Ed.), *The extended care facility: a handbook for the medical society.* Chicago: American Medical Association.

Health and Human Services. (2011). *A report on the actuarial, marketing, and legal analyses of the CLASS program.* Retrieved January 3, 2012, from http://aspe.hhs.gov/daltcp/reports/2011/class/index.shtml

Houser, A. (2007). *Nursing homes.* AARP Public Policy Institute, October 2007. Retrieved March 15, 2011, from http://www.aarp.org/home-garden/livable-communities/info-2007/fs10r_homes.html

Iwashyna, T., & Chang, V. (2002). Racial and ethnic differences in place of death: United States, 1993. *Journal of the American Geriatric Society, 50*(6), 1113–1117.

Johnson, R. W., & Uccello, C. E. (2005). *Is private long-term care insurance the answer?* (No. 29). Boston: Center for Retirement Research at Boston College.

Kaiser Commission on Medicaid Facts. (2011). *Medicaid and long-term care services and supports.* Retrieved March 14, 2011, from http://www.kff.org/medicaid/upload/2186-08.pdf

Kaiser Family Foundation. (2009a). *Statehealthfacts: Total number of residents in certified nursing facilities, 2009.* Retrieved March 15, 2011, from http://www.statehealth-facts.org/comparemaptable.jsp?ind=408&cat=8&sort=a

Kaiser Family Foundation. (2009b). *The Community Living Assistance Services and Supports (CLASS) Act.* Retrieved April 21, 2011, from http://www.kff.org/healthre form/upload/7996.pdf

Kaiser Family Foundation. (2010a). *Statehealthfacts: Distribution of nursing care facilities by ownership type, 2003.* Retrieved March 18, 2011, from http://statehealthfacts.org

Kaiser Family Foundation. (2010b). *Statehealthfacts: Average annual growth in medicaid spending, FY1990–FY2009.* Retrieved April 21, 2011, from http://www.state healthfacts.org/comparetable.jsp?cat=4&ind=181

Kane, R., Kane, R., & Ladd, R. (1998). *The heart of long-term care.* New York: Oxford University Press.

Kanter, J. (1989). Clinical case management: Definition, principles, components. *Hospital and Community Psychiatry, 40*(4), 361–368.

Legal Information Institute. *Opinion of the court: Long Island Care at Home, Ltd., et al v. Evelyn Coke.* Retrieved March 18, 2011, from http://www.law.cornell.edu/supct/pdf/06-593P.ZO

Manard, B., Kart, C., & Gils, D. V. (1975). *Old age institutions.* Lexington, MA: Lexington Books.

Martin, D. (2009). Evelyn Coke, home care aide who fought pay rule, is dead at 74. *New York Times,* August 9, 2009.

Merlis, M. (1999). *Financing long-term care in the twenty-first century: The public and private roles.* New York: Institute for Policy Solutions.

Mor, V., Zinn, J., Angelleli, J., Teno, J., & Miller, S. (2004). Driven to tiers: Socioeconomic and racial disparities in the quality of nursing home care. *The Milbank Quarterly, 82*(2), 227–256.

Morony, R., & Kurtz, N. (1975). The evolution of long-term care institutions. In S. Sherwood (Ed.), *Long-term care: A handbook for researchers, planners, and providers.* New York: Spectrum Publications.

National Council on Aging. (2009). *CLASS Act summary.* Retrieved April 22, 2011, from http://www.ncoa.org/independence-dignity/class-act-summary.html

National Health Care Policy Forum. (2011). *The basics: Long term services and supports.* Retrieved March 28, 2011, from http://www.nhpf.org/library/the-basics/Basics_LongTermServicesSupports_03-15-11.pdf

NHPCO. (2006). *History of hospice care.* Retrieved May 3, 2006, from http://www.nhpco.org/i4a/pages/index.cfm?pageid=3285

O'Brien, J. (1988). *The three sector nursing home industry.* Unpublished doctoral dissertation, University of Washington, Seattle.

O'Brien, J., Saxberg, B., & Smith, H. (1983). For-profit nursing homes: Does it matter? *The Gerontologist, 23,* 341–347.

OECD. (2010). *Economic Outlook, 2* (88). Annex Table 1, Real GDP: Percentage Change from Previous Year. Organisation for Economic Co-operation and Development, Paris, France.

Pegals, C. (1981). *Health care and the elderly.* Rockville, MD: Aspen Systems Corporation.

Rabin, D., & Stockton, D. (1987). *Longterm care for the elderly: A factbook.* New York: Oxford University Press.

Rawls, J. (2001). *Justice as fairness.* Cambridge, MA: Harvard University Press.

Roemer, M. I. (1961). Bed supply and hospital utilization: A natural experiment. *Hospitals, 35,* 36–42.

Ruger, J. P. (2007). The moral foundations of health insurance. *QJM, 100,* 53–57.

Seelbach, W., & Sauer, W. (1977). Filial responsibility expectations and morale among the aged. *The Gerontologist, 17*(6), 492–499.

Select Committee on Aging. (1987). *Exploding the myth: Caregiving in America.* Washington, DC: U.S. Congress, House of Representatives.

Shi, L., & Singh, D. (2001). *Delivering health care in America: A systems approach.* Gaithersburg, MD: Aspen.

Shrestha, L. (2006). *Age dependency ratios and social security solvency: CRS Report for Congress,* Oct. 27, 2006. Retrieved March 21, 2011 from http://aging.senate.gov/crs/ss4.pdf

Spector, W. D., Fleishman, J. A., Pezzin, L. E., & Spillman, B. C. (2000). *The characteristics of long-term care users.* Rockville, MD: Agency for Health Care Policy and Research.

Spector, W. D., Seldon, T., & Cohen, J. (1998). The impact of ownership type on nursing home outcomes. *Health Economics, 7,* 639–653.

The Urban Institute. (2001). *Long-term care: Consumers, providers, and financing: A chart book.* Washington, DC: The Urban Institute.

Thomas, W. (1969). *Nursing homes and public policy: Drift and decision in New York State.* Ithaca, NY: Cornell University Press.

Treas, J. (1977). Family support systems and the aged: Some social and demographic considerations. *The Gerontologist, 17,* 486–491.

U.S. Census Bureau. (2004). *2002 economic census: Nursing homes and residential care facilities* (No. EC02-62I-03). Washington, DC: U.S. Department of Commerce.

U.S. Census Bureau. (2005a). *Table 2: Annual estimates of the population by selected age groups and sex for the United States: April 1, 2000 to July 1, 2004 (NC-EST2004-02).* Washington, DC: U.S. Census Bureau.

U.S. Census Bureau. (2005b). *Table 2a: Projected population of the United States, by age and sex: 2000 to 2050.* Washington, DC: U.S. Census Bureau.

Vladeck, B. (1980). *Unloving care: The nursing home tragedy.* New York: Basic Books.

Weissert, W. (1985). Seven reasons why it is so difficult to make community-based long-term care cost-effective. *Health Services Research, 20*(4), 423–433.

Wilson, C., & Weissert, W. (1989). Private long-term care insurance: After coverage restrictions is there anything left? *Inquiry, 26*(4), 493–507.

World Health Organization. (2011). *WHO definition of palliative care [Electronic Version],* 1. Retrieved March 13, 2011, from http://www.who.int/cancer/palliative/definition/en/print.html

CHAPTER SIX

DISPARITIES IN HEALTH AND HEALTH CARE

*T*he central concern of this chapter encompasses the relationships between social inequality, health, and health care policy. This is the first of two chapters that examines the incidence and causes of disparities in health and in health care in the United States. Although the two chapters both have descriptive and causal components, they differ in their emphasis. This chapter concerns itself primarily with the descriptive aspects of disparities in health and health care, while the next focuses on the causal aspects of these disparities.

CONCEPTUALIZING DISPARITIES IN HEALTH AND HEALTH CARE

The National Institutes of Health defines *disparities in health* as "differences in the incidence, prevalence, mortality, and burden of diseases and other adverse health conditions that exist among specific population groups in the United States" (NIH, 2001a). The U.S. Department of Health and Human Services (HHS) employs a more encompassing definition that includes both the *health* and *health care* dimensions of disparity (AHRQ, 2004; HHS, 2000). According to HHS, "All differences among populations in measures of *health* and *health care* are considered evidence of disparities ..." (AHRQ, 2004, p. 7). The distinction between *disparities in health* and *disparities in health care* is a huge one, both conceptually and politically. Disparities in health concern differences between populations and population subgroups in the overall level of health and the distributions of disease and death, while disparities in health care encompass both health care outcomes and other dimensions of health care that include access, quality, and equity.

Although the above definitions of *disparities in health* are generally accepted, the position of HHS that "all differences among populations in measures of *health care* are considered evidence of disparities" is far more controversial. In its analysis of racial and ethnic disparities in health care, the Institute of Medicine (IOM) limited its definition of disparities in health care to differences in "the quality of healthcare that are not due to access-related factors or clinical needs, preferences, and appropriateness of intervention" (IOM, 2003, p. 32).[1] A similarly limited conceptualization of disparities in health care was put forth in a related article in *Annals of Internal Medicine,* in which disparities in health care are argued to be limited to differences in health care that:

1. Represent shortfalls in appropriate care that are both associated with adverse health consequences and
2. Cannot be explained by differences in patient factors, such as needs and preferences (Rathore & Krumholz, 2004).

As exemplified in the IOM definition of health care disparities, the choice of a narrow conceptualization of health care disparities has significant political implications.[2] While the U.S. Congress charged the IOM with the task of analyzing health care disparities, the mandate given IOM very deliberately excluded analysis of disparities in health care that arise from access factors. By shaping the discourse on health care disparities in this way, Congress has historically avoided or at least significantly deflected discussions of disparities in health care access that provide political leverage for advocates of radical health care reform. On the other hand, the limited conceptualization of health care disparities conveyed in the *Annals of Internal Medicine* represents resistance within the medical profession to a definition of health care disparities that implies a general culpability on the part of physicians and other clinicians for any and all differences in health care that are correlated with race, ethnicity, sex, and other characteristics linked with social inequality.

In part, the medical profession's reluctance to embrace a more encompassing definition of disparities in health care is provoked by the implicit (and often explicit) tendency in much of the literature on health care disparities to cite any and all differences in health care as further evidence of the multiple biases in the diagnosis and treatment of various patients from disadvantaged groups. Although the medical profession is indeed deeply implicated in multiple aspects of disparities in health care, including the evolvement of a system of finance that keeps millions of U.S. residents from various disadvantaged groups out of the health care system altogether (Starr, 1982), it is important to concede four points in favor of the defenders of the medical profession's concerns about the conceptualization and methods used to investigate disparities in health care:

1. Much of the literature on disparities in health care confuses correlation with causality.
2. Disparities in health care can arise from patient need and preferences, the system, or the health care practitioner.
3. All of the health professions share culpability for disparities in health care.
4. Some differences in health care by such factors as gender, race, or income level are not in and of themselves, either malevolent in intent or detrimental in outcome.[3]

However, there are two troubling aspects of a perspective on health care disparities that narrows the definition of health care disparities to factors that exclude issues of *access* and individual *needs and preferences* for health care.

Concerning access, it is well established that access to health care in the United States varies by income, race, gender, nativity, and a variety of other factors related to status, material resources, and social power. Further, it is also well established that groups that encounter barriers to health care access have poorer health (AHRQ, 2004). Thus, it is arbitrary if not disingenuous to limit the definition of disparities in health care only to differences in health care for those privileged to receive it. A similarly restricted definition of malnutrition would exclude differences in the nutritional status of individuals who, for any number of reasons, are kept from food. The effect of excluding issues of access as a key component of the definition of disparities in health care is a denial and negation of the culpability of all individuals and groups responsible for the delivery of care (political actors, policy makers, hospital boards, hospital administrators, physicians, and allied health professionals) for any and all aspects of differences in health that arise from issues of access.

In this regard, the IOM correctly concedes that multiple factors related to access cannot be kept distinct from other processes affecting the quality of health care provided (IOM, 2003, p. 31). For example, although a Medicaid voucher may provide the appearance of access to care, the stigma attached to being a Medicaid patient can bias the clinical assessment of health care needs as well as a patient's willingness to articulate preferences (Gurwitz et al., 2002; Obst, Nauenberg, & Buck, 2001).

Excluding *needs and preferences* from the calculus of health care disparities denies the very subtle ways in which individual preferences are shaped through the clinical encounter. There is a central paradox embedded in the clinical encounter that arises from a conflict between the criteria for achieving an unbiased expression of patient preference for care and the patient's dependence on the clinician for critical information. The achievement of unbiased patient preference requires that the patient possesses the same information about risks and benefits of treatment as that possessed by the clinician. Although the ethical principles espoused in Western medicine obligate the physician to provide information about the risks and benefits of various treatment alternatives in an unbiased fashion, these conversations occur in a context of differences in race, socioeconomic class, ethnicity, gender, and age that profoundly influence perceptions of choice, best interests, and the norms of expressing preference. Put another way, the patient preferences are rarely antecedent to, or independent of, the sociology of the clinical encounter.[4]

The summary point of the preceding discussion of the definition of health care disparities is this: Although some differences in health care by such characteristics as race, ethnicity, and gender may be either benign or even beneficial, all differences in health care from any source qualify as disparities that are inherently suspect, and therefore worthy of thoughtful investigation.

The Three Dimensions of Disparities Relevant to Health Care Policy

As shown in Figure 6.1, there are huge differences in age-adjusted death rates in the United States by race and Hispanic ethnicity.[5] Among the groups compared, non-Hispanic Black (NH Black) have the highest death rates, about 200 deaths/100,000 persons per year relative to the age-adjusted death rates of non-Hispanic Whites (NH Whites) and more than 400 deaths/100,000 per year relative to the death rates for Hispanics. It is also clear that American Indians and Alaska Natives (AIANs) may have death rates that are significantly above those for both Hispanics and those that are categorized Asian and Pacific Islanders (API).

Differences in age-adjusted death rates are illuminating because they reflect the cumulative and combined effects of disparities between population subgroups in three key dimensions of disparities in health: in the *burden of disease* carried by a subgroup, in the subgroup's relative *access to health care*, and in the *quality of health care* available to the subgroup. All three dimensions of disparity are of central concern to health care policy, however, the *burden of disease* is the most complex and influential dimension of disparity.

Conceptually, any population's (or population subgroup's) *burden of disease* refers to the prevalence and distribution of diseases, disabilities, and mortality that is carried by the population. Depending upon the application

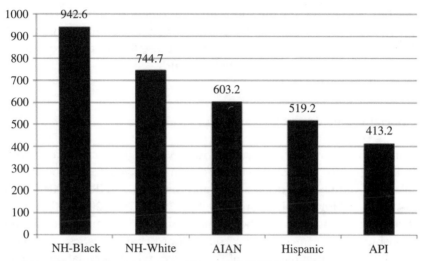

Source: Miniño, A. *Death in the United States, 2009*. NCHS Data Brief
No. 64, July 2011. Figure 1 Age-Adjusted Death Rates, by Race and Hispanic
Origin: United States, preliminary 2009.

Figure 6.1 *Age-adjusted deaths per 100,000 persons, U.S. 2009.*

and central questions, *burden of disease* measures can be highly specific to one particular disease or cluster of related diseases, or can be global measures of population health that capture the overall impact of disease, disability, and death on a population.[6] The *burden of disease* that is carried by a population or population subgroup incorporates the susceptibilities and exposures to disease that arise from the interaction of biology and social environment as well as those differences in health that can be attributed to disparities in health care arising from such factors as ethnic and racial discrimination.

Unlike disparities in the *burden of disease*, which in part are produced by disparities in health care access and outcomes, disparities in *access to health care* and *quality of health care* do not in and of themselves reflect differences in health. From the perspectives of health care policy and, more broadly, public health, this is a critical distinction. For example, the higher *burden of disease* that is reflected in the mortality rates of non-Hispanic Black Americans relative to those of other racial/ethnic groups (per Figure 6.1) can likely be reduced by policy initiatives aimed at eliminating the disparities in health care access and quality experienced by both groups (AHRQ, 2004)—but only to a limited degree given sources of disease, death, and disability that lie outside of the health care system (e.g., economic displacement, disadvantages in education, and racial segregation). Although health and health care policy encompasses consideration of all factors that are relevant health disparities, specific policy questions and interventions must make clear the distinction between factors that are most closely linked to the organization and processes of the health care system and those factors that are tied to the larger structural context of disparities in health.[7]

The Social Production of Disparities in Health

Disparities in health are associated with a variety of social characteristics, including age, race, ethnicity, gender, foreign birth, geographic location, and social class (education, occupation, and income) (AHRQ, 2004; Collins, Davis, Doty, & Ho, 2004; Denton & Walters, 1999; Finch, 2003). Although the next chapter will address the theories and evidence pertaining to the causal relationships between particular population characteristics and health, what follows is a brief overview of the ways in which population character- istics interact with the health care system to produce disparities in health.

As shown in the heuristic model[8] depicted in Figure 6.2, health dispar- ities (aggregate population differences in the burden of disease) are associated with social characteristics in two ways. The first, a direct causal pathway is depicted by the downward arrow at the right side of the model. The term *direct causal pathway* is used to convey the idea that there are particular

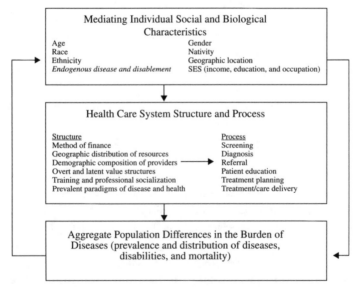

Figure 6.2 *A heuristic model of health disparity generation.*

social and biological characteristics of individuals (age, race, gender, etc.) that act as mediators for the determinants of disease prevalence in populations. As one example, race is less a direct determinant of disease than it is a social and biological characteristic that acts as mediator of various determinants of disease risk that have complex biological and social origins. The same relationship holds for age, gender, ethnicity and the other mediating characteristics shown in the top box of Figure 6.2. The middle pathway, shown in the downward arrows that connect the three boxes, conveys the idea that social characteristics also have an indirect effect on disease prevalence that is mediated through the health care system. For example, to the extent that there are racial characteristics of individuals that have detrimental effects on the availability and quality of health care, those same racial characteristics will lead to a higher burden of disease in the racial population.

The third arrow, pointing upward on the left side of the model, depicts a complex but important relationship between the differences in the burden of disease and the social and biological characteristics referred to as *endogenous disease and disablement*.

The term *endogenous* refers to the existence of a causal relationship that is internal to a model. As shown in Figure 6.2, an endogenous process takes place as particular diseases and disablements have a detrimental effect on the availability and quality of health care in ways that (in turn) lead to an even higher burden of disease. For example, the stigma attached to HIV disease has in many instances been detrimental to the treatment of the disease, thus increasing the burden of disease both in terms of prevalence and severity in the populations at risk for HIV. In general, persons with high levels of chronic illness and disability confront various barriers to appropriate care related to stigma. Other examples of this endogenous causal process include sexually transmitted diseases (STDs), asthma, cancer, epilepsy, tuberculosis, obesity, and general psychiatric conditions (Becker, Janson-Bjerklie, Benner, Slobin, & Ferketich, 1993; Hayes, Vaughan, Medeiros, & Dubuque, 2002; Jacoby, Snape, & Baker, 2005; Joachim & Acorn, 2000; Michielutte & Diseker, 1982; Rogge, Greenwald, & Golden, 2004).

The relationship between diabetes and the Native American population illustrates the ways in which health disparities observed at the population level flow directly through individuals and are further generated through the health care system. Relative to persons racially identified as White, Native Americans are twice as likely to have diabetes listed as their cause of death (U.S. Census, 2012a). Embedded in this statistic are differences between Whites and Native Americans in both the incidence and severity of diabetes. Although meeting the criteria for inclusion in the Native American racial category is a significant risk factor for diabetes, being classified as a

Native American does not "cause" either the incidence or the severity of the disease. Rather, Native American origin is correlated with multiple causal determinants of diabetes, including but not limited to diet, obesity, lack of exercise, smoking, and genetic susceptibilities (Gohdes, 1995; NIH, 2001b). Although it is impossible to reconstruct the prevalence rates of diabetes among Native Americans preceding the conquest and displacement of indigenous peoples by Europeans, there is little doubt that the root causes of disproportionate prevalence of diabetes among Native Americans are embedded in the near eradication of indigenous culture that accompanied contact with Europeans. Specifically, a principal casualty of the socio-cultural genocide that accompanied the European conquest involved the elimination of ancient ways of food production, acquisition, and consumption that functioned together as crucial protective factors against diabetes. As a result of these aggregated individual level predisposing factors (and as shown in the right-hand arrow of Figure 6.2), there is a high and increasing prevalence of diabetes in the population of Native Americans that precedes exposure to the health care system.

As the U.S. health care system is structured, Native Americans confront a kind of double jeopardy: health care disparities that arise from race and health care disparities that arise from lower socioeconomic status (SES). Although the Indian Health Service (IHS) has existed since 1955 to provide health care services to Native Americans, the IHS provides services to only about 60% of the Native Population (Acton et al., 2002). This, in large part, is because a significant proportion of the Native American population is geographically isolated from IHS services. The 40% of the Native Americans that are not served by IHS must rely on a system of health care that disadvantages persons of lower SES above and beyond issues of race. Notably, Native Americans lag in all three dimensions of SES: income, occupation, and education (OMH, 2012). Aside from confronting barriers in *access* to health care, individuals of lower SES also receive lower *quality of care* in a variety of dimensions, including patient–provider communication, respectful treatment, timeliness of appointments, preventative treatment, and the provision of care that is appropriate to the condition (AHRQ, 2004). In the case of diabetic care, the clinical management of the disease that is critical to slowing its progression is shown to be significantly inferior for persons of lower SES (AHRQ, 2004). Although it is difficult to clearly disentangle the disparities that arise from socioeconomic disadvantage from those that arise from disadvantaged treatment on the basis of race, the evidence is irrefutable that Native Americans (1) continue to experience significant disparities in multiple dimensions of health care quality and access and (2) have a burden of diabetic disease that is disproportionately large and growing relative to other racial groups in the United States (Acton et al., 2002; AHRQ, 2004; Hoyert, Kung, & Smith, 2005).

These disparities in care and outcomes can be traced to specific structures and processes within the U.S. health care system (see the middle box of Figure 6.2). For example, the *method of finance* is clearly unfavorable to the working poor—a social class disproportionately representative of Native Americans. Relative to non-Hispanic Whites, Native Americans are nearly three times more likely to live in poverty (OMH, 2012). As pointed out previously, the *geographic structure* of the health care system is very problematic to Native Americans in that a large proportion of Native Americans are spatially isolated from INS clinics. The *demographic composition of providers* is also very unfavorable to Native Americans. Of all racial groups in the United States, Native Americans are the least likely to encounter a provider of their own race (American Medical Association, 2005; U.S. Census, 2003). In fact, the lack of Native American providers in the health care system both reflects and perpetuates all of the structural origins of disparities in health care shown in Figure 6.2, including *detrimental, overt, and latent value structures*[9] inadequate *training and professional socialization of non-Native American providers*, and *prevalent paradigms of disease and health* that conflict with indigenous conceptions of health, illness, and healing (AHRQ, 2004; Garroutte, Kunovich, Jacobsen, & Goldberg, 2004).

All of the processes of health care shown in Figure 6.2 (screening, diagnosis, referral, patient education, treatment planning, and treatment/care delivery) are determined by the structural components just discussed. Conceptually, it is useful to speculate on the extent to which any structural component depicted increases or decreases the likelihood that any particular process of health care will occur in a way that promotes health care disparities. For example, it is easy to see how a system of health care finance that makes it more likely that a health care provider will be reimbursed less for seeing a low-income patient than a middle-income patient impacts on the provider's willingness to invest equally in the clinical encounter with a low-income patient—thus negatively affecting screening, diagnosis, patient education, and treatment planning and delivery. It is also readily apparent to see the ways in which dramatic differences between the race and class composition of providers and patients affect the trust and communication between patient and provider that influences all aspects of patient care. Given the interaction of health care financing and the class and race composition of health care providers, it is hardly surprising to find that low-income and minority patients perceive less respect on the part of providers, feel less listened to, and (in apparent consequence) receive generally poorer health care that contributes to a higher burden of disease (AHRQ, 2004; IOM, 2003).

MEASURING DISPARITIES IN HEALTH AND HEALTH CARE

As mentioned at the beginning of this chapter, measures of disparities involve three general categories of health and health care delivery: *burden of disease*, *access to health care*, and *quality of health care*. However, measures of disparity often overlap across categories. For example, the incidence rates of diseases that are sensitive to prevention (e.g., diabetes) act as measures of a population's *burden of disease* and reflect disparities in *health care access* and *health care quality* as well. In answer to this dilemma, both the IOM and the Agency for Healthcare Research and Quality (AHRQ) have engaged in a significant effort to identify measures of disparity that tend to be specific to key aspects of health care as it is organized and delivered in the United States. In contrast, some of the most innovative *burden of disease* measures have evolved from international health studies.

Measuring Disparities in Burden of Disease

Earlier in this chapter it was stated that any population's *burden of disease* refers to the prevalence and distribution of diseases, disabilities, and mortality that is carried by the population. So the first characteristic that typically determines one burden of disease measure from another is whether the measure concerns morbidity or mortality. *Morbidity* measures involve incidence rates of disease and/or disability in nonfatal or prefatal stages, while *mortality* measures refer to death rates. In recent decades, burden of disease measures have been widely used for international comparisons that combine morbidity and mortality, such as the DALY (disability adjusted life year) measure discussed previously, and the HALE (health-adjusted life expectancy) measure. While the DALY estimates the number of life years lost to premature death and years of healthy life lost due to disabling conditions, HALE is interpreted as the number of years at birth a person can expect to live in full health (i.e., unencumbered by either ill-health or disability) (World Health Organization, 2001). The DALY has the advantage of being disease or disabling condition specific (Murray & Lopez, 1996), while the HALE is useful as a summary measure of population health. Other burden of disease measures, again developed at the international level, involve the estimation of disparities in population morbidity and mortality that are due to specific risk factors—such as exposure to environmental toxins and the prevalence of tobacco use (Ezzati, Lopez, Rodgers, Vander Hoorn, & Murray, 2002). The advantage of these types of burden of disease measures is that they are directly linked to important sources of health disparities and critical areas of risk that can be addressed by targeted health care policies.

Although burden of disease measures that have applied to the problem of health disparities in the domestic context have been limited to either disease-specific measures or very general measures of population health like life expectancy at birth or infant mortality, there have been revealing exceptions. For example, Kominski et al. (2002) employed the DALY measure to examine the burden of disease disparities by race, ethnicity, and gender in Los Angeles County. Aside from finding that African Americans were the most disadvantaged of all groups in terms of the overall burden of disease, it was found that employing the DALY measure established a different ranking of diseases in terms of overall population burden than the more typical approach based solely upon mortality rates.

Turning to the prevalent measures for burden of disease in the United States, the most dominant of the global measures of population burden of disease involve two closely related indices of population health, the infant mortality rate and life expectancy. Life expectancy refers to the average number of remaining years for a person at a given age, given the prevailing pattern of population mortality. Although life expectancy at birth is the most frequently cited life expectancy statistic, tables of population life expectancy typically calculated in single-, 5-, and 10-year intervals that allow estimation of life expectancy at multiple ages for different populations. The National Center for Health Statistics regularly estimates and publishes updated life expectancies at the state and national levels by general categories of race, ethnicity, and gender, and there are multiple studies of life expectancies for very specific subpopulations published in the public health literature.[10] As a general measure of population mortality, life expectancy is invaluable as an overall measure of the relative health disadvantages confronting some groups. For most people, the observation that the life expectancy of African Americans is over 4 years less than the average for White Americans has more impact than citing the disparities in age-specific death rates that determine estimates of life expectancy (U.S. Census, 2012b). However, the biggest disadvantage of life expectancy as a general measure of health is that it can be badly distorted by high death rates in younger ages—particularly in infancy. Thus, while African American male individuals have an average life expectancy at birth that is 4.1 years less than the average of that for Whites, a significant component of that racial disparity is attributable to infant death rates.

Disparities in life expectancy that are attributable to particular causes of death can also be calculated by the use of multiple decrement life table methods and related life table methods.[11] Basically, such methods identify life years that are lost to a population due to particular diseases or social characteristics associated with premature mortality (Schryock & Siegal, 1976).

An often utilized general burden of disease measure that is yielded by such methods is the summary "years of potential life lost" (YPLL) statistic, which refers to the life years that are lost due to all deaths that occur prior to a selected benchmark of average life expectancy. YPLL can also be calculated for specific causes of death associated with premature mortality (e.g., lung cancer, diabetes, accidental deaths, and homicide). As an example, the Centers for Disease Control (CDC) estimates YPLL per 100,000 persons for each state by race due to deaths by injury (both intentional and nonintentional). Death rates due to injury are highest among groups that are socially and economically disadvantaged (Rogers, Hummer, & Nam, 2000), such as Native Americans. According the CDC estimates for the year 2009, the Native American/Alaska Native age-adjusted YPPL/100,000 due to all categories of injury exceeded that for all other races combined by 172 YPLL/ 100,000 persons—a difference of 35% (CDC, 2012). This in itself is disturbing, but when the age-adjusted YPPL due to injury among Native Americans living in South Dakota are compared with the age-adjusted YPLL for all races nationwide, the differences in YPPL/100,000 among South Dakota's Native American population is 2194.9 (or a difference in relative magnitude of more than 5:1). At least part of the explanation for the drastically higher YPPL for Native Americans living in South Dakota is the fact that South Dakota's Pine Ridge Indian Reservation is among the most economically deprived communities in the country.

Of the many *burden of disease* measures, the one that is most often used in referencing health disparities is cause-specific death rates. *Cause-specific death rates* are calculated from cause of death data extracted from death certificates by county and state public health authorities, with the "underlying cause of death" typically used as the statistically relevant cause of death. Although multiple disease processes often contribute to death events, the underlying cause of death represents the coroner's evaluation of the disease process that is the most determinant causal factor of a person's death.[12] Thus, while a person might have advanced heart disease, diabetes, and lung cancer, heart disease is identified as the cause of death only if it is the factor most implicated in the series of physiological events which resulted in death. This is an important point, because it should now be clear that cause-specific death rates do not by themselves reflect the full burden of disease carried by individuals or populations. However, for a variety of reasons discussed in more detail below, it is a powerful and highly informative measure of both health disparities and the root causes of disparities. The cause-specific death rate is typically calculated as the number of deaths per 100,000 persons from a given cause in a given year or month. However, there are also methods to adjust for differences in population age distribution, which for disease processes like cancer are often necessary to capture the relevant sources of disparity.

There are several reasons why cause-specific death rates are favored as a burden of disease measure that is illustrative of health disparities. Among the most important is the fact that in most countries, and all parts of the United States, all deaths are registered along with the determinant causes of death. Also, diagnoses in death records are more complete and scrutinized than other health records. Although death records are not immune to error and even fraud, on the whole they are much more accurate than clinical encounter records, and, moreover, ultimately capture disease prevalence rates from persons who do not ordinarily utilize health care. Another important advantage of cause-specific death rates is that they both measure the most critical health disparities (as death is considered the most extreme form of health disparity) and often reflect underlying social causes.

To illustrate this key point, the cause-specific death rates shown in Table 6.1 provide a glimpse of the health care disparities between persons that are classified as Hispanic versus those classified as non-Hispanic White. It is important to note that the cause-specific death rates shown in Table 6.1 are described as age-adjusted, meaning that the death rates estimates are adjusted to eliminate the effects of the differences in the age compositions between the Hispanic and non-Hispanic White populations. If age-adjusted death rates were not used, the younger age composition of the Hispanics relative to non-Hispanic Whites would produce significantly misleading estimates of the differences in death rates.[13]

For most leading causes of death, Hispanics have lower death rates than non-Hispanic Whites. This phenomenon is referred to generally as the "Hispanic Paradox," because the SES of Hispanics relative to non-Hispanic Whites would predict a significant mortality disadvantage. Although there are competing causal explanations for the Hispanic Paradox, there is compelling evidence that much of the Hispanic mortality advantage is driven by the prevalence of low adult mortality among the foreign born—which suggests that selective migration plays an important role in the Hispanic mortality advantage (Palloni & Aria, 2004). The basic idea of selective migration is that Hispanic immigrants to the United States tend to be drawn from the healthiest of adults (those able to both work and withstand the rigors of the migratory journey). There is also the possibility of a selective return migration effect that arises as Hispanic immigrants who become too ill to work return to their country of origin before dying (also known as the so-called "salmon hypothesis"). However, there is also strong evidence to suggest that cultural factors play a protective role, in particular the protective factors of close

Table 6.1 *Age-Adjusted Death Rates (per 100,000) for Selected Causes of Death by Hispanic Origin*

	Hispanic or Latin	White, Not Hispanic	Difference	Ration Hisp/White N-H
All causes	546.1	749.4	−203.3	0.7
Diseases of the heart	136.0	187.8	−51.8	0.7
Ischemic heart disease	97.8	125.5	−27.7	0.8
Cerebrovascular disease	32.7	40.5	−7.8	0.8
Malignant neoplasms	116.2	177.5	−61.3	0.7
Trachchea, bronchus, lung	20.9	51.2	−30.3	0.4
Colon, rectum, and anus	12.0	16.4	−4.4	0.7
Chronic lower respiratory diseases	17.5	43.0	−25.5	0.4
Influenza and pneumonia	13.1	16.0	−2.9	0.8
Chronic liver disease and cirrhosis	13.8	9.4	4.4	1.5
Diabetes mellitus	28.9	20.5	8.4	1.4
HIV disease	4.1	1.9	2.2	2.2
Unintentional injuries	30.1	41.5	−11.4	0.7
Motor vehicle accidents	13.3	14.8	−1.5	0.9
Poisoning	5.8	10.6	−4.8	0.5
Suicide	6.0	12.5	−6.5	0.5
Homicide	6.9	3.7	3.2	1.9

Source: NCHS, Health, United States, 2010. Data from Table 24. Age adjusted death rates for selected causes according to sex, race and Hispatnic origin, United States, selected years 1950–2007. Hyattesville, Maryland.

family and community ties. Although some very rigorous studies failed to find clear evidence that cultural factors, as opposed to selective factors, accounted for the Hispanic mortality advantage (Palloni & Aria, 2004), it is also clear that for some selected health outcomes (e.g., substance abuse, obesity, and low birthweight), there is a negative acculturation effect on Hispanics—meaning that as Hispanic immigrants and their children have adopted the cultural beliefs and practices of the dominant society, the detrimental health behaviors of the dominant culture replace the beneficial ones that characterized their culture of origin (Lara, Gamboa, Kahramanian, Morales, & Bautista, 2005).

As shown in Table 6.1, Hispanic residents of the United States have a mortality disadvantage relative to non-Hispanic Whites in only four of the 13 leading cause of death categories: chronic liver disease and cirrhosis, diabetes, HIV, and homicide. What is significant in this pattern is that this particular cluster of diseases is consistent with a working age mortality pattern found among the most highly disadvantaged African Americans (Guest, Almgren, & Hussey, 1998; Palazzo, Guest, & Almgren, 2003). All four causes of death are associated with premature death during what should be the most productive years of adulthood, and three of the four (chronic liver disease, HIV, and homicide) arise from detrimental exposures (interpersonal violence) and risky health behaviors (alcoholism, I.V. drug abuse). These particular risks and exposures are associated with disadvantages in stable employment, and fit with the employment barriers that confront Hispanics immigrants—in particular, undocumented workers. Diabetes is associated with dietary practices and exercise, which implicate the negative aspects of acculturation.

Measuring Disparities in Access to Health Care

Access to health care is generally defined as the ability to engage in timely use of the health care services that achieve the optimal health outcomes (IOM, 1993). As noted by the *2004 National Health Care Disparities Report* (AHRQ, 2004), access to health care involves gaining entry, getting to the geographic and physical locations where the needed health care is delivered, and finding appropriate providers for the needed care. Obviously, access barriers can arise in any one or all of these three steps to gaining access. The approach to measuring access that was undertaken by the Agency for Healthcare Research and Quality (a sub-agency within the U.S. Department of Health and Human Services) involves three general categories of access measures: structural measures, patient assessments of care, and measures of health care utilization (AHRQ, 2004, p. 59). Structural measures involve the presence or absence of resources that enable health care (e.g., health insurance, health care providers within geographic proximity). Patient assessments of care, while subjective, are critically important to the process of seeking and acquiring appropriate care. Measures of health care utilization provide a more objective appraisal of the adequacy of the connection between health risk and conditions and the health services accessed.

Disparities in access to health care, and the measures that reflect them, revolve around issues of equity. Equity of access actually involves two conceptually distinct dimensions of equity, *need-based equity* and *similar treatment for similar cases* (Aday & Andersen, 1981). Equity based on need acknowledges that differences between groups in health care utilization or the allocation of health care resources do not in and of themselves suggest disparities in health care access. For example, fewer oncologists and fewer hospital beds dedicated to oncology care within some Hispanic communities might reflect the lower prevalence of cancer among the Hispanic population (even though it is more likely that socioeconomic disadvantage of Hispanic communities is the primary reason). On the other hand, to the extent that diabetes is more prevalent among Hispanics, a *need-based* approach to equity would require a higher level of specialized services for the prevention and treatment of diabetes among Hispanics than other groups at lower risk. *Similar treatment for similar cases* refers to the notion that given the same identified health care need, access to appropriate care should not differ by such extraneous factors such as race, social class, gender, age, geographic location, or insurance status.

Although differences in health insurance coverage by income, race, and employment status are the most frequently cited measures of disparities in access to health care, another important measure is the extent to which there are differences in having a source of regular and ongoing health care. Having a usual source of health care matters, because people who must rely upon hospital emergency rooms and urgent care clinics for their health care needs are unlikely to either build a trusting relationship with a physician or receive essential preventative care.

Figure 6.3, provided by the *National Health Care Disparities Report, 2010* (AHRQ, 2011), shows that race, ethnicity, and income are all predictive of the likelihood of having a usual source of primary care. Of all groups, Hispanics are the least likely to report having a usual source of primary care, while about 80% of non-Hispanic Whites are the most likely to have a usual source of primary care. Although American Indians and Alaska Natives (shown as AIAN) experienced dramatic gains in having a regular and ongoing source of care during the first half of the decade, between 2006 and 2007 these gains evaporated (AHRQ, 2011, p. 242). In the lower graph in Figure 6.3, it

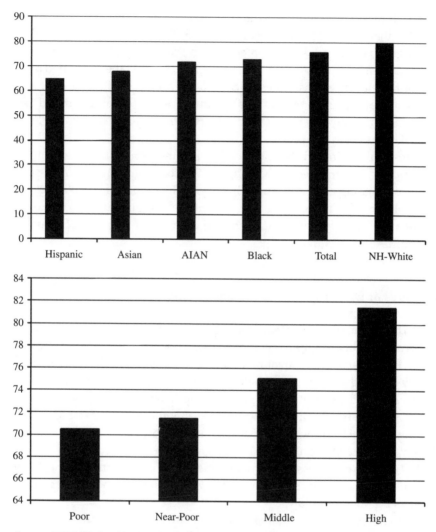

Source: AHRO. National health care disparities report, 2010. Rockville, MD: U.S. Department Health and Human Services. Adapted from Figure 9.8.

Figure 6.3 *Percentage with usual source of primary care by race, ethnicity, and income, 2007.*

can be seen that income has a powerful effect on the probability of having a usual source of primary care, one factor among many that explains the poorer health of low-income populations. Perhaps surprising to some is the particularly dramatic increase in the likelihood of having a usual source of primary care when persons of middle income are compared with persons of high income. In part, this may reflect the ever-increasing burden of out-of-pocket health expenditures on middle-income families—as discussed in Chapter 4. It should be noted that since the beginning of the decade through 2007, the general trend for all groups showed almost no change in the likelihood of having a usual source of primary care (AHRQ, 2011), which may reflect the continued devolution of the employer-based health care insurance system and the off-setting benefits of public investments in alternatives to the employer-based health care—most notably the State Children's Health Insurance Program (SCHIP) as also discussed in Chapter 4.

It should be noted that no racial or income group shown in Figure 6.3 achieved the Healthy People 2010 goal of 96% of Americans having a specific source of ongoing care. Although those with the highest income are closer to this goal than others, the number of Americans without a usual source of care remains far in excess of what might be predicted by the level of national expenditures on health care.

Measures of Disparity in Health Care Quality

As can be surmised at this point, the measurement of disparities in health care access and quality is a highly complex enterprise. In fact, there are decades of research on the conceptualization and measurement of health care access and quality—with the escalating debate concerning disparities in health care even further raising the stakes. The approach undertaken by the Agency for Healthcare Research and Quality (AHRQ) represents the most current and encompassing approach to measuring disparities in health care quality and access (Kelley, Moy, & Dayton, 2005). Although a more complete overview of the AHRQ model of access and quality measurement is provided by Kelley et al. (2005), the graphic version of the AHRQ model shown in Figure 6.4 conveys the fundamentals.

First, it is shown that all aspects of health care access and quality serve four very general purposes: promoting health, recovering from illness, living with chronic disease and disability, and coping with the end of life. It is also shown that quality of care is conceptualized as encompassing four specific aspects: effectiveness, safety, timeliness, and patient centeredness. The quality aspect that perhaps is the most abstract, patient centeredness, incorporates the notion that the care provided "is respectful of and responsive to individual patient preferences, needs, and values" (AHRQ, 2004, p. 21). Figure 6.4 also depicts the idea that access to care and quality of care are in part relative to the level of health care need, and that disparities in health care by race, ethnicity, and social class are observed in multiple aspects of health care access and quality.

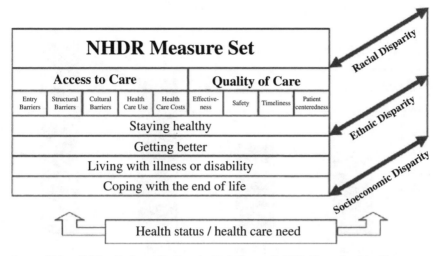

Source: Kelley, E. Moy, E., Stryer, D., Burstin, H. & Clancy, C. 2005. The national healthcare quality and disparities reports: An overview. *Medical Care*, 43(3), 3–8. Figure 2. Used with permission.

Figure 6.4 *The agency for health care research and quality's approach to the conceptualization and measurement of disparities.*

An example regarding application of the AHRQ framework for disparities in quality of health care, shown in Figure 6.5, concerns the racial disparities in the *patient safety* aspect of quality—specifically in the incidence of postoperative sepsis. Sepsis is a life-threatening infection of the bloodstream, and always a risk whenever surgery is performed. Protections against postoperative sepsis include a sterile surgical field, sterilization of surgical instruments, the rituals of vigorous hand and arm scrubbing, "gowning-up" in the sterile vestments of surgery, proper wound care following surgery, and the use of prophylactic antibiotics (AHRQ, 2011). The risk of sepsis is minimized to the extent that hospitals and surgical staff are vigilant in all aspects of sterile procedure, and made substantial where there is inattention to patient safety at any point prior to, during, or after surgery.

As shown in Figure 6.5, the national rates of postoperative sepsis vary by race and ethnicity, with the rate of postoperative sepsis much higher among Asians and African Americans than either Hispanic patients or non-Hispanic Whites. Although the postoperative sepsis rates for Hispanics have declined dramatically in the most recent data available, for all groups rates have increased relative to their levels at the beginning of the decade (AHRQ, 2011). It is also the case that patients on Medicare, Medicaid, and the uninsured run a substantially higher risk of contracting postoperative sepsis

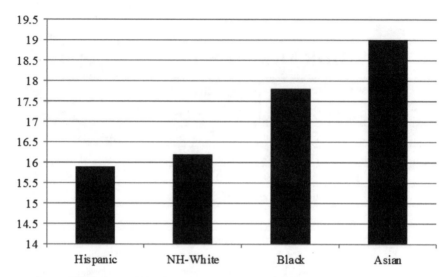

Source: AHRQ *National Health Care Disparities Report, 2010* Rockville,
MD. U.S. Department of Health and Human Services.

Figure 6.5 *Postoperative sepsis by race/ethnicity. 2007 (Cases per 1000 hospital discharges).*

than patients on private insurance (AHRQ 2011, p. 153). The reasons as to why any of this should be so are unclear, particularly given the existence of the knowledge of how to prevent postoperative sepsis, the financial investments in health care that are the highest in the world, and the billions expended annually in malpractice litigation.

SOCIAL CHARACTERISTICS ASSOCIATED WITH DISPARITIES IN HEALTH AND HEALTH CARE

Disparities in health and health care are structural in origin, meaning that they reflect the multiple forms of social hierarchy that are embedded in the organization of social relationships at all levels of society. According to "fundamental social cause" theory,[14] disparities in the burden of disease (and ergo in health care) arise wherever and whenever there are differences between groups in access to power, knowledge, and resources that are critical to health (Link & Phelan, 1995). In the United States, and to a greater or lesser extent elsewhere, differences in power, knowledge, and access to resources are associated with a broad variety of social characteristics, including age, race, SES (education, occupation, and income), gender, nativity (U.S. vs. foreign born), and also geography. As previously mentioned in this chapter, because disease and various forms of disablement are sources of disempowerment and deprivation, they further accentuate health disparities that may have arisen from other determinant factors (e.g., poverty).

Given the breadth of social characteristics associated with disparities in health and in health care, the evidence concerning either is difficult to summarize in a way that is adequately comprehensive. However, the remainder of this chapter draws from the findings from three ambitious attempts to do so: *Living and Dying in the U.S.A.*, a sociological analysis of the adult mortality undertaken by Rogers et al. (2000); the *National Health Care Disparities Report* series, published annually by the U.S. Department of Health and Human Services; and *Unequal Treatment: Confronting Racial and Ethnic Disparities in Health Care*, the IOM's groundbreaking analysis of disparities in the delivery of health care. As rigorous and comprehensive as these studies are, even in total they provide only an incomplete portrayal of the disparities that arise in the wealthiest nation on earth with the most expensive and technologically advanced health care system. Occasionally, data from other sources will be added to at least somewhat complete this tragic and ironic picture.

DISPARITIES IN HEALTH AND BURDEN OF DISEASE: GENERAL FINDINGS

Before examining the specific factors that are correlated with disparities in health, a few exemplars are provided to offer some sense of the magnitude of the disadvantages. First to be considered are disparities by sex, race, and ethnicity reflected in the "years of potential life lost" (YPLL) statistic described earlier in the chapter. Again, the YPLL statistic refers to either the life years lost in a population due to all deaths that occur prior to a selected benchmark of average life expectancy or life years lost due to specific causes of death associated with premature mortality. Figure 6.6 shows the recent time trends by sex, race, and ethnicity in the years of potential years of life lost (per 100,000 persons) from all causes of premature death combined.[15]

The top graph shows that between 1990 and 2077, the years of potential life lost among male and female individuals declined, and for males the decline was particularly dramatic. Still, a yawning gender gap remains between the life years lost due to premature death—though it has slightly closed over the past two decades. The higher levels of premature mortality among male

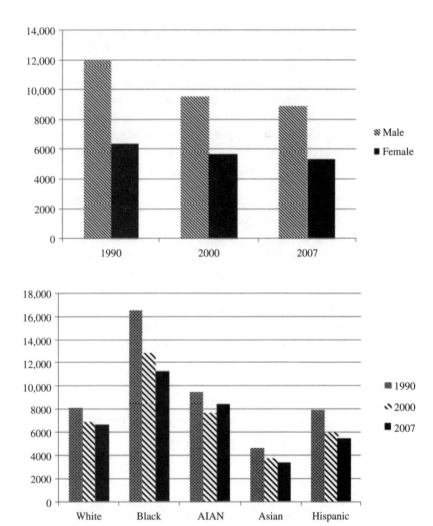

Source: NCHS, *Health, United States 2010.* Hyattesville, MD. Table 25 Years of potential life lost before age 75 for selected causes of death, by sex, race, and Hispanic origin: United States, selected years 1980–2007. The racial category White includes both Hispanic and Non-Hispanic Whites, and Hispanics include all races. AIAN refers to Native Americans/Alaska Natives.

Figure 6.6 *Years of potential life lost (YPLL) before age 75 per 100,000 persons, 1990–2007 according to sex, race, and ethnicity for all causes of death (age adjusted).*

relative to female individuals is a phenomenon common to post-industrial societies, attributable in significant part to the tendency of male individuals to engage in higher risk health behaviors (Denton & Walters, 1999).

The bottom graph in Figure 6.6 shows the disparities in years of potential life lost by different racial and ethnic categories, and the extent to which the premature deaths for each group have declined during recent decades. First, it can be seen that of the racial/ethnic grouping compared, the disparities in premature deaths are most pronounced among the Black (African American) population. While the declines in premature mortality for this population are large and encouraging, the disparity in premature death rates of African Americans relative to Whites has actually slightly increased. That is, African American premature death rates have declined, but not as rapidly as among Whites. We also once again see evidence of the mortality advantage of Hispanics relative to Whites, despite the disadvantages that encumber Hispanics in education and income. The Asian category has the benefit of the lowest levels of premature mortality and is continuing to show improvements in premature mortality—though it should be recognized that within different subcategories of Asians there are significant differences in premature mortality. Finally, the Native American/Alaska Native (AIAN) population, while it has also experienced improvements in premature mortality over the most recent two decades, shows a worrisome trend in the most recent data towards a resurgence in premature mortality (AHRQ, 2011).

The take-home message from this small representation of a vast compendium of health disparities research is that, for a variety of complex reasons (some well established and others more elusive), large disparities in health by sex, race, and ethnicity persist—despite continued improvements in the general population health.

A second exemplar of disparities in health illuminates the role of education on the prevalence of low birthweight infants (birthweights under 2500 g). Low birthweight is highly correlated with infant mortality, as well as a range of factors associated with social disadvantage. As shown in Figure 6.7, while there has been a gradual increase in the percentage of low birthweight infants over most recent decades that reflects gains in the survival of very low birthweight infants, there is a remarkably consistent educational benefit among mothers of newborns with 13 or more years of education.[16] That is, the percentage of low birthweight infants among live births to mothers with higher levels of education is consistently lower than that observed for mothers with lower levels of education. Why should maternal education decrease the likelihood of a low birthweight pregnancy outcome? First, a higher level of education suggests that throughout the maternal life course there has been less exposure to poverty and psychosocial stress (Denton & Walters, 1999). Second, mothers with higher levels of education are more likely to engage in beneficial health behaviors and avoid detrimental

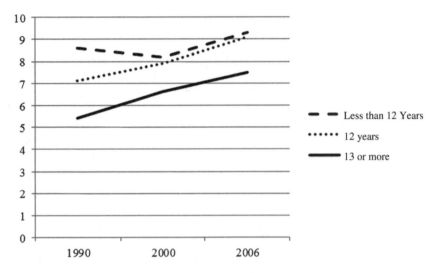

Source: NCHS. *Health, United States 2009*. Hyattesville, MD. Table 12. Low birthweight, live births among mothers aged 20 and above, by detailed race, hispanic origin, and education of mother: United States, selected years and reporting areas.

Figure 6.7 *Percent low birthweight births/1000 live births by education level of mother, 1900–2006.*

ones (Denton & Walters, 1999). Finally, mothers with higher levels of education are more likely to have access to appropriate prenatal care (AHRQ, 2011). Interestingly enough, the last few decades have seen a reduction in the disparity of low birthweight outcomes among women with less than a high school education relative to those with 12 years of education. This possibly reflects, among other factors, the extension of prenatal care to low-income women under the States Children's Health Insurance Program (SCHIP). This is a plausible inference because the decrease in the prevalence of low birthweight outcomes among women in the lowest education category coincides with the implementation of SCHIP beginning in 1998.

Another illuminating health disparities comparison is the examination of the prevalence of premature mortality from communicable diseases, also by education. In contrast to chronic conditions such as heart disease or diabetes, communicable diseases are generally more likely to be acquired and progress to premature mortality as a function of disadvantaged SES than to act as a determinant of socioeconomic disadvantage. That is, while it can be speculated that a person with a chronic disease may experience some disadvantages in educational attainment and employment due to their health condition, the acute nature of communicable diseases makes it more likely that disadvantages in education and income play a causal role in the disease rather than the other way around. As shown in Figure 6.8, the mortality disadvantages of lower SES (as measured by fewer years of education) are quite substantial where communicable diseases are the immediate cause of mortality. It is also apparent that despite significant improvements in the risk of death from communicable diseases during the mid-1990s (mostly attributable to decreased mortality from AIDS), the disparities by level of education remained little changed. For example, the lightest gray bar in Figure 6.8 shows that the most extreme education gap in age-adjusted mortality rates from communicable diseases remained well in excess of 30 deaths per 100,000 persons between 1994 and 2002—despite rather dramatic changes in the overall death rates.

Taken together, the exemplars shown in Figures 6.6 through 6.8 illuminate two critical aspects of disparities in health. First, disparities by race and SES are substantial. Second, despite general improvements in the overall level of health across all race and education over the recent decades, relative mortality disadvantages tend to persist. What can't be surmised from these trends is the relative influence of race and social class on disparities in health. For

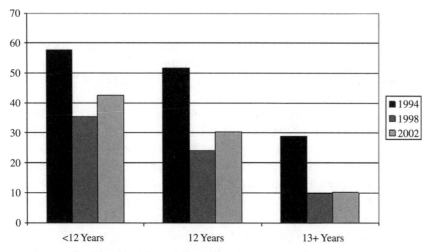

Source: *Health, United States 2004.* N.C.H.S. Hyattesville, Maryland.
Table 34. Age adjusted chronic and noncommunicable disease dearth rates for adults aged 25–64. United States, selected years 1994–2002.

Figure 6.8 *Age-adjusted death rates from communicable diseases for persons aged 25–64, by years of education (in deaths per 100,000).*

that, we turn to the groundbreaking and exhaustive sociological analysis of disparities in adult mortality undertaken by Rogers et al. in *Living and Dying in the USA* (2000).

Assessing the Relative Effects of Social Characteristics on Disparities in Health

Findings From Living and Dying in the USA

To the extent that SES is associated with race, as is the case in the United States, determining the relative causal influence of either race or SES on disparities in health is not possible absent the ability to examine the lives of individuals with different racial and educational characteristics over time. The same is true for ethnicity, nativity (country of birth), marital status, sex, and a variety of other social characteristics that are associated with both health and SES.

Rogers et al. (2000) tackled this problem by employing data prepared by the National Center for Health Statistics that linked survey information on individual social characteristics, health status, and health relevant behaviors to the death records of survey respondents who subsequently died. The linked survey and death records spanned a 9-year period (1986–1995) and involved a nationally representative sample—thus permitting generalization of multiple findings to the U.S. population as a whole.[17] Although the details of the study are fairly complex, the statistical strategy employed by Rogers et al. produced findings that are straightforward to explain and interpret. In essence, the disparities in health that are attributable to different social characteristics are presented as "adjusted mortality differentials," that is, differences in the risk of death associated with a given social characteristic when all other factors are statistically controlled.

The graph shown in Figure 6.9 summarizes the findings from only one enlightening component of the exhaustive analysis of health disparities undertaken by Rogers et al. Essentially, each social characteristic shown in Figure 6.9 is expressed as an adjusted mortality differential, meaning its effects on mortality are statistically adjusted for other potentially confounding factors—age, income, employment status, and marital status.[18] For racial/ ethnic characteristics, all differences shown are relative to the mortality risks associated with White Americans. Thus it can be seen that being of Asian-American descent reduces the likelihood of mortality something akin to 20% relative to White Americans when other relevant factors are taken into account. Conversely, there are distinct disadvantages in mortality risk attributable to those of African American or Puerto Rican descent relative to White Americans.

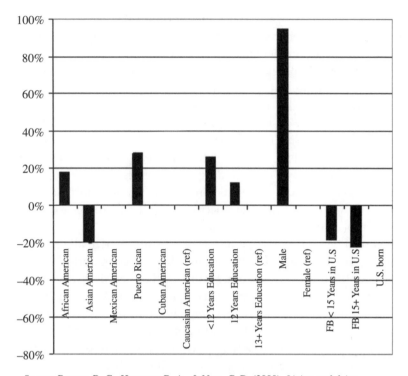

Source: Rogers, R. G., Hummer, R. A., & Nam, C. B. (2000). *Living and dying in the USA: Behavioral, health, and social differentials of adult mortality.* San Diego: Academic Press. Adapted from Table 4.3.

Figure 6.9 *Mortality differentials by race, education, sex, and nativity, adjusted for all social characteristics shown plus age, income, employment status, and marital status. All reference social characteristics (those used for relative comparison) show a 0% mortality differential.*

The mortality risks by lower levels of education are relative to the mortality levels of persons with 13+ years of education (shown in Figure 6.9 as the reference category). It is readily apparent that net of the effects of race, ethnicity, gender and other social characteristics; the mortality disadvantages of limited education are powerful. Specifically, persons having only 12 years of education (equivalent to a high school education), relative to those that have 13+ years of education, have about a 15% mortality risk disadvantage, and persons of less than 12 years of education have about a 30% mortality risk disadvantage. Although the education and race/ethnicity effects on relative mortality risks are substantial, the most powerful social characteristic is gender. Relative to female individuals (the reference or comparison category), male individuals carry nearly twice the mortality risk of female individuals when all other social characteristics are taken into account. The reason that male individuals do not actually die at twice the rate of female individuals is that (on an individual level) male individuals are buffered by such protective factors as income, education, employment, relative age, and favorable marital status. Still, the mortality disadvantage in male individuals is expressed in a variety of statistics, including a 5-year disadvantage in life expectancy at birth (NCHS, 2011). Interestingly, being of foreign birth decreases mortality risk, again, where differences in income, education, race/ethnicity, and other confounding social characteristics are taken into account. The most likely dynamic in the favorable mortality effects of foreign birth has to do with the selective migration process explained previously in this chapter (Palloni & Aria, 2004).

It is well beyond the scope of this text to summarize all of the findings from the exhaustive analysis of mortality disparities undertaken by Rogers et al. Indeed, the findings shown in Figure 6.9 that pertain to social characteristics associated with significant disparities in mortality are but a small but illuminating glimpse of their complete analysis. The other structural sources of disparities in mortality addressed in their investigation include the role of the occupational hierarchy,[19] disabilities, mental illness and addictions, and the mediating effects of specific health behaviors (e.g. exercise, smoking, and alcohol consumption). These issues are considered in more depth in Chapter 7.

Social Characteristics Related to Disparities in Health Care

2010 National Healthcare Disparities Report: Background and Key Findings

The *2010 National Healthcare Disparities Report* (2010 NHDR) is actually the seventh in a series of annual studies authorized by the U.S. Congress and organized by the Agency for Healthcare Research and Quality.[20] Each of these studies (the first was in 2003) are viewed as the foundation of an ongoing effort to describe and monitor disparities in health care delivery as they "relate to racial and socioeconomic factors in priority populations" (AHRQ, 2004, p. 7). The 2010 NHDR, in addition to focusing on health care disparities by race, ethnicity, income, education, age, and gender, provides a special focus on examining the care received by residents of inner-city and rural areas. The 2010 NHDR measures disparities within two distinct domains: health care access and health care quality. Most importantly, the

NHDR series tracks the national progress toward the reduction of health care disparities by tracking trends across a wide range of health disparity measures. The complete 2010 NHDR is a textbook-length report packed with tables and graphs of data pertaining to different aspects of disparities in health care—some of which have been highlighted previously (see Figure 6.5).

Among the most illuminating findings in the *2010 National Health Care Disparities Report* is a summary chart of the disparities in *core health care quality measures* by race, ethnicity, and income. Core health care quality measures that are compared across groups number in the dozens, and collectively address the crucial aspects of patient care—effectiveness, timeliness, and "patient centeredness."[21] Although the number of core quality measures available to assess the evidence of health care disparities varies by the specific groups being compared, even the most limited comparison summarized in this report employs no fewer than 23 core quality measures.

Figure 6.10 is a reduced version of the *2010 National Health Care Disparities Report* summary chart of health care disparities by core health care quality measures, abbreviated to highlight the extent to which different groups fare worse in multiple measures of health care quality. Racial/ethnic comparisons utilize Whites as the reference category, since in overall health care quality Whites benefit from higher standards of health care quality.[22] First, it can be seen that among the racial/ethnic comparisons of health care quality, the Hispanics encounter health care disparities in just over 50% of the core measures of health care quality relative to non-Hispanic Whites. Although it has been shown at an earlier point in this chapter that Hispanics fare better than non-Hispanic Whites in overall health (as measured by age-adjusted death rates, see Figure 6.1), the relative health advantage of Hispanics relative to non-Hispanic Whites and most other groups occurs despite the disparities in health care access and quality Hispanics encounter. Among the racial comparisons shown in Figure 6.10, the most disadvantaged group relative to Whites are persons in the Black and American Indian/Alaska Native (AIAN) categories. Asians actually fare slightly better than Whites in the core measures of health care quality, in that they fare worse in only 21% of core health care quality measures while faring better in 26% of such measures (AHRQ, 2011, p. 4). The most dramatic dimension of health care quality disparities, though, is that of income. Relative to persons of high income, the poor in the American health care system encounter inferior care in over 80% of measures of health care quality. This is an astonishing level of health care disparity, particularly when it is considered that the public expenditures on health care in the United States are nearly equal to private expenditures on health care (see Chapter 3, Table 3.1). In large part though, the failure of public expenditures

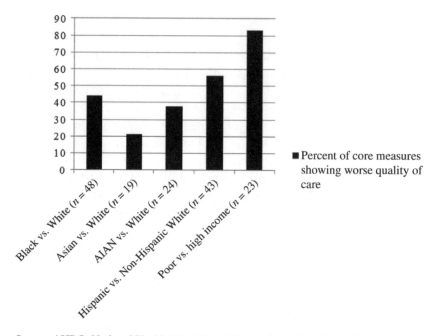

Source: AHRQ. National Health Care Disparities, Report: 2010. Rockville, MD. U.S. Department of Health and Human Services. Adapted from Figure H.1.

Figure 6.10 *Percent of quality measures for which members of selected groups experienced worse quality of care as compared with reference group.*

in health care to produce anything approaching equity in the quality of health care received by the poor reflects the fact that public expenditures in health care entail largely middle-class entitlements like Medicare.

One of the core dimensions of quality that the NHDR series devotes considerable attention to is *patient centeredness,* defined as "[H]ealth care that establishes a partnership among practitioners, patients, and their families (when appropriate) to ensure that decisions respect patients' wants, needs, and preferences and that patients have the education and support they need to make decisions and participate in their own care" (AHRQ, 2011, p. 169). A core measure of *patient centeredness* that the NHDR series employs is the extent to which patients believe they have been consulted by their health care provider in the making of treatment decisions. As it happens, the culture of American health care appears to place inadequate emphasis on the practice of involving patients in their treatment decisions. As shown in Figure 6.11, depending on their demographic characteristics, from 10% to

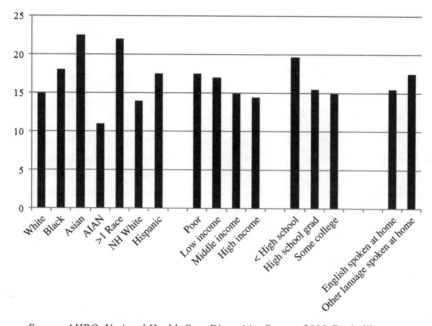

Source: AHRQ. *National Health Care Disparities Report: 2010.* Rockville, MD: U.S. Department of Health and Human Services. Adapted from Figure 5.12.

Figure 6.11 *Percent of adults with usual source of care whose health providers sometimes or never asked for the patient's help to make treatment decisions, by race, income, education, and english proficience.*
Note: **AIAN refers to American Indian Alaska Native.**

30% of adult patients report that their health care providers only sometimes or never ask for their help in making the treatment decisions affecting their health care and health. Predictably enough, race, ethnicity, income, education, and language spoken all influence the likelihood that patients experience involvement in their health care decisions. As with other aspects of health care access and quality, Whites are *less likely* to report that they have little or no involvement in treatment decisions, while most racial and ethnic minorities *are more likely* to report their health care providers only sometimes or never consult them in treatment decisions affecting their health.[23] Consistent with the detrimental effects of educational disadvantage on health, Figure 6.11 shows that patients with less than a high school education are among the least likely to be consulted in decisions affecting their health. Finally, it is apparent that lower income patients have less involvement in their health care decisions than higher income ones. The central thread through all of these findings is the relationship between the social status and power of a patient (as determined by such factors as race, income, and education) and the extent to which they are therefore likely to be consulted by health care providers in decisions affecting their health.

Findings From the IOM

The IOM is a branch of the National Academy of Sciences established to seek and secure analysis of critical health policy issues from the most eminent scientists of medicine. Although the American Medical Association can be described as the most influential voice of the medical profession's political interests, the IOM can be described as the medical profession's most authoritative voice in matters of scientifically informed health care practice and policy. Earlier in this chapter, it was pointed out that the IOM restricted its definition of health care to differences in health care that did not involve issues of access, patient needs, and patient preferences (IOM, 2003, p. 32). As a result, the IOM's *Unequal Treatment* [24] report (IOM-UTR) largely restricts its focus on disparities that arise within the health care system's structural context of clinical practice and sources of disparity that arise from patient–provider-level discrimination. Also, the IOM-UTR is principally concerned with racial and ethnic discrimination among selected groups (primarily African Americans, Hispanics, and non-Hispanic Whites) as opposed to discrimination based upon age, income, gender, and other social characteristics. Nonetheless, the IOM-UTR made pioneering contributions in its illumination of the institutional context of disparities in health care, and in highlighting the complex processes that produce disparities in health care. Moreover, the IOM-UTR provides an important historic baseline against which our national progress in the eradication of health care disparities can be assessed.

According to the IOM-UTR's conceptual framework, the sources of disparity in health care occur at three levels: at the health care system level, at the patient level, and at the practitioner level (IOM, 2003, p. 126). As noted by the IOM-UTR, it is the clinical encounter[25] during the process of care that links sources of disparity with the various manifestations of unequal treatment. Although the cultural ideal of the clinical encounter is a face-to-face interaction between patient and provider that is founded upon mutual trust, honesty, empathy, objectivity, scientific knowledge, and deep concern for the patient's preferences and best interests, a variety of factors make this ideal exceedingly difficult to accomplish. In the reality of American health care, the clinical encounter typically involves three actors: the clinician (e.g., physician, nurse practitioner, or physical therapist), the physically absent but omnipresent utilization manager, and the patient. All three actors have the capacity to exercise discretion in what is shared and offered, and all three actors bring their own very subjective orientation to the "facts," purposes, and priorities of the encounter. Moreover, all three actors are encumbered by uncertainty and specific disadvantages with respect to critical information. Thus, the clinical encounter is not solely governed by objectivity, science, and clarity of purpose—but also by a fog of uncertainty and discretion. To paraphrase the IOM-UTR on this point, despite benign intent, "discretion and ambiguity create the conditions within which race and ethnicity may become salient and operative in ways that are more likely to produce disparities in health care" (IOM, 2003, p. 128).

As noted in the IOM-UTR, there are a number of ways in which each actor in the clinical encounter introduces the potential for disparities in care—absent the distrust, malicious intent, or overt negligence that is often assumed to be the basis of disparities in health care. For example, there is a substantial body of evidence from the literature in the behavior and social sciences establishing that patients vary greatly in their perception of symptoms, reporting of pain, in their particular conceptual frameworks of health and illness, and in health-seeking behavior—and that some of this variation correlates with race and ethnicity.[26] Differences between the patient and clinician by race, ethnicity, and social class only serve to compound the difficulties in clinical perception and interpretation. The sources of uncertainty that encumber the clinician include the often limited diagnostic information available from objective diagnostic tests, the often equivocal evidence concerning the relative efficacy of different therapeutic alternatives, and the often very limited knowledge or shared experience with the patient's world—thus leaving a large place for the clinician's subjective appraisal of the patient's needs and best interests. This, of course, is fertile ground for the introduction of stereotypes and biases into the process of health care (IOM, 2003).

Although the IOM-UTR takes the position that there is "no direct evidence that racism, bias, or prejudice among health care professionals affects the quality of care for minority patients" (IOM, 2003, p. 176), this conclusion turns on a very narrow definition of direct evidence—perfectly controlled experimental conditions. Instead, the IOM-UTR adopts the position that "indirect evidence from several lines of research" supports the statement that "[b]ias, stereotyping, prejudice, and clinical uncertainty on the part of healthcare providers *may* [italics not in original] contribute to racial and ethnic disparities in healthcare" (IOM, 2003, p. 178). In view of the multiple studies cited and summarized by the IOM-UTR demonstrating various examples of race-based discrimination in diagnosis and treatment, the logic of this equivocal conclusion appears tortured at best. A small partial sampling of the *indirect evidence* cited in the IOM-UTR includes studies that show:

- The lower probability of cardiac catheterization referral for African-American women relative to White men and women. (Schulman et al., 1999)[27]
- The tendency of a White male physician to treat severe pain more aggressively for White patients than for African American patients suffering from identical symptoms. (Weisse, Sorum, Sanders, & Syat, 2001)
- The propensity of White medical students (relative to minority medical students) to assess angina symptoms more seriously in White males that African American females. (Rathore et al., 2000)
- The likelihood that African American patients are assessed more negatively on a variety of personal and clinical traits than White patients despite controls for socioeconomic status, personality attributes, and severity of illness (Van-Ryn & Burke, 2000); and
- The lower incidence of cardiac bypass surgery and the higher 5-year mortality for African American heart disease patients relative to Whites despite similar clinical characteristics. (Peterson et al., 1997)

In fact, of the 13 studies on racial disparities in clinical care and outcomes selected by the IOM-UTR (all of which had appropriate controls for potentially confounding clinical characteristics) 11 (85%) found distinct patterns of racial disparities in care that could not be explained by patient characteristics other than race (IOM, 2003, pp. 380–383).

In evolutionary terms, these findings should not be in any way surprising. As pointed out by Princeton University sociologist Douglas Massey in his definitive analysis of social stratification in American Society,[28] human beings are psychologically "hardwired" to classify or categorize others in accordance with highly simplistic and generally subconscious schemas (learned memory structures). Such categorizations are essential and endemic to social interactions, and do not need to be either malevolent or conscious to result in biased perceptions and discriminatory health care. Interestingly, as cautious as the IOM-UTR language is regarding empirical support for the conclusion that personal biases and prejudices undermine equitable health care for racial and ethnic minorities, the theoretical case that the IOM-UTR provides for the scientific basis of stereotyping and discrimination in health care (like Massey's subsequent 2007 analysis) that appears to make such a conclusion inevitable.[29]

CONCLUDING COMMENTS: THE DEEP ROOTS OF DISPARITIES IN HEALTH CARE

In contrast to the equivocal posture of the IOM-UTR, the position taken here is that the combined evidence from Rogers et al., *Living and Dying in the U.S.A.*, the *National Health Care Disparities Report* series, and the multiple studies cited in the IOM-UTR leads to one undeniable conclusion—disparities in U.S. health care system exist on the basis of a wide variety of social characteristics associated with other forms of social oppression and disadvantage. Differences in health care quality and outcomes are correlated with particular social characteristics because:

1. The psychological processes of stereotyping are deeply embedded in our collective evolutionary history,
2. The reinforcement of stereotypes have historically benefitted the dominant groups in human societies,
3. Many organizations and individuals resist the acknowledgement of biases and prejudice and,
4. The health care system is embedded in a societal context that values and privileges some groups over others.

Although disparities based on race are the most controversial and emotionally charged, all social forms of health care disparities are pervasive and pernicious, and involve both structural and individual-level processes.

Pertaining to racism specifically, it can be argued that the IOM-UTR's reluctance to make a stronger statement on the effects of racism the equitable delivery of health care, despite overwhelming evidence to the contrary, perpetuates a key process in the production of health care disparities—institutional racism. Institutional racism, defined generally as institutional-level structures and processes that sustain the mechanisms of racial oppression with or without individual-level awareness or malicious intent, thrives where plausible denial of racism is permitted to exist. Among the more deeply rooted and most difficult to eradicate sources of disparities in health care is the denial of institutional and individual agency in the processes that produce differences in care by race, ethnicity, and income. Despite its groundbreaking contributions toward the understanding of many of the ways health care disparities are manifested and generating in the health care system, the IOM-UTR contention that there is "no direct evidence that racism, bias, or prejudice among health care professionals affects the quality of care for minority patients" (IOM, 2003, p. 176) contributes to the perpetuation of the social problem it seeks to solve.[30]

In the next chapter, these issues are explored in more depth. In addition, the chapter that follows considers theories that explain why disparities in health persist even where equity in health care is achieved.

NOTES

1. Established in 1970, the Institute of Medicine (IOM) is the voice of the National Academy of Sciences on national issues pertaining to health, health care, and the practice of medicine.
2. The IOM developed this narrow definition of health care disparities in response to the limited definition of disparities conveyed by the U.S. Congress in its original charge to the IOM to perform an analysis of health care disparities. Although the IOM acknowledges that the exclusion of access factors from the definition of health care disparities results in a definitional distinction that is "artificial" (IOM, 2003, p. 30), it is argued here that the IOM's narrow definition of health care also serves to downplay the role of access factors in production of health care disparities.
3. For example, the risk for sickle cell diseases is substantially higher among children of African, Mediterranean, Caribbean, South and Central American, Arabian, or East Indian heritage, a factor which for the right reasons may affect investments in newborn screening tests and the diagnostic considerations in children in high-risk groups that express symptoms consistent with sickle cell disorders. That said, there are very few racial and ethnic differences in health and burden of disease that have a genetic basis, as opposed to enormous and enduring influence of social factors (Williams Mohammed, Leavell, & Collins, 2010).
4. A useful anecdotal example (and sadly not a hypothetical one) is a physician that elected to prescribe less-expensive medications to Medicaid patients due to personal biases against public assistance recipients.
5. Age-adjusted death rates are used to compare the death rates of populations having different age compositions by statistically controlling for the effects of differences in population age composition on death rate comparisons. In contrast, crude death rates do not adjust for the effects of population age composition.
6. An example of a global burden of disease measure is the Disability Adjusted Life Year (DALY), developed for the World Health Organization by the Harvard School of Public Health (Murray & Lopez, 1996). In essence, The DALY estimates the number of life years lost to premature death and years of healthy life lost due to disabling conditions. DALY estimates can be disease specific (e.g., years of healthy life lost due to breast cancer) or can be calculated to measure the summed impact of all diseases.
7. Even though disparities in access to health care and quality of health care do not "in and of themselves" reflect differences in health, they are correlated with them to the extent that there are patterns of disease that influence health care access and quality. An example of this is treatment of HIV, which remains encumbered with fear, stigma, and denial of appropriate care.

8. The term "heuristic" is attached to the model as an acknowledgment of the model's simplification of extremely complex processes. In particular, the model shown omits the social and biological determinants that link the manifestations of disease to particular individual characteristics. These issues are taken up in the chapter that follows.

9. Overt value structures are those values that are espoused through formal statements, professional credos, rules of conduct, and laws, for example, statements pertaining to patient rights and provider responsibilities, laws pertaining to patient consent and confidentiality, and formal statements pertaining to issues like patient autonomy. Latent values are those expressed through the de facto effects of policies and the attitudes and actions of health care providers. For example, most health care organizations now espouse the value of "culturally competent practice" while at the same time retaining institutionalized structures and processes that reinforce the dominant culture.

10. Life expectancies are generally calculated from vital records (birth and death records) and population counts, although there are also methods to calculate life expectancies from household-level survey data.

11. It should be pointed out that multiple decrement life tables are only a crude approximation of differences in life expectancy that are due to the impact of particular causes of death, because individuals dying of natural causes often have other potentially fatal co-morbid conditions

12. Causes of death are based upon an internationally recognized method for classifying diseases and causes of death, currently the World Health Organization *International Statistical Classification of Diseases and Related Health Problems Manual— Revised Version 10* (commonly called the ICD-10). In the parlance of ICD-10, accidents and acts of violence are coded as externally caused diseases.

13. For example, homicide is more prevalent among young adults. Therefore, absent adjustments for the differences in the age composition between Hispanics and non-Hispanic Whites, it would make it appear that the relative prevalence of homicides among Hispanics is even higher because there are fewer young adults among the non-Hispanic White population.

14. The theory of "fundamental social causes of disease" (Link & Phelan, 1995) will be covered extensively in the next chapter, which is devoted more specifically to social epidemiology.

15. Premature deaths are deaths that occur from diseases that can either be delayed until old age or death from external causes that are preventable (e.g., accidents, interpersonal violence).

16. Paradoxically, the general increase in the percentage of low birthweight live births reflects some progress in prenatal health care, in that the survival of very low birthweight infants has increased over this period–thus yielding a higher percentage of low birthweight live births (Fanaroff et al., 2007).

17. There are caveats and important limitations that Rogers et al. explain in detail. Interested readers are referred to Rogers et al. (2000, pp. 18–20).

18. The relative mortality risks shown in Figure 6.9 are derived from multivariate techniques that statistically control for the confounding effects of all other social characteristics shown in Figure 6.9, plus age, income, employment status, and marital status. Thus, for example, the 28% mortality disadvantage associated with being of Puerto Rican descent (as opposed to being of White American descent) is not

in addition to whatever mortality disadvantages are imposed by lower education levels, lower income, unfavorable marital status, age effects, and even being male.

19. Notably, Rogers, Hummer, and Nam find that persons in the lowest status jobs experience a 25% excess risk of mortality, even when the effects of income and education are taken into account (Rogers et al., 2000, p. 155).

20. The Agency for Healthcare Research and Quality is under the U.S. Department of Health and Human Services. The NHDR process was authorized by Congress under the Healthcare Research and Quality Act of 1999 (Public Law 106-129).

21. In this report, *patient centeredness* is defined as "[H]ealth care that establishes a partnership among practitioners, patients, and their families (when appropriate) to ensure that decisions respect patients' wants, needs, and preferences and that patients have the education and support they need to make decisions and participate in their own care" (AHRQ, 2011, p. 169).

22. For the comparisons in Figure 6.10 between Whites and Blacks, Asians and AIAN (American Indians/Alaska Natives), the category of Whites includes both Hispanic and non-Hispanic Whites.

23. Interestingly, American Indians and Alaska Natives appear less likely than other racial/ethnic groups to report to have been either sometimes or never consulted by their health care provider in treatment decisions affecting their care. It is possible that this finding may reflect the fact that because the questions are asked of American Indians and Alaska Natives with a usual source of care, there may be a high proportion of respondents receiving their care from the Indian Health Service clinics and practitioners—which place a particular emphasis on patient centeredness.

24. Institute of Medicine, Committee on Understanding and Eliminating Racial and Ethnic Disparities in Health Care (2003). *Unequal treatment: Confronting racial and ethnic disparities in health care.* Washington, DC: National Academy Press.

25. As it is used here, the term clinical encounter is meant to refer to the typical face-to-face dialog between patient and health care provider that is focused upon the process of diagnosis and treatment.

26. This is a good instance to remember the oft-ignored adage that "correlation is not causality."

27. This paper has attracted significant criticism on the basis of methods and findings, however, the central findings that race and gender affected referral to catheterization are well defended by the evidence.

28. Douglas Massey, *Categorically Unequal: The American Stratification System.* 2007, Sage Publications: New York.

29. See the discussion in Chapter 4 of the IOM-UTR, pp. 169–174.

30. The full sentence from the IOM-UTR reads "In summary, the committee found no direct evidence that racism, bias, or prejudice among healthcare professionals affects the quality of care for minority patients, such as that which might be available from audit studies where 'testers' from different racial or ethnic groups present in clinical settings with similar clinical complaints, histories and symptoms to assess possible differences in the quality of their treatment" (IOM, 2003, p. 176). As pointed out earlier in this chapter, this is an exceedingly narrow definition of "direct evidence."

REFERENCES

Acton, K. J., Rios Burrows, N., Moore, K., Querec, L., Geiss, L. S., & Engelgau, M. M. (2002). Trends in diabetes prevalence among American Indian and Alaska Native children, adolescents, and young adults. *American Journal of Public Health, 92*(9), 1485–1490.

Aday, L. A., & Andersen, R. (1981). Equity of access to medical care. *Medical Care, 19*(12), 4–27.

AHRQ. (2004). *2004 National healthcare disparities report.* Rockville, MD: U.S. Department of Health and Human Services.

AHRQ. (2011). *National health care disparities report, 2010.* Rockville, MD: U.S. Department of Health and Human Services.

American Medical Association. (2005). *Total physicians by race/ethnicity—2003.* Retrieved March 21, 2005, from http://www.ama-assn.org/ama/pub/category/12930.html

Becker, G., Janson-Bjerklie, S., Benner, P., Slobin, K., & Ferketich, S. (1993). The dilemma of seeking urgent care: Asthma episodes and emergency service use. *Social Science and Medicine, 37*(3), 305–313.

CDC. (2012). *National Center for Injury Prevention and Control: WISQARS Years of Potential Life Lost (YPLL) Reports, 1999–2009.* Retrieved February 1, 2012, from http://webappa.cdc.gov/sasweb/ncipc/ypll10.html#Advanced Options

Collins, S. R., Davis, K., Doty, M. M., & Ho, A. (2004). *Wages, health benefits, and worker's health.* New York: The Commonwealth Fund.

Denton, M., & Walters, V. (1999). Gender differences in structural and behavioral determinants of health: An analysis of the social production of health. *Social Science & Medicine, 48*(9), 1221–1222.

Ezzati, M., Lopez, A. D., Rodgers, A., Vander Hoorn, S., & Murray, C. J. (2002). Selected major risk factors and global and regional burden of disease. *The Lancet, 360*(9343), 1347–1360.

Fanaroff, A. A., Stoll, B. J., Wright, L. L., Carlo, W. A., Ehrenkranz, R. A., Stark, A. R., Bauer, C. R., Donovan, E. F., Korones, S. B., Laptook, A. R., Lemons, J. A., Oh, W., Papile, L. A., Shankaran, S., Stevenson, D. K., Tyson, J. E. & Poole, W. K. (2007). Trends in neonatal morbidity and mortality for very low birthweight infants. *American Journal of Obstetrics & Gynecology, 196*(2), 147.e1–147.e8.

Finch, B. K. (2003). Early origins of the gradient: The relationship between socioeconomic status and infant mortality in the United States. *Demography, 40*(4), 675–699.

Garroutte, E. M., Kunovich, R. M., Jacobsen, C., & Goldberg, J. (2004). Patient satisfaction and ethnic identity among American Indian older adults. *Social Science & Medicine, 59*(11), 2233–2244.

Gohdes, D. (1995). *Diabetes in North American Indians and Alaska Natives* (NIH Publication No. 95-1468). Bethesda, MD: National Institute of Diabetes and Digestive and Kidney Diseases, National Institutes of Health.

Guest, A., Almgren, G., & Hussey, J. (1998). The ecology of race and socioeconomic distress: Infant and working-age mortality in Chicago. *Demography, 35*(1), 23–35.

Gurwitz, J. H., Goldberg, R. J., Malmgren, J. A., Barron, H. V., Tiefenbrunn, A. J., Frederick, P. D. et al. (2002). Hospital transfer of patients with acute myocardial infarction: The effects of age, race, and insurance type. *American Journal of Medicine, 112*(7), 528–534.

Hayes, R. A., Vaughan, C., Medeiros, T., & Dubuque, E. (2002). Stigma directed toward chronic illness is resistant to change through education and exposure. *Psychology Reports, 90*(3 Pt 2), 1161–1173.

HHS. (2000). *Healthy people 2010.* Washington, DC: U.S. Department of Health and Human Services.

Hoyert, D., Kung, H., & Smith, B. (2005). *Deaths: Preliminary data for 2003.* Hyattsville, MD: National Center for Health Statistics.

IOM. (1993). *Access to health care in America.* Washington, DC: National Academy Press.

IOM. (2003). *Unequal treatment: Confronting racial and ethnic disparities in health care.* Washington, DC: National Academy Press.

Jacoby, A., Snape, D., & Baker, G. A. (2005). Epilepsy and social identity: The stigma of a chronic neurological disorder. *Lancet Neurology, 4*(3), 171–178.

Joachim, G., & Acorn, S. (2000). Stigma of visible and invisible chronic conditions. *Journal of Advanced Nursing, 32*(1), 243–248.

Kelley, E. P., Moy, E. M. D., & Dayton, E. M. A. (2005). Health care quality and disparities: Lessons from the first national reports. [Miscellaneous]. *Medical Care, 43*(3), 3–8.

Kominski, G., Simon, P., Ho, A., Luck, J., Lim, Y., & Fielding, J. (2002). Assessing the burden of disease and injury in Los Angeles County using disability-adjusted life years. *Public Health Reports, 117*(2), 185–191.

Lara, M., Gamboa, C., Kahramanian, M., Morales, L., & Bautista, D. (2005). Acculturation and Latino health in the United States: A review of the literature. *Annual Review of Public Health, 26,* 367–397.

Link, B. G., & Phelan, J. (1995). Social conditions as fundamental causes of disease. *Journal of Health and Social Behavior,* Special Issue, 80–94.

Massey, D. (2007). *Categorically unequal: The American stratification system.* New York: Russell Sage Foundation.

Michielutte, R., & Diseker, R. A. (1982). Children's perceptions of cancer in comparison to other chronic illnesses. *Journal of Chronic Disease, 35*(11), 843–852.

Murray, C., & Lopez, A. (Eds.). (1996). *The global burden of disease: A comprehensive assessment of mortality and disability from diseases, injuries and risk factors in 1990 and projected to 2020 (Vol. 1).* Cambridge, MA: Harvard School of Public Health on behalf of the World Health Organization and the World Bank.

NCHS. (2011). *Health, United States 2010.* Hyattsville, MD: National Center for Health Statistics.

NIH. (2001a). *Addressing health disparities: The NIH program of action.* Retrieved March 15, 2005, from http://healthdisparities.nih.gov/whatare.html

NIH. (2001b, August 2001). *Diabetes in American Indians and Alaska Natives.* Retrieved March 16, 2005, from http://diabetes.niddk.nih.gov/dm/pubs/americanindian/index.htm

Obst, T. E., Nauenberg, E., & Buck, G. M. (2001). Maternal health insurance coverage as a determinant of obstetrical anesthesia care. *Journal of Health Care for the Poor Underserved, 12*(2), 177–191.

OMH. (2012). *American Indian Alaska Native Profile.* U.S. Department of Health an Human Services Office of Minority Health. Retrieved February 1, 2012 from http://minorityhealth.hhs.gov/templates/browse.aspx?lvl=2&lvlID=52/

Palazzo, L., Guest, A., & Almgren, G. (2003). Economic distress and cause-of-death patterns for Black and non-Black men in Chicago: Reconsidering the relevance of classic epidemiological transition theory. *Social Biology, 50*(1/2), 102–127.

Palloni, A., & Aria, C. (2004). Paradox lost: Explaining the Hispanic adult mortality advantage. *Demography, 41*(3), 385–415.

Peterson, E., Shaw, L., DeLong, E., Pryor, D., Califf, R., & Mark, D. (1997). Racial variation in the use of coronary-revascularization procedures: Are the differences real? Do they matter? *New England Journal of Medicine, 336*, 480–486.

Rathore, S., Lenert, L., Weinfurt, K., Tinoco, A., Taleghani, C., Harless, W. et al. (2000). The effects of patient sex and race on medical students' ratings of quality of life. *American Journal of Medicine, 108*(7), 561–566.

Rathore, S. S., & Krumholz, H. M. (2004). Differences, disparities, and biases: Clarifying racial variations in health care use. *Annals of Internal Medicine, 141*(8), 635–638.

Rogers, R. G., Hummer, R. A., & Nam, C. B. (2000). *Living and dying in the USA: Behavioral, health, and social differentials of adult mortality.* San Diego, CA: Academic Press.

Rogge, M. M., Greenwald, M., & Golden, A. (2004). Obesity, stigma, and civilized oppression. *Advanced Nursing Science, 27*(4), 301–315.

Schryock, H., & Siegal, J. (1976). *The methods and materials of demography.* San Diego, CA: Academic Press.

Schulman, K., Berlin, J., Harless, W., Kerner, J., Sistrunk, S., Gersh, B. et al. (1999). The effect of race and sex on physicians' recommendations for cardiac catheterization. *New England Journal of Medicine, 340*(8), 618–626.

Starr, P. (1982). *The social transformation of American medicine.* New York: Basic Books.

U.S. Census. (2003). *2000 census of population and housing, characteristics of American Indians and Alaska Natives by tribe and language: 2000* (No. PHC-5). Washington, DC: U.S. Census Bureau.

U.S. Census. (2012a). *The 2012 statistical abstract.* Table 118, Leading Causes of Death by Race, 2007. Retrieved February 1, 2012, from: http://www.census.gov/compendia/statab/2012/tables/12s0118.pdf

U.S. Census. (2012b). *The 2012 statistical abstract.* Table 105 Life Expectancy by Race, Age and Sex, 2008. Retrieved February 1, 2012, from http://www.census.gov/compendia/statab/2012/tables/12s0105.pdf

Van-Ryn, M., & Burke, J. (2000). The effect of patient race and socio-economic status on physician's perceptions of patients. *Social Science & Medicine, 50*, 813–828.

Weisse, C., Sorum, P., Sanders, K., & Syat, B. (2001). Do gender and race affect decisions about pain management? *Journal of General Internal Medicine, 16*(4), 211–217.

Williams, D., Mohammed, S., Leavell, J., & Collins, C. (2010). Race, socioeconomic status and health: Complexities, ongoing challenges and research opportunities. *Annals of the New York Academy of Sciences, 1186*, 69–101.

World Health Organization. (2001). *World Health report 2001, statistical annex.* Retrieved March 28, 2005, from http://www.who.int/trade/glossary/story036/en/.

CHAPTER SEVEN

SOCIAL EPIDEMIOLOGY: UNRAVELING THE SOCIAL DETERMINANTS OF DISPARITIES IN HEALTH

*T*he term *social epidemiology* first appeared in the scientific literature in 1950, in the title of an article in the *American Sociological Review* that addressed the linkage between infant mortality and racial segregation (Krieger, 2001c; Yankauer, 1950). The author later became the editor of the *American Journal of Public Health*, which in a serendipitous way underscores the interdisciplinary pedigree of social epidemiology in the more firmly established disciplines of sociology and public health (Krieger, 2001c).

Although inquiries into the social conditions that give rise to disease date back many centuries, arguably the French sociologist and philosopher Emile Durkheim is as much the founder of social epidemiology as he is of sociology. Rather than investigating suicide from the standpoint of an individual act with an internally embedded chain of causality, Durkheim approached the incidence of suicide as a social fact (sociological phenomenon) with a structural explanation (Kawachi, 2002, p. 1740). In fact, Durkheim's work on suicide captured the defining feature of the discipline of social epidemiology: inquiries that focus upon structural explanations for the level and distribution of morbidity and mortality in human populations (Kawachi, 2002). Unlike traditional epidemiology, which incorporates social context as a background to its investigation on biological processes, social epidemiology "is distinguished by its insistence upon explicitly investigating the social determinants of population distributions of health, disease, and wellbeing ..." (Krieger, 2002, p. 7).

THE DISCIPLINE OF SOCIAL EPIDEMIOLOGY

Despite the legitimacy of its early origins, social epidemiology's recognition as a distinct discipline with its own place in the scientific community has been very recent and even then somewhat tenuous. In fact, the first textbook that employed "social epidemiology" in its title did not emerge until 2000 (Berkman & Kawachi, 2000; Krieger, 2001c). Many reasons account for this. Chief among them is the fact that several well-established disciplines have significant bodies of research that in one way or another address linkages between social structure and population health outcomes, including among them medical sociology, social demography, anthropology, medical geography, political science, and public health. A second and related reason is the slow development, until the last decade, of any significant disciplinary infrastructure in social epidemiology: such as doctoral training programs, dedicated journals, and well-funded research centers. The glacial emergence of a disciplinary infrastructure in social epidemiology is largely a consequence of social epidemiology's inherent character as a multidisciplinary enterprise and the tendency of scientific and academic recognition and reward structures to be very discipline-specific and conservative. A third reason for social epidemiology's tenuous hold as a unique discipline has to do with an arguably weak and underdeveloped theoretical structure in social epidemiology—a point taken up by critics within the discipline who identify themselves as social epidemiologists as well as those who consider social epidemiology to be a little more than a pretentious fad (Kaplan, 2004; Kasl & Jones, 2002; Macdonald, 2001; Zielhuis & Kiemeney, 2001). Fourth, (but not exhaustively), social epidemiology is an inherently radical discipline. The central theme and line of inquiry of social epidemiology is, after all, the notion that inequalities in the distribution of disease in a population are a function of social inequalities.

Although it can be acknowledged that medical science and traditional epidemiology espouse as their ultimate purpose improvement of the human condition through knowledge of disease processes and treatment, neither is linked to an explicit agenda to identify and change the structural arrangements implicated in the prevalence and distribution of human diseases. As mentioned previously, Krieger defines social epidemiology as a scientific discipline that is "distinguished by its insistence upon explicitly investigating the social determinants of population distributions of health, disease, and well-being" (Krieger, 2002, p. 7). In the scientific community, where dispassionate objectivity and repudiation of a political agenda are central to the ethos, a field of inquiry that is predicated upon the assumption and illumination of detrimental social conditions is often regarded as an anathema to the integrity of science. Moreover, many of the central constructs employed by social epidemiologists in their theories and measures (e.g., discrimination, racism, sexism, social inequality) are derived directly from the discourse of the political left. Finally, social epidemiologists in general make little effort to distance their discipline from a view of a healthy society as one that is materially and socially egalitarian and driven by a deep respect for fundamental human rights (Burris, 2002). The prediction that arises from these observations is that, despite whatever significant advancements are made in the theories and methods of social epidemiology, to the extent that the theories and findings of social epidemiologists fundamentally challenge embedded hierarchies of power and privilege, the discipline will remain clouded in questions about its legitimacy.

The Theories and Methods of Social Epidemiology

The historical evolvement and current state of theory in social epidemiology have been well summarized in a series of articles written by social epidemiologist Nancy Krieger (Krieger, 1994, 1999, 2000, 2001a, 2001b, 2001c, 2002; Krieger & Davey Smith, 2000, 2004). As noted by Krieger, the theoretical landscape of social epidemiology is dominated by three major frameworks that are listed in their order of emergence: psychosocial theories, political economy/social production of disease theories, and theories that derive from the ecological perspective (Krieger, 2001c).

The Psychosocial Theoretical Framework

The earliest to emerge, this model operates within the host–pathogen environment paradigm and focuses upon the selective susceptibilities to disease that are created by the psychosocial context. Although structural constructs such as dominance hierarchies, material deprivation, victimization, and social isolation are identified as the fundamental social determinants, the chronic stress produced by these determinants and effect of chronic stress on the individual's biological defenses is viewed as the intervening mechanism of host–pathogen susceptibility (Krieger, 2001c, p. 669).

The mediating effects of stress are central to the arguments employed by Richard Wilkinson to bring social epidemiology to the forefront of the contemporary public health discourse (Wilkinson, 1996). In Wilkinson's pioneering book, *Unhealthy Societies: The Afflictions of Inequality*, chronic stress is emphasized as a critical intermediate mechanism through which societies embedded with status hierarchies both perpetuate the socioeconomic status (SES) gradient and suppress population life expectancy—despite significant advances in health care infrastructure and per capita income. Although the hierarchy–stress–susceptibility link was not original to Wilkinson,[1] his extension of this paradigm as part of the explanation for emergence of a social inequality–mortality gradient at the societal level afforded the hypothesis renewed attention.

In Wilkinson's theoretical narratives (Wilkinson, 1996, 1999; Wilkinson & Pickens, 2010), the lower levels of social cohesion, trust, and social support that are prevalent in hierarchical societies promote both material deprivation and a pathogenic quality of social relationships that have direct effects on an individual's defenses against a wide array of diseases. In making his causal arguments, Wilkinson (1996) cites the linkage between social relationships and neuroendocrine system function at the individual level that were identified 20 years earlier by epidemiologist John Cassel (1976). Wilkinson also extends the identification of intermediate mechanisms to such factors as depression and interpersonal violence.

Political Economy/Social Production of Disease Theoretical Framework

This theoretical framework encompasses theories that derive from the classic political economy formulation of Adam Smith and the 19th century Marxist critique of industrial capitalism (Swingwood, 2000). Central to this perspective is the assumption that the root causes of health inequalities are embedded in the economic and political structures and processes that promote and perpetuate economic and social privilege (Krieger, 2001c, p. 670). The main foci of this theoretical framework are the various structural determinants of health that are linked to disparities in social and economic power, such as poverty, detrimental working conditions, and spatial isolation from health care.

An important variant of this perspective places emphasis on disease as an outcome of a production function that serves the interest of the dominant social classes (Diamond, 1992). One can think about the production function of disease occurring in a number of ways: the direct exposure of disadvantaged populations to pathogens in a way that benefits the dominant class, the selective privileging of some threats to the health and well-being over others, and in the social construction of disease and therapeutics.

The most obvious example of the first, exposure to pathogens, is easily and tragically exemplified in the class and race-targeted promotion of smoking in order to benefit investors in the tobacco industry (Balbach, Gasior, & Barbeau, 2003; Barbeau, Wolin, Naumova, & Balbach, 2005). An example of the selective privileging of some threats to health over others is observed in the juxtaposition of the influenza vaccine shortage of 2005 with the intense television advertising campaigns touting competing patent remedies for erectile dysfunction. Concerning the social construction of disease and therapeutics, there is extensive literature on historic linkages between the financial interests of the medical profession and the development of standards of practice related to the diagnosis and treatment of a variety of conditions (Starr, 1982), such as the extensive incidence of medically unnecessary hysterectomies (Broder, Kanouse, Mittman, & Bernstein, 2000; Dicker et al., 1982; Haas, Acker, Donahue, & Katz, 1993; Travis, 1985; West & Dranov, 1994).

In a classic example of a social epidemiology investigation framed by a political economy perspective, Roderick Wallace linked patterns of homicide, suicide, drug abuse, low birthweight, and deaths from AIDS in the Bronx section of New York City to the class- and race-based withdrawal of basic municipal services—including fire protection (Wallace, 1990). Rather than attributing the high death rates of the African American and Hispanic inhabitants of the Bronx to the internal characteristics and social pathologies of their neighborhoods, Wallace's study showed how deliberate and targeted policies of "planned shrinkage" propelled these neighborhoods into chaos. In Wallace's political economy perspective, the high death rates among Bronx inhabitants were less an outcome of poverty and political neglect than they were of a calculated policy of race and class-based neighborhood abandonment by the economic and political elites of the city.

It can be claimed without much controversy that the *Political Economy/ Social Production of Disease* framework has dominated the empiricism of social epidemiology. A case can also be made that this theoretical dominance has been promoted by methodological innovations over the past several years, greatly aided by innovations in computer technology that can more precisely estimate the relative contributions of individual characteristics from contextual effects on health outcomes. Sometimes referred to generally as mixed, hierarchical, or multilevel modeling techniques, these approaches allow researchers to deal with the statistical anomalies that occur when observations at the individual level (e.g., health outcomes or specific behaviors) are nested within larger social units such as families, neighborhoods, or large communities. The ability to more precisely sort out the unique contributions of social context from individual characteristics has thus enabled social epidemiologists to better model and validate the theoretically suggested causal linkages between structural determinants at the societal level, the effects of proximate social context, and intervening mechanisms of disease at the individual level. Although in one way this synergy of theory and method represents a significant advance in science, in another way it has embedded social epidemiology further in a linear model of causality that fails to account for the complex, dynamic, and mutually generative interactions between social structure and biology that occurs at all levels.

The Ecosocial Theoretical Framework

As explained by Krieger (1994, 1999, 2001c), the ecosocial framework applies to a class of theories that move the ecological perspective from a general metaphor to a wide array of testable propositions based on a model of human health that situates "humans as one notable species among many co-habiting, evolving on, and altering our dynamic planet" (Krieger, 2001c, p. 671). This is a significant advancement over the linear, albeit hierarchical model of social epidemiology that is the basis of the *political economy/social production of disease* model.

Briefly described, the ecosocial framework greatly enriches the theoretical basis of social epidemiology in several respects. First, it incorporates and contextualizes the basic principles and processes of the social production of the disease model within the framework of an ecological analysis (Krieger, 2001c). Thus it is a theoretical framework that is inherently concerned with the ways in which structural relationships are implicated in, and accountable for, the creation and perpetuation of inequalities in health. Second, the ecosocial framework is not driven by or confined within linear models and methods. Instead, the ecosocial perspective merges social and biological analyses in a way that examines their dynamic interplay at multiple levels as opposed to an analysis that is a linear and hierarchical approximation of reality. Third, the ecosocial perspective invites and embraces an array of theories that operate within and across different ecological levels that, in synthesis, promote an enhanced understanding of the complex and simultaneous processes through which particular social constructs and processes become biologically incorporated and expressed in disease (Krieger, 2002).

Ecosocial theory is built around four central concepts: *embodiment, pathways of embodiment, cumulative interplay between exposure, susceptibility, resistance*, and *accountability and agency* (Krieger, 2001c). *Embodiment* refers to the means by which human beings "literally incorporate, biologically; the material and social world, from conception to death." *Pathways to embodiment* (the means of incorporation) are structured simultaneously by societal arrangements, the limits of possibilities of the biology that is shaped by evolution, and individual biological and social history. *Cumulative interplay between exposure, susceptibility, and resistance* is expressed in pathways to embodiment, with each of these factors and their respective distributions conceptualized at multiple ecological levels and in multiple domains, and manifested in processes at multiple *scales*[2] of time and space. *Accountability and agency* occurs in relation to social units at various levels of structure: institutions, households, and individuals—but also extending to the agents and agencies of science that privilege some theories and ignore others in the production of explanations for social inequalities in health (Krieger, 2001c, p. 672). In essence, these four central constructs function as heuristic lenses through which social epidemiologists can unveil and illuminate the patterns of health and disease that are a function of the complex interrelationships between the biological and social aspects of causality.

As Krieger suggests, the ecosocial perspective, aside from being derived from evolutionary theory, is akin to it as a general perspective for inquiry (Krieger, 2001c, p. 671). In the way that evolutionary theory provides the biological sciences with general guidance toward specific propositions, the ecosocial theoretical framework guides inquiry in social epidemiology toward "specificity within complexity." One way to conceptualize this notion is to examine the myriad ways in which race is *embodied* in the relative mortality levels of Native Americans living on the Pine Ridge Reservation.

By way of background, the Pine Ridge Ogala Lakota (Sioux) Reservation is located in a three-counties area at the southwest corner of South Dakota, and is home to approximately 15,000 Native Americans, and is the second-largest Native American reservation within the United States (Schwartz, 2006; South Dakota Department of Public Health, 2009). Comprised of the barren Badlands, rolling hills and dry prairielands, the Pine Ridge Reservation devoid of a sustainable economic base of its own and is 120 miles from the nearest labor market in Rapid City, SD (Schwartz, 2006). The Pine Ridge Reservation is also the sight of the most tragic and reprehensible military action in United States history—the slaughter of nearly 300 members of the Lakota Sioux tribe by the Seventh Calvary on December 29, 1890 at Wounded Knee Creek. Following the massacre at Wounded Knee, which was the last armed conflict between the U.S. Army and Native American Tribes, the U.S. Census Bureau declared the American Frontier to be officially closed (USHistory.org, 2012).[3]

Thus, Pine Ridge Reservations stands out, in both symbolic and literal terms, as the preeminent icon of the nation's historic and contemporary oppression of indigenous peoples. Since nearly 80% of the tribal population of the Pine Ridge Reservation is located in Shannon County, South Dakota, Shannon County data are used here to provide the economic and epidemiological portrait of Pine Ridge Reservation.

Table 7.1 shows the age-adjusted death rates, reproductive health statistics, and the poverty rate for the Lakota (Sioux) Tribe inhabitants of Shannon County relative to the nation as a whole. Notably, the 53.5% poverty rate among the Lakota of Pine Ridge is nearly 4 times that of the

Table 7.1 *Health Indicator Profile of Pine Ridge Tribal Reservation (Shannon County, South Dakota) Relative to the Entire United States*

	United States	Shannon County, South Dakota	Ratio
Mortality			
All cause	760.2	1856.7	2.4
Heart disease	190.9	354.6	1.9
Acute myocardial infarction	41.4	156.4	3.8
Heart failure	17.3	14.4	0.8
Malignant neoplasma	178.4	285.6	1.6
Trachea, bronchus, and lung	50.6	76.3	1.5
Colon, rectum, and anus	16.9	33.5	2.0
Female breast	22.9	29.3	1.3
Pancreas	10.8	14.7	1.4
Cerebrovascular disease	45.1	80.4	1.8
Chronic lower respiratory disease	42.4	117.6	2.8
Accidents	41.0	209.2	5.1
Motor vehicle accidents	14.6	137.4	9.4
Diabetes mellitus	23.7	173.8	7.3
Influenza and pneumonia	17.5	41.4	2.4
Suicide	11.5	25.6	2.2
Chronic liver disease and cirrhosis	9.7	121.3	12.5
Infant mortality	6.8	18.4	2.7
Natality			
Percent low birthweight infants	8.2%	7.3%	0.9
Percent of mothers receiving care in 1st trimester	70.8%	54.8%	0.8
Percent of mothers used tobacco while pregnant	10.4%	20.9%	2.0
Percent of birth <27 weeks gestation	12.7%	10.2%	0.8
Average age of mother	27.4	24.1	0.9
Teenage pregnancy rate	40.2	86.6	2.2
Population/Socioeconomic indicators			
Percent Native American	0.9%	96.8%	107.5
Percent of population under 100% of poverty level	14.3%	53.5%	3.7

Notes: Mortality rates except for infant mortality rates are age-adjusted per 100,000 population. Infant mortality rates and teenage pregnancy rates are per 1000 population (respectively live births and females aged 15–17). All health status indicators are based on 2005–2007 vital events and calculated in accordance with the 2000 Census estimates. Population and socioeconomic indicators are based on Census 2010 estimates.

Source: South Dakota Department of Public Health, *2009 South Dakota Vital Statistics Report, Health Profiles by County.*

national average. For comparison of relative mortality rates, Table 7.1 shows the age-adjusted death rates for selected leading causes of death for both the U.S. population and the population of Shannon County in the first two columns, followed by their Shannon County ratios in the third column. Because 97% of Shannon County's inhabitants are Pine Ridge Lakota, the Shannon County epidemiological statistics shown in Table 7.1 are treated as equivalent to Pine Ridge Lakota estimates.

First, it can be seen that Pine Ridge Lakota die at over twice the rate of other residents of the United States, and for some causes of death (motor vehicle accidents, diabetes, and chronic liver disease/cirrhosis) the death rates among the Pine Ridge Lakota are several times that of the national average. In epidemiologic terms, Pine Ridge is a disaster zone, but not one that results from an act of God or nature—but rather one that is a function of deliberate national policies for which every generation of Americans is implicated.[4] That is, each of the dramatically higher mortality rates among the Pine Ridge Lakota represents what Krieger's ecosocial theory refers to a *pathway to embodiment* that incorporates and expresses both contemporary structural oppression and historical trauma.[5]

As just one example among many, the "embodiment of structural oppression" is reflected in the relationship between the death rates from motor vehicle accidents that are 9.4 times the national average. Motor vehicle accidents on Pine Ridge reservation reflect, among other things, the combination of treacherous rural roads, aging and unsafe vehicles, inadequate law enforcement resources, and alcoholism. All four of these causal factors are associated with rural poverty and high levels of unemployment. Similarly, the disproportionally high rates of death from very treatable infectious diseases (influenza and respiratory diseases) are reflective of both crowded housing conditions and inadequate access to timely health care services. Another example of the "embodiment of structural oppression" is the suicide rate among the Pine Ridge Lakota, which is over twice the national average. Although causal pathways to suicide are complex, chronic unemployment is prominent among them. Similarly, high rates of infant mortality within the borders of otherwise affluent nations are attributable to racial segregation and endemic poverty and unemployment (Guest, Almgren, & Hussey, 1998). Finally, the high death rates from diabetes among the Pine Ridge Lakota (7.3 times the national average) can be attributed in significant part to the biological consequences of intergenerational nutritional stress (Benysheka, Martin, & Johnston, 2001).

In sum, the *pathways to embodiment* that are created and sustained by racial oppression include a tribal history and contemporary replication of racial isolation and deprivation; social policies that continue to promote endemic poverty and expropriation of resources by nonnatives; and the embedded exposures and susceptibilities to early death that are manifest in the harsh natural environment, dilapidated housing, diet, and contaminated water.[6] *Accountability and agency* are seen not only in the U.S. government's historically genocidal policies toward Native Americans, but in the willful ignorance of the American mainstream—both in the historic and contemporary sense. Although the Pine Ridge Lakota were briefly in the national spotlight in the 2004 elections as potentially the only pocket of Democratic votes that could keep Senate minority leader Thomas Daschle from being swept from office, there was far more media attention to the political tactics aimed at either recruiting or disenfranchising the Lakota voters than on their dire living conditions and short life spans. Sadly, in the near decade since, the poverty rate among the Pine Ridge Lakota has remained essentially the same and the disparities in mortality have actually worsened.[7]

THE "FUNDAMENTAL SOCIAL CAUSES" HYPOTHESIS

Although the ecosocial perspective represents the most elaborate and encompassing framework with which to advance the field of social epidemiology, at this stage of its development the most influential general theory in social epidemiology is the "fundamental social causes hypothesis" (Link & Phelan, 1995). Arising from the *political economy/social production of disease* perspective, this hypothesis resolves two enduring paradoxes of population health:

1. The growth of disparities in mortality and longevity by such factors as race, gender, and social class that follow significant advancements in the knowledge base, methods, and technologies of health care.
2. The tendency of intergroup disparities in mortality to persist even though the specific disease mechanisms linked to disparities in mortality change significantly over time.

More than a dozen years ago sociologists Bruce Link and Jo Phelan advanced the theory that disparities in mortality endure over time because the "fundamental social causes" of health disparities arise from pernicious social inequalities rather than the intervening disease mechanisms that happen to link social inequalities to health disparities at any given point in time (Link & Phelan, 1995). Although this proposition may seem intuitive to many, it has not guided the thinking of the majority of the work in either investigating the causes of health disparities or ameliorating them through policy initiatives.

Rather, the focus of attention of social epidemiology has been on the prevailing and transitory intervening mechanisms of group mortality differences (i.e., diseases, risk, and protective factors) that are operative at the historical moment (Phelan, Link, Diez-Roux, Kawachi, & Levin, 2004).

The result of this skewed attention toward intervening variables is a phenomenon somewhat akin to an epidemiological shell game. At the first stage of the game, science uncovers a salient linkage between a social factor such as race and selective mechanisms of disease, differential risk, and specific health behaviors or health care access issues that are causally implicated in racial health disparities. At the next stage, policy interventions take place that reduce the incidence of risk and disease for the disadvantaged group and it is widely assumed that health disparities associated with race will in turn be reduced. However, since disease ecology is a dynamic process that is in large part shaped by fundamental underlying social inequalities, racial disparities in health reemerge in the form of other diseases with different clusters of risk and protective factors that advantage one racial group over the other. This is the third stage of the epidemiological shell game and the point to begin anew with another disease-focused inquiry.

The mortality patterns that reflect this process are clearly visible as the most recent 60-year trend in both overall disparities in life expectancy by race and age-adjusted death rate are examined. As Figure 7.1 shows, although dramatic improvements in life expectancy for both Whites and African Americans occurred over this period, a significant disparity in the life expectancy of African Americans relative to Whites persisted (NCHS, 2011). At the conclusion of a 60-year period marked by dramatic improvements in standards of living, expansion of civil rights, monumental advances in medical technology and health care system infrastructure, and the election of the nation's first African American President in 2008, a racial gap in life expectancy of 4.3 years remained. The persistence of disparities by race is the first mortality pattern that conforms to the epidemiological shell game.[8]

The second conforming trend, as shown in Table 7.2, is the shift of the intervening disease mechanisms of mortality disparities between African Americans and Whites over the most recent nearly six decades from one set of mechanisms to another—despite the persistence of the overall African American disadvantage in average life expectancy (as shown in Figure 7.1). The age-adjusted death rates shown in Table 7.2 identify the African American/White mortality disparities for specific causes of death during three different periods: 1950, 1980, and 2007. First, it should be noted that between 1950 and 2007 the mortality ratios from age-adjusted deaths by "all causes combined" actually became slightly less favorable to African Americans in 2007 than in 1950 (see the tops of both the fourth column and

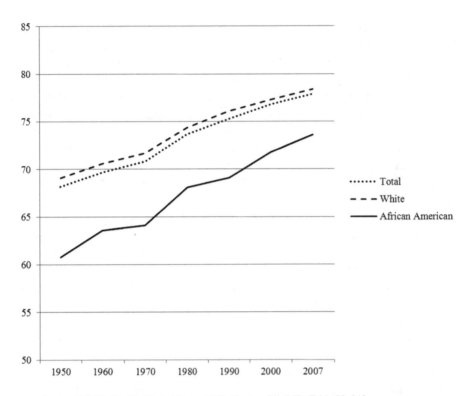

Source: NCHS. *Health, United States 2010.* Hyattesville, MD. Table 22. Life expectancy at birth, at 65 years of age, and at 75 years of age, by race and sex: United States, selected years 1900–2007.

Figure 7.1 *Population life expectancy trends 1950–2007: Total, White and African American (both sexes).*

the final column of Table 7.2).[9] That is, in 1950 the mortality ratio from all causes of death among African Americans was 1.2, whereas in 2007 this same ratio had increased to 1.3. In 1950, the specific causes of death that showed the most dramatic African American disparities (shown in bold) were cerebrovascular disease, influenza and pneumonia, and homicide. However, by 1980, disease of the heart and cancer replaced influenza and pneumonia as the primary mechanisms of health disparities among African Americans. More recently (between 1980 and 2007), ischemic heart disease has shifted from a cause of death that had lower rates among African Americans relative to Whites, to a cause of death that is more prevalent among African Americans.

As a general pattern over the last half-century, as shown in Table 7.2, the African American mortality disadvantage has largely shifted toward a cluster

Table 7.2 *Age-Adjusted Death Rates (per 100,000) for Selected Causes of Death According to Race, 1950, 1980, and 2007*

	1950		Period		1980		Period		2007		Period	
	White	AA	Dif	Ratio	White	AA	Dif	Ratio	White	AA	Dif	Ratio
All causes	1410.8	1722.1	311.3	1.2	1012.7	1314.8	302.1	1.3	749.4	958.0	208.6	1.3
Natural causes	—	—	—	—	945.0	1206.0	261.0	1.3	—	—	—	—
Diseases of heart	584.8	586.7	1.9	1.0	409.4	455.3	**45.9**	1.1	187.8	247.3	**59.5**	1.3
Ischemic heart disease	—	—	—	—	347.6	334.5	-13.1	1.0	125.5	150.6	25.1	1.2
Cerebrovascular diseases	175.5	233.6	**58.1**	1.3	93.2	129.1	35.9	1.4	40.5	60.3	19.8	1.5
Malignant neoplasms	194.6	176.4	-18.2	0.9	204.2	256.4	**52.2**	1.3	177.5	215.5	**38.0**	1.2
Trachea, bronchus, and lung	15.2	11.1	-4.1	0.7	49.2	59.7	10.5	1.2	51.2	55.6	4.4	1.1
Colon, rectum, and anus	—	—	—	—	27.4	28.3	0.9	1.0	16.4	23.5	7.1	1.4
Prostate	28.4	30.9	2.5	1.1	30.5	61.1	30.6	2.0	—	—	—	—
Breast	32.4	25.3	-7.1	0.8	32.1	31.7	-0.4	1.0	—	—	—	—
Chronic lower respiratory diseases	6.8	6.2	-0.6	0.9	29.3	19.2	-10.1	0.7	43.0	28.1	-14.9	0.7
Influenza and pneumonia	44.8	76.7	**31.9**	1.7	30.9	34.4	3.5	1.1	16.0	18.4	2.4	1.2
Chronic liver disease and cirrhosis	11.5	9.0	-2.5	0.8	13.9	25.0	11.1	1.8	9.4	7.4	-2.0	0.8
Diabetes mellitus	22.9	23.5	0.6	1.0	16.7	32.7	16.0	2.0	20.5	42.8	22.3	2.1
HIV disease	—	—	—	—	—	—	—	—	1.9	17.3	15.4	**9.1**
External causes	—	—	—	—	67.7	108.8	**41.1**	1.6	—	—	—	—
Unintentional injuries	77.0	79.9	2.9	1.0	45.3	57.6	12.3	1.3	41.5	36.6	-4.9	0.9
Motor vehicle-related injuries	24.4	26.0	1.6	1.1	22.6	20.2	-2.4	0.9	14.8	14.1	-0.7	1.0
Suicide	13.9	4.5	-9.4	0.3	13.0	6.5	-6.5	0.5	12.5	5.0	-7.5	0.4
Homicide	2.6	28.3	25.7	10.9	6.7	39.0	32.3	5.8	3.7	21.1	17.4	5.7

Source: NCHS. *Health, United States 2002*, Data from Table 30 Age-Adjusted Death rates for selected causes according to sex, race and hispanic origin, United States, Selected Years 1950–1999 Hyattsville, Maryland. NCHS. *Health, United States 2010*. Table 24 Age-Adjusted Death rates for selected causes of death, by sex, race, and hispanic origin: United States, Selected Years 1950–2007, Hyattesvillem, MD.

of diseases that are either (1) highly influenced by early detection, treatment, and close management (such as ischemic heart disease and cancer) or (2) reflective of disproportionate exposure to violence and intravenous drug abuse—causes of death that tied to life in racially segregated neighborhoods with high concentrations of poverty (HIV disease and homicide). In the discussion of fundamental social cause theory that follows, it will be shown that the shift from one set of intervening disease mechanisms of disparity to another is not random, but instead is reflective of the advantaged group's differential access to critical adaptive social resources.

The specific propositions of fundamental social causes theory have been advanced by Link and Phelan in a series of collaborative articles published over a decade (Link & Phelan, 1995, 1996, 2002; Phelan et al., 2004). Their central ideas are summarized in five main points:

1. *The focus of epidemiology, both in research and public dissemination of findings, has largely been centered on the proximate risk factors and specific causes of disease and related disparities in health outcomes reduced to the individual level. The emphasis on individual agency over structural context, because it resonates with the individualistic orientation of Western culture, has contributed to a bias in contemporary epidemiology toward individually based risk and protective factors to the neglect of the fundamental causes of disparities in health—the pervasive causal influence of social inequalities (Link & Phelan, 1995, pp. 80–81).*[10]

2. *Although policy and program measures aimed at the intervening mechanisms of disease that link disparities in health outcomes to fundamental social causes might ameliorate health disparities in the short run, fundamental social causes will over time exert their effects in other intervening mechanisms (Phelan et al., 2004, p. 280).*

3. *The enduring nature of fundamental causes of disease, in essence, the capacity to create and sustain disparities in health outcomes despite changes in the prevailing intervening mechanisms of disease, arises from structural disparities in access to resources that are critical to the avoidance of disease risk; and where disease occurs, minimization of its detrimental consequences. Resources that are critical to the avoidance of disease, and attenuation of its detriments to individual health, involve and include such social assets as "money, knowledge, power, prestige and social connectedness" (Link & Phelan, 1995, p. 87).*

4. *Ultimately, sustained reductions or eradications of disparities in health outcomes cannot be achieved through exclusive focus on the ever-changing mechanisms of disease and risk to the detriment of the attention given to the social structures and processes that determine access to critical adaptive resources:*

e.g., money, knowledge, power, prestige, and various aspects of social capital (Link & Phelan, 1995, p. 89, 1996, p. 472).

5. *The common features of the fundamental social causes within population disparities in mortality are that they (1) influence multiple disease outcomes, (2) affect disease outcomes through multiple disease factors, (3) reproduce their effects on mortality over time via the replacement of intervening disease and risk factor mechanisms, and (4) "involve access to resources that can be used to avoid risks or to minimize the consequences of disease when it occurs" (Link & Phelan, 1995, p. 87; Phelan et al., 2004, p. 268).*

Evidence for the "Fundamental Social Causes" Hypothesis

At this point in its development, the field of social epidemiology is dominated by studies that have focused on the identification of the prevailing intervening mechanisms that link disparities in mortality to various dimensions of social inequality (e.g., gender, race, ethnicity, social class). However, the limited number of studies that have sought to rigorously examine evidence for fundamental cause processes provides compelling support for the theory. For example, one test of the fundamental cause hypothesis would be to examine whether higher socioeconomic status confers mortality advantages through differential access to knowledge about health behaviors that would avoid and ameliorate the effects of "preventable" causes of death over the life course as opposed to "non-preventable" causes of death that are by their nature not amenable to individual advantages in knowledge, money, power, prestige, or social capital.

Presumably, if SES confers significant advantages to the individual in knowledge and other resources critical to the reduction of the risk of death from any number of preventable causes, death rates from preventable causes of death should reflect a significantly stronger SES advantage than death rates from "non-preventable" causes of death. If, on the other hand, the SES effect on death rates is generally similar across both preventable and nonpreventable causes of death, this would undermine a key proposition of fundamental cause theory, namely that SES confers advantage in critical knowledge and other social assets tied to disease prevention.

To test the validity of this proposition, Phelan et al. (2004) employed data from the National Longitudinal Mortality Study to discern whether national population mortality patterns in fact conformed with theoretical expectations. Briefly described, they examined both the income and education dimensions of SES on the cause and age-specific death rates of a sample of 368,585 individuals representing a cross section of the U.S. adult population (those over age 25). Their central question was whether the magnitudes of the SES effects on death rates from preventable diseases were significantly larger for preventable causes than nonpreventable causes of death (Frisbie, Song, Powers, & Street, 2004). Although the details of the Phelan et al. analysis are far more complex than are reported here, the mortality trajectories by education for persons aged 25 to 44 shown by Figure 7.2 serve as a good example of their general findings.

Figure 7.2 depicts a series of survival trajectories observed over a 9.5-year (114-month) period for adults aged 25–44. As can be seen on the graph, the survival curves for individuals with different levels of education depict a very modest education effect for causes of death that have low probability of prevention, while for the highly preventable causes of death the survival curves differ dramatically by levels of education. Since education functions as an important component and measure of SES, the patterns observed fully conform to the theoretical proposition that SES confers significant advantages in access to knowledge and other resources that are tied to an individual's capacity to reduce the probability of preventable death. Notably, the Phelan et al. study found that SES effects on preventable causes of death are far less dramatic in old age, perhaps reflecting the

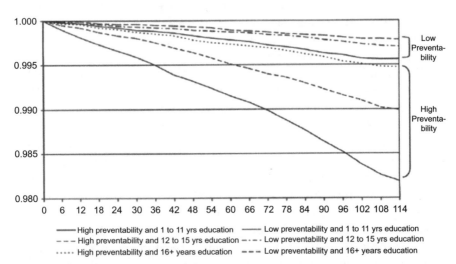

Source: Phelan, Link, Diez-Roux, Kawachi, and Levin. (2004). "Fundamental Causes" of Social Inequalities in Mortality: A Test of the Theory. *Journal of Health and Social Behavior*, 45(3), Figure 1. Used with permission.

Figure 7.2 *Cumulative survival by education and preventability of death, ages 25–44 at baseline.*

cumulative effects of frailty on the effectiveness of interventions (Phelan et al., 2004, p. 278).

A second study that provides compelling support for the fundamental social causes hypothesis (Frisbie et al., 2004) examined the patterns of disparities in infant mortality by race. Race, like SES, is argued to fit the criteria as a "fundamental social cause" of disparities in health because its effects are at once pervasive and enduring despite significant changes in the prevailing regimes of morbidity and mortality. Although it is well established that disparities in infant mortality between Whites and African Americans have increased over the past 2 decades despite significant reductions in the overall rates of infant mortality for both groups, there is little scientific consensus on the chief reasons. Employing the fundamental social causes hypothesis as their framework (Link & Phelan, 1995, 1996, 2002), Frisbie et al. speculated that the growth in infant mortality disparities by race over the past 2 decades reflects the tendency of more advantaged groups to have earlier access to new innovations in health care, due to their differential access to the critical resources of knowledge, money, power, prestige, and interpersonal connections identified by Link and Phelan (1995, p. 87).

As a test of their proposition, Frisbie and his colleagues examined the national data on infant death rates from respiratory distress syndrome (RDS) over two periods that represented different conditions in the availability of an important innovation in the treatment of RDS. During the first period (1989–1990), when the new RDS treatment was not available, African American infants were slightly less likely to die from RDS than White infants once disparities in prenatal care and other important factors relevant to infant survival were accounted for. During the second period (1995–1998), when the new innovation for treatment of RDS was made available, the relative risks of dying from RDS became higher for African American infants—as well as the risk of dying from all other causes (Frisbie et al., 2004, p. 789). These findings conform to the central tenet of fundamental social causes theory that racism, as one among several fundamental forms of social inequality, affords some racial groups more access to innovations in health care technology than others due to their privileged access to knowledge and the resources critical to their capacity to utilize it.

Racial Segregation as a Fundamental Social Cause of Health Disparities. For some additional evidence in support Fundamental Social Cause theory, we return to Figure 7.1, which, as previously mentioned, shows a very encouraging narrowing of the gap between African American and White average life expectancies over the most recent decade (from a 5.7 difference in life expectancy to a difference of 4.3 years). In accordance with Fundamental Cause Theory, this favorable change in African American life expectancy relative to White life expectancy should correspond to some fundamental change in the social structure that reduces the detriments to the health of the African American population across a broad range of health risks and conditions. Contrary to what may seem obvious possibilities, it was not disparities in either income or education. While the 1990s witnessed a slight reduction in the income gap between African American families and White families that was sustained over the most recent decade (U.S. Census Bureau, 2012), this improvement in relative income was of insufficient magnitude to explain the 25% improvement in the relative life expectancy of African Americans that was observed over this same period.[11] As to the possibility of the reduction of educational disparities between Whites and African Americans, despite an increase in the educational attainment of African Americans in recent decades (as measured by the percentage of 28-year olds with a completed 4-year degree), the education gap between African Americans and Whites has not diminished (McDaniel, DiPrete, Buchmann, & Shwed, 2009).

However, over the most recent decades there has been one profound change in the structure of American society that has been deeply implicated in the health disparities of the African American population—a sustained decline in the level of residential racial segregation across all of the nation's large cities. Residential racial segregation, which entails the concentration of the African American population of cities within defined neighborhoods that are typically economically disadvantaged, fits the criteria identified as a "fundamental social cause" of health disparities because residential racial segregation is a structural arrangement of society that isolates the urban African American population from resources that are critical both to the avoidance of disease risk, and where disease occurs, the minimization of its detrimental consequences (Link & Phelan, 1995, p. 87).[12] In its most extreme but sadly too common form among the nation's large cities, residential racial segregation is represented as the urban ghetto—a neighborhood or segment of a city that is inhabited almost solely by low income African American families enmired in poverty and surrounded by dilapidated buildings and violent crime. Such neighborhoods are devoid of good schools, parks, adequate health care clinics and hospitals, and also (most critically) opportunities for employment.

The primary causes of racial segregation include decades of housing policies and practices that were motivated and sustained by the racism of the dominant White majority, including neighborhood covenants that would not allow the sale of housing to African Americans, mortgage lending policies and practices that excluded African Americans from home loans (particularly in formerly White neighborhoods), urban planning policies that deliberately established and reinforced the racial boundaries between African American neighborhoods and White ones, and the disadvantages in income and education that kept African Americans from migrating from low-income African American neighborhoods to more affluent neighborhoods inhabited by Whites. During the most recent decade, particularly dramatic gains were made in the de-segregation of the nation's largest cities, such that by the 2010 Census, the most segregated of the nation's largest cities had experienced an average decline in segregation of 29% relative to its 1970 level (Glaesar & Vigdor, 2012).[13] Most critically, this decline in the average level of racial segregation among the nation's large cities involved the gradual transformation of many of the nation's worse urban ghettos through either de-population (more people moving out than in) and racial integration and gentrification (Glaeser & Vigdor, 2012).

While as a society we are a very long way from achieving the kind of broad decline in racial segregation that would eliminate racial segregation as a fundamental social cause of African American disparities in health, a compelling argument can be made that the recent unprecedented reduction of the life expectancy gap between African Americans and Whites is attributable in part to a sustained decline in the level of racial segregation among the nation's most segregated cities. The substantial and sustained decline in the racial segregation of African Americans is implicated in the recent reduction of the African American/White disparity in average life expectancy because racial segregation has been so devastating to the health of African Americans through a number of well-established causal pathways. As summarized by Willams and Collins (2001), the detrimental impacts of racial segregation on the health of African Americans are mediated through such factors as the creation and reinforcement of socioeconomic disadvantage, living in decayed neighborhoods with high levels of concentrated poverty and violent crime, scarce and inadequate resources for medical care, exposure to endemic violent crime, and exposure to factors conducive to unhealthy behaviors (e.g., limited access to affordable healthy foods and safe parks for recreation and exercise, exposure to targeted advertising by the alcohol and tobacco industries). As shown by Guest, Almgren, and Hussey (1998), this results in a distinctive pattern of premature mortality among ghettoized neighborhoods, including very high levels of infant mortality along with death from an array of preventable causes during the working ages (e.g., accidents, homicides, liver disease, and HIV disease). In fact, a number of studies have shown that mortality rates and limited life expectancies in the most highly segregated neighborhoods are consistent with those found in the world's poorest countries (Guest, Almgren, & Hussey, 1998; McCord & Freeman, 1990). In sum, it is not merely coincidental that there has been a promising reduction in the average life expectancy gap between African Americans and Whites as the African American ghetto appears (albeit gradually) to be a receding feature of the American urban landscape.

INCOME INEQUALITY AS A SOCIAL DETERMINANT OF HEALTH

Thus far, the disparities in health that are the central concern of social epidemiology have been those that occur within populations, such as the socioeconomic class gradient in life expectancy. As discussed in the prior chapter, there is a powerful linear relationship between socioeconomic status and health that persists to varying degrees throughout the life course on a variety of dimensions of health and across all three dimensions of social class (income, occupation, and education). In an intriguing and related development over the last 2 decades, a second line of research has emerged that seeks to explain the relationship between income inequality and various indices of health at the population level. In part, the surge of interest in the role income inequality plays on health may have been fueled by rising levels of income inequality observed among wealthy nations in the wake of economic globalization (Alderson & Nielsen, 2002).

The earliest published study finding a relationship between population mortality and population income distribution appeared in 1979 (Rodgers, 1979), and by the mid-1990s a significant body of research had emerged from multiple sources of international data that implicated income inequality as a determinant of population mortality (Wilkinson, 1995). Although British social epidemiologist Richard Wilkinson was the chief proponent (and defendant) of the hypothesis that income inequality at the population level exerts a powerful effect on population mortality that is not explained by such factors as the absolute level of poverty, per capita income, population literacy, or the accessibility to health services, the "income inequality–population health hypothesis" garnered broad empirical support from other investigators. Remarkably, findings consistent with the "income inequality–population health hypothesis" from an array of investigations using different data and methods also appeared to extend this hypothesis to populations at multiple ecological levels (e.g., states, communities), and not just national populations (Kaplan, Lynch, Cohen, & Balfour, 1996; Kawachi & Kennedy, 1997; Wilkinson, 1996).

As an example of this research, Figure 7.3 shows the findings of analysis of the relationship between income inequality and health among U.S. states,

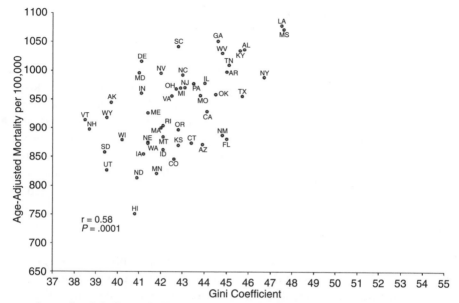

Source: Lynch, J., Harper, S., Kaplan, G., & Smith, G. (2005). Associations between income inequality and mortality among U.S. states: The importance of time period and source of data. *American Journal of Public Health*, 95(8): Figure 2 Cross-sectional association between income inequality and age-adjusted mortality based on (a) U.S. Census Data. Used by permission.

Figure 7.3 *Cross-sectional association between income inequality and age-adjusted mortality for 50 U.S. States based on U.S. Census data (A) and Internal revenue service tax return data (B), 1989.*

based on health statistics and U.S. Census data on household income. As Figure 7.3 shows, there is a modest linear relationship ($r = .58$, $p < .001$) between the age-adjusted mortality rate and the level of income inequality within each state, as measured by the Gini coefficient.[14] Although the Gini coefficient depicted in Figure 7.3 is the most widely used measure of income inequality, the relationship between income inequality and health has also been shown to be quite consistent across several other measures in income inequality (Kawachi & Kennedy, 1997).

Findings of this sort, replicated many times by various investigators, provoked two closely linked debates in emerging discipline of social epidemiology, one theoretical and the other methodological. The methodological debate considers whether these findings in fact reflect biased or flawed data and analyses, while the theoretical debate considers the causal linkages between income inequality and health. The first to be discussed will be the theoretical debate.

THEORETICAL DEBATES CONCERNING INCOME INEQUALITY EFFECTS

Setting aside the methodological questions for the time being, why *should* higher levels of population income inequality be associated with lower levels of population health? While at the individual level there are multiple well-established causal connections between relative deprivation and poor health (e.g., nutrition, exposure to occupational hazards, access to health care), at the population level the causal connections are far more contested. The theoretical and empirical debates aimed at illuminating the relationship between income inequality and population health have been dominated by two perspectives: a psychosocial perspective and one that takes a materialist political economy approach. While income inequality can influence health through material conditions, the quality of social participation, and the capacity to exercise choice (Marmot, 2002), the psychosocial perspective places far more emphasis on the importance of the latter two factors.

As mentioned previously in this chapter, the main proponent of the psychosocial perspective has been Richard Wilkinson (Wilkinson, 1992, 1995, 1996, 1999; Wilkinson, Kawachi, & Kennedy, 1998). The central thrust of this perspective is that extremes of income inequality are both associated with and implicated causally in the qualities of the social environment encountered by individuals at all strata of society. Accordingly, societies with high levels of income inequality are characterized by lower levels of "social cohesion," endemic distrust, and the pervasive social anxieties attendant with hierarchical relationships and low social status. The pathogenic mechanisms of the psychosocial environment identified by Wilkinson (and others) center around the quality of interpersonal relations and include such factors as depression, low attachment in early childhood, interpersonal violence, and (per the earlier work of John Cassel) disease susceptibilities linked to psychosocial stress. On the other hand, according to this perspective, societies with low levels of income inequality have qualities of social cohesion, egalitarian relationships, and mutual trust that "are essential in ameliorating the effects of stress and poor living conditions" (Wilkinson et al., 1998, p. 35).

For the better part of the 1990s, the psychosocial perspective on the income inequality–population health link occupied center stage in the theoretical discourse of social epidemiology. To a large extent, this can be attributed to a prevailing ideology within the field of social epidemiology that postulates the inherently detrimental nature of inequality in all of its forms—including social class. However, the popularity of the psychosocial perspective on income inequality–population health was also elevated considerably by its synthesis with social capital theory in sociology (Kawachi, Kennedy, Lochner, & Prothrow-Stith, 1997; Lomas, 1998; Wilkinson et al., 1998). While at the individual level, social capital refers to the quality and extent of a person's interpersonal networks, at the societal level social capital is defined as features of social organization that promote collective action toward mutual benefit, such as civic engagement, norms of reciprocity and high levels of interpersonal trust, and norms of mutual aid and reciprocity (Kawachi et al., 1997; Lochner, Kawachi, & Kennedy, 1999).

Aside from the intuitive appeal of the connections between income inequality, social capital, and health, by the late 1990s a growing body of empirical support for these linkages had emerged in the public health literature. A seminal article in this line of research was a Harvard School of Public Health study that tested the evidence of linkages between income inequality, social capital, and population mortality (Kawachi et al., 1997). Using state-level data on income distribution and key dimensions of social capital and mortality, Ichiro Kawachi and his collaborators showed that states with higher levels of income inequality showed lower levels of social capital in three key areas: group membership, social trust, and perceptions of the helpfulness of others.[15] Consistent with theoretical expectations, higher levels of population mortality (adjusted for age) were in turn linked to lower levels of social capital. Also consistent with theoretical expectations, their findings showed that the mortality effects of income inequality were largely mediated by the dimensions of social capital evaluated—in particular, beliefs about trust and fairness.

In contrast to psychosocial explanations of the link between income inequality and health, the materialist/political economy perspective concerns itself with the overall structural context that determines the distribution of power, status, and material resources (Lynch et al., 2001, 2004; Lynch, Smith, Kaplan, & House, 2000; Muntaner, 1999, 2001; Muntaner, Lynch, & Smith, 2001; Muntaner et al., 2002; Navarro & Shi, 2001). Thus, the materialist/political economy perspective encompasses race, gender, social class, cultural norms, history, and political traditions. This makes the perspective an inherently far more complex one than the psychosocial perspective, which places its explanatory emphasis on a few key constructs—most notably social status and social capital. The basic narrative of the materialist/political economy perspective is that linkages between income inequality and overall levels of population arise from their shared association with "a combination of negative exposures and lack of resources held by individuals, along with systematic underinvestment across a wide range of human, physical, health, and social infrastructure" (Lynch et al., 2000, p. 1202).[16]

Since income inequalities and population health are both manifestations of material conditions, they are often associated. However, in the materialist/ political economy explanation, there is no one common process that links income inequalities to population health across all populations—but many that are determined by the history, culture, and political economy that is specific to each population. A critical policy implication of this proposition is that income inequality and population health are not always associated, that is, structural arrangements that benefit health can occur that are independent of the income distribution (Lynch et al., 2000, 2004).

There is an important strain in the materialist/political economy perspective that places emphasis on social class over other structural determinants (Muntaner, 1999; Muntaner et al., 2002; Navarro & Shi, 2001). The basic argument of the class structure proponents is that vigorous labor movements and other aspects of working class power are associated with higher levels of income inequality, greater political representation for women, a more generous welfare state, and higher levels of population health. Although the social class perspective is not new, it was reinvigorated as a critique of the psychosocial perspective's neglect of the role of social class in health and the power of social class relations within societies to shape differences in population health outcomes. The central thrust of the social class critique of the psychosocial perspective is that the concept of social class and its effects encompass both the material and status inequalities that operate as key structural determinants of health, and that the social capital and "social cohesion" effects on population health touted by the psychosocial perspective are actually consequent to the structural effects of class. Accordingly, the road to increased population health lies in political change and not through strategies to enhance the quality of interpersonal relationships (Muntaner, 1999).

Toward a Convergence of Materialist and Psychosocial Explanations of the Effects of Income Inequality on Health

It should be apparent that the psychosocial and materialist explanations of the pathways through which high levels of income inequality detrimentally affect health are not mutually exclusive. However, it could be said that over time the materialist explanations tended to attract more proponents because the psychosocial framework lacked the same degree of theoretical specificity and evidence. That said, in recent years, bio-behavioral researchers have made significant theoretical and evidence-based advancements, unraveling the ways in which both material deprivation and hierarchical status disadvantage each have distinct effects on health through disease-specific consequences of sustained and cumulative stress. This line of research, in addition to strengthening the theoretical and empirical basis of the psychosocial approach to the income inequality–health hypothesis, brings both theories closer to convergence within an encompassing framework. In essence, this encompassing framework focuses on the ways in which differences in socioeconomic status (SES), as a type of dominance hierarchy, translate to disparities in health through the neurobiology of cumulative stress exposure.

Briefly summarized, dominance hierarchies are common to animal societies as well as human ones, and have been shown to be linked to the distribution of quality of life, disease, and survival in both (Sapolsky, 2005). In modern human societies, the most ubiquitous form of hierarchy is SES, measured as an individual or group's position relative to others in income, occupation, and education. SES (also commonly referred to as social class),[17] is a dominance hierarchy that is based upon the possession of advantage in material capital, human capital, and social status—as opposed to the capacity to dominate others through physical attributes such as size, agility, and strength. The effects of low SES on health are both material and symbolic, with the former conventionally linked to such factors as nutritional deprivation, exposure to toxins, detrimental health behaviors, and access to health care—as opposed to neurobiological linkages that entail cognitive responses to material deprivation.

However, as recently summarized by McEwen and Gianaros (2010), there is emerging theory and evidence illuminating the cognitive pathways through which the deleterious effects of both low SES and high levels of income equality on health can entail stress responses that arise independently both from material insecurity and the emotional consequences of occupying a position of low status in a dominance hierarchy.

> For example, the chronic experience of low SES at the individual level could involve enduring financial hardships, a sense of insecurity regarding future prosperity, and the possible demoralizing feelings of marginalization or social exclusion attributable to comparative social, occupational, or material disadvantage. Further, an individual's perception of her or his relative standing or ranking in a social hierarchy, formally termed subjective social status, may affect an individual's pattern of emotional, behavioral and physiological reactivity to and recovery from life stressors, consequently impacting risk for ill health. (p. 191)

In particular, the evidence summarized by McEwen and Gianaros (2010) suggests that while biological stress responses are adaptive in the short term, exposure to chronic stress leads to biological responses that are maladaptive over time. That is, exposure to chronic stress ultimately leads to a "deregulation" of allostasis—the human organism's capacity to achieve stability of its biological processes through the activation and deactivation of its allostatic systems (immune, automatic nervous, and neuroendocrine systems). In physiological terms, deregulation of allostatis (through the mechanism of a sustained high allostatic load) lends itself to such pathologies as cardiovascular disease, obesity, and susceptibility to infectious disease through impaired immune system response (McEwen & Gianaros, 2010). In sum, these advancements in the neurobiology of material and status disadvantage have undermined the justification for sustaining an artificial dichotomy between material and psychosocial explanations of the deleterious effects of income inequality on health.

Methodological Debates Concerning Income Inequality Effects

Ten years after the *British Medical Journal's* publication of Richard Wilkinson's seminal paper showing a dramatic negative correlation between income inequality and life expectancy among wealthy nations (Wilkinson, 1992), an editorial in the very same journal conceded that the empirical support for the income inequality–population health hypothesis was rapidly waning—at least in cross-national population comparisons (Mackenbach, 2002). While income inequality effects at the population level appeared evident within the United States in comparisons between states (Lynch et al., 2004), by the early 2000s there was an emerging consensus among social epidemiologists that (1) the correlations observed in earlier studies between income inequality and life expectancy at the international level were largely an outcome of significant flaws in data and methods and (2) the effects of income inequality on population health are far more complex and contextual than simple and generalized (Lynch et al., 2004, p. 81). The methodological critiques of the income inequality–population health hypothesis fall into two areas, the first concerned with the measurement of key constructs, and the second concerned with statistical modeling and sample selection effects.

Within the key constructs critique, most of the criticism pertains to the psychosocial perspective on the health effects of income inequality—specifically the constructs of social capital and social cohesion. As the critics note, social capital theory was developed in sociology at the level of the individual—not as a construct of societies or populations. As a result, within the psychosocial perspective there is theoretical ambiguity concerning the meanings of social capital and social cohesion that extends to a lack of specificity and consistency in measurement (Lomas, 1998). This problem is then compounded by the ad hoc measurement of these concepts via conveniently available population surveys (Forbes & Wainwright, 2001). The effect of all this is to cast serious doubt on whether particular statistical relationships used to support causal arguments have a clear theoretical interpretation.

The primary measurement critique specific to the materialist political economy perspective pertains to the measurement of income inequality. Although the relationship between income inequalities and population health has proved robust across a variety of measures in the context of the United States (Kawachi & Kennedy, 1997), the relationship at the cross-national level has been shown to be quite sensitive to the measure of income inequality employed (Judge, 1995). A second measurement problem that cuts across theoretical perspectives involves the measures of population health that are chosen. In essence, the critique here is that some of the most influential studies used to argue a relationship between income inequality and population health relied upon a small set of very general indicators, such as average life expectancy, infant mortality, and homicide (Lynch et al., 2004).

At the heart of the sample selection critique of the income inequality—population health literature is the appearance of a statistical correlation that can arise when a small sample of cases is used. In fact, this was the case in the most famous of the early international studies used to argue the income inequality–population health hypothesis.[18] A second and related problem is that, under such circumstances, a few atypical cases can drive the results and lead to an erroneous conclusion. In fact, several studies that were able to capture data on a larger number of countries have shown this to be the case (Judge, 1995; Lynch et al., 2001). The concluding critique is one that involves both issues of sample selection and statistical design; the spurious correlation between income inequality and health at the aggregate (population) level that arises where the effects of individual income on health are smaller as income rises (Gravelle, 1998). Since the diminishing returns of income on health correspond to the general pattern, this statistical artifact poses a significant problem to the evaluation of the income inequality–population health hypothesis. Although the use of multilevel (population and individual) data and methods can mitigate this problem, until recent years this approach was largely ignored in favor of population-level only studies (Lynch et al., 2004).

To illuminate some of these methodological concerns, Figure 7.4 shows the different estimates of the relationship between income inequality that were produced by Lynch, Harper, Kaplan, and Smith (2005) when alternative sources of data for household income are used. The top graph (labeled "a"), is the same as that shown in Figure 7.3—which, as discussed previously, shows

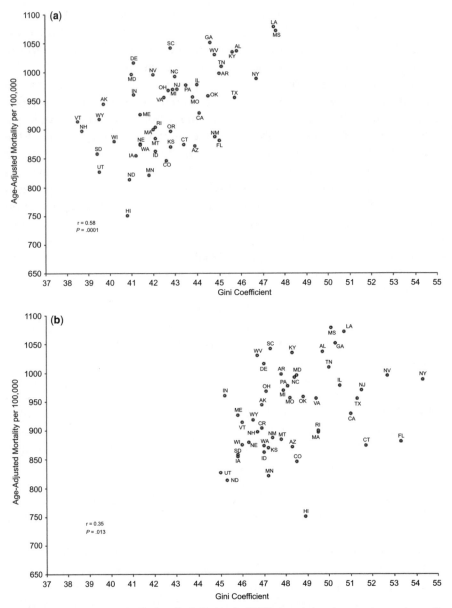

Source: Lynch, J., Harper, S., Kaplan, G., & Smith, G. (2005). Associations between income inequality and mortality among U.S. states: The importance of time period and source of data. *American Journal of Public Health*, *95*(8): Figure 2 Cross-sectional association between income inequality and age-adjusted mortality based on (a) U.S. Census data. Used by permission.

Figure 7.4 *Cross-sectional association between income inequality and age-adjusted mortality for 50 U.S. States based on U.S. Census data (a) and internal revenue service tax return data (b), 1989.*

a very robust relationship between income inequality and age-adjusted mortality (a correlation coefficient of .58, $p < .001$). It should be noted that data source for income inequality estimates in the top graph, consistent with many other similar studies, is national census data. The bottom graph, (b) in Figure 7.4, based on the less commonly used but more valid IRS tax returns, shows a more dispersed and much weaker estimate of the relationship between income inequality and age-adjusted mortality—in fact, one that fails to meet the $p < .01$ criteria for statistical significance (a correlation coefficient of .35 and $p < .013$). While the contrasting results shown in Figure 7.4 do not themselves refute the income inequality-health disparities hypothesis, they demonstrate the extent to which the findings in much of this research can be misleading—even when widely accepted data sources and measures are used.[19]

Does Income Inequality Directly Affect Population Health?

Debates about the relative importance of the psychosocial effects as opposed to the material effects of income inequality of health are predicated on the assumption that income inequality is a pervasive determinant of population health. So, theoretical pathways aside, we are left with the central question of whether or not income inequality affects health. On the basis of a comprehensive review involving the 98 studies published on this question between 1979 and 2004, John Lynch and his collaborators concluded that, *as a general phenomenon* among wealthy nations, *income inequality itself is not associated with population health differences* (Lynch et al., 2004, p. 81). However, their conclusion came with several important caveats:

1. First and most important, the lack of a consistent association between income inequality and population health at the international level does not preclude the effect of a relationship between income inequality and health *within* countries—in fact, such seems to be the case in the United States, where there appears to be persistent state-level income inequality effects on health despite controls for a variety of confounding factors. As Lynch suggests, the income inequality effects on health may be more pronounced in national contexts (like the United States), where extremes of income inequality are juxtaposed with less evenly distributed social investments in goods and services that are relevant to health, such as high-quality public education and health care (Lynch et al., 2001).
2. Income inequality, as a characteristic of a social system, can in many ways shape the life chances of individuals in ways that are not readily

observable at the individual level (Lynch et al., 2004, p. 82). The fact that such "system effects" of income inequality are not as obvious and universal at the international level as once assumed does not mean that they are not important or in fact quite powerful—rather, it suggests that they are complex and highly contextualized by the nation's specific cultural, historical, and political factors that affect health.[20]

3. Finally, Lynch and his collaborators earnestly point out that income inequality statistics at the population level reflect aggregate income disadvantages for individuals that are linked to poor health—thus implying the same fundamental public policy interventions; specifically, those policy interventions aimed at raising the income levels of the most disadvantaged (Lynch et al., 2004, p. 83).

Central to Lynch et al.'s (2004) conclusion that the income inequality effects in population health are not generalized among wealthy nations was the lack of evidence of an income inequality effect on population health based on studies that employed multilevel data and statistical methods. In this kind of research, it is crucial to identify the relative contributions of individual and aggregate effects (such as neighborhood population effects), and only multilevel data and methods can do so. In the years subsequent to this critique, numerous studies have been published that meet these criteria. In a meta-analysis of 9 cohort and 19 cross-sectional multilevel studies that examined the relationship between income inequality and self-rated health, Kondo et al. (2009) found a modest adverse effect in income inequality and health and, in particular, evidence of a threshhold effect, which means that the adverse effects of income inequality on health only begin to emerge after a certain "tipping point" of income inequality occurs—in these findings, a Gini coefficient of income inequality in excess of .30.[21] Adding to this more recent and credible evidence of an association between income inequality and health is a cross-sectional and time trend analysis of the relationship between income inequality and infant mortality, life expectancy and homicide using World Bank Data on 134 countries from 1970 through 1995. This study (Babones, 2008) found that changes in income inequality were significantly related to both life expectancy and infant mortality.

In sum, despite continued controversy over such questions as: (1) the precise magnitude of the income inequality effect on population health, (2) the degree to which the relationship is linear, and (3) the possibility of contextual effects on the association between income inequality and health—the evidence of a deleterious linkage between income inequality and health is far more substantial than it was a decade ago.

Prospects for the Advancement of Social Epidemiology as a Discipline

Although the claims and controversies pertaining to the health effects of income inequality were heavily featured in social epidemiology's emergence as a distinct discipline over the last roughly 15 years, income inequality is but one potential structural determinant of health among many. In fact, the rejection or revisions of popular theory on empirical grounds are the hallmark of a maturing discipline. The richness and scientific relevance that is inherent in the discipline of social epidemiology is not tied to the fate of any one meta-theory or unifying idea, but in what the discipline brings to the epistemologies of causality. In this regard, the future of social epidemiology is very promising.

Perhaps social epidemiology's prospects as a discipline have been best articulated through an essay by Nancy Krieger published in the *International Journal of Epidemiology*, ironically in response to an editorial questioning the legitimacy of social epidemiology as a field of scientific endeavor (Zielhuis & Kiemeney, 2001).[22] As argued by Krieger, any complete explanation of disease, whether at the individual level or the population level, must take account of the fact that humans exist as both social and biological beings (Krieger, 2001a). Thus, "epidemiologically adequate explanations of current and changing distributions of population disease [must] entail simultaneous social and biological explanations" (Krieger, 2001a, p. 44). By implication, there is an inherent merit to a discipline that affords a niche for theoretical and methodological syntheses between the social and biological sciences.

However, because the disciplinary paradigm of social epidemiology encompasses at once the social and biological, it is exceedingly complex as well. Social epidemiologist George Kaplan illustrates this point by reference to his own work, specifically the Kaplan and Lynch model of the social epidemiology of cardiovascular disease depicted in Figure 7.5 (Kaplan & Lynch, 1999). As noted by Kaplan, the array of factors at multiple levels that are considered in Figure 7.5 is far more broad and complex than the models typically employed in other branches of science. While the model shown offers a general sense of the intricate web of causality that links structural determinants of health to specific mechanisms, it is still a gross oversimplification of the causal processes implied by a social and biological paradigm of disease.

In order for social epidemiology to advance as a discipline and prove useful as a tool of medicine and social policy, complex multilevel models like that shown in Figure 7.5 need to be validated and refined through empirical investigation. However, this imposes formidable challenges that have been well summarized by Kaplan in a general critique of the discipline (Kaplan, 2004). These challenges include surmounting obstacles in the acquisition of

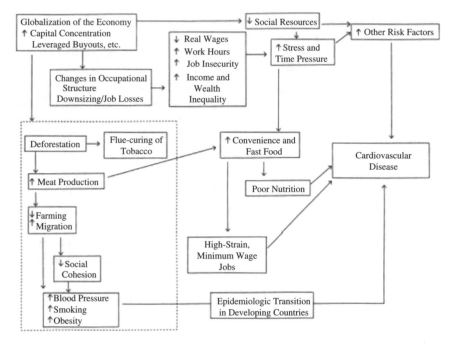

Source: Kaplan, G. A., &Lynch, G. W. (1999). Socioeconomic considerations in the primordial prevention of cardiovascular disease. *Prevention Medicine*, 29: Figure 2 Example of impact of macroeconomic factors on primordial and primary prevention. Used by permission.

Figure 7.5 *The Kaplan and Lynch model of the social epidemiology of cardiovascular disease.*

theory-relevant data at multiple levels (e.g., individual, household, and neighborhood level data) data relevant to psychosocial support networks, data pertaining to occupational status and work environment, data on the local health care infrastructure, and macro level data pertaining to such factors as job outsourcing. Aside from these formidable data challenges, Kaplan also identified such challenges as gaining disciplinary consensus on the meaning and measurement of key constructs (e.g., social cohesion), contending with the statistical complexities involved in estimating relative effects of variables at different ecological levels, contending with issues of temporal effects and reciprocal causality, and overcoming the tendency to substitute general constructs (such as social class, gender, and race) for specific causal factors that are confounded with measures of the general construct. Although such impediments to disciplinary progress are not unique to social epidemiology, they are perhaps more daunting given the complex nature of the theoretical paradigms in social epidemiology.

CONCLUDING COMMENTS: SOCIAL EPIDEMIOLOGY
AS A TOOL OF SOCIAL POLICY

This chapter began with Nancy Krieger's observation that social epidemiology "is distinguished [from other sciences and branches of epidemiology] by its insistence upon explicitly investigating the social determinants of population distributions of health, disease, and wellbeing ..." (Krieger, 2002, p. 7). As much as this distinct purpose lends relevancy to the discipline, it also imposes a paradox in managing the boundaries between scientific inquiry, theory building, and political ideology. This paradox arises because (1) the social determinants of health tend to be structural in origin, and (2) such structural determinants of health are intertwined with hierarchies of power and privilege. Further (to reinforce a point made in the opening paragraphs of the chapter), to the extent that the theories and findings of social epidemiologists fundamentally challenge embedded hierarchies of power and privilege, the discipline will remain encumbered by questions about its legitimacy. There is one sense in which social epidemiology should embrace and celebrate challenges to its legitimacy, and another sense in which social epidemiology should be worried.

Challenges to legitimacy that arise because the scientific inquiries of social epidemiologists either uncover or highlight social arrangements that are detrimental to health should be regarded as an affirmation that the social epidemiology is fulfilling a critical social purpose. Indeed, it seems that the more credible the theory and evidence that links power and privilege to detrimental social arrangements, the louder will be the outcry from the interests benefiting from the status quo. Examples of this include the tobacco industry's decades long disinformation campaign aimed at discrediting the irrefutable findings by well-established scientific disciplines that tobacco usage in multiple forms is a principle cause of cancer, and, in more recent years, the attempts by a host of industries and their sponsored politicians to discredit the science behind the discovery and measurement of global warming.[23] Ultimately, though, such outraged protests about scientific legitimacy often portend the introduction of scientifically informed social policies.

On the other hand, to the extent that social epidemiologists fall into the trap of confounding the advancement of egalitarian political ideology with the advancement of epidemiological theory, other challenges to legitimacy arise that ultimately undermine the credibility of social epidemiology as a scientific discipline. This seems to have occurred in the popular consumption of theories that identify income inequality as a general determinant of population

health, rather than as a more complex dimension of material and status deprivation with highly contextualized effects. While the proposition that income
inequality functions as a readily observable *general determinant* of population
health remains unsubstantiated due to contradictory evidence and a formidable array of methodological challenges, there is far more empirical support
for the conclusion that income inequality appears to have had significant detrimental effects on population health under a variety of specific circumstances
(Balbones, 2008; Kondo et al., 2009). In order to illuminate these more nuanced
and policy relevant linkages between income inequality and population
health, the discipline of social epidemiology will need to continue to
advance in theoretical specificity and methodological rigor. This, of course,
is the challenge that confronts all scientific disciplines and gives meaning to
the term "scientific progress."

NOTES

1. As noted by Krieger (2001c), John Cassel introduced the idea that both hierarchical
   social relationships and marginalized status are implicated in the impairment of
   individual-level biological defense mechanisms (Cassel, 1976).
2. Krieger defines scales as "quantifiable dimensions" of spatial and temporal
   phenomenon, for example, kilometers and nanoseconds (2001, p. 372).
3. The Seventh Calvary that conducted the massacre and Wounded Knee was the
   same military unit as that originally commanded by General George Armstrong
   Custer, reconstituted after the infamous annaliation of Custer and his troops in
   the Battle of Little Big Horn in 1876. At Wounded Knee, the soldiers of the
   Seventh Calvary opened fire on all of the Sioux men, women, and children
   present—killing the Chief of the tribe in his tent as he lay recovering from pneumonia and cutting down others as they ran. Despite the consensus among historians
   that Wounded Knee was essentially an unprovoked slaughter of innocents rather
   than an armed conflict between opposing forces, more Congressional Medals of
   Honor were awarded to U.S. soldiers for the action at Wounded Knee than any
   military action in history (U.S. History.org, 2012).
4. While the reservation system evolved over the 19th century as territories
   inhabited by indigenous peoples were expropriated by European Americans,
   more recent generations of Americans have failed to either redress violations of
   treaty obligations or invest in national policies that would significantly reduce
   the economic and health disparities that continue to persist within the reservation
   system.
5. Historical trauma is defined by Brave Heart (1999) as a distinct form of trauma that
   reflects the shared consequences of a collective experience of a traumatic event (or
   series of traumatic events). In contrast to other forms of trauma, which are individual, historical trauma is a collective phenomena that can be transmitted from one
   generation to the next. Historical trauma is attributed to such events as genocide
   and territorial displacement.

6. Aside from contamination of the ground water from nonnative sources of agricultural pesticides and residues from mining operations, over a third of homes on the reservations lack running water and sewage systems (Schwartz, 2002).

7. The earlier edition of this book, published in 2007, had an identical version of Table 7.1 with data based on 2003 vital records. In preparing this edition, it was distressing to discover that almost all of the relative mortality rates had increased between editions. An exception to this general pattern was the relative death rates among the Pine Ridge Lakota for lower respiratory disease, which have dramatically declined. This improvement suggests the effect of targeted health care interventions.

8. During the period between 2000 and 2007, the disparity between average life expectancy for Whites and African Americans narrowed from 5.7 to 4.3 years. This improvement is consistent with Fundamental Social Cause theory, in that during the most recent decades, African American racial segregation has dramatically declined (Glaesar & Vigdor, 2012). The multiple pathways through which racial segregation is implicated in African American health disparities will be explored in more depth at a later point in this chapter.

9. Age-adjusted death rates for 1999 are used as estimates for the 2000 period and are sufficient for the particular comparisons made here.

10. Italicized type is employed to identify ideas that are closely paraphrased from the source articles.

11. Between 1990 and 2000, the real (constant dollar) income gap between White and African American family households declined slightly but significantly, by 2%. This is because while both racial groups experienced gains in real median income, the gains in real median income among African American families during this prosperous decade were nearly twice that of White families. During the most recent economically difficult decade (between 2000 and 2009), while both White and African American families endured significant declines in real income, the income gap between White and African American families remained essentially unchanged (U.S. Census Bureau, 2012).

12. The residential racial segregation of African Americans refers to two interrelated phenomena, the concentration of African Americans within particular neighborhoods of the nation's large cities, and the exclusion of African Americans from neighborhoods that are populated by non-African Americans—in particular, neighborhoods inhabited by Whites. For a complete history of urban racial segregation in America, see Massey and Denton's *American Apartheid: Segregation and the Making of the Underclass*, Harvard University Press, 1993.

13. The decline in segregation is measured by a reduction in the index of dissimilarity, the standard indice of racial segregation employed by sociologists to measure the level of residential segregation between two groups—in most comparisons, African Americans vs. Whites. An index of dissimilarity value of 100 in a given city indicates a city where there are no neighborhoods that have inhabitants of both races, whereas a dissimilarity value of 0 means that all neighborhoods within a city have an equally proportionate representation of both races. In 1970, the 10 most segregated of America's largest cities had an index of dissimilarity that averaged 89; by 2010 this average had declined to 64 (calculated from Glaesar and Vigdor (2012), Table 4 Long-run Segregation Trends in the Nation's Most Segregated Cities).

14. The Gini coefficient is widely used as a measure of income inequality that varies between 0 and 1, with 0 representing perfect equality and 1 representing the total concentration of income. In essence, a Gini coefficient of .58 represents the proportion of national household income that would have to be redistributed to create income equity across all households.

15. These dimensions of social capital were measured on the bases of selected responses to the General Social Science Survey (the GSS), averaged over the 5-year period between 1986 and 1999. The GSS is a national probability sample survey of adults on an array of social attitudes, beliefs, and behaviors that is conducted annually by the National Opinion Research Center at the University of Chicago. Although the investigators suggest that the selected GSS questions they employed measure four dimensions of social capital, two of the survey items employed appear to represent the same underlying dimension (see Kawachi et al., 1997, p. 1492).

16. Lynch et al. use the term "neo-material" for this perspective rather than the "materialist/political economy" label applied here. The latter is preferred here because the principal origin of the perspective resides in political economy theory.

17. Although SES and social class are often used synonymously, there are distinctions that are specific to their societal context. In some societies, social class is regarded as an inherited attribute (e.g., "being well-bred" or as in a caste system). In others such as the United States, the inherited attributes of social class are de-emphasized in favor of attributes that are presumed to reflect personal achievement (income, education, and occupational status).

18. This was Richard Wilkinson's (1992) *British Medical Journal* article that employed data from nine industrialized democracies to show a strong negative correlation between income inequality and life expectancy.

19. In this same paper Lynch, Harper, Kaplan, and Smith (2005) also demonstrate that association between income equality and health observed among U.S. states fluctuates widely by the decade observed, suggesting that there are important historical period effects that are not fully captured by the magnitude of income inequality.

20. This more nuanced and contextualized view of the income inequality effects on health is quite consistent with the "fundamental social causes of disease" theory reviewed at an earlier point in the chapter. In essence, this theory suggests that the intervening mechanisms of disease through which income inequality influences health are likely to vary by historical period and social context—thus leading to inconsistency of results in cross-national comparisons of income inequality.

21. The average Gini coefficient among OECD countries in the most recently available estimates is .31. According to the OECD's most recent estimates, the U.S. (after tax and transfer) Gini coefficient stands at .38, which exceeds that of all comparably affluent democracies (OECD, 2012).

22. Zielhuis and Kiemeney's essay seeks to keep epidemiology in the realm of the biological, and rejects the notion that investigators trained in social science can make meaningful contributions to epidemiology in the absence of formal training in the biological sciences. Krieger's essay in response is one of several compelling rebuttals to this point of view.

23. As a specific example, during the 2012 presidential primary election candidate, former U.S. Senator Rick Santorum made the claim in a February 20, 2012

campaign speech in Ohio that global warming is "not climate science, but political science" (reported and quoted by Jeffrey Brown, *PBS Newshour*, aired February 20, 2012). In making this claim, Santorum contradicted the scientific conclusions reached by the National Academy of Sciences (see, e.g., *America's Climate Choices: Report in Brief*. 2011, National Academies Press, Washington, DC), as well as denigrated the scientific integrity of some of the nation's most eminent oceanographers, climatologists, and earth scientists. In Santorum's defense, the use of unpopular scientific conclusions as political fodder is nothing new in American politics.

REFERENCES

Alderson, A., & Nielsen, N. (2002). Globalization and the great U-Turn: Income inequality trends in 16 OECD countries. *American Journal of Sociology, 107*(5), 1244–1257.

Babones, S. (2008). Income inequality and population health: Correlation and causality. *Social Science & Medicine, 66,* 1614–1626.

Balbach, E. D., Gasior, R. J., & Barbeau, E. M. (2003). R.J. Reynolds' targeting of African Americans: 1988–2000. *American Journal of Public Health, 93*(5), 822–827.

Barbeau, E. M., Wolin, K. Y., Naumova, E. N., & Balbach, E. (2005). Tobacco advertising in communities: Associations with race and class. *Preventative Medicine, 40*(1), 16–22.

Benysheka, D., Martin, B., & Johnston, C. (2001). A reconsideration of the origins of the type 2 diabetes epidemic among native Americans and the implications for intervention policy. *Medical Anthropology: Cross-Cultural Studies in Health and Illness, 20*(1), 25–64.

Berkman, I., & Kawachi, I.(Eds.) (2000). *Social epidemiology.* Oxford: Oxford University Press, 2000.

Brave Heart, M. (1999). Gender differences in the historical trauma response among the Lakota. *Journal of Health & Social Policy, 10*(4), 1–21.

Broder, M. S., Kanouse, D. E., Mittman, B. S., & Bernstein, S. J. (2000). The appropriateness of recommendations for hysterectomy. *Obstetrics & Gynecology, 95*(2), 199–205.

Burris, S. (2002). Introduction: Merging law, human rights, and social epidemiology. *Journal of Law and Medical Ethics, 30*(4), 498–509.

Cassel, J. (1976). The contribution of the social environment to host resistance: The fourth Wade Hampton Frost lecture. *American Journal of Epidemiology, 104*(2), 107–123.

Diamond, T. (1992). *Making gray gold: Narratives of nursing home care.* Chicago, IL: University of Chicago Press.

Dicker, R. C., Scally, M. J., Greenspan, J. R., Layde, P. M., Ory, H. W., Maze, J. M. et al. (1982). Hysterectomy among women of reproductive age. Trends in the United States, 1970–1978. *Journal of the American Medical Association, 248*(3), 323–327.

Forbes, A., & Wainwright, S. P. (2001). On the methodological, theoretical and philosophical context of health inequalities research: A critique. *Social Science & Medicine, 53*(6), 801–816.

Frisbie, W. P., Song, S. E., Powers, D. A., & Street, J. A. (2004). The increasing racial disparity in infant mortality: Respiratory distress syndrome and other causes. *Demography, 41*(4), 773–800.

Glaesar, E., & Vigdor, J. (2012). The end of the segregated century: Racial separation in America's neighborhoods, 1890–2010. Manhatten Institute for Policy Research: Civic Report No. 6. Retrieved February 13, 2012, from http://www.manhattan-institute.org/html/cr_6.htm

Gravelle, H. (1998). How much of the relation between population mortality and unequal distribution of income is a statistical artefact? *British Medical Journal, 316*(7128), 382–385.

Guest, A., Almgren, G., & Hussey, J. (1998). The ecology of socio-economic distress: Infant and working age mortality in Chicago. *Demography, 35*(1).

Haas, S., Acker, D., Donahue, C., & Katz, M. E. (1993). Variation in hysterectomy rates across small geographic areas of Massachusetts. *American Journal of Obstetrics and Gynecology, 169*(1), 150–154.

Judge, K. (1995). Income distribution and life expectancy: A critical appraisal. *British Medical Journal, 311*(7015), 1282–1285.

Kaplan, G. A. (2004). What's wrong with social epidemiology, and how can we make it better? *Epidemiology Review, 26,* 124–135.

Kaplan, G. A., & Lynch, J. W. (1999). Socioeconomic considerations in the primordial prevention of cardiovascular disease. *Preventive Medicine, 29*(6), S30–S35.

Kaplan, G. A., Lynch, J. W., Cohen, R. D., & Balfour, J. (1996). Inequality in income and mortality in the United States: Analysis of mortality and potential pathways. *British Medical Journal, 312*(7037), 999–1003.

Kasl, S. V., & Jones, B. A. (2002). Social epidemiology: Towards a better understanding of the field. *International Journal of Epidemiology, 31*(6), 1094–1097.

Kawachi, I. (2002). Social epidemiology. *Social Science and Medicine, 54*(12), 1739–1741.

Kawachi, I., & Kennedy, B. P. (1997). The relationship of income inequality to mortality: Does the choice of indicator matter? *Social Science and Medicine, 45*(7), 1121–1127.

Kawachi, I., Kennedy, B. P., Lochner, K., & Prothrow-Stith, D. (1997). Social capital, income inequality, and mortality. *American Journal of Public Health, 87*(9), 1491–1498.

Kondo, N., Sembajwe, G., Kawachi, I., van Dam, R., Subramanian, S., & Yamagata, Z. (2009). Income inequality, mortality, and self rated health: Metaanalysis of multilevel studies. *BMJ 339,* b4471 doi:10.1136/bmj.b4471.

Krieger, N. (1994). Epidemiology and the web of causation: Has anyone seen the spider? *Social Science and Medicine, 39,* 887–903.

Krieger, N. (1999). Sticky webs, hungry spiders, buzzing flies, and fractal metaphors: On the misleading juxtaposition of "risk factor" versus "social" epidemiology. *Journal of Epidemiology and Community Health, 53*(11), 678–680.

Krieger, N. (2000). Epidemiology and social sciences: Towards a critical reengagement in the 21st century. *Epidemiology Review, 22*(1), 155–163.

Krieger, N. (2001a). Commentary: Society, biology and the logic of social epidemiology. *International Journal of Epidemiology, 30*(1), 44–46.

Krieger, N. (2001b). Historical roots of social epidemiology: Socioeconomic gradients in health and contextual analysis. *International Journal of Epidemiology, 30*(4), 899–900.

Krieger, N. (2001c). Theories for social epidemiology in the 21st century: An ecosocial perspective. *International Journal of Epidemiology, 30*(4), 668–677.

Krieger, N. (2002). A glossary for social epidemiology. *Epidemiology Bulletin, 23*(1), 7–11.

Krieger, N., & Smith, G. D. (2000). Re: "Seeking causal explanations in social epidemiology." *American Journal of Epidemiology, 151*(8), 831–833.

Krieger, N., & Smith, G. D. (2004). "Bodies count," and body counts: Social epidemiology and embodying inequality. *Epidemiology Review, 26*, 92–103.

Link, B. G., & Phelan, J. (1995). Social conditions as fundamental causes of disease. *Journal of Health and Social Behavior*, Spec No., 80–94.

Link, B. G., & Phelan, J. (1996). Understanding sociodemographic differences in health—The role of fundamental causes. *American Journal of Public Health, 86*(4), 471–473.

Link, B. G., & Phelan, J. C. (2002). McKeown and the idea that social conditions are fundamental causes of disease. *American Journal of Public Health, 92*(5), 730–732.

Lochner, K., Kawachi, I., & Kennedy, B. P. (1999). Social capital: A guide to its measurement. *Health & Place, 5*(4), 259–270.

Lomas, J. (1998). Social capital and health: Implications for public health and epidemiology. *Social Science and Medicine, 47*(9), 1181–1188.

Lynch, J., Harper, S., Kaplan, G., & Smith, G. (2005). Associations between income inequality and mortality among U.S. states: The importance of time period and source of data. *American Journal of Public Health, 95*(8),1424–1430.

Lynch, J., Smith, G. D., Harper, S., Hillemeie, M., Ross, N., Kaplan, G. et al. (2004). Is income inequality a determinant of population health? Part 1. A systematic review. *Milbank Quarterly, 82*(1), 5–99.

Lynch, J., Smith, G. D., Hillemeier, M., Shaw, M., Raghunathan, T., & Kaplan, G. (2001). Income inequality, the psychosocial environment, and health: Comparisons of wealthy nations. *Lancet, 358*(9277), 194–200.

Lynch, J. W., Smith, G. D., Kaplan, G. A., & House, J. S. (2000). Income inequality and mortality: Importance to health of individual income, psychosocial environment, or material conditions. *British Medical Journal, 320*(7243), 1200–1204.

Macdonald, K. (2001). Commentary: Social epidemiology. A way? *International Journal of Epidemiology, 30*(1), 46–47.

Mackenbach, J. P. (2002). Income inequality and population health. *British Medical Journal, 324*(7328), 1–2.

Marmot, M. (2002). The influence of income on health: Views of an epidemiologist. *Health Affairs, 21*(2), 31–46.

McCord, C., & Freeman, H. (1990). Excess mortality in Harlem. *New England Journal of Medicine, 322*, 173–177.

McDaniel, A., DiPrete, T. N., Buchmann, C., & Shwed, U. (2009). *The Black gender gap in educational attainment: Historical trends and racial comparisons.* Unpublished manuscript. Retrieved February 15, 2012, from http://www.ssc.wisc.edu/soc/faculty/docs/diprete/Race%20Paper%2009232009.pdf.

McEwen, B. S., & Gianaros, P. J. (2010). Central role of the brain in stress and adaptation: Links to socioeconomic status, health, and disease. *Annals of the New York Academy of Sciences, 1186,* 190–222.

Muntaner, C. (1999). Invited commentary: Social mechanisms, race, and social epidemiology. *American Journal of Epidemiology, 150*(2), 121–126; discussion 127–128.

Muntaner, C. (2001). Social epidemiology: No way back. A response to Zielhuis and Kiemeney. *International Journal of Epidemiology, 30*(3), 625–626.

Muntaner, C., Lynch, J., & Smith, G. D. (2001). Social capital, disorganized communities, and the third way: Understanding the retreat from structural inequalities in epidemiology and public health. *International Journal of Health Services, 31*(2), 213–237.

Muntaner, C., Lynch, J. W., Hillemeie, M., Lee, J. H., David, R., Benach, J. et al. (2002). Economic inequality, working-class power, social capital, and cause-specific mortality in wealthy countries. *International Journal of Health Services, 32*(3), 423–432.

Navarro, V., & Shi, L. (2001). The political context of social inequalities and health. *Social Science & Medicine, 52*(3), 481–491.

NCHS. (2011). *Health, United States 2010.* Hyattesville, MD. Table 2. Life expectancy at birth, at 65 years of age, and at 75 years of age, by race and sex: United States, selected years 1900–2007.

OECD. (2012). OECD.statExtracts: *Income distribution-Inequality.* Retrieved February 15, 2012, from http://stats.oecd.org/Index.aspx?DataSetCode=INEQUALITY

Phelan, J. C., Link, B. G., Diez-Roux, A., Kawachi, I., & Levin, B. (2004). "Fundamental causes" of social inequalities in mortality: A test of the theory. *Journal of Health and Social Behavior, 45*(3), 265–285.

Rodgers, G. (1979). Income and inequality as determinants of mortality: An international cross-section analysis. *Population Studies, 33,* 343–351.

Sapolsky, R. M. (2005). The influence of social hierarchy on primate health. *Science, 308,* 648–652.

Schwartz, S. (2002). *"Hidden away, in the land of plenty .... 2002 current statistics concerning the Pine Ridge Oglala Lakota (Sioux) Reservation."* Retrieved February 20, 2005, from http://www.wambliho.homestead.com

Schwartz, S. (2006). The arrogance of ignorance; Hidden away, out of sight and out of mind: *The Link Center Foundation: The Life and Conditions on the Pine Ridge Ogala.-Lakota (Sioux) Reservation of South Dakota.* Retrieved February 10, 2012, from http://www.linkcenterfoundation.org/id24.html

South Dakota Department of Public Health. (2009). *2009 South Dakota Vital Statistics Report: A state and county comparison of leading health indicators.* Retrieved February 10, 2012, from http://doh.sd.gov/Statistics/2009Vital/HealthStatusByCounty.pdf.

Starr, P. (1982). *The social transformation of American medicine.* New York: Basic Books.

Swingwood, A. (2000). *A short history of social thought* (3rd ed.). New York: St. Martin's Press.

Travis, C. (1985). Medical decision making and elective surgery: The case of hysterectomy. *Risk Analysis, 5*(3), 241–251.

U.S. History.Org. (2012). The Wounded Knee massacre. *The U.S. History Online Textbook.* Retrieved February 10, 2012, from http://www.ushistory.org/us/40e.asp.

U.S. Census Bureau. (2012). Statistical Abstract of the United States: 2012. Table 697. Money Income of Families—Median Income by Race and Hispanic Origin in Current and Constant (2009) Dollars: 1990–2009.

Wallace, R. (1990). Urban desertification, public health and public order: "Planned shrinkage," violent death, substance abuse and AIDS in the Bronx. *Social Science and Medicine, 31*(7), 801–813.

West, S., & Dranov, P. (1994). *The hysterectomy hoax* (3rd ed.). New York: Doubleday.

Wilkinson, R. G. (1992). Income distribution and life expectancy. *British Medical Journal (Clinical Research Ed.), 304*(6820), 165–168.

Wilkinson, R. G. (1995). Commentary: A reply to Ken Judge: Mistaken criticisms ignore overwhelming evidence. *British Medical Journal, 311*(7015), pp. 1285–1287

Wilkinson, R. G. (1996). *Unhealthy societies: The afflictions of inequality.* London: Routledge.

Wilkinson, R. G. (1999). Health, hierarchy, and social anxiety. *Annals of the New York Academy of Sciences, 896*(1), 48–63.

Wilkinson, R. G., & Pickens, K. (2010). *The spirit level: Why greater equality makes societies stronger.* New York: Bloomsbury Press.

Wilkinson, R. G., Kawachi, I., & Kennedy, B. (1998). Mortality, the social environment, crime and violence. In M. Bartley, D. Blane, & G. Davey-Smith (Eds.), *The sociology of health inequalities* (pp. 19–38). Oxford, UK: Oxford Sociology of Health and Illness Monograph.

Willams, D., & Collins, C. (2001). Racial residential segregation: A fundamental cause of racial disparities in health. *Public Health Reports, 116*, 404–416.

Yankauer, A. (1950). The relationship of fetal and infant mortality to residential segregation: An inquiry into social epidemiology. *ASR, 15*(6), 644–648.

Zielhuis, G. A., & Kiemeney, L. A. (2001). Social epidemiology? No way. *International Journal of Epidemiology, 30*(1), 43–44; discussion 51.

CHAPTER EIGHT

PROSPECTS FOR JUST HEALTH CARE SYSTEM REFORM: A POLITICAL AND PRINCIPLED ANALYSIS

*T*he task taken up by this last chapter entails a review of the dominant and stable array of policy agendas arising from different interests and segments of the body politic. A pragmatic understanding of the policy priorities and arguments of the health care system's key stakeholders must be taken into account in any effort toward health care reform, whether incremental or fundamental. The Patient Protection and Affordable Care Act (PPACA) is then summarized and critiqued both as a politically viable approach to health care reform, and in accordance with the central principles of alternative theories of social justice. The chapter concludes with a synopsis of an approach to health care reform that would satisfy the demands of justice articulated in the theory of John Rawls.

THE SOCIAL AND POLITICAL CONTEXT OF HEALTH CARE REFORM

Virtually every presidential administration since Lyndon Johnson's has needed to confront "the crisis in American health care," however it has been defined. Conservative politicians have tended to frame the crisis in terms of an unsustainable level of growth in federal health care spending and the disastrous consequences on the national economy that follow. In contrast, liberal politicians have typically framed the crisis in health care by the well-documented failures of the health care system to ensure the availability of essential health care for millions of Americans. Both positions are fundamentally correct. As discussed at length in an earlier chapter (Chapter 3,

"Health Care Finance"), four decades of mostly continuous health care inflation have been paralleled by the growth of federal expenditures for health care—principally via the Medicare and Medicaid programs. Conservatives rightly point out that over this same 40-year period there have been multiple expansions in the entitlements of both programs, as well. On the other hand, just as liberals claim, the American health care system remains replete with disparities in access to health care across multiple categories of race, ethnicity, and social class.

Presidential administrations have tended to follow suit by defining the nature of the health care crisis largely in terms of one of these two perspectives—but not always in ways that are consistent with political party affiliation. The presidential administrations that have framed the health care crisis primarily as one of rising costs include Nixon (1969–1974), Carter (1977–1981), and Reagan (1981–1989). Each of these administrations introduced cost containment reforms with varying degrees of success that range from negligible to modest. In contrast, the Clinton administration (1993–2001) and the Obama administration (2009–present) are the only presidencies in recent history that defined the crisis in health care principally in terms of the lack of universal health insurance coverage. Two other recent administrations, those of George H. W. Bush (1989–1993) and George W. Bush (2001–2008), have framed the crisis in health care in fairly narrow terms and thus have pursued narrowly targeted reforms.[1]

The Obama presidency is the first administration in recent history that has sought to actually reform the health care system in ways that would pursue both the curbing of health care inflation and assure near universal access to health care. Even Clinton deferred from pursuing a health care reform agenda that would overtly challenge the key vested interests within the health care industry opposed to more than incremental reform—including the large share of physicians committed to the lucrative rewards of medical free enterprise, the for-profit and voluntary sectors of the hospital industry, the health care insurance industry, the pharmaceutical industry, and a significant share of the organized labor movement.

Public Preferences for Health Care Reform

Despite the fact that personal health care expenditures and the affordability of health care have been an ongoing concern of Americans for most of the last century, public opinion on the nature and extent of the crisis in health care has varied dramatically from one national election to the next. In part, this is due to immediate economic and political issues that either illuminate or overshadow the problems embedded in the health care system. As a case in point, the 2004 presidential election witnessed the overshadowing of health care issues by the war in Iraq and related national security concerns— despite the resurgence of health care inflation and an increase in the number of both employed and unemployed Americans without health insurance (Kaiser Commission on Medicaid and the Uninsured, 2006). More recently, the Obama administration's implementation of the PPACA has been jeopardized by a sustained economic depression.

Public opinion on the nature and extent of the crisis in health care, as well as the most viable options for reform, has also been influenced by the *political framing* of the health care issue by politicians and the interests they represent. Briefly described, *political framing* is a rhetorical tactic that reduces highly complex issues to simple ideas, assumptions, and contrasts that are put forth in highly biased terms. Sometimes referred to as "defining the terms of the debate," political framing tactics thrive where there is a convergence between public issue complexity, voter ambivalence about policy trade-offs, and strong vested interests in policy alternatives.

During the debates over the health care reform measures proposed by both the Clinton administration and the Obama administration, the crisis in health care and related reform proposals were politically framed as a tradeoff between extending health care coverage to a small minority of uninsured Americans and the surrendering of individual free choice in health care for all Americans and a "government takeover of health care." This was a very effective use of this tactic that clearly contributed to the decay of public support for the Clinton plan (which failed to achieve congressional approval), and the PPACA—which while signed into law encounters major political obstacles to its implementation.

Although these factors have contributed to a high level of inconsistency in public opinion pertaining to the adequacy of the health care system and health care reform, over time there has been tremendous stability in public opinion pertaining to the role of the government in assuring access to health care. Since 1972, the General Social Survey has regularly asked a nationally representative sample of adults the same question pertaining to the role of the government (as opposed to the individual) in assuring affordable access to health care. Interestingly, the proportion of those surveyed during each decade since 1972 who believed the federal government should have little to no role in helping individuals to pay for doctors and hospitals has never exceeded 20%.[2] In contrast, most of those surveyed feel the government should either assume a large role in helping persons to pay for health care (48%) or at least assume a significant share of the responsibility (30–32%; National Opinion Research Center, 2006). Consistent with the General Social Survey findings, a series of public opinion polls conducted by the Kaiser Family Foundation and the Pew Research Center during the past decade also show that most Americans favor a strong federal role in assuring that all Americans have access to health care and health care insurance—even if it involves an increase in taxes (Kaiser Family Foundation, 2006; Pew Research Center, 2006). Most significantly, President Barack Obama was elected to presidency in 2008 by the largest majority in recent history on a platform including a commitment to universal access to health insurance for all Americans through expanded public entitlements to health care and health insurance industry reforms. Although the public support for the specific approach to health care reform undertaken by the Obama administration became mixed during its implementation, most Americans (64%) believe that the government should guarantee health care for all.[3]

Despite a generally favorable attitude toward universal entitlement to health care, public opinion can best be described as fragmented and ambivalent when it comes to solutions. Among the lessons learned in the wake of the demise of the Clinton plan and the more recent mixed popularity of the PPACA (to be discussed later in this chapter) is the fact that while most Americans share a moral commitment to the uninsured, this value will not by itself create the impetus for fundamental health care system reform. As stated by Blendon et al. (1994, p. 283), "... moral concern by itself will not spur the 85 percent of Americans who have health coverage into action on behalf of the 15 percent who do not." The American public still tends to distrust its government, is resistant to even low-level tax increases, and in particular is resistant to reform strategies that are at all suggestive of diminished health care choice or access (Blendon et al., 1994).

In addition, solutions to universal coverage that entail compulsory insurance coverage (as essential as they are to assuring universal access to affordable coverage) are generally unpopular. This perhaps is the most important lesson of the Obama administration's PPACA. In addition to encountering a Constitutional challenge pertaining to the authority of the Congress to mandate the purchase of health insurance coverage (even when subsidized by the government), the evidence from public opinion research indicates that broad objections to this one "individual mandate" provision undermined the favorability of the health care reform package as a whole. That is, while most major provisions of the PPACA received more than $\frac{2}{3}$ majority support, the general $\frac{2}{3}$ objection to the individual mandate translated an even divide between those holding favorable and unfavorable views of the PPACA as a whole (Kaiser Family Foundation, 2012).

Stakeholder Interests and Competing Agendas for Health Care Reform

In the contemporary rhetoric of public policy, the term stakeholders is often employed to refer to the groups and organizations that have a compelling interest in the outcome of any policy-making process. Simply stated, these are the groups and organizations that stand to either gain or lose dependent upon what policy alternatives are implemented. It is also the case that some stakeholders have more power in the policy-making process than others, sometimes because of legitimate authority but often because of other sources of political capital.[4] Because the interests of stakeholders typically conflict in some areas and converge in others, the policy alternatives that are most likely to be implemented are those that serve the overlapping interests of the most powerful stakeholders. Conversely, the policy alternatives that are least likely to be implemented are those that conflict with these overlapping interests. Thus, the pragmatics of social policy formulation and implementation must involve a rigorous appraisal of the political context of policy making: the identification of the stakeholders, their conflicting and overlapping interests, their overt and latent policy agendas, and the authority and political capital that each stakeholder is able and willing to bring to the policy-making process.

Since health care reform can be defined as any action by the federal government that significantly alters the financing, structure, and delivery of health care services, it is obvious that health care reform has a great many stakeholders. From the consumption side, there are stakeholder groups that are relatively well served by the current health care system and those that are not. Well-served consumer groups include middle income citizens, employees of industries that have relatively generous health care benefits, and persons employed by the federal government. Consumer stakeholders that are not well served by the current health care system include undocumented workers, service industry employees, Native Americans who are geographically isolated from IHS clinics, and both the working and nonworking poor. On the provider side of the health care system, the principal stakeholders include different sectors of the medical profession, the nursing profession and other health care professionals, different sectors of the hospital and nursing home industries, the health care insurance industry, the bioengineering industry, and the pharmaceutical industry. Given the employment-based financial structure of the U.S. health care system, different groups of employers also must be defined as key stakeholders in health care reform—often with very different interests. For example, associations representing the interests of large employers are less likely to oppose mandated employee health insurance benefits than associations representing the interests of small employers.

Other key stakeholders in health care reform are state governments. Because Medicaid funding is structured as a shared partnership between states and the federal government, any health care reforms that either expand or contract Medicaid program participation and expenditures have a significant fiscal impact on states. In general, state governments oppose any expansions in Medicaid eligibility or benefits that place a higher burden on states, and favor reform proposals that shift the costs of health care for the poor and the uninsured to the federal government.

The Health Care Reform Agenda of Disenfranchised vs. Enfranchised Health Care Consumers

In the U.S. health care system, one is "enfranchised," or eligible, to receive nonstigmatized health care on the basis of health care insurance. For Americans under the age of 65, stable employment in the right kind of job in the right kind of industry are the essential requisites for adequate health insurance coverage. Because Medicaid recipients are subjected to the stigma of public welfare, it cannot be said that Medicaid eligibility or the possession of a Medicaid voucher yields the same level of dignified entitlement to health care as an insurance card. Thus, the disenfranchised health care consumers include those on Medicaid, the marginally employed and the unemployed, and those who work in the low-wage economy. For this group of consumer stakeholders, the disenfranchised, the health care reform agenda involves the dismantlement of the employment-based health insurance in favor of a publicly funded system of universal health insurance coverage. Thus, when California voters were given the opportunity to consider a proposition that would have created a single-payer insurance plan (Proposition 186, in 1994), the health care consumer groups that were the strongest supporters included Hispanics (64%) and the uninsured (58%; Kaiser Family Foundation, 1994).[5]

Nationally, surveys on health care reform options show that only about 50% of the public favor abandonment of the employment-based health care system in favor of a single-payer public insurance fund (Kaiser Family Foundation, 2009). Generally, Americans who have health care insurance coverage tend to be satisfied with their current level of access to health care and distrust change (Blendon Brodie, Altman, Benson, & Hamel, 2005). For the enfranchised health care consumers, comprising the majority of the voting public, the health care reform agenda can be characterized as a general desire to achieve universal health insurance coverage with a minimum of personal sacrifice—either in tax burden or perceived quality of health care.

The Health Care Reform Agenda of the Medical Profession

Throughout most of the last century, the medical profession could be regarded as a single stakeholder group when it came to issues of health care reform. Until the 1960s, the AMA could claim with some legitimacy that it represented the unified voice of the medical profession. Over the past 50 years, however, the medical profession has become far more diverse in its views on health care reform and a much smaller proportion of physicians align themselves with the AMA's historic opposition to compulsory national health insurance. At the apex of the AMA's influence, the model of medical practice was medical free enterprise characterized by the private physician in independent practice. However, the physician labor force is now represented by a high proportion of physicians who work in salaried positions or are dependent upon various forms of publicly funded health care programs for a large share of their practice income. Thus, there are sectors of the medical profession that support the expansion of publicly funded health care programs and other sectors of the medical profession that remain vigorously opposed to any expansion of publicly sponsored health care. It is also true that the modern medical profession is challenged by the "democratization" of medical knowledge, meaning that the consumers of health care have multiple sources of information about prevention, disease management, and treatment alternatives aside from the physician—most notably the Internet (Hernes, 2001). In effect, this means that the medical profession is no longer able to retain the same level of authority over health care policy alternatives it had once exerted, even if it could achieve internal consensus. Finally, physicians no longer wholly equate the bureaucratization of medicine solely with publicly financed health care. Managed care plans sponsored through the private insurance industry burden physicians with mountains of paperwork, are notorious for their interference with the clinical judgments of physicians, and are likely a permanent feature of the employment-based health insurance industry.

Despite these developments, there are cross-cutting interests and "hot button" issues that tend to unite physicians around a common policy agenda. These include:

- The preservation of the medical profession's privileged position in terms of authority, prestige, and the economic rewards of medicine;
- The protection of the doctor–patient relationship, both with respect to confidentiality and with respect to physicians' ability to act in the best interests of their patients;
- A promotion of the purchasing power of health care consumers;

- A promotion of public and private investments in medical science and health care technology;
- Assuring a minimal standard of access to essential health care for all citizens; and
- Antagonism toward policies that appear to promote or sanction the overt rationing of health care.[6]

Although this is not an exhaustive list of the political issues that tend to bring physicians together, it can be seen that collectively they reflect themes of both professional altruism and professional self-interest. In this respect, the medical profession is not distinctly different from other socially rewarding professions (e.g., lawyers, dentists, military officers, and university professors). However, in historical terms, physicians have been uniquely successful relative to other professions in blurring the lines between professional altruism, scientific authority, and collective self-interest (Hernes, 2001; Starr, 1982).

In significant respects the political agenda of the medical profession has always resembled Abraham Maslow's hierarchy of needs (Maslow, 1970),[7] in the sense that the profession has been willing (or at least less opposed) to health care reform initiatives that serve both the public good and the medically disenfranchised only after the profession's more basic concerns around economic sustenance, preservation of authority, and professional autonomy have been satisfied. In historic terms, this was evident in the policy compromises that ultimately produced the inflationary financial structure of Medicare (Starr, 1982). In a contemporary context, this dynamic is evident in the prominence of tort reform on the political agenda of the medical profession relative to the profession's concerns about endemic disparities in health and access to health care. The former undermines the economic viability of medical free enterprise, while the latter concerns the broader humanitarian concerns of the medical profession.

The Health Care Reform Agenda of the Hospital Industry

Except for incremental measures that expand health insurance coverage without introducing extreme cost controls, there is no single health care reform agenda or strategy for health care reform that unites the disparate sectors of the hospital industry. In part this is due to the fact that the American Hospital Association, as the most powerful hospital industry organization, is compelled by its membership composition to represent the different interests of all three ownership sectors of the hospital industry (investor owned, voluntary not-for-profit, and public hospitals).[8] Thus, the AHA cannot go too far in endorsing either private market-based solutions (favored by the investor-owned hospitals) or public sector financing solutions (favored by public hospitals and the more progressive members of the voluntary hospital industry sector).[9] There is another, perhaps more cynical, argument that suggests that all three sectors of the hospital industry at least tacitly support the status quo in health care finance, because each sector of the hospital industry is well served by the system just as it exists. Investor-owned hospital corporations are able to return healthy profits to their shareholders, the voluntary hospitals also see acceptable returns on equity through their capacities to attract a sufficient proportion of insured patients, and public hospitals risk losing their patient base to the other more prestigious (or less stigmatized) privately owned hospitals should health insurance coverage be greatly expanded (Oliver & Dowell, 1994).[10]

Oliver and Dowell (1994) describe an instructive "natural experiment" of hospital industry behavior in the face of various potentially politically viable reform alternatives which occurred in California in the early 1990s. In 1992, when California's population of uninsured had reached one-quarter of the nonelderly, three different health insurance market reform proposals were introduced that for a time gained some political traction among either legislators or voters. The first was a plan that would have radically changed the rules of health insurance underwriting with the intended effect of making health insurance more accessible and affordable, while the second was a health insurance proposal that would have required all employers to provide basic health benefits for all employees and their dependents and absorb 75% of the cost health insurance premiums. The third proposal would have provided a uniform health insurance benefit package paid from payroll taxes and means-based worker contributions, framed by a managed competition restructuring of the insurance industry (Oliver & Dowell, 1994).

As noted by Oliver and Dowell (1994, p. 129), the fragmented ownership structure and internal divisions among California's hospitals precluded the industry from doing much more that "staying on the sidelines," while other groups fought for and against alternative reforms. Where the industry did take a clear stand, it involved opposition to proposals that would have introduced cost controls and insufficient hospital benefit provisions. Given the fact that this occurred at a point when one-quarter of California's working age families were not covered by health insurance, the lesson from the California hospital industry example seems to suggest that the hospital industry is unlikely to support fundamental health care reform to the extent that it involves significant compromise on the part of any particular sector of industry. Yet fundamental reforms in health care financing by definition must include such compromises. Thus, it seems that the prospects for fundamental health care reform are bleak to the extent that consensus from within the hospital industry is a precondition—at least barring a complete collapse of the mixed private and public insurance system that places all sectors of the industry in jeopardy.

The Health Care Reform Agendas of Disparate Employer Groups

As mentioned previously, employers are divided in their interests where major health care reforms are concerned. Large employers in industries that absorb the expenses of health care insurance premiums in their labor costs are not strongly averse to mandated health care coverage, though on principle large employers are in sympathy with small ones when it comes to resisting government regulation. To the extent that the insurance and tax burdens on large employers are increased by the health care costs of the uninsured, their interests diverge from those of small employers and sectors of the large employer industry that evade health benefit costs. Small employers, in large part represented by the National Federation of Independent Businesses and the U.S. Chamber of Commerce, oppose mandated employer health care insurance coverage for a variety of reasons, some more debatable than others.

Among the most debatable is the contention that the profit margins of small employers are insufficient to absorb the costs of health insurance. Strictly speaking, this is true, in that as long as some small employers in a given market can evade the costs of health insurance while others are burdened by them, those that absorb the significant costs of health insurance are less price competitive and more likely to go broke. Conversely though, proponents of mandated insurance coverage argue that universal employer mandates level the pricing playing field for all competitors. However, it must be acknowledged that in some small employer industries with a high degree of price-sensitive demand (like the restaurant industry), an across-the-board increase in prices might hurt the industry as a whole. Although the public supports universal health care coverage, it is not at all certain that they are willing to absorb the added costs of health care coverage for such incidental luxuries as a restaurant meal, a new permanent, or a visit to a movie theatre.

A less debatable issue behind the resistance of small employers to health insurance mandates is the fact that small employers, relative to large ones, are enormously disadvantaged when it comes to the costs of health insurance. As discussed in the chapter on health care finance (Chapter 3), small employers lack the capacity to self-insure like large ones, have less clout when it comes to negotiating health insurance premium pricing, and, most importantly, tend to draw a labor pool that is more disadvantaged with respect to education, income, and health. The kinds of health insurance reforms that small employers do support involve reforms in the regulation of the health insurance industry that would make health care coverage more affordable for many small employers. For example, the U.S. Chamber of Commerce supports a number of insurance reform aims of the PPACA although it characterizes the PPACA as a "1-2 trillion dollar takeover of health care" (U.S. Chamber of Commerce, 2009).

Where the interests and policy agenda of small employers and large employers from all sectors of the economy (manufacturing, service, union, and nonunion) most clearly converge are reforms that promise to constrain health insurance inflation and lower the costs of insurance premiums. Dominant among these reform measures are forms of health care insurance that place a higher threshold on the consumption of health care, like Health Savings Accounts, that make employees responsible for the first dollar costs of health care. In large part this agenda is driven by the globalization of markets that place U.S. industries at a disadvantage due to relative health insurance benefit costs, and the reemergence of rampant health care inflation after a temporary slowing in the early 1990s. Employers from all sectors of the economy have totally lost faith in the motivation and capacity of providers to reduce health care costs, and are now far more committed to a policy agenda that focuses on the demand side of health care costs—specifically the health utilization behaviors of consumers.

Perhaps the most significant recent development in the domain of employer stakeholders in health care policy has been the emergence of a new large employer business model that seeks aggressively to evade both unionization and health care benefits. In past decades, the dominant strategy of large nonunion employers seeking to avoid collective bargaining agreements involved the co-option of workers through preemptive wage and benefit concessions. In contrast, the Wal-Mart strategy both aggressively fights unionization and also recruits a labor force that is less likely (or able) to demand adequate health care benefits as a condition of employment. The success of this model has enabled Wal-Mart to undercut the pricing of other large retail employers, and it is speculated that this model will ultimately move beyond the retail industry into sectors of the economy that are becoming increasingly vulnerable to global competition (Inglehart, 2006). In the retail sector of the economy, this development has caused some convergence of interests between some traditional large employers that are striving to compete with Wal-Mart and organized labor in the promotion of state-level health care policy legislation that would require the largest employers to allocate a minimum proportion of their payroll to health care benefits.

The Health Care Reform Agenda of Organized Labor

Today, only roughly 1 in 10 American workers belongs to a labor union, in contrast to 50 years ago when the ratio was 1 in 3 (Bowers, 2005). However, the organized labor still speaks for the interests and agendas of the nation's nonmanagerial and nonprofessional workers. Indeed, the historical evidence strongly credits the organized labor movement for creating the governmental and nongovernmental social and health insurance systems that benefit all workers and their families (Rosner & Markowitz, 2003). Perhaps ironically, a significant share of the blame for the failure of national health insurance to take hold in the United States can also be laid at the feet of organized labor. Despite the voicing of at least nominal support for national health insurance at various junctures during the post-World War II era, in reality, the leaders of organized labor have often been as committed to a private employment-based health system as the health insurance industry itself. The central reason for this paradox has been the conflict between organized labor's espoused mission of promoting the health and welfare of American workers and their families and the role that health benefits have served as a tool of union recruitment since the Taft–Hartley Act of 1947 (Quadagno, 2004).[11] The historic ambivalence of organized labor toward national health insurance is also reflective of divisions within the labor movement between radicals and moderates, and between the workers of low-wage/benefit occupations (e.g., farm and service industry workers) and the more advantaged occupations (manufacturing and construction industry workers). Tragically for national health insurance, in the decades since the labor movement has become more unified in its support of radical health care, reform union membership has declined and the labor movement has lost much of its political clout.

The most interesting development, however, is at least the suggestion of a renascence of the labor movement represented by the ascendance of the Service Employees International Union (SEIU). Currently boasting in excess of 2.1 million members, the SEIU has been growing at a time when other unions struggle to maintain their membership. Because it represents the now dominant service sector of the economy, the SEIU has in many respects upstaged the venerable AFL-CIO as the leading edge of the American labor movement.[12] Unlike the AFL-CIO, which is heavily invested in the manufacturing sector of the economy and the survival of specific employers, the SEIU (like the building trades) is occupation-based and therefore much more portable in a dynamic economy where specific employers rapidly come and go (Milkman, 2005).

Both labor organizations support universal health care coverage as an alternative to what each decries as the collapse of the employer-based system, and both the AFL-CIO and SEIU endorse a single-payer approach as the ultimate solution (Healthcare-Now, 2009; SEUI, 2009). Both labor organizations also identify a similar short-term and long-term health care agenda. The short-term agenda highlights issues such as the protection of the existing health care benefits of workers and their families, supporting state and federal legislation that requires large employers to commit a proportion of their payroll to health benefits, and protecting the health care benefits of retired workers. The longer term health care agenda is the realization of universal health care insurance, and the political consensus on the mandated features of universal health insurance. As defined by the SEIU, these mandated features include (in addition to universal coverage) lowering the costs of health care, placing an emphasis on prevention, and assuring individual choice of doctors and health plans (SEIU, 2006). Despite the appeal of these policy objectives with labor and the public in general, it should be noted that there is an inherent and difficult to reconcile conflict between the objective to lower the costs of health care and the SEIU's mission to increase the wages and benefits of health care workers.

The Health Care Reform Agenda of the Health Insurance Industry

As described in Chapter 2, at a critical juncture during the administration of Franklin Roosevelt, the country turned toward a patchwork system of employer-sponsored voluntary health insurance and away from a federally sponsored health care trust fund that would have provided universal health care coverage. The critical force that propelled this choice was the vigorous opposition of the AMA to compulsory government health insurance. In more recent decades, the political clout of the AMA has greatly diminished and the fight has been taken up by AHIP (America's Health Insurance Plans, created by the merger of the Health Insurance Association of America and the American Association of Health Plans). AHIP is an organization that both reflects the political conservatism that is the hallmark of the finance and insurance industries and the particular interests that health insurance corporations have in protecting the private insurance market. Despite the not-for-profit roots of the health insurance industry and the original conceptions of health insurance coverage as a quasi-public good, the health insurance industry of today (both in the profit and the not-for-profit sectors) exists as a lucrative corporate enterprise with what many perceive as a pernicious grip on national health care policy.

The transformation of the health insurance industry from a beneficent arrangement between employers, workers, and providers to assure the affordability of health care to an industry largely dedicated to the interests of highly paid executives and shareholders occurred in stages over several decades. Clearly though, by the early 1960s the employment-based health insurance industry had enrolled enough of the labor force to become a major force in American health care policy with a clear stake in opposing publicly sponsored health care insurance (Scofea, 1994). Notably, the health insurance industry did not test its clout in opposition to the Medicare legislation of 1965, in large part because the industry's earlier forays into health insurance for the elderly had not been profitable. Instead, the insurance industry successfully sought to carve out a role for itself as the claims intermediary for the Medicare program and as the underwriter of supplemental insurance or the so-called Medigap policies (Quadagno, 2004). Thus, the health insurance industry's core interests are tied to the preservation of the fragmented patchwork of public and private health care financing arrangements that characterize the U.S. health care system's fundamental weaknesses.

Although there are multiple issues of interest to the health insurance industry that can be connected to the rubric of health care reform, the central interests of the industry converge on the general issues of cost control and protecting itself from further significant expansions of publicly financed health care—in particular, in the form of a single-payer health insurance trust fund that would marginalize the role of private health insurance to supplementary coverage.[13] The stake that the health insurance industry has in cost control has mostly to do with two overlapping issues: the insurance industry's general interest in tort reform that would place limits on the rewards of malpractice litigation, and the worry that unconstrained health care inflation will lead to the final collapse of employment-based insurance. Should that come to pass, a government takeover of health care financing appears all but inevitable.

Given all this, the private health insurance industry's core interests are best served by encouraging incremental solutions to health care inflation, the growing millions of uninsured, and the related problem of uncompensated care that threatens the health care safety net. The incremental approach both preserves the status quo and, if effectively pursued, keeps more radical reform on the margins of public opinion.

With respect to the PPACA, while the AHIP endorses its general approach of preserving a mix of public and private health insurance through subsidies to health insurance purchasing power of small employers and individuals and limited expansion of entitlement programs, AHIP vehemently opposes the insurance market provisions of the PPACA that threaten the profit margins of the industry. Central to this concern are the PPACA's provision that place a limit on insurance premium tax deductions for high-end health insurance plans and limits on the proportion of health insurance premiums that can be allocated to administrative expenditures and profits (AHIP, 2011).[14]

The Health Care Reform Agenda of the Pharmaceutical Industry

The lifeblood of the pharmaceutical industry is innovation and the preservation of profit margins sufficient to keep all types of investors happy.[15] As a result, for this industry, the optimal form of health care reform legislation involves the enactment of provisions that increase the subsidies to pharmaceutical consumers while both constraining competition and government price controls. The pharmaceutical industry has long recognized that to the extent that health care is financed by the federal government, the government has a larger stake in employing its regulatory power and market clout to limit the profits of the industry.[16] Thus, like the health insurance industry, the pharmaceutical industry has historically been a vigorous opponent of health care reform that would expand the federal role in the financing of health care (Common Cause, 1992; Quadagno, 2004).

In defense of the pharmaceutical industry's worries, the evidence from Europe indeed suggests that publicly financed health care brings with it lower profits for the pharmaceutical industry and a significant role in the targeting of the research and development (R&D) investment. However, evidence from the European experience does not suggest that either leads to a diminished commitment to R&D or inferior public benefits (Hutton, Borowitz, Oleksy, & Luce, 1994).

In the most recent decade, the pharmaceutical industry has abandoned its general opposition to expanded federal financing of health care for a more nuanced strategy that better achieves its vision of optimal policy (as previously stated, policies that increase the purchasing subsidies of consumers while constraining competition and federal cost controls). This can be characterized as a strategy that embraces selective opposition, cooperation, and co-option. This was first evidenced in the Medicare drug benefit package passed by Congress in 2003 (the Medicare Modernization Act of 2003), which critics claim was a piece of legislation written by the pharmaceutical industry for the pharmaceutical industry (Kuttner, 2006). The Medicare Modernization Act at once expanded the purchasing power of Medicare program beneficiaries but precluded the federal government from using its formidable pharmaceutical purchasing clout to negotiate favorable drug pricing. Thus the Medicare Modernization Act met the pharmaceutical industry's two key criteria for optimal health reform legislation: expansion of consumer purchasing power for pharmaceutical consumers without either constraints on the industry's anticompetitive practices or the incursion of government price controls (Iglehart, 2004).

The pharmaceutical industry's strategic shift toward cooperation and co-option has been most recently evidenced in PhRMA's (Pharmaceutical Research and Manufacturers of America) support of the PPACA in exchange for the Obama administration's pledge not to include provisions that would allow the federal government to negotiate for lower prescription drug prices for Medicare Prescription Drug Plans (Part D) beneficiaries, or sanction the importation of cheaper drugs from Canada or Europe (Medicare Newsgroup, 2012). Instead of being a major opponent of health care reform, as was the case with the Clinton administration's unsuccessful health reform effort, PhRMA was a major ally of the Obama administration's effort to pass the PPACA–to the tune of $150 million advertising campaign in support of health reform (Medicare Newsgroup, 2012). Whether or not this strategy pays out for the pharmaceutical industry in the long run is an open question. Certainly it can be said that in contrast to health insurance industry, the pharmaceutical industry has been largely spared from disparaging media attacks by proponents of health care reform and the Obama administration. On the other hand, to the extent that the PPACA provisions designed "bend the health care inflation curve" are effective, the pharmaceutical companies represented by PhRMA also stand to lose billions in future profits.[17] Whether this turns out to be the case likely depends upon the ultimate balance between reduced pharmaceutical expenditures for current public and private insurance plan beneficiaries, and the benefits accrued to the industry through expansion of insurance coverage to another 30 million Americans.

THE PATIENT PROTECTION AND AFFORDABLE CARE ACT (PPACA)

Background

The PPACA (P.L. 111–148) was signed into law by President Barack Obama on March 23, 2010, followed his signing of the Health Care and Education Reconciliation Act (P.L. 111–152) 1 week later.

Together, both pieces of legislation comprise the legislative framework of the PPACA, a comprehensive health care reform package that seeks to expand health insurance coverage to 93% of the national population,[18] control rising health care costs, and improve the health care delivery system. The structure of the PPACA is essentially consistent with the approach to health care reform advocated by Obama's 2008 presidential campaign platform; that is, the PPACA seeks to expand health insurance coverage to near universal coverage through a combination of regulatory insurance market reforms, insurance purchase mandates for individuals and employers, and expansions of public entitlement programs (Obama '08 Campaign, 2008). From the standpoint of history, the PPACA also represents the first successful effort by any of several presidential administrations (beginning with Franklin Delano Roosevelt in the 1930s) to pass legislation that would extend universal health insurance coverage to all American citizens.[19]

In contrast to other more radical approaches to health care reform, in particular, some form of a single-payer social insurance fund that would entail universal enrollment of all U.S. citizens and legal residents, the PPACA is a middle ground approach to health care reform that leaves the employment-based system of private health insurance intact while expanding both health insurance purchase subsidies to low-income households and public entitlement programs. The PPACA also imposes consumer-oriented health insurance market reforms, but favors the expansion of commercial health insurance enrollment over publicly funded health insurance. Finally, while the PPACA imposes some direct cost reductions on health care providers and eliminates a few inherently inflationary provider practices, the PPACA's central strategy for reducing the unsustainable growth in national health care expenditures focuses on the fostering of cost-effective approaches to health care through a combination of funding resources for the development of innovative practice models and financial incentives for cost-efficient provider organizations. The PPACA's implementation strategy is incremental; that is, the specific regulatory and entitlement provisions of the PPACA are phased in over a period of 8 years (2010 through 2018)—though most provisions are scheduled to be implemented by the end of 2014.

While years of public opinion surveys have consistently found strong majority for the idea of a government guarantee of health care for all who need it (Bodenheimer, 2005) and the PPACA is the first legislation intended to achieve that guarantee, the public is equally divided between those who favor the PPACA and those who oppose it (Kaiser Family Foundation, 2012). In part, this is attributable to the PPACA's complexity and a variety of misperceptions that have been promulgated by opponents—representing both adversely affected segments of the health care industry and groups who object to the PPACA on ideological grounds. However, the PPACA also has engendered worries among the general public about the growth in costly government entitlement programs and concerns about the effect of the PPACA on health care quality and choice.

The most controversial feature of the PPACA is the so-called "individual mandate," which requires U.S. citizens and legal residents to have qualifying health coverage by the year 2014. While the origins of the individual mandate as a legitimate and essential tool of health care policy are traced to the conservative Heritage Foundation and have been included in a number of health care reform proposals sponsored by Republican members of congress (Butler, 1989; Procon.org, 2012),[20] the PPACA's individual mandate has galvanized the libertarian wing of the Republican party (represented in the "Tea Party Movement") and been heavily exploited as a symbol of government overreach in electoral politics.[21] The individual mandate also raised a fundamental Constitutional question pertaining to the authority of the federal government to require that persons purchase commercial goods or services, which was the basis of a U.S. Supreme Court litigation considered by the court during the Spring of 2012.[22] This same package of U.S. Supreme Court litigation included a lawsuit filed by 26 states in opposition to the PPACA's requirement that states expand the number of state residents eligible for Medicaid program enrollment. While the Supreme Court ultimately upheld the Constitutionality of the individual mandate by a narrow majority, the court held that the federal government could not coerce states into expanding Medicaid enrollment.

Overview of the Essential Features of the PPACA

Since the PPACA seeks to expand health insurance enrollment to over 90% of the nation's population, increase in health care quality, and "bend the curve" of ever rising health care costs, while at the same time leaving an extremely complex mixed private/public model of health care financing intact, the PPACA is among the most complex packages of legislation ever promulgated by the federal government—which of course is saying a lot. Because the PPACA is over 2500 pages in length and entails 92 major provisions, only the PPACA's basic architecture and main features will be summarized, beginning with the PPACA's three major components: Insurance Market Reform, Coverage Expansion, and Health Care System Delivery Reform.

Insurance Market Reforms

The central paradox of the American health care system's approach to health care finance is that for the majority of the population that is dependent on commercial health insurance (those younger than 65 years and thus ineligible for Medicare), the more likely you are to need health care the less likely it is that you are covered by health insurance. There are four primary reasons for this:

- Ill health and disability are disproportionately prevalent among persons who are not eligible for affordable health insurance in the employment-based health insurance system—the unemployed and low-wage workers.
- Persons with preexisting health conditions are typically precluded from health insurance plan enrollment, and consistent with very basic principles of risk and insurance, health insurance underwriters are incentivized to market their services to only persons in good health—or to employers with healthier workers.
- For the sickest of the sick fortunate enough to possess an insurance card, their health care expenditures often exceed the limits and conditions of their health insurance coverage.
- For many potential purchasers of health insurance, particularly the young and healthy, it seems rational to avoid the high costs of health insurance and risk medical bankruptcy in the unlikely event of catastrophic illness or injury. In fact, for lower income persons in good health, it is a very rational decision to pay for rent, food, and other necessities of a decent life before paying for health insurance.

As discussed in Chapters 2 and 3, the emergence of this paradox was decades in the making, and can only be dismantled through either (1) the creation of a social insurance plan for health care or (2) fundamental reforms of the health insurance market that would impose new requirements on individuals, employers, and the private health insurance industry.

The PPACA of course represents the second approach, and it has provisions that address the following seven major reforms of the nation's private health insurance market:[23]

1. Elimination of lifetime limits on coverage for health care expenditures.
   Beginning in 2014, prohibit individual and group health plans from placing annual limits on the dollar value of coverage.
2. Elimination of "pre-exisiting conditions" clauses that exclude ill or disabled persons from insurance eligibility.
   Prohibit preexisting condition exclusions for children (effective 6 months following enactment) and prohibitions on preexisting condition exclusions for adults (effective 2014).
3. Imposing limits on out-of-pocket expense requirements.
   Create an essential health benefits package that provides a comprehensive set of services, covers at least 60% of the actuarial value of the covered benefits, limits

annual cost-sharing to the current law, establishes Health Savings Accounts (HSA) out-of-pocket limits ($5950 individual and $11,900 family in 2010), and is not more extensive than the typical employer plan. Require the Secretary to define and annually update the benefit package through a transparent and public process. (Effective 2014).

4. Imposing limits on the proportion of insurance premium costs that originate from administrative costs and profits.

   Require health plans to report the proportion of premium dollars spent on clinical services, quality, and other costs and provide rebates to consumers for the amount of the premium spent on clinical services and quality that is less than 85% for plans in the large group market and 80% for plans in the individual and small group markets. (Requirement to report medical loss ratio effective plan year 2010; requirement to provide rebates effective 2011.)

5. Requiring employers to provide employees with health insurance and individuals who are not eligible for employer insurance to purchase health insurance. These mandates are facilitated by tax penalties for enforcement and subsidies for the affordability of health insurance.

   (A) The Employer Mandate

   Assess employers with 50 or more employees that do not offer coverage (and have at least one full time employee who receives a premium tax credit) a fee of $2000 per full time employee, excluding the first 30 employees from the assessment. Employers with 50 or more full-time employees that offer coverage but have at least one full-time employee receiving a premium tax credit will pay the lesser of $3000 for each employee receiving a premium credit or $2000 for each full-time employee, excluding the first 30 employees from the assessment. Require employers with more than 200 employees to automatically enroll employees into health insurance plans offered by the employer. Employees may opt out of coverage. (Effective 2014).

   (B) The Individual Mandate

   Require U.S. citizens and legal residents to have qualifying health coverage. Those without coverage pay a tax penalty of the greater of $695 per year up to a maximum of 3 times that amount ($2085) per family or 2.5% of household income. The penalty will be phased-in according to the following schedule: $95 in 2014, $325 in 2015, and $695 in 2016 for the flat fee or 1.0% of taxable income in 2014, 2.0% of taxable income in 2015, and 2.5% of taxable income in 2016. Beginning after 2016, the penalty will be increased annually by the cost-of-living adjustment. Exemptions will be granted for financial hardship, religious objections, American Indians, those without coverage for less than 3 months,

> *undocumented immigrants, incarcerated individuals, those for whom the lowest cost plan option exceeds 8% of an individual's income, and those with incomes below the tax filing threshold.*

6. Defining and requiring a basic minimum benefit package for individual and group health insurance plans.

   Create an essential health benefits package that provides a comprehensive set of services, covers at least 60% of the actuarial value[24] of the covered benefits, limits annual cost-sharing to the current law HSA limits ($5950/individual and $11,900/family in 2010), and is not more extensive than the typical employer plan. Require the Secretary to define and annually update the benefit package through a transparent and public process. Further, require (except grandfathered individual and employer-sponsored plans) to offer at least the essential health benefits package. (Effective 2014).

7. Creating at the state level, health insurance co-ops and insurance exchanges in order to enhance the health insurance purchasing power of smaller employers and individuals.

   Create state-based American Health Benefit Exchanges and Small Business Health Options Program (SHOP) Exchanges, administered by a governmental agency or nonprofit organization, through which individuals and small businesses with up to 100 employees can purchase qualified coverage. Permit states to allow businesses with more than 100 employees to purchase coverage in the SHOP Exchange beginning in 2017. States may form regional Exchanges or allow more than one Exchange to operate in a state as long as each Exchange serves a distinct geographic area. (Funding available to states to establish Exchanges within one year of enactment and until January 1, 2015.)

Collectively, these seven reforms of the nation's private health insurance market represent very fundamental reforms that if fully implemented; (1) tip the balance in favor of the purchasers and consumers of health insurance over the financial interests of the insurance industry, (2) at least to a large extent, restore the private insurance industry to its original societal purpose—the promotion of access to health care and the protection of households from medical bankruptcy, (3) facilitate the affordability of health insurance to small employers and middle- to low-income Americans, and (4) make it far more possible for millions of sick and disabled persons to acquire affordable health insurance.[25]

First, by limiting the amount of health insurance coverage costs that can be applied to administrative expenditures and profits, the PPACA both rewards administrative efficiency and makes it more difficult for insurance companies (both profit and not-for-profit) to sustain lavish salary and benefit structures for high-level administrators. The profit limits in the PPACA also reduce the incentives for health insurance companies to engage in practices that compromise health care in order to enhance their bottomline (such as arbitrarily disallowing coverage for medically necessary care and imposing formidable bureaucratic obstacles to fair review). Second, by imposing individual and employer insurance coverage mandates, the PPACA reduces the extent to which problems of *moral hazard* and *adverse selection* undermine the viability and affordability of health insurance for individuals and populations that are at higher risk for health problems. That is, both mandates will facilitate the addition of healthy persons into the insurance pool, thereby reducing coverage costs for lower income and higher risk individuals. The individual mandate will also reduce the incentive for people to avoid the purchase of health insurance until they have reasons to need it, thus reducing the *moral hazard* problem that makes it necessary for health insurance plans to exclude coverage for pre-existing conditions. Third, by creating insurance exchanges and health insurance purchasing co-ops for individuals and small businesses, both individual insurance purchasers and small businesses can pool insurance risk and enjoy more bargaining clout in the health insurance marketplace. Finally, by imposing limits on out-of-pocket expenditures for insured persons and eliminating annual limits on coverage, the PPACA goes a long way toward eliminating the specter of medical bankruptcy among middle- and low-income individuals and households that carry health insurance.

As promising as these insurance market reform provisions of the PPACA are argued to be, they are functionally interdependent and must be fully implemented as planned. They also must work in accordance with the predictions of the insurance theory principles they are founded upon, at least largely, if not perfectly. Sweeping social policy provisions never work out completely as intended, but often in history have achieved their social aims through subsequent revisions and improvements. Whether or not this will be the case with the PPACA's health insurance market reforms depends in significant part on the politics of implementation—a subject to be considered in more depth at a later point in this chapter.

Health Insurance Coverage Expansion

The term "health insurance coverage" is being used broadly in the discussion that follows, to extend to public health care entitlement programs such as Medicaid as well as to private health insurance. As it is being used here for purposes of simplicity, having "health insurance coverage" means walking into a clinic or hospital with a plastic coverage card from a public or private health care plan that affords access to necessary care. At the point that the PPACA was signed into law in 2010, about 50 million persons in the United

States lacked such a coverage card, although disproportionately representative of the low income and poor increasingly representative of the middle class. By the time that the PPACA is fully implemented in 2019, the numbers of uninsured are predicted to be reduced (in proportional terms) to 21 million.[26] Although this leaves the population of uninsured at about 7% of U.S. residents, it brings the United States in alignment with the OECD's general standard of universal health insurance coverage for citizens and legal residents.[27] This approximation of universal health insurance coverage is achieved through three main PPACA policy strategies:

1. The provision of various forms of subsidies to individuals and employers for the purchase of health insurance, along with employer and individual insurance coverage mandates (as previously described).[28]

   (A) Individual subsidies

   Citizens and legal U.S. residents who are not provided qualifying health insurance through employment are eligible to receive health insurance premium tax credits and cost-sharing subsidies for health insurance plans offered by Health Insurances Exchanges.[29] Premium tax credits are available to individuals and families with incomes between 133% and 400% of the Federal Poverty Line. Premium tax credits apply to basic benefit insurance plans that pay on average 70% of covered health insurance benefits. What follows is the maximum premium contribution that an individual or family is required to provide as a share of annual income, at different levels of the Federal Poverty Line (FPL).[30]
   100–150% FPL: 94%
   150–200% FPL: 87%
   200–250% FPL: 73%
   250–400% FPL: 70%
   Cost-sharing subsidies, on the other hand, are provisions that protect lower income individuals and households (those below 250% of the FPL) from unaffordable out-of-pocket expenditures through allowing them to enroll in insurance plans that pay a greater share of covered benefits. The amount of additional protection varies with income, as follows:
   100–150% FPL: 94%
   150–200% FPL: 87%
   200–250% FPL: 73%

   (B) Employer Subsidies

   Small employers (less than 25 full-time equivalent employees) with an average employee salary of less than $50,000 dollars are eligible for health insurance benefit tax credits of up to 35% of the employer's contributions to health insurance for the years 2010 through 2013. Beginning

2014 and thereafter, the maximum small employer tax credit for health insurance contributions will be increased to 50%.[31]

2. The expansion of mandatory Medicaid eligibility criteria, supported by increased federal subsidies to states for newly eligible Medicaid enrollees.[32]

   Expands Medicaid eligibility to citizens and legal residents under age 65 (children, pregnant women, parents, and adults without dependent children) with incomes up to 133% FPL, based on modified adjusted gross income. To fund this Medicaid entitlement expansion, the PPACA provides federal funding to states for those who were not previously eligible for at least benchmark equivalent coverage, those who were eligible for a capped program but were not enrolled, or those who were enrolled in state-funded programs. States will receive 100% federal funding for these costs in the years 2014 through 2016, 95% federal financing in 2017, 94% federal financing in 2018, 93% federal financing in 2019, and 90% federal financing for 2020 and subsequent years.[33]

3. The promotion of state level "basic health plan" options

   The PPACA permits states to create a Basic Health Plan option for uninsured low-income individuals (those with incomes between 133% and 200% of the FPL), who would otherwise be eligible for health insurance premium subsidies for plans offered through Health Insurance Exchanges. These state "basic health plans" are required to offer basic insurance at the same premium cost as equivalent plans offered through Health Insurance Exchanges. The PPACA provides funds to states for their "basic health plan option" that is 95% of what would have been paid in premium tax credits and cost-sharing in Health Insurance Exchange sponsored plans.

In addition to the above three major strategies for the expansion of health insurance coverage to the currently uninsured, there are other important but relatively easily implemented measures, such as requiring that all individual and group plans extend the maximum age of coverage for adult children up to age 26 (this provision became effective in 2010).

The Basic Architecture of the PPACA's Approach to Health Insurance Market Regulation and Coverage Expansion.

Since the PPACA seeks to expand the affordability of health insurance to households at all levels of income, while at the same time reducing the pace of health care inflation within the structure of a mixed private and public health care system, it is very difficult to boil down to a concise and coherent synopsis. Figure 8.1 will at least provide readers with a basic schematic overview of the PPACA's major components of reform. The PPACA is described in Figure 8.1 as a "carrot and sticks" approach, because it entails mandated

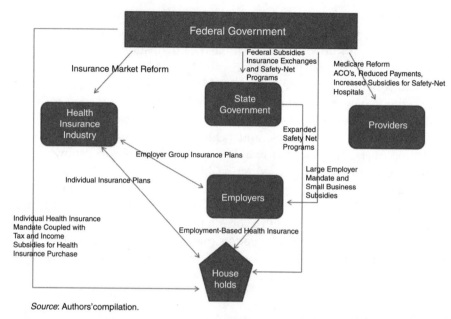

Source: Authors'compilation.

Figure 8.1 *The basic architecture of the PPACA's carrots and sticks approach to health care reform.*

directives, financial penalties for noncompliance (*sticks*), and subsidies and rewards (*carrots*) to facilitate choices by all of the players in the health care system that will lead to expanded health care coverage while curtailing the growth in national health care costs. The players in the health care system of course include the health insurance industry, employers, health care providers, state governments, and health care consumer households.[34]

To summarize the main points of Figure 8.1, under the PPACA, the federal government imposes reforms on the health insurance industry designed to make health insurance more accessible and affordable to households, while at the same time mandating that households either carry employment-based insurance, individual insurance, or if financially eligible enroll in means-based health care entitlement programs (e.g., Medicaid, SCHIP). The first line of federal provisions, shown on the far left of Figure 8.1, entails insurance coverage mandates and insurance purchase subsidies to households. The PPACA's second line of federal provisions involves health insurance market reforms that facilitate the affordability of basic health insurance to more households, particularly those that are disadvantaged in income and health status. The PPACA's third line of federal provision provides funds to states for both the creation of Health Insurance Exchanges and the expansion of means-tested health care entitlement programs (aka Safety-net programs). These state-targeted actions make health insurance coverage more affordable to individual health insurance purchasers and small businesses and expands the accessibility of health care entitlement programs to low-income households. The PPACA's fourth line of provisions targets the expansion of employment-based insurance coverage to households, through medium and large employer mandates to provide health insurance plans to employees, and health insurance benefit subsidies for small employers. The fifth and final line of federal provisions, shown on the far right of Figure 8.1, is focused on health care provider reforms that will: (1) protect the health care safety-net (those hospitals and clinics providing a disproportion share of care to the poor), (2) curb health care entitlement program inflation by reducing payments to providers, and (3) facilitate the creation of health care delivery models that will lead to higher quality care at lower cost. It is to this component of the PPACA's reform agenda we now turn—health care delivery system reforms.

Health Care Delivery System Reforms

A primary impediment to the universal health insurance coverage is that U.S. health care is already the most expensive health care system in the world, even with 50 million uninsured persons. As has been pointed out in previous chapters, at 17.3% of the GDP, the U.S. health care system is already outspending its OECD counterparts approximately 2:1. Perhaps one of the few areas of agreement between politicians from both the left and the right is the shared conviction that even current publically financed health care entitlements are unsustainable without some fundamental reforms of the health care delivery system. In addition, despite being the most technologically sophisticated health care system in the world, the U.S. health care system also has deeply embedded health care quality problems (IOM, 2000). Both of these deficits of the nation's current health care system are products of two interrelated aspects of the health care delivery system; fragmentation of patient care and provider incentives that reward higher levels of health care utilization rather than better patient outcomes. The health care delivery system reform components of the PPACA that are intended to address these fundamental problems include:

- Heavy investment in preventative health services
- Increased investment and payment incentives in primary care
- Significant investment in innovative approaches to the management of chronic disease

- Payment mechanisms that reward cost-effective clinical care
- Identification and elimination of inflationary provider incentives (such as proprietary doctor-owned hospitals)

While the specific details of these reforms of the health care delivery system go well beyond the scope of this brief synopsis of the PPACA, one particularly important PPACA delivery system reform provision will be considered in more depth—the nationwide development of Accountable Health Care Organizations for Medicare program beneficiaries.

Briefly described, Accountable Health Care Organizations (ACOs) are health care provider organizations that agree to be accountable for the overall care of their Medicare beneficiaries in return for the opportunity to participate in Medicare program cost savings. In order to qualify as an ACO, the organization must include primary care providers that care for at least 5000 Medicare beneficiaries; have a formal legal structure that includes a leadership and management structure; has systems in place that will provide data on health care cost and quality; and practice in accordance with the principles of evidence-based medicine, patient engagement, and patient centeredness (Lieberman & Bertko, 2011, p. 24). The evidence from studies that have found dramatic regional variation in the average Medicare lifetime costs per beneficiary, despite no evidence of differences in health outcomes, suggests that ACOs have the potential of dramatically reducing the growth in Medicare program expenditures without compromising quality (Wennberg, Fisher, & Skinner, 2002). For example, the Dartmouth Medical Atlas project's analysis of 2008 Medicare expenditures found that the difference between annual medical expenditures per beneficiary between Portland, Oregon ($6971) and Miami Florida ($15,571) was $8600—even with statistical controls for age, race, sex, and price (Skinner, Gottlieb, & Carmichael, 2011).[35] Although the PPACA regulations permit ACOs to adopt a variety of structures, because ACOs are accountable for the cost and quality of all services received by Medicare beneficiaries enrolled in the ACO, the ACOs must integrate care and reimbursement across the full range of care (Leiberman & Bertko, 2011). That is, instead of each component of care operating within its own patient care data management and fee-generating "silo," successful ACOs will have to create integrated patient care data managements systems, clinical case management models, and payment structures that flow between the traditionally isolated "silos" of primary care, specialty care, acute hospital care, rehabilitation care, skilled nursing home care, and home health care.

Figure 8.2 provides an illustration of the difference between the traditional Medicare beneficiary "silo" provider structure, and a model ACO provider structure that is promoted under the Medicare program reforms

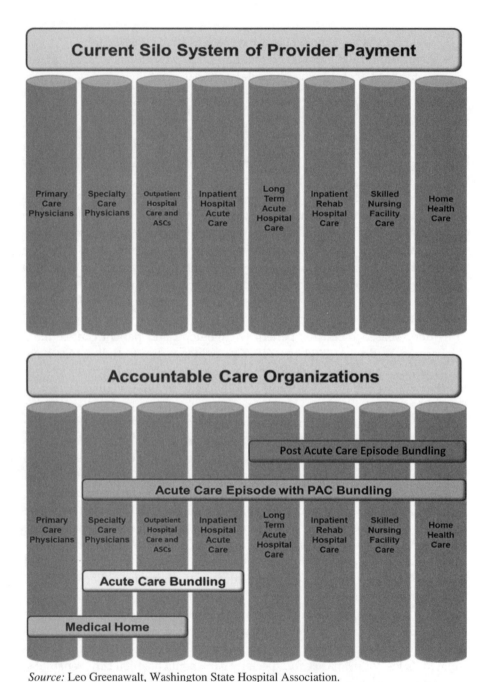

Source: Leo Greenawalt, Washington State Hospital Association.
Lecture UW School of Social Work, October 19, 2010. Used by permission.

Figure 8.2 *Illustration of accountable health care organization (ACO) Medicare reform provision.*

embedded in the PPACA. The "medical home" component of the ACO (also referred as the "patient-centered medical home") is a model of primary care that operates on a set of principles that include an ongoing relationship with a medical provider, a whole person orientation that includes care for all stages of life; acute care; chronic care; preventive services; and end-of-life care and care that is coordinated and integrated across all elements of the complex health care system.[36] "Bundling" refers to a provision of the PPACA that encourages the use of a single negotiated payment for all provider services used during a single episode of care, as opposed to individual fees for each health care service. Aside from being a simpler reimbursement structure, the bundled payment approach creates incentives to provide more cost-efficient integrated care (PAC refers to "post-acute care" payment bundling).

Political Analysis of the PPACA as Successful Social Policy

Successful social policy entails three accomplishments. First, the policy must be implemented as designed. Second, the policy must achieve its basic aims. Third, the policy's unintended consequences must not be so detrimental as to outweigh its intended benefits. Most social policy innovations, at least in their initial form, end up falling short on at least one of these criteria of success. For comprehensive omnibus social policy innovations that entail complex regulations and political actors at multilevels of government, this is particularly the case. Historically, such complex and sweeping policy innovations, where ultimately successful, achieve their accomplishments in a protracted series of revisions that adapt both to political realities and what is learned over the course of implementation. In this vein, social policy historian Theda Skocpol draws parallels between the PPACA and both the Social Security Act of 1935 and the 1965 expansion of the Social Security Act that established Medicare. Similar to the PPACA in scope and complexity, both of these ultimately successful examples of comprehensive social legislation underwent significant reforms between initial versions and their current forms (Skocpol, 2010).

There are at least eight major political threats to the implementation and ultimate success of PPAC:

The PPACA's Usefulness as a Target and Tool of Partisan Politics

On March 24, 2010, the day after President Barack Obama signed the PPACA into law, the Des Moines Register published a guest opinion article by the then House Minority Leader John Boehner that called the health care reform legislation a "massive government takeover of health care" and pledged that his party repeal it (Boehner, 2010). This characterization of the PPACA belies the fact that the PPACA is largely based on an approach to health care that seeks to preserve a system of health care that is predicated on medical free enterprise, consumer choice, and a system of financing that places emphasis on the expansion of commercial health insurance. It is also a plan of health care that implements, a national scale, the approach to universal health insurance advocated and implemented by Republican party presidential candidate Mitt Romney during his tenure as governor of Massachusetts. These inconsistencies suggest that the vehement and vitriolic condemnation of the PPACA (derisively referred to as Obamacare)[37] is far more political than genuinely ideological. That is, the PPACA standing as the most significant social legislation of the Obama presidency means that it is in the opposition party electoral interests to attack the legislation on whatever grounds are likely to appeal to the doubts and fears of the American public. Because the PPACA is complex, difficult to comprehend, and inclusive of a number of provisions that adversely affect the interests of powerful stakeholders, its vilification is strategically irresistible and also essential to the opposition party—independent of either its potential merits or deficits as sound social policy.

PPACA's Status as Redistributive Social Welfare Policy

Although there is little direct reference to it in partisan attacks on the PPACA, the PPACA is redistributive social legislation. That is, there are provisions of the PPACA that benefit the poor and low income at net cost to the better off. A particular example of this are the PPACA's imposition of an excise tax on the health insurance premiums of the most expensive high benefit plans— those health insurance plans that are more prevalent among high-income households.[38] While the intent of this provision is to reduce some of the inflationary incentives that are built into the health care system, in effect, it takes from the rich (at least in the health care benefits sense) in order to make health care more affordable to everyone else—particularly the low income. In addition, by expanding means-tested health insurance entitlements, the PPACA is subsidizing low-income and poor households through federal and state taxes on the more affluent. Redistributive are an anathema to conservatives and libertarians, and even more centrist voters place a high threshold on the justifiability of redistributive social policies (Katz, 2008; Skocpol, 2010).

The Vulnerability of PPACA to "Death From 1000 Cuts" Through Litigation and Legislation at All Levels

As pointed out previously, the PPACA is a massive package of legislation that entails hundreds of new and amended regulations across multiple agencies at both the federal and state levels of government, as well as myriad policy guidelines that will be written as PPACA is implemented (CMS, 2010; Skocpol, 2010). While new regulations have the force law, they also can be opposed by local governments and agencies in the judicial branch. Within the first year of its being signed into law, 26 states had sued in opposition to both the individual mandate and the PPACA's mandatory expansion of Medicaid eligibility standards, and even though the PPACA survived this initial legal challenge more are sure to follow. In addition, even unambiguous policy initiatives with limited scope are subject to the slings and arrows of oppositional and recalcitrant state-level bureaucrats. In metaphorical terms, the PPACA is akin to a large ship of unproven design, headed for a distant destination shore across uncharted waters, with a muttering if not mutinous crew, a few bickering officers, and some very worried passengers.[39]

Constitutional Challenges

The litigation brought before the U.S. Supreme Court in opposition to the PPACA in 2012 concerned three issues: (1) whether the powers given to the federal government under the U.S, Constitution's "commerce clause" extend to the imposition of individual mandates to either carry or purchase health insurance, (2) whether, in the event that the individual mandate is found unconstitutional, other PPACA provisions that are not directly related to the individual mandate can remain the law of the land, and (3) whether or not the federal government can require that states expand the number of people eligible for assistance from the state under the Medicaid program.[40] The first issue was the most crucial. Without the individual mandate to carry insurance being the law of the land, the PPACA's insurance regulations requiring insurance companies to issue insurance policies to persons with preexisting conditions would have been economically unviable; in not requiring that healthy younger individuals enter insurance risk pools, health insurance will be unaffordable to higher risk segments of the population (Congressional Research Service, 2011). The general consensus among health policy experts was that should the individual mandate provision have been ruled unconstitutional, the PPACA as a whole would ultimately be deemed a policy failure.

In a decision that stunned legal experts from both sides of the PPACA litigation before the U.S. Supreme Court, in the early summer of 2012 the court narrowly ruled in a 5 to 4 decision in favor of the constitutionality of the individual mandate—but not as lawful extension of the federal government's authority to regulate interstate commerce as had been argued by lawyers representing the Obama administration. Instead, the majority opinion argument in favor of the constitutionality of the PPACA's individual mandate (as another shocker written by conservative Chief Justice John Roberts) found that the enforcement provisions of the individual mandate fell within the federal government's constitutional authority to levy taxes.

With respect to the PPACA's Medicaid expansion provisions, the 2012 Supreme Court ruling was more mixed. In essence, while the court held that the federal government could induce states to expand Medicaid eligibility to a larger share of the uninsured through the availability of additional federal Medicaid dollars, the federal government could not coerce states to expand Medicaid eligibility through the withholding of federal Medicaid dollars for already established programs. In effect, this means that some states may choose to forgo millions in added federal dollars to reduce the ranks of their uninsured in favor of fairly meager savings in state Medicaid funds. To the extent that states make this policy choice for either fiscal or ideological reasons, as several had voiced the intent to do so in the wake of the Supreme Court's 2012 ruling, the PPACA's ability to achieve near universal health care will be substantially undermined.

In sum, while in 2012 the U.S. Supreme Court ruled largely in favor of the constitutionality of the PPACA's core provisions, as other parts of this complex legislation are implemented over the next several years, well financed opponents are likely to raise other constitutional challenges on a piecemeal basis—with results that are as difficult to predict as the PPACA litigation that was considered by the court in 2012.

The Complexity of the PPACA

If the United States is to achieve near universal coverage within the framework of a mixed public and private system that seeks to preserve both medical free enterprise and a high level of consumer choice over health plans and providers, it must necessarily be complex. Even a relatively concise synopsis of the PPACA's essentials consumed many pages of this book—targeted as it is to an already knowledgeable audience of health care professionals. For the general public, even the most basic public explanations of the PPACA are subject to obfuscation and political framing by adversely affected health care industry stakeholders and politicians, leaving about half of the American adults polled with a sense of confusion about both the specifics of the PPACA and whether or not their interests are served by the PPACA (Kaiser Family Foundation Tracking Poll, 2012).

Among Progressives, Ideological Division and Ambivalence About the PPACA

According to the results of a national tracking poll conducted by the Kaiser Family Foundation in March of 2012 (Kaiser Family Foundation, 2012), while most people who identify with the Democratic party expressed support of the PPACA (64%), that support was nearly evenly split between those who strongly favor the PPACA and those who identify themselves as only "somewhat favorable." On the other hand, respondents to the same national tracking poll who identified with the Republican party were much more unified in their strong opposition to the PPACA. The somewhat lukewarm support for the PPACA among political progressives is largely attributable to a preference for a more radical and inclusive approach to health care reform; specifically, a single-payer social insurance fund that would cover more of the insured, be less expensive and complex to administrate, and would also be more egalitarian. That is, there is pervasive sentiment among the more left leaning political progressives that the PPACA retains too much of a broken and unfair health care system. In addition, the PPACA's exclusion of undocumented immigrant workers from eligibility for health insurance coverage is troubling to the many progressives who recognize the essential contributions that undocumented workers make to the national economy.

Opposition of Powerful Stakeholders, Most Notably AHIP

In contrast to the Clinton administration's health care reform legislation of two decades ago, the PPACA has enjoyed more support from health care industry key stakeholder groups—in particular, the powerful pharmaceutical industry.[41] On the other hand, other critical players in the health care industry strongly oppose the PPACA—at least in its current form. The most powerful stakeholder in the oppositional camp is America's Health Insurance Plans (or AHIP), which opposes the PPACA on a number of grounds, in particular, the provision that reduces the share of health insurance premium dollars can be used for the insurance company's administrative costs and profit margin (AHIP, 2011). While most other key health care industry stakeholder groups have voiced general support for the PPACA in order to retain their political influence over its provisions, as compromise legislation the PPACA requires that every health care industry stakeholder make sacrifices. In effect, this means that to the extent that different provisions of the PPACA run counter to the interests of any particular health care industry stakeholder, they will continue to make efforts to amend or repeal unfavorable provisions on a piecemeal basis—even if the PPACA as a whole is not directly opposed. Thus, the proponents of the PPACA need to worry as much about the possibility that the PPACA will be fatally co-opted by lukewarm stakeholders as much as they must worry about the possibility of outright repeal.

Unintended Consequences

As mentioned earlier in this chapter, all social policies that make their way to enactment create unintended consequences. This is because social policies are at their core are a social experiment based on selected theories of collective human behavior, which tend to have flaws either in principle or in application. For example, a particularly worrisome plausible unintended consequence of the PPACA is the possibility that adding millions of previously uninsured to the demand base for primary care will overwhelm already strained primary care clinics and thus compromise quality of care, as happened when universal coverage was implemented in the state of Massachusetts (Sack, 2008). The other possibility is that the expansion of Medicaid coverage to near poor adults will cost much more than has been predicted as health conditions that have been previously undiagnosed become the basis of unprecedented levels of health care utilization among the previously uninsured. While on the one hand, the reduction of health care access disparities among the low income is central to the PPACA's purpose, on the other, the costs of treating heretofore neglected health conditions on an unprecedented scale may be far more extensive than anticipated. There are also unintended consequences that pertain to the social divisions that arise as over social policies that entail a universalistic approach. This has already occurred with the political backlash that ensued in response to the PPACA's inclusion of coverage for contraception as the minimum requirements for basic benefits were defined by the Department of Health and Human Services (HSS) in late 2011, which brought vehement opposition from some groups representing religiously affiliated employers who argued that the PPACA compelled them to provide benefits that ran counter to their religious principles.[42] As more of the specific guidelines and administrative regulations of the PPACA are fleshed out in the process implementation, we can expect similar kinds of "culture war" backlashes.

Principled Analysis of the PPACA as Just Social Policy

A principled analysis of the PPACA refers to examining the merits of the legislation's approach to health care reform in light of the basic principles of alternative theories of social justice. Since an in-depth principled analysis of the PPACA through the lens of the five theories of justice highlighted in this book could easily extend to at least another book or two, we must content ourselves with a very basic and concise synopsis of the ways in which the PPACA either reflects or runs counter the basic principles of these five theories. Following the order of the theories as they were considered in Chapter 1, we will begin with the Libertarian approach to social justice.

A Libertarian Analysis of the PPACA

The Libertarian perspective, because its principles place its primary emphasis on limited government, individual self-responsibility, and unencumbered free choice, would oppose the PPACA on a number of grounds. Primary among them are the PPACA's expansion of the federal government's financing and regulatory control of the health care industry, the PPACA's expansion of publically financed entitlement programs and nature as redistributive social policy, and finally and most fatally from a Libertarian perspective, the requirement that individuals carry some form of health insurance—which represents both an abrogation of individual liberty rights and government intrusion into private health and health care choices. From a Libertarian point of view, the only fundamental features of the PPACA that might win favor is that it preserves the private insurance market from medical free enterprise, and significant consumer choice in the selection of insurance plans and health care providers. That is to say, from a Libertarian perspective, the PPACA is favorable only to the extent that it is a lesser evil than a social insurance approach to universal health care (in essence, some form of a single-payer plan).

A Utilitarian Analysis of the PPACA

The central evaluation from a Utilitarian perspective is whether the PPACA in its full implementation achieves the maximum good averaged over the maximum number of people (Rescher, 1966). In the context of health care, this would be generally defined as the systems of health care that would yield the highest levels of average population health relative to dollars invested in health care. While the PPACA seeks to expand the capacity of the health care system while restraining the growth in expenditures, consistent with the core Utilitarian principle, it preserves a mixed private and public model of health care delivery that is far less efficient than other approaches that yield far better population health outcomes relative to the dollars invested in health care. From this perspective, while the PPACA is a policy improvement over the status quo in American health care, it does not nearly approach the efficiency of reform models that place more emphasis on a public social insurance approach and a direct government role in health care infrastructure investments. From a Utilitarian perspective, France, which has the lowest death rate from health conditions that are amenable to health care of all OECD nation states despite spending only one half of the dollars per capita for health care than is spent in the U.S. (Nolte & McKee, 2008; OECD, 2011), would be a far superior model of health care reform. In contrast to the PPACA approach, which preserves private health insurance as the dominant form of coverage, France finances 75% of its health care through a universal public insurance fund and private health insurance plays only a supplementary role.

A Marxist Analysis of the PPACA

The Marxist perspective is quite forthright in its assertion that in a just society there is a positive right to health care that extends to all. As pointed out in Chapter 1, Marx's famous dictum that a post-revolutionary socialist society would assure that "each contributes according to their ability and receives according to their need" strongly suggests themes of equity and commonwealth as core to the purposes of society and its social welfare provisions (Wolff, 2003). In addition, Marxist social philosophy also is particularly hostile to the exploitation of labor and private ownership of the means of production. The PPACA only reflects Marxist principles to the extent that it both seeks to expand health insurance coverage to a larger share of workers and their families and define a set of minimum health care benefits that are commiserate with fundamental human needs. Where the PPACA particularly fails by Marxist social philosophy is (1) its treatment of health care as a marketable commodity vs. a universal need-based entitlement, (2) its preservation of a system of health care financing that allocates quality of health care by social class, (3) its accommodation of private ownership of much of the nation's health care infrastructure, and (4) the PPACA's exclusion of a significant segment of the working class from entitlement to even basic health care—specifically undocumented workers and their dependents. In sum, because the PPACA attempts to create only a partially inclusive limited health care entitlement to health care while preserving the essential features of a capitalist medical industrial complex,[43] it is inherently inconsistent with a Marxist social justice framework.

A Liberal Theory Analysis of the PPACA

As discussed in Chapter 1, while John Rawls argued for a positive right for health care based upon his "fair equality of opportunity" principle in his final reformulation of his theory,[44] it was left to philosopher Norman Daniels to fully extend Rawls's theory to the specifics of a positive right to health care (Daniels, 2008). To recapitulate, readers might recall that Daniels emphasized that realization of "fair equality of opportunity" would necessarily encompass six health needs essential to "normal human functioning," which in turn would be a precondition to "fair equality of opportunity." These six health needs were identified by Daniels (2008, pp. 42–43) as

1. Adequate nutrition
2. Sanitary, safe, unpolluted living and working conditions
3. Exercise, rest, and such important lifestyle features as avoiding substance abuse and practicing safe sex
4. Preventative, curative, rehabilitative, and compensatory personal medical services (and devices)
5. Nonmedical personal and social support services
6. An appropriate distribution of other social determinants of health.

The PPACA, because it concerns itself with the promotion of universal access to basic and essential health *care*, limits its provisions primarily to the health needs subsumed under "4. Preventative, curative, rehabilitative, and compensatory personal medical services (and devices)." The remaining five health needs pertain primarily to the *social* determinants of health that reside outside the health care system, for example, structural arrangements and social policies that prevent and alleviate poverty. That said, there are some provisions of the PPACA that can be extended to "3. Exercise, rest, and such important lifestyle features as avoiding substance abuse and practicing safe sex;" in particular, those components of the PPACA that address preventative health care.

Aside from the extent to which the PPACA provides universal coverage of provisions that satisfy the six health needs that are argued to be essential to the realization of "fair equality of opportunity," there is the question of whether the mixed public and private health care model of health care financing also satisfies Liberalism's particular concerns with equity. In Daniel's interpretation of Rawls's Liberal Theory of justice, the primary good that carries the full weight of Liberalism's equity principle is "fair equality of opportunity," not health care per se (Daniels, 2008, p. 57). That is, if a health care system satisfies the health needs that pertain specifically to fair equality of opportunity, equity of health care is not a principled concern. Thus, Daniels takes a somewhat agnostic position toward the various ways a health care system might be organized to satisfy Liberalism's principles of justice:

"What forms of organization—public or private administration and financing—are implied is not a question to which just health provides a unique answer. There are probably an array of 'just enough' institutional structures that can provide the needed protection of opportunity" (2008, p. 144).

However, Daniels is unequivocal about the central principle of the Liberal justification for a positive right to health care; that "fair equality of opportunity" requires universal access to health care for all that is devoid of all obstacles–financial, geographic, racial, etc." (p. 143). This is then the primary lens through which we evaluate the extent to which the PPACA satisfies Liberalism's criteria for reform of the American health care system that meets the demands of justice.

Since the PPACA, if fully implemented, both expands access to heretofore uninsured segments of the population (primarily the working poor and lower income individuals and families in general) and also defines a basic benefits package for all health insurance plans that satisfies the health needs that pertain specifically to health care (preventative, curative, rehabilitative, and compensatory personal medical services and devices), Liberalism would hold that the PPACA is a major moral improvement over the current health care system. A Liberal theory evaluation of the PPACA's insistence on the preservation of a mixed public and private system of health care financing and delivery would also find the PPACA to be acceptable, as long as there would be no obstacles to universal access to health care that are consequent to the mixed public and private approach to health care favored by the PPACA.

As it happens, though, there are significant shortcomings in the PPACA that create formidable obstacles to health care access for various segments of the population. First and foremost, because the PPACA excludes undocumented workers and their dependents from the PPACA, it perpetuates obstacles to care that correspond to race, ethnicity, and class. While it might be argued that as noncitizens and unlawful residents, undocumented immigrants are not party to the social contract that is the foundation of Rawls's Liberal theory of justice, this runs completely counter to Rawls's theory of a just society as a "unified and fair system of cooperation for reciprocal advantage between free and equal citizens" (Rawls, 2001, p. 22). That is to say, because exploitive immigration and labor market policies that promote the use of undocumented immigrant labor as a means of raising the standard of living for those granted the privilege of citizenship care are an anathema to Rawls's vision of a just society, the undocumented stratus of immigrant workers and their dependents cannot serve as a just basis for exclusion from otherwise universal entitlements to health care.

A second major shortcoming of the PPACA by the criteria of "absence of obstacles to universal health care–financial, geographic, racial, etc." pertains to the PPACA's lack of sufficient attention to significant disparities in access to health care by geography, race, and the intersections of both. As discussed in Chapter 2, the provider infrastructure of the American health care system (physicians, diagnostic and curative technologies, and hospitals) has been driven more by the geography of affluence and the incentives of medical free enterprise than by the geography of population health disparities. In particular, both the urban poor and poor rural populations encounter significant obstacles to health care access that are as much about the lack of local health care infrastructure as health insurance status (AHRQ, 2011). While the PPACA contains provisions that are intended to ameliorate geographic and income disparities in health care infrastructure, they are of insufficient scope and magnitude to largely eliminate the obstacles to health care that reflect decades of disparities in health care infrastructure investment.

A third major shortcoming of the PPACA from the standpoint of Liberalism's central health care access principle, is its emphasis on the expansion of a highly stigmatized means-tested entitlement program, Medicaid, as the principle form of health insurance for the poor and low income, as opposed to an approach that would either incorporate a public health insurance option open to enrollees at all income levels or a private insurance voucher approach. As pointed out in Chapter 3, the possession of a Medicaid card does not translate to the same level of health care access as the possession of a health insurance card. In part, this is because Medicaid reimbursement for provider services is often inadequate to the expenses incurred and administratively cumbersome to recover. Beyond this problem, the possession of a Medicaid card also carries with it the stigma of poverty and dependency (Stuber & Kronebusch, 2004; Stuber & Schlenger, 2006), thus imposing a shaming penalty on the bearer for accessing care.

While the three Liberal theory objections to the PPACA described here are not necessarily the only ones, they are significant. That said, it should be recognized that the PPACA also represents the most ambitious health care reform legislation signed into law in nearly 50 years, and in full implementation would afford access to health care for well over 90% of the population. Perhaps most crucially, even in flawed form, the PPACA represents an unprecedented societal commitment to the idea of health care as a universal entitlement that is justified by the moral principle of "fair equality of opportunity."

A Capabilities Approach Analysis of the PPACA

As a comparative framework of social justice, the Capabilities Approach (CA) does not specify any particular model of just social arrangements or specific policies that would realize a vision of perfect justice (Sen, 2009). As discussed in Chapter 1, the CA evaluates the moral superiority of different societal arrangements and policies through the extent to which they fulfill the manifest obligation of society to foster the real opportunities (capabilities) of individuals to do and be what they have reason to value. As also discussed in Chapter 1, the most well formulated and comprehensive application of the CA to question of just health and health care policy comes from Sridhar Venkatapuram's *Health Justice* (Polity Press, 2012). Drawing on the CA writings of Martha Nussbaum (*Women and Human Development: The Capabilities Approach*, Cambridge University Press, 2000), Venkatapuram (2012) defines the "Capability to be Healthy" (CH) as a person's ability to achieve or exercise a cluster of basic capabilities and functioning—which in turn are understood as a "meta-capability" to achieve and exercise Nussbaum's 10 central human capabilities (p. 143).[45] The CH (as a "meta-capability") would therefore necessitate conceptualization of a right to health as a "cluster-right," that is, an entitlement that can only be realized through a combination of other rights, claims, privileges, protections, and powers (p. 163)—which include health care entitlements. In sum, in the CH framework, the PPACA would be seen not as comprehensive health policy, but as an approach to the provision and financing of health care entitlements.

Since CH has not advanced to the point where specific health care entitlements are delineated in a systematic way (Venkatapuram, 2012), we are left to discern the ways in which the PPACA approach to health care entitlements advances the most basic of all health capabilities; life itself. In the language of Nussbaum's list of Central Human Capabilities, this would be "[B]eing able to live to the end of a human life of normal length; not dying prematurely, or before one's life is so reduced as to be not worth living" (Nussbaum, 2000, p. 78). From this perspective, the PPACA is clearly a moral improvement over the current system of heath care entitlements—primarily because it improves access to needed health care at all stages of the life course for a larger share of the national population. The PPACA also seeks to promote a model of health care that is holistic and patient centered, which is responsive to other Central Human Capabilities as identified by Nussbaum. However, the flaws of the PPACA that conflict with the principles of Liberal theory would also extend to the CH framework: exclusion of coverage to immigrant workers, the PPACA's limited provisions for the amelioration of geographic and racial disparities in health care infrastructure, and the PPACA's reliance on stigmatizing means-tested Medicaid entitlements for those already marginalized by poverty and low-wage employment.

CONCLUDING COMMENTS: TOWARD A PROGRESSIVE VISION OF UNIVERSAL HEALTH CARE

Despite its flaws and uncertain future, the PPACA represents a sea of change in politics of health care reform. No matter what happens to individual parts of the PPACA or the legislative package as a whole, its passage in 2010 shifted the national discourse toward the ideological premises and pragmatics of a health care system that provides universal health care coverage—as opposed to debates over the legitimacy of universal health care coverage as a priority of just governance. In political terms, the proponents of the PPACA are at risk for the public opinion fallout that will ensue should the PPACA fail to achieve its goals of expanding coverage while "bending the cost curve" and create significant unintended consequences. On the other hand, the politicians that have condemned the PPACA and advocated its repeal take full ownership of a health care system that is fundamentally broken and fiscally unsustainable.[46]

Ultimately, health care reform is inevitable, whether or not it takes the form of the PPACA or other legislation. In fact, in the very possible event that the PPACA is either repealed by Congress or extensively modified, what *should* health care reform look like—either as an improved version of the PPACA or an altogether different approach in the near future?

From the standpoint of Rawls's final formulation of his theory of justice (*Justice as Fairness: A Reformulation*, Harvard University Press, 2001), most of the PPACA's provisions that pertain to a universal minimum standard of basic health care benefits, improvements in health care quality, and cost reductions would be entirely consistent with the Rawls's principles of justice. In this respect, the interpretation of how Rawls's theory might view the PPACA seems consistent with that of Norman Daniel's most extension of Rawls's theory of justice to just health and health care policy (*Just Health: Meeting Health Needs Fairly*, Cambridge University Press, 2008). Where this book differs from Daniel's (2008) account of the minimal requirements of a just health care system is more specificity on the health care financing arrangements that are essential to the requirements of justice.

Limited Entitlement Universal Social Insurance Fund/Private Insurance Residual

DESCRIPTION

A limited array of primary goods health care entitlements through a universal trust fund, specifically those "that are deemed essential to fair equality of opportunity and each individual's capacity to take advantage of the basic rights and liberties essential to citizenship" (paraphrased from Rawls, 2001, p. 174). The distribution of these primary good health care entitlements will be based upon the two principles of justice, modified from Rawls (2001, pp. 42–43) to read as follows:

1. Each person has the same claim to a full adequate scheme of equal basic health care entitlements, which scheme is compatible with the same scheme of entitlements for all; and
2. Disparities in either access to essential health care entitlements, or in the quality of health care entitlements provided, are presumptively unjust, and defensible only where they are demonstrably linked to superior health care benefits for the least advantaged.

Health care benefits that are of lower order, in that they provide coverage for health care services and technologies that attend to individual ends like happiness, life satisfaction, and subjective quality of life rather than fair equality of opportunity, are treated as ordinary commodities obtained through either voluntary health insurance or out-of-pocket purchase.

While Daniels (2008, p. 144) correctly observes that "[t]here are probably an array of 'just enough' institutional structures that can provide the needed protection of opportunity," it is argued here that approaches to health care financing that relegate the most disadvantaged segments of the population to means-tested health care entitlement programs are inherently incompatible with the demands of justice. Means-tested entitlement programs, unlike social insurance programs, are perpetually subject to unstable funding allocations and the stigmatizing of beneficiaries. Thus, means-tested health care entitlement programs cannot satisfy Daniel's central principle of the Liberal justification for a positive right to health care; that 'fair equality of opportunity' requires universal access to health care for all that is devoid of all obstacles—financial, geographic, racial, etc." (p. 143). Taking the specific example of New Orleans in August of 2005 (Hurricane Katrina), the possession of a Medicaid card placed patients in Charity Hospital and the abandonment that followed, whereas the possession of a private health insurance card placed patients in Tulane University hospital and evacuation to safety.

A system of health care financing that is more compatible with the demands of justice while accommodating tastes and demands for health care that are not essential to "fair equality of opportunity," is an approach that combines a universal social insurance fund essential health care entitlements with a vibrant private health insurance market. This structure of health care financing, which is akin to the Medicare program for adults aged 65+, both limits the scope of universal benefits to those that are deemed essential and directly related to critical domains of social functioning and provides an outlet for less essential health care demands to the private health insurance.

While such an approach retains some semblance of a two-tiered health care system, the evidence from international comparisons demonstrates that this is unavoidable in a heterogeneous society with market economy (OECD, 2011). The approach that is advocated here as that which is most compatible with Rawls's to principles of justice is summarized in the highlighted box on page 368.

There are two fundamental challenges to this model of health care reform. The first of course is political. The PPACA only squeaked through Congress under the condition that a federal public insurance option that had been in the original framework of the PPACA be dropped, largely at the behest of Connecticut Senator Joe Lieberman, who had close ties with the private health insurance industry.[47] The health insurance industry *correctly* viewed the public insurance option as a "Trojan Horse" federalized public insurance structure that would both bring down health insurance prices and speed the transition to a universal health care entitlement based on a social insurance model. With or without the PPACA success, this remains a distinct possibility as a future path to a universal social insurance fund for health care for three reasons:

1. There is strong public support for a public health insurance option. As the structure for the PPACA was being considered in 2009, 67% of adults surveyed in a nationally representative poll expressed support for a public health insurance option as a means of achieving universal health care.[48]
2. Support for the public insurance option tends to be stronger among younger voters.[49]
3. There is no assurance that the Health Insurance Exchanges included with the PPACA will necessarily work as intended to increase the accessibility and affordability of private health insurance. This concept is as yet untested on a national scale and is likely to work far better in some states than others.

The popularity of the public option among young adult voters is particularly critical to the eventual political viability of a public health insurance option, because as younger cohorts age and become more politically active their perspectives alter the political landscape on a range of social issues—as evidenced by the recognition of same-sex marriage as a civil right. In sum, it seems more likely than not that at some point in the not-too-distant future a public health insurance option will reemerge as a strategy for realizing the universal accessibility of affordable health care. This, in turn, sets the table for an eventual transition to a basic universal health insurance entitlement based on a social insurance model.

The second fundamental challenge to a universal social insurance plan that is built upon Rawls's principles of justice is scientific, that is the ability to identify the particular health care services and technologies that are directly determinate of fair equality of opportunity and as such qualify as "primary good" health care entitlements. There are also very formidable problems having to do with the slippery slope of some kinds of health care benefits that are made to become so highly desirable from a consumer marketing perspective that they eventually confer significant social and political advantage—thus, ultimately transforming lower order health care consumption preferences to primary good entitlements.[50] However, in search of a health care system that is more cost-effective, universally accessible, and ultimately just—these are challenges to be embraced.

NOTES

1. The George H. W. Bush administration (1989–1992) minimized the scope of the crisis in health care and disavowed any electoral mandate for health care reform (Roper, 1989). The George W. Bush administration framed the crisis in health care in terms of the "affordability" of health care for ordinary Americans, and pursued a reform platform that emphasizes tort reforms intended to reduce the burden of medical malpractice costs and the addition of Medicare prescription drug coverage for older Americans. The significant health care cost control measures implemented by the George W. Bush administration, primarily affecting the poor, were labeled as "deficit reduction" legislation.
2. The precise wording of the General Social Survey question is "In general, some people think that it is the responsibility of the government in Washington to see to it that people have help in paying for doctors and hospital bills. Others think that these matters are not the responsibility of the federal government and that people should take care of these things themselves." Respondents are then asked to place themselves on a scale that ranges between 1 and 5, with 5 indicating strong agreement with the sentiment that people should "take care of themselves." The combined tabulations for the 1972–1982, 1983–1987, 1988–1991, and the 1998

survey all show that less than 20% of respondents place themselves above a score of 4 on the question. In contrast, nearly 50% place themselves at the opposite end of the scale, which indicates a strong preference toward a significant role of the federal government in helping persons pay for health care (National Opinion Research Center, 2006).

3. Joal Roberts. Poll: The politics of health care. *CBS News: Opinion*. June 24, 2010.

4. Broadly speaking, political capital refers to possessing the assets needed to influence the decisions of other key actors in any political process. It can involve material things such as campaign funds or the ability to perform favors, as well as nonmaterial assets such as scientific credibility or moral authority.

5. Proposition 186 was defeated by a wide margin, in excess of 2:1 (Kaiser Family Foundation, 1994).

6. While physicians, like most Americans, strongly oppose the idea of overtly rationing health care, the reality is that the employment-based health insurance system rations health care by race, social class, nativity, and a variety of other nonclinical social characteristics having to do with prestige and power. Historically, the medical profession has supported the latter version of health care rationing in preference to equitable access to health care.

7. Maslow's famous hierarchy of needs has been broadly applied in education, business, and the health professions to explain human needs and behavioral motivations. In essence, Maslow's theory holds that humans seek to satisfy lower-order needs like survival and basic safety before they seek higher-order needs such as self-actualization and the kinds of more noble ends that yield the supreme achievements of humanity.

8. Another key hospital industry stakeholder group, although not strictly aligned with any one form of hospital ownership, is comprised of teaching hospitals. The interests of teaching hospitals are principally represented by two organizations, the Association of Academic Health Centers and the Association of American Medical Colleges. The central policy concerns of teaching hospitals include adequate reimbursement for uncompensated care, cost allowances from public programs and private insurance carriers that account for the added costs of these hospitals' teaching function, and support for health care research.

9. To many of its critics, the AHA is heavily biased toward market-based solutions to health care and is a significant obstacle to more radical reform measures that would promote equitable access to health care for all Americans. This impression was reinforced when the AHA's Vice President of Executive Branch Relations hosted a Bush–Cheney campaign fund-raising event in October, 2003 (Tieman & Fong, 2003), despite the AHA's official policy of not becoming involved in presidential elections.

10. The policy statement of the organization representing public hospitals (the National Association of Public Hospitals and Health Systems, 2003) has endorsed universal health care coverage and continued institutional coverage for the safety-net hospitals and clinics serving a disproportionate share of the poor (NAPH, 2009). Notably, the organization's policy statement does not specifically endorse a publicly funded single-payer plan as a preferred alternative, which would be more likely to place public hospitals in direct competition with the other sectors of the hospital industry.

11. The Taft–Hartley Act greatly constrained the union recruitment activities of union organizers, which left bargaining for fringe benefits a more critical priority of union leadership (Quadagno, 2004).

12. In 2005 the SEIU broke away from the AFL-CIO, a move which many progressives fear (and many conservatives hope) will ultimately weaken the labor movement. Others adopt a different view, believing that the SEIU's break with the AFL-CIO represents a much needed challenge to American labor's institutional inertia.

13. Should the employment-based health insurance system be entirely supplanted by a single-payer plan, under any credible scenario there would still be a significant market for supplemental health insurance to cover policy gaps and attend to the demands of privileged consumers. A single-payer system will not by itself create a single-tiered health care system.

14. This is a provision of the PPACA that places a cap on the "Medical Loss Ratio," that is, the proportion of the insurance premium that goes to administrative expenditures and profits rather than health care benefit expenditures.

15. Small shareholders, institutional investors, and venture capitalists.

16. The pharmaceutical industry has good reason to be worried about federally financed health care. As a case in point, Veterans Affairs health care system has been very successful in its use of a national drug formulary in terms of influencing physician prescribing behavior toward the selected drugs, the achievement of sizable price reductions from manufacturers, and in reducing drug expenditures (Huskamp, Epstein, & Blumenthal, 2003).

17. It is claimed by some that PhRMA's chief lobbyist, former congressman Billy Tauzin, was fired after the passage of the PPACA because drug manufacturers concluded he had unnecessarily bargained away too much of the industry's profits. That is, he had allowed PhRMA to be co-opted by the Obama administration rather than the opposite (Medicare Newsgroup, 2012; Wayne & Armstrong, 2011).

18. This estimate of the health insurance coverage effects of the PPACA is taken from the Centers for Medicaid and Medicare Service (CMS) actuarial estimates provided to the U.S. Congress on April 22, 2010 (CMS, 2010), combined with U.S. Census projections for the U.S. population as of 2019 (U.S. Census, 2008), the point at which the PPACA is fully implemented. Absent the PPACA, CMS estimates that by 2019 the size of the population of uninsured would rise to 57 million—leaving 17% of the nation's population without health insurance.

19. The PPACA excludes undocumented immigrants from health insurance coverage, either through private insurance market regulations or public entitlement programs. Thus, even if fully implemented, the PPACA would leave over 23 million U.S. residents uninsured—largely comprised of undocumented workers and their dependents. While it should be noted that the exclusion of undocumented immigrants from health insurance coverage is prevalent among countries that are credited with providing "universal insurance coverage," the U.S. economy is dependent upon both the labor and the taxes of undocumented workers.

20. To quote Heritage Foundation policy scholar Stuart Butler's argument in favor of an individual mandate to carry health insurance directly: "... it assumes there that there is an implicit contact between households and society, based on the notion that health insurance is not like other forms of insurance. If a young man wrecks his Porsche and has not had the foresight to obtain insurance, we may

commiserate, but society feels no obligation to repair his car. But health care is different. If a man is struck down by a heart attack in the street, Americans will care for him whether or not he has insurance . . . . even if it means more prudent citizens end up paying the tab." (Butler, 1989, p. 6).

21. Historically speaking, candidates from both major political parties have used the individual mandate as a symbol of government overreach, including at one point then-Democratic party presidential primary candidate Barack Obama. In a February 28, 2008 interview on the *Ellen DeGeneres* show about his divergent views with Hillary Clinton, Obama declared: "... she mandates that everybody buy health care. She'd have the government force every individual to buy insurance and I don't have such a mandate because I don't think the problem is that people don't want health insurance, it's that they can't afford it" (Procon.org, 2012, p. 1). In the more recent Republic party presidential primary, presidential primary candidate Mitt Romney repeatedly declared his opposition to individual mandates as part of his broader criticism of the Obama administration's to health care reform, while as governor of Massachusetts he imposed just such an individual mandate on Massachusetts state residents. These reversals reflect two contradictory aspects of the individual mandate to carry some form of health insurance: (1) as a symbol of government overreach the individual mandate is irresistible as a tool of electoral politics and (2) as any credible health economist will tell you, the individual mandate is essential to any plan of universal health insurance coverage that depends upon the commercial health insurance market.

22. The litigation brought before the U.S. Supreme Court in opposition to the PPACA concerned three issues: (1) whether the powers given to the federal government under the U.S., Constitution's "commerce clause" extend to the imposition of individual mandates to either carry or purchase health insurance, (2) whether, in the event that the individual mandate is found unconstitutional, other PPACA provisions that are not directly related to the individual mandate can remain the law of the land, and (3) whether or not the federal government require that states expand the number of people eligible for assistance from the state under the Medicaid program. The three cases that comprise these issues were *The National Federation of Independent Business v. Sebelius, No. 11-393; U.S. Department of Health and Human Services v. Florida, No. 11-398*; and *Florida v. Department of Health and Human Services, No. 11-400* (Vincini, 2012).

23. The source for this summary of PPACA insurance market provisions is the Kaiser Family Foundation's *Focus on Health Care Reform: Summary of New Health Reform Law*, http://www.kff.org/healthreform/upload/8061.pdf. Italicized text is either a direct quote or close paraphrasing of selected content from this document.

24. The term "actuarial value" means the average proportion that the insurance plans actually pays toward the total expenses of covered benefits. An insurance plan with a 60% actuarial covers, on an average basis, 60% of total medical expenses for benefits that are covered by the plan—thus leaving 40% as an out-of-pocket expenditure to the enrollee (which for lower income patients frequently becomes uncompensated care for the provider).

25. Between the 2010 enactment of the PPACA and the implementation of the provisions that disallow exclusions from health insurance enrollment for preexisting conditions in 2014, the PPACA establishes a temporary national high-risk pool

to provide health coverage to individuals with preexisting medical conditions. U.S. citizens and legal immigrants who have a preexisting medical condition and who have been uninsured for at least 6 months will be eligible to enroll in the high-risk pool and receive subsidized premiums.

26. Accounting for U.S. Census population growth projections, the numbers of uninsured with full implementation of the PPACA will be about 23 million (CMS, 2010). The 21 million figure cited here holds the U.S. population at its 2010 level to better illustrate the net effects of the PPACA on the size of the uninsured population.

27. As noted previously, the PPACA excludes undocumented workers and their dependents from either public or private insurance plan coverage. Although this is the prevalent practice among other OECD countries that are counted among those with universal coverage, from a variety of social justice perspectives this would not be considered either universal coverage or in any way just. This is an issue that will be considered in more depth in the section devoted to a principled analysis of the PPACA.

28. The italicized text in this section is either directly quoted or closely paraphrased text from a Kaiser Family Foundation summary of PPACA health insurance premium subsidies (Kaiser Family Foundation, 2010).

29. The premium credits will be provided as advanceable, refundable federal tax credits ultimately calculated through individual tax returns (although the credit payments will go directly to insurers). The credits can only be obtained by qualifying individuals who file tax returns (Congressional Research Service, 2010).

30. The Federal Poverty Line (FPL) is defined annually by the Census Bureau as the income threshold of poverty, adjusted for family size and age composition of the family household. As an example, in 2011 the income threshold for poverty (100% of the FPL) for a family of four with two children under age 18 was an annual income of $22,811, while a family of four at 400% of the FPL in 2011 would have an annual income of $91,244 (U.S. Census Bureau, 2012).

31. Text in italics summarized from *Health care reform: A primer for employers*, published online by Nixon Peabody International, retrieved March 22, 2012 from http:// www.nixonpeabody.com/publications_detail3.asp?ID=3233. The details pertaining to PPACA employer subsidies are quite complex, interested readers are referred to this excellent synopsis.

32. The source for this summary of PPACA Medicaid provisions is the Kaiser Family Foundation's *Focus on Health Care Reform: Summary of New Health Reform Law*, http://www.kff.org/healthreform/upload/8061.pdf. Italicized text is either a direct quote or close paraphrasing of selected content from this document.

33. The State Children's Health Insurance Program (SCHIP) will also be in line for increased federal subsidies under the PPACA. States will be required to maintain current income eligibility levels for children on Medicaid and the Children's Health Insurance Program (CHIP) until 2019, and beginning in 2015 will receive increased federal subsidies.

34. While individuals consume health care and purchase health insurance, health care consumption decisions more typically encompass family households.

35. Dartmouth Atlas Project at the Center for Health Policy Research at Dartmouth College is funded by a broad coalition of private and public funders, led by the Robert Wood Johnson Foundation.

36. The "patient-centered medical home" model that is endorsed by the American Academy of Family Physicians (AAFP), the American Academy of Pediatrics (AAP), the American College of Physicians (ACP), and the American Osteopathic Association (AOA) contains seven principles of care. For a full statement see the "Joint Principles of the Patient-Centered Medical Home, March 2007," available through the following URL: http://www.medicalhomeinfo.org/downloads/pdfs/jointstatement.pdf.

37. Proponents of the PPACA later embraced this label.

38. This provision imposes and excise tax on insurers of employer-sponsored health plans with aggregate values that exceed $10,200 for individual coverage and $27,500 for family coverage (indexed for inflation and effective 2018). The excise tax is quite substantial; 40% of the value of the plan that exceeds the threshold.

39. On the other hand, proponents of health care reform would point out it better than staying aboard the *Titanic* (in metaphorical imagery, the current unsustainable health care system).

40. The three cases that represented these issues were *The National Federation of Independent Business v. Sebelius, No. 11-393; U.S. Department of Health and Human Services v. Florida, No. 11-398;* and *Florida v. Department of Health and Human Services, No. 11-400* (Vincini, 2012).

41. "In the final analysis, we believe the Senate bill provides the best blueprint for reform. It offers the kind of change that will benefit patients today without putting medical progress at risk in the future. Today, we believe the Senate voted with America's best interests and future in mind" (PhRMA, Statement of Senate Health Care Reform Bill, December 24, 2009).

42. The point of controversy was a basic benefit regulation defined by the U.S. Department of Health and Human Services that was based on standards for women's health care that were established by nonpartisan Institute of Medicine. The basic benefit regulation required that individual and group plans provide a package of women's basic health benefits that includes (without patient cost-sharing) contraceptives approved by the FDA, screening for gestational diabetes, sexually transmitted infection counseling, breastfeeding supplies and counseling, and domestic violence screening and counseling (Bell, 2011). The U.S. Conference of Bishops vehemently opposed the mandatory inclusion of contraceptive coverage for religiously affiliated employers (United States Conference of Catholic Bishops, 2012), which then became politically framed by opponents of the PPACA as an example of egregious federal violation of religious freedom. While the Obama administration offered a compromise that would not require that religious organizations fund the benefit, this compromise was rejected by the Conference of Bishops. Ironically, despite this policy dispute, such a mandatory contraceptive benefit provision had already been in force in the majority of states preceding the PPACA's being either signed into law or even contemplated by Congress. Also, the Catholic Health Association, representing the nation's largest group of nonprofit health care systems, broke with the Conference of Bishops in fully endorsing the compromise that would preserve contraception as a required basic benefit of health insurance for women (Tapper, 2012).

43. Although the "medical industrial complex" has many definitions, the term refers to capital class ownership and/or control of the health care industry to the benefit and interests of capital: for example, hospital systems, health care insurance companies,

the pharmaceutical industry, the nursing home industry, and the health care research and education infrastructures.

44. "…. provision for medical care, as with primary goods generally, is to meet the needs and requirements of citizens as free and equal. Such care falls under the general means necessary to underwrite fair equality of opportunity [italics added in this text for emphasis] and our capacity to take advantage of our basic rights and liberties, and thus to be normal and fully cooperating members of society over a complete life" (Rawls, 2001, p. 174).

45. Nussbaum's 10 Central Human Capabilities are listed in Chapter 1, pp 30–31. In the language of the Capabilities Approach, a "meta capability" is defined as an overarching capability to be and to do things that make up a minimally good human life in the contemporary world' (Venkatapuram, 2012, p. 20).

46. This observation was also made by Democratic Party strategist and political pundit James Carville on a CNN interview on March 27, 2012 on the day that the Supreme Court heard oral arguments in favor of repealing the PPACA. Said Carville, "Just as a professional Democrat, there's nothing better to me than overturning this thing 5-4 and then the Republican Party will own the health care system for the foreseeable future. And I really believe that. That is not spin." As cited from Darius Dixon, "James Carville: Court loss 'best thing' for Democrats." *Politico,* March 28, 2012.

47. Mike Lillis, "Why Lieberman Opposed the Public Option." The Washington Independent, December 21, 2009 and Adam Smith, "Watchdog Group Says Ties to Health Insurance Companies Make Sen, Joe Lieberman an 'Insurance Puppet'." *Public Campaign Action Fund*, December 2, 2009. According to the latter source, Senator Lieberman had received $448 thousand in campaign contributions from the health insurance industry.

48. Kaiser Family Foundation Poll, April 2009.

49. During the 2008 campaign, Obama ran on a platform that emphasized an insurance reform approach that would include a public health insurance option. Obama's largest majority (66%) was among voters 18–29. Roper Public Opinion Archives, http://www.ropercenter.uconn.edu/elections/how_groups_voted/voted_08.html.

50. A plausible example is the increasingly widespread use of laser surgery as a substitute for eyeglasses, leading to the wearing of eyeglasses to eventually become a marker of social class.

REFERENCES

AHIP. (2011). *The unintended consequences and regulatory burdens of the new medical loss ratio requirements: Testimony for House Energy and Commerce Committee Subcommittee on Health.* Retrieved March 26, 2012, from http://www.ahip.org/Issues/Affordable-Care-Act/

AHRQ. (2011). *2010 National Health Care Disparities Report.* Rockville, MD: Agency for Healthcare Research and Quality.

Bell, A. (2011). *PPACA: Feds add contraception to preventive care package.* Retrieved March 26, 2012, from http://www.lifehealthpro.com/2011/08/01/ppaca-feds-add-contraception-to-preventive-care-pa

Blendon, R. J., Brodie, M., Altman, D. E., Benson, J. M., & Hamel, E. C. (2005). Voters and health care in the 2004 election. *Health Affairs*, W5, 86–96.

Blendon, R. J., Marttila, J., Benson, J. M., Shelter, M. C., Connolly, F. J., & Kiley, T. (1994). The beliefs and values shaping today's health reform debate. *Health Affairs*, *13*(1), 274–284.

Bodenheimer, T. (2005). The political divide in health care: A liberal perspective. *Health Affairs*, *24*(6), 1426–1435.

Boehner, J. (2010). Guest opinion: Why Republicans will fight to repeal health-care takeover. *Des Moines Register*, March 24, 2010.

Bowers, C. (2005, July 25). Big unions break from AFL-CIO. *CBS News*.

Butler, S. (1989). *Assuring affordable health care for all Americans. The Heritage foundation*. Retrieved March 21, 2012, from http://www.policyarchive.org/handle/10207/bitstreams/13354.pdf

CMS. (2010). Office of the Actuary: *Estimated financial effects of the "patient protection and affordable care act*. Retrieved March 20, 2012, from https://www.cms.gov/ActuarialStudies/downloads/PPACA_2010-04-22.pdf

Common Cause. (1992). Why the United States does not have a national health program: The medical-industry complex and its pac contributions to Congressional candidates, January 1, 1981, Through June 30, 1991. *International Journal of Health Services*, 22, 619–644.

Congressional Research Service. (2010). *Health Insurance Premium Credits Under PPACA (P.L. 111–148)*. Retrieved March 22, 2012, from http://liberalarts.iupui.edu/economics/uploads/docs/jeanabrahamcrscredits.pdf

Congressional Research Service. (2011). PPACA: *A Brief Overview of the Law, Implementation, and Legal Challenges*. Washington, DC.

Daniels, N. (2008). *Just health: Meeting health needs fairly*. New York: Cambridge University Press.

Healthcare-Now. (2009). AFL-CIO Convention Endorses Single-Payer. September 15, 2009. Retrieved March 31, 2012, from http://www.healthcare-now.org/afl-cio-convention-endorses-single-payer/

Hernes, G. (2001). The medical profession and health care reform—Friend or foe? *Social Science & Medicine*, *52*(2), 175–177.

Huskamp, H. A., Epstein, A. M., & Blumenthal, D. (2003). The impact of a national prescription drug formulary on prices, market share, and spending: Lessons for Medicare? *Health Affairs*, *22*(3), 149–158.

Hutton, J., Borowitz, M., Oleksy, I., & Luce, B. R. (1994). The pharmaceutical industry and health reform: Lessons from Europe *Health Affairs*, *13*(3), 98–111.

Iglehart, J. (2004). The new Medicare prescription–drug benefit: A pure power play. *New England Journal of Medicine*, *350*(8), 826–833.

Inglehart, J. (2006). U.S. hospitals: Mission versus market. *Health Affairs*, *25*(1), 10.

IOM. (2000). *Crossing the quality chasm: A new Health System for the 21st Century*. Washington, DC: National Academy Press.

Kaiser Commission on Medicaid and the Uninsured. (2006). *The uninsured: A primer*. Washington, DC: Henry J. Kaiser Family Foundation.

Kaiser Family Foundation. (1994). *Statewide survey of California: Publication No. 1026*. Menlo Park, CA: Henry J. Kaiser Family Foundation.

Kaiser Family Foundation. (2006, October). *Kaiser public opinion spotlight: The uninsured*. Retrieved April 14, 2006, from http://www.kff.org/spotlight/ uninsured/6.cfm

Kaiser Family Foundation (2009). *Public opinion on health care issues: July 2009*. Retrieved March 30, 2012, from http://www.kff.org/kaiserpolls/upload/7945.pdf

Kaiser Family Foundation. (2010). *Explaining health care reform: Questions about health insurance subsidies*. Retrieved March 22, 2012, from http://www.kff.org/healthreform/upload/7962-02.pdf

Kaiser Family Foundation. (2012). Health Tracking Poll: Exploring the Public's Views on the Affordable Care Act (ACA). Retrieved March 20, 2012, from http://healthreform.kff.org/public-opinion.aspx

Katz, M. (2008). *The price of citizenship: Redefining the American Welfare State*. New York: Holt.

Kuttner, R. (2006, January 2). *Medicare misery: The new Medicare bill is about to kick in, and what it offers to seniors isn't pretty*. Retrieved April 21, 2006, from http://www.prospect.org/web/page.ww?section=root&name=ViewWeb&articleId=10792

Lieberman, S., & Bertko, J. (2011). Building regulatory and operational flexibility into accountable care organization and "shared savings." *Health Affairs, 30*(1), 23–31.

Maslow, A. (1970). *Motivation and personality [by] Abraham H. Maslow*. New York: Harper & Row.

Medicare Newsgroup. (2012). *What is the pharmaceutical industry's position on the Affordable Care Act?* Retrieved March 31, 2012, from http://www.medicarenewsgroup.com/newsroom/medicare-faqs/individual-faq?faqId=f25bdc56-513a-41fa-8efc-2f18af4107a1

Milkman, R. (2005). The SEIU and the future of US labor. *Labor History, 46*(3),376–387.

NAPH (2009). *Safety net health systems: Health care reform principles*. Retrieved March 30, 2012, from http://www.naph.org/Main-Menu-Category/Our-Work/Health-Care-Reform/Health-Reform-Debate-Resources/HCR-Principles.aspx?FT=.pdf

National Association of Public Hospitals and Health Systems. (2003). *Improving access to health care for the uninsured*. Retrieved April 18, 2006, from www.naph.org

National Opinion Research Center (2006). General Social Survey Codebook. Retrieved April 13, 2006, from http://webapp.icpst.umich.edu/GSS/.

Nolte, E., & McKee, C. (2008). Measuring the health of nations: Updating an earlier analysis. *Health Affairs, 27*(1), 58–71.

Nussbaum, M. (2000) *Women and human development: The capabilities approach*. New York: Cambridge University Press.

Obama '08 Campaign. (2008). *Barack Obama's Plan for a Health America: Lowering health care costs and ensuring affordable, high-quality health care for all*. Retrieved March 20, 2012, from http://www.nytimes.com/packages/pdf/politics/factsheet_healthcare.pdf

OECD (2011). *Health data, 2011*. Retrieved March 27, 2012, from http://www.oecd.org/document/16/0,3746,en_2649_33929_2085200_1_1_1_1,00.html

Oliver, T. R., & Dowell, E. B. (1994). Interest groups and health reform: Lessons from California. *Health Affairs, 13*(2), 123–141.

Pew Research Center. (2006). *News release, February 1–5 national survey*. Washington, DC: The Pew Research Center for the People and the Press.

Procon.org. (2012). *History of the individual health insurance mandate, 1989–2010: Republican origins of democratic health care provision*. Retrieved March 21, 2012, from http://healthcarereform.procon.org/view.resource.php?resourceID=004182#heritage-1989

Quadagno, J. (2004). Why the United States has no national health insurance: Stakeholder mobilization against the welfare state, 1945–1996. *Journal of Health and Social Behavior, 45*(Extra Issue), 25–44.

Rawls, J. (2001). *Justice as fairness: A reformulation.* Cambridge, MA: Harvard University Press.

Rescher, N. (1966). *Distributive justice: A constructive critique of the utilitarian theory of distribution.* New York: Bobbs-Merrill.

Roper, W. L. (1989). Financing health care: A view from the White House. *Health Affairs, 8*(4), 97–102.

Rosner, D., & Markowitz, G. (2003). The struggle over employee benefits: The role of labor in influencing modern health policy. *The Milbank Quarterly, 81*(1), 45–73.

Sack, K. (2008). In Massachusetts, Universal Coverage Strains Care. *New York Times,* April 5, 2008.

Scofea, L. A. (1994). The development and growth of employer-provided health insurance. *Monthly Labor Review, 117*(3), 3–10.

SEIU. (2006). *It's time for an American solution to our health care crisis.* Retrieved April 20, 2006, from http://www.seiu.org/issues/ american solution.cfm

SEIU (2009). *Press release: SEIU, CNA/NNOC announce major accord. May 19, 2009.* Retrieved March 31, 2012, from http://www.seiu.org/2009/03/seiu-cnannoc-announce-major-accord.php

Sen, A. (2009). *The idea of justice.* Cambridge, MA: Belknap Press of Harvard University Press.

Skinner, J., Gottlieb, D., & Carmichael, D. (2011) *A new series of Medicare expenditure measures by hospital referral region: 2003–2008, executivesummary.* Retrieved March 26, 2012, from http://www.dartmouthatlas.org/downloads/reports/ PA_Spending_Report_0611.pdf

Skocpol, T. (2010). The political challenges that may undermine health reform. *Health Affairs, 29*(7), 1288–1292.

Starr, P. (1982). *The social transformation of American medicine.* New York: Basic Books.

Stuber, J., & Kronebusch, K. (2004). Stigma and other determinants of participation in TANF and Medicaid. *Journal of Policy Analysis and Management, 23*(3), 509–530.

Stuber, J., & Schlenger, M. (2006). The sources of stigma in means-tested programs. *Social Science and Medicine, 63*(4),933–945.

Tapper, J. (2012). Both Catholic health assn and planned parenthood say they're pleased with contraception rule announcement. *ABC News,* February 12, 2012. Retrieved March 27, 2012, from http://abcnews.go.com/blogs/politics/2012/ 02/both-catholic-health-assn-and-planned-parenthood-say-theyre-pleased-with-contraception-rule-announcement/

Tieman, J., & Fong, T. (2003). Mixing politics with pleasure. *Modern Healthcare, 33*(40), 6–7.

U.S. Census. (2008). *Projections of the population and components of change for the United States: 2010 to 2050.* Retrieved March 20, 2012, from http://www.census.gov/ population/www/projections/summarytables.html

U.S. Census Bureau. (2012). *Poverty thresholds by size of family and number of children: 2011.* Retrieved March 22, 2012, from http://www.census.gov/hhes/www/ poverty/data/threshld/index.html

U.S. Chamber of Commerce. (2009). *Health care reform we support.* Retrieved March 30, 2012, from http://www.freeenterprise.com/2009/10/health-reform-we-support

United States Conference of Catholic Bishops. (2012). *Open letter to the U.S. Senate: February 15, 2012.* Retrieved March 26, 2012, from http://nchla.org/datasource/idocuments/S1467-2-15-12.pdf

Venkatapuram, S. (2012). *Health justice.* Cambridge, UK: Polity Press.

Vincini, J. (2012). U.S. healthcare legal issues at Supreme Court. *Rueters news service, published online March 14, 2012.* Retrieved March 21, 2012, from http://www.reuters.com/article/2012/03/14/us-healthcare-court-idUSBRE82D11N20120314

Wayne, A., & Armstrong, D. (2011). Tauzin's $11.6 million made him highest-paid health-law lobbyist. *Bloomberg News,* November 28, 2011. Retrieved March 31, 2012, from http://www.bloomberg.com/news/2011-11-29/tauzin-s-11-6-million-made-him-highest-paid-health-law-lobbyist.html

Wennberg, J., Fisher, E., & Skinner, J. (2002). Geography and the debate over medicare reform. *Health Affairs* (21), W96–W114.

Wolff, J. (2003). Karl Marx: Life and works. In E. N. Zalta (Ed.), *The Stanford encyclopedia of philosophy.* Palo Alto, CA.

GLOSSARY

Access to Health Care   According to the Institute of Medicine,[1] access to health care is generally defined as the ability to engage in timely use of the health care services that achieve the optimal health outcomes. Access to health care involves having the financial resources essential to entering the health care system, getting to the geographic and physical locations where the needed health care is delivered, and finding appropriate providers for the needed care.

Accountable Health Care Organizations (ACOs)   A Medicare program health care provider structure that integrates patient care management, patient care data management systems, clinical case management models, and payment mechanisms across primary care, specialty care, acute hospital care, rehabilitation care, skilled nursing home care, and home health care.

Adverse Selection   Adverse selection occurs when individual purchasers of insurance or those selected for inclusion to the insurance pool actually have a level of insurance risk that is significantly in excess of the risk and costs assumed in the calculation of the insurance premium.

Burden of Disease   The prevalence and distribution of diseases, disabilities, and mortality that is carried by the population. The burden of disease that is carried by a population or population subgroup incorporates the susceptibilities and exposures to disease that arise from the interaction of biology and social environment, as well as those differences in health that can be attributed to disparities in health care.

Capabilities Approach   An approach to social justice that is based on the theoretical framework developed by Amartya Sen and Martha Nussbaum. The Capabilities Approach posits that (1) the freedom to achieve well-being is of primary moral importance and (2) the freedom to achieve well-being is to be understood as function of human capabilities—their real (as opposed to hypothetical and elusive) opportunities to do and to be what they have reason to value.

Capital-Based Competition The use of competitive advantages in physical facilities and/or health care technologies to either preserve or expand a health care provider's market share. In contrast to price-based competition, it is inherently inflationary.

Capitation A system of health care financing that is based on the application of a flat rate of reimbursement over a specified period on a per cap (per person) basis, in contrast to reimbursement that is based on fees for specified health services.

Carve-Outs The selective use of either subcontracting the management and provision of a segment of the benefits package to a specialty provider or making some benefits available on a discounted fee-for-service basis through an external provider contract.

Case Management Case management has a variety of definitions and approaches, but in health care it generally means the assignment of a care coordination specialist to a patient with a difficult-to-manage disease profile or one that involves high utilization of resources.

Centers for Medicare & Medicaid Services (CMS) The federal agency that administers Medicare, Medicaid, and the State Children's Health Insurance program. CMS, in addition to its administrative functions, is also a prominent source of health services research and statistics.

Community Health Centers (CHCs) A diverse group of not-for-profit and public health care clinics that are federally funded under the provisions of the Public Health Service Act to provide an array of primary health care services to low-income and medically underserved communities.

Community Rating An insurance fund and premium pricing estimation method that is based on geographic residence, generally by county. This method of insurance pricing is more favorable to persons of low income because their higher risks and insurance costs are averaged in with the lower risks and costs of higher income persons residing in the same community.

Cost-Shifting The practice through which hospitals and other providers recover losses from uninsured patients through higher charges to insured patients.

Critical Access Hospital (CAH) A rural hospital that has been certified as a CAH by the federal government to receive cost-based reimbursement from Medicare, by meeting certain requirements (small size, geographic isolation from other hospitals and status as sole local provider of essential acute and semi-acute hospital services).

Diagnosis-Related Groups (DRGs)   A DRG is determined at hospital discharge and involves a select array of factors that include the patient's final diagnosis and other case characteristics that have proven to be predictive of hospital care costs (e.g., patient age, sex, type of surgery, if any, or presence of comorbid conditions). There are roughly 500 DRGs to which a patient may be assigned, depending upon individual case characteristics.

Difference Principle   Central to John Rawls's theory of justice, this principle establishes the very limiting circumstances under which inequalities in wealth, power, and status are just. The difference principle states that "just" social and economic inequalities must satisfy two conditions: first, they are to be attached to offices and positions that are open to all under fair conditions of equality of opportunity; and second, they are to be the greatest benefit to the least-advantaged members of society.

Distributive Justice   A political theory or system of thought that is concerned with the just allocation of limited benefits and resources.

Employer Rating   An insurance fund and premium pricing estimation method that is based on employer characteristics. This method of insurance pricing is unfavorable to persons of low income and education and their employers because their higher insurance costs are not averaged in with persons having more income and education that tend to work for different kinds of employers.

Health   The absence of pathologies that prevent or inhibit "human normal functioning"; "normal human functioning" is understood to incorporate both biological and social contextual criteria.[2]

Health Insurance Cooperatives   A not-for-profit, member-owned insurance organization that provides a structure through which members can pool their insurance risks and enhance their purchasing power in the health insurance marketplace. The PPACA includes the Consumer Operated and Oriented Plan (CO-OP) Program to establish regulatory guidelines and promote the development of health insurance cooperatives.

Health Insurance Exchanges   The PPACA requires that each state establish a "health insurance exchange" for the individual and small business health insurance market, which serves as a marketplace for the selling of health insurance plans that meet minimum standards and are less expensive than health insurance policies sold on the open market.

Health Insurance Portability and Accountability Act of 1996 (HIPAA) A comprehensive package of federal legislation that includes a variety of provisions pertaining to health insurance market reforms intended to promote the affordability and accessibility of health insurance, and other provisions that impose very stringent procedural requirements on providers pertaining to the protection of patient confidentiality.

Health Maintenance Organizations (HMOs) Managed care organizations that provide a comprehensive array of health services through capitated financing.

Health Rights Universal entitlements pertaining to health care and other determinants of health, in accordance with different theories of social justice.

Independent Practice Associations (IPAs) A structure through which physicians in private practice can join together and negotiate managed care contracts with health insurance plans.

Insurance Pool A set of individuals assigned to a common insurance fund, assumed to share the average risks and related losses (costs) for the occurrence of the insured events.

Libertarianism A social and political philosophy that advocates maximum individual freedom and minimum government. At the heart of libertarianism is the idea that societies must be governed, but only to the extent necessary to assure the protection of an explicit set of individual rights. Classic libertarianism holds that government's legitimate functions pertain only to basic protections against foreign or domestic threats to life, property, or the exercise of personal autonomy.

Life Expectancy The average number of remaining years of life for a person at a given age, given the prevailing pattern of mortality in the population. The most commonly used measure of life expectancy is life expectancy at birth.

Long-Term Care The health, personal care, and related social services provided over a sustained period of time to people who have lost or never developed certain measurable functional abilities.[3] Long-term care policies and services encompass the aged, the developmentally disabled, the chronically ill, and persons disabled by trauma.

Managed Care   Managed care is defined in multiple ways, but it commonly encompasses various activities by health care underwriters to control health care costs, quality, and access.[4]

Marxism   A social and political theory based on historical materialism, which holds that the particular social arrangements that compose different forms of society (social systems) are determined by the modes of production that are dominant in any given historical epoch. Class exploitation and conflict lie at the heart of the Marxist perspective of the nature of industrialized societies, as well as the belief that the oppressive nature of capitalism will ultimately lead to the revolutionary establishment of socialist states.

Medicaid   Established in 1965 through amendments to the Social Security Act, Medicaid is a means-based program for medical assistance for financially needy persons of all ages. Medicaid is funded jointly by individual states and the federal government through general tax revenues. In contrast to Medicare, Medicaid is not structured as a federalized social insurance fund, does not have consistent eligibility criteria and benefits from state to state, and often incurs both stigma and discrimination from providers.

Medical Free Enterprise   A health care provider model is based on the selling of professional services in the marketplace. The medical free enterprise model incentivizes the medical provider to select the most profitable professional services and attract and retain the customers (patients or their sponsoring insurance plans) that are willing and able to pay the highest fees.

Medicare   Established in 1965 through amendments to the Social Security Act, Medicare is a federally funded health insurance entitlement program for persons over age 65, persons under age 65 with certain disabilities, and persons with permanent kidney failure requiring dialysis or a kidney transplant. In contrast to Medicaid, which is a means-based program for medical assistance for needy persons, Medicare is structured as a form of social insurance with eligibility based on age and disability criteria.

Moral Hazard   The problem of "moral hazard" arises when the state of being insured for a given event leads the insured person to become less averse to the event occurring—thus altering his or her risk-related behavior. In the context of health insurance, the risk event is an "episode of health care" or use of health care. The fact of having health insurance often makes people less averse to episodes of health care and generally more inclined toward using health care.

National Health Insurance   In classic form, national health insurance entails universal coverage for a comprehensive array of health care services, financed through a tax-based public health insurance fund.

Negative Rights   Negative rights involve constraints on others to not impede our actions and preferences, do something to us, or take something from us. Negative rights, where they apply to the actions of the state or governments, are commonly referred to as "liberty rights."

OECD   The Organisation for Economic Co-operation and Development (OECD) was founded in 1961, replacing the Organisation for European Economic Co-operation, which had been established in 1948 under the Marshall Plan. The OECD is comprised of 34 member states, each having a democratic form of governance and a market economy.

Patient Protection and Affordable Care Act, PL 111-148 (PPACA)   A comprehensive health care reform act signed into law by President Barack Obama on March 23, 2010. Its provisions are intended to expand health insurance and public health care entitlements to U.S. citizens and lawful residents, improve health care quality, and reduce the pace of health care inflation—while retaining a health care financing structure that is largely based on employment-based health insurance.

Point-of-Service (POS) Providers   A form of preferred provider arrangement that permits the health care consumer to choose one's provider, who may or may not be a part of a preferred provider panel, who then functions as the "gatekeeper" for other health care services related to the episode of care. The consumer may choose another provider for a subsequent episode of care.

Positive Rights   Rights that pertain to what is owed to us or what we can legitimately claim we should be provided. Depending upon the theory of justice applied, positive rights may include such rights as personal safety, basic education, employment opportunity, a just minimum wage, and basic health care.

Preferred Provider Organizations (PPOs)   Networks of providers (e.g., physician groups, hospitals, pharmacies) that contract with health insurance underwriters to furnish an array of health care services and products at a discounted price.

Prospective Payment System (PPS)   A system of reimbursement implemented in 1983 as amendments to the Social Security Act. It changed the basis of Medicare payments to hospitals from a fee-for-service-based system to one based on the patient's assignment to a Diagnosis-Related Group (see DRG).

Rawlsian Theoretical Perspective (aka Rawlsian Liberalism)   Viewpoints and positions on issues of social justice that are directly derived from the theoretical works of John Rawls on social justice, in particular his two principles of justice.

Right to Health Care   The right to health care entails a societal obligation to furnish individuals and/or populations with some established array of health care services that may be preventative, curative, or even restorative.[5]

Roemer's Law   A principle of health care economics that states *supply tends to induce its own demand where a third party guarantees reimbursement of use.* In the context of institutional care such as hospitals and nursing homes, this law suggests the extent that public funds are available to subsidize the costs of care, a market dynamic of "build the beds and they will come" emerges. Roemer's Law is named after its founder, the late Milton Roemer, formerly a Professor of Health Services at UCLA.

Safety Net   The health care system safety net is generally defined as the clinics, hospitals, and individual health care providers that care for a disproportionate share of the poor, the uninsured, those afflicted by stigmatizing health conditions, and persons otherwise isolated from the mainstream health care system.

SES Gradient   In the context of social epidemiology and health care policy, the SES gradient refers to the linear relationship that prevails worldwide between socioeconomic status (income, education, and occupation) and health. Higher SES demonstrates a positive linear relationship to health and longevity, even within very affluent populations and income groups.

Single-Payer System   A system of health care financing that provides for payment of health care services through a single insurance fund, most typically as an essential function of government and through a social insurance program supported by tax revenues.

Social Epidemiology   A scientific discipline that has, as its primary and explicit concern, the investigation of the *social* determinants of population distributions of health, disease, and wellbeing.

Social Health Maintenance Organization (S/HMO)   A comprehensive community-based long-term care program that integrates medical care and social supports under a model of capitated financing. Typical S/HMO benefits include case management, personal in-home support services, adult day care, respite care (including short-term nursing home care), and coverage for pharmaceuticals.

Social Justice   A philosophical construct that refers to a political theory or system of thought used to determine what mutual obligations flow between the individual and society. A theory of social justice identifies what society as a whole owes to its individual members and, in turn, what individual members owe to society.

Stakeholders   Groups and organizations that have a compelling interest in the outcome of any policy-making process. In essence, the groups and organizations that stand to either gain or lose, dependent upon what policy alternatives are implemented.

Two-Tiered System of Health Care   Two-tiered systems of health care entail disparities in health care access and delivery wherein there is one system of health care for the segment of the population with adequate health care insurance coverage, and another for those dependent upon either inadequate public subsidies for health care or "charity care" from the limited number of health care providers willing to provide it.

Uncompensated Care   Care that is provided without payment and without obligation to pay for persons unable to afford it, and also care that incurs bad debt—which represents a provider's decision to write off fees for health care that are deemed uncollectible. Both forms of uncompensated care comprise a significant source of the financing for health care delivered to the poor and the uninsured.

U.S. Public Health Service (PHS)   Originally founded in 1798 as the Marine Hospital Service, the PHS exists as a function of the Department of Health and Human Services. The central mission of the PHS and its eight major divisions entails the protection and advancement of the public's health.

Utilitarianism   A theory of distributive justice, often extended to a social and political philosophy, that is founded upon the *principle of utility*: the idea that utility (whatever is valued as a good thing) should be distributed in accordance with whichever scheme yields the maximum good to the maximum number of people.

Utilization Review   The auditing of clinical records for the purposes of identifying care delivery by providers that fails to meet explicit standards of care established by the insurance underwriter. This includes care that is deemed either unnecessary or care that is of poor quality.

Voluntary Health Insurance   Health insurance plans that are funded from purchasers that include individuals, private and public employers, employment industry purchasing cooperatives, beneficent societies, and labor unions. The term "voluntary" refers to the voluntary nature of participation in the insurance plan, in contrast to the compulsory nature of a tax-based public health insurance fund (see national health insurance).

NOTES

1. IOM. (1993). *Access to health care in America*. Washington, DC: National Academy of Sciences.
2. This definition draws on the arguments of Norman Daniels, in *Just health: Meeting health needs fairly*. Cambridge: Cambridge University Press, 2008.
3. Per Kane, R., Kane, R., & Ladd, R. (1998). *The heart of long term care* (p. 314). New York: Oxford University Press.
4. Per Baily, M. A. (2003). Managed care organizations and the rationing problem. *The Hastings Center Report, 33*(1), 34–42.
5. Per Hessler, K., & Buchanan, A. (2002). Specifying the content of the human right to health care. In R. Rhodes, M. Battin, & A. Silvers (Eds.), *Medicine and social justice*. New York: Oxford University.

INDEX